Photoshop Artistry

A Master Class for Photographers and Artists

Barry Haynes and Wendy Crumpler

SYBEX

San Francisco ◆ Paris ◆ Düsseldorf ◆ Soest

PHOTOSHOP ARTISTRY
A MASTER CLASS FOR PHOTOGRAPHERS AND ARTISTS

Barry Haynes and Wendy Crumpler

Acquisitions Manager: Kristine Plachy

Associate Publisher: Amy Romanoff

Editor: Alex Miloradovich

Project Editor: Malcolm Faulds

Technical Editors: Rita Amladi and Mike Birch

Book Design and Production: Wendy Crumpler

Color Separations: Barry Haynes

Indexer: Matthew Spence

Cover Design: Barry Haynes and Wendy Crumpler

Cover Photograph: Barry Haynes

SYBEX is a registered trademark of SYBEX Inc.

Adobe Photoshop® is a trademark of Adobe Systems Incorporated. Used with permission.

TRADEMARKS

SYBEX has attempted throughout this book to distinguish proprietary trademarks from descriptive terms by following the capitalization style used by the manufacturer.

NOTICE OF LIABILITY

Every effort has been made to supply complete and accurate information. However, neither SYBEX nor the authors and contributors assume any responsibility for its use, nor do they assume any liability for any infringement of the intellectual property rights of third parties which would result from such use.

Library of Congress Card Number: 95-69356
ISBN: 0-7821-1774-0

Manufactured in the United States of America
10   9   8   7   6   5   4   3   2   1

DEDICATION

To Max, our son due August 20, 1995, and to Chumley, our best friend and companion dog, both of whom have patiently put up with our seemingly unending work on this book.

ACKNOWLEDGMENTS

There are many people who have helped us on our way in life and with this book.

I, Barry, would like to thank Mike Liebhold for the positive way he helped me get into digital imaging and a new mind space at Apple; Bill Atkinson for his advice on dealing with my own needs versus the desires of corporations; Dave Nagel for support in following my dreams in photography; Steve Wozniak and Dan Sokol for their interest and the dye-sub printer; Charles McConathy and MicroNet; Jerry De Avila and Daystar; John Taylor and many others at Radius/SuperMac for supporting my projects; Jim Rich for his comradery, friendship and separation expertise; Bruce Ashley for his ideas, images, and friendship, and for blazing the digital imaging trails with me; Marc Simon for his images and creativity; Al Hoffman, Mary Cadloni, Bruce Hodge and Liz Weal for their support and friendship over the years; Mom for always believing in me and being there to help; all the people I worked with at Apple for bringing personal computers from 40 column black-and-white systems to the 24-bit color creation environments we have today, and of course my wife, Wendy, for being a wonderful person and a great partner and for making the creation of this book, our son, and all my dreams come true.

I, Wendy, would like to thank Goldie Ferrell for instilling in me the love of language and teaching; Peter Lewis for his financial, moral and artistic support and for some of the best business advice I've ever heard; Pat Miller for her wisdom, laughter and encouragement; Lynne Morris for helping me learn to believe in myself; Curvin O'Rielly for always believing that I could do anything; Diane Wicks for her continued guidance, acceptance, faith and faithfulness; Luke Neal for making me compute and laugh; and Susie Hellerer for magic. Also a word of thanks to the people who have helped me develop technical and creative skills—my clients, my students and my coworkers. Thanks to Barry for insisting that we could do this book our own way, for pushing me forward creatively, for giving me time to rest, and for being a wonderful partner in every sense of the word.

We'd both like to thank Rita Amladi for doing a creative technical review and for all her help and ideas; Mike Birch for the PC technical edit, the screen grabs, and the sense of calm at the end of a long project; the eagle-eyed Alex Miloradovich for a very detailed edit and for leading us through the process of putting a book together; Amy Romanoff for her marketing skills and for having so much enthusiasm about our book; Kristine Plachy for all her patience; Jim Curran for helping us produce our vision of a beautiful book; Margaret Rowlands for her help with the many cover ideas; Malcolm Faulds for smiling and keeping us all on schedule; Rodnay Zaks, Rudy Langer, and Barbara Gordon for approving this project; Celeste Grinage for tech edit support; Judy Jigarjian for publicity, tracking down titles, and being ever so pleasant; Sarah Lemas for proofreading; Matthew Spence for the index; Randall Goodall and Lorrie Fink of Seventeenth Street Studios for their help in dealing with design issues of every type; Marcella Smith of Barnes & Noble for sharing her knowledge of the publishing industry, for her support, and for being a great friend; Brad Bunnin for his happy voice and his great legal advice; Julia Held for rushing in to help with production; Bruce Hodge, Jeff Myers, Michael Kienitz, Al Hoffman, Steve Clark, Dave Forrest, Victor DeNigris and Ed Velandria for their comments.

We want to say a special word for Rudy Langer. We feel that this project happened because of his commitment and support for it. Although we had only recently met him, we feel a great sadness at Rudy's passing. He was truly a gentleman.

Finally, and most importantly, our personal thanks to the Divine Creator who led us here and through this project.

TABLE OF CONTENTS

vi

PHOTOGRAPHY AND OVERALL COLOR CORRECTION

Here we show you what makes a good photograph technically—both traditionally, using the Zone System, and digitally by evaluating histograms. Seeing how to bring traditional photography skills into the digital realm gives you better scans, calibration and overall color correction for the best possible output.

IMPROVING COLOR AND MOOD WITH SELECTIONS AND MASKS

Once you have done overall color correction, you will want to use selections to isolate specific areas of your image and change their color or make them lighter or darker. Many of these techniques, including color matching different color objects, making a fine black-and-white print and changing the color of objects, demonstrate the finer artistic control you have with digital photography.

An overview discussion of the differences between and uses of selections, masks and channels to help you feel comfortable with these concepts. Read this before doing the rest of the examples in this part of the book.

Selecting a complex object within a photo using the Magic Wand, Lasso and Quick Mask tools and changing its color using Hue/Saturation.

When overall color correction is done, fine tune the GrandCanyon image by removing spots and scratches, and by dodging or burning dark and light image areas—things you could do in a normal darkroom, but digitally it's a lot easier, and you have greater control.

Final adjustments of particular off-color and dark areas using Selections, dealing with out-of-gamut colors and using Unsharp Mask to sharpen this Photo CD scan.

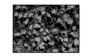

Using Color Range and Replace Color to easily isolate all the yellow flowers and change their colors. Using Selective Color to fine tune those colors after RGB to CMYK conversion.

Making a fine black-and-white print, with detailed dodging and burning; how to darken the edges of the print using Curves, and do some detailed tweaks to remove unwanted blemishes and objects.

LAYERS FOR COMPOSITING
AND PROTOTYPING

Layers are the most powerful set of features added to Photoshop 3.0. The examples in this part of the book show you many of the possibilities for better color correction and effects when combining images using Layers. The following chapters also show you how to use Layers as a great prototyping tool.

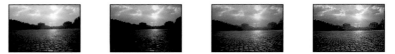
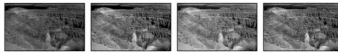

Using the Layers palette and Layer options including Clipping Groups, Layer Masks and Drag & Drop; reordering layers, and understanding when to merge layers and/or flatten the image as you create a final composite with 14 layers and 8 original images. How to use Layers to set up your Photoshop files to show yourself, or your clients, unlimited variations of a composite or effect quickly, without losing any of those variations.

CALCULATIONS, PATTERNS, FILTERS AND EFFECTS

The examples in this section use Layers, Filters, Bitmaps and Calculations in combination with each other to achieve a variety of special effects including motion simulation, drop shadows , pattern creation, text with shadows, line drawings and many others.

Detailed explanations of the Blend modes in all the tools (painting tools, the Fill command, Layers, Calculations and Apply Image); the many variations and uses of the Apply Image and Calculations commands are demonstrated and demystified.

Combining a positive and negative version of the same image, creating and placing neon text with the Calculations command and combining Illustrator text with Photoshop drop shadows for more creative control and higher quality PostScript text output.

Creating texture and pattern effects using Posterize, Bitmaps, Layers and Patterns—cool stuff!

FOREWORD

In his autobiography, discussing the decision to make his original negatives available for future photographers to print, Ansel Adams wrote:

> *"Photographers are, in a sense, composers and the negatives are their scores. ...In the electronic age, I am sure that scanning techniques will be developed to achieve prints of extraordinary subtlety from the original negative scores. If I could return in twenty years or so I would hope to see astounding interpretations of my most expressive images. It is true no one could print my negatives as I did, but they might well get more out of them by electronic means. Image quality is not the product of a machine, but of the person who directs the machine, and there are no limits to imagination and expression."*

Ansel Adams had a good vision for the future that we are now living. We hope this book will help you experience that vision in your photographic work.

Seeing an image on the computer screen is a beautiful thing. You bring it up from the scanner and you begin to think, "Now what do I really want this to look like?" If you know the Zone System, developed by Ansel Adams in traditional photography, then you know the type of control you can have while taking a photo or printing it in the darkroom. On the computer screen, you can have this control and much more. You can try numerous variations, making extreme or subtle changes easily and quickly. The computer is a new tool for the photographer to get precisely what he or she wants.

Many people think of using computer imaging for its proven ability to create special effects and image composites. It is very good at this, and we will show you how to create images that cannot be done optically in the darkroom. I very often use my computer darkroom, however, to make a print of nature and to have much finer control in making that print. Realistic photography is another area where we will show you things that can be done on the computer that can't be done easily or at all in the darkroom.

This book has developed from the Photoshop courses I started teaching in 1990. It's not an exhaustive book that goes through each menu bar and each feature and lists them in order. The examples in *Photoshop Artistry* teach you how to use Photoshop 3.0 by working with typical situations that you encounter as a photographer, artist or designer. This is Photoshop for creating fine images that are sometimes high quality reproductions of reality and sometimes fine renditions of composites and effects.

For each situation, the detailed, step by step process has been spelled out in the book. You can practice the technique yourself since the original images, masks and progress steps as well as the final images for each example are on the *Photoshop Artistry* CD included with the book. These examples have been taught over the past five years to thousands of students across the country. Their feedback has helped us refine these exercises to make them easy to understand, concise, and full of special tips for more advanced users. In addition to student tested, step by step instructions, *Photoshop Artistry* also includes explanations of concepts like color correction, calibration, duotones, selections, masking, layers, and channels, so you really understand what you are doing and are not just blindly following directions. Understanding allows you to expand the ideas in this book as you apply them to your own situations and creations without wasting your time on unnecessary issues.

We start with simple examples like how to crop and color correct a photograph. Color correction is covered in great depth. Then we move into things that you would normally do in the darkroom like changing the contrast, burning and dodging, removing spots and scratches, and making a nice photographic print. Before we get into compositing and special effects, we talk about having absolute control over the colors in your photographs. The masters of color photography use contrast reduction masks, shadow, highlight and color masks in the darkroom to make very fine Cibachrome, C and dye transfer art prints. With these techniques you can make specific colors pop by increasing their saturation and changing their relationship to the rest of the photograph. *Photoshop Artistry* shows you how to do all these things digitally and how to generate art quality output to dye sublimation or ink jet printers. We will also talk about enhancing an image for output back to 4x5 and 8x10 film as well as output to separations for printing on a press. We will use the above techniques along with sharpening to get great quality prints from Photo CD and Pro Photo CD scans. The preferences and separation sections of the book include tips and references from my friend, Jim Rich, who has over 20 years experience doing color separations and scans for organizations like National Geographic, Crossfield and Scitex.

Once you understand how to make a fine color print with Photoshop, we will make extensive use of Layers and image compositing techniques. Most commercial compositing techniques can easily be done with Photoshop. We will go through the step by step examples for some simple compositing jobs and then some more complex examples using hard and soft edge masks as well as a variety of shadow and drop shadow effects and all the features of Layers. The Apply Image and Calculations commands and their many Blend Mode variations are explained in detail along with examples of where to use them in both still photography and motion picture situations.

Photoshop Artistry also includes many tips and techniques on how to get the most from the Photoshop filters including some of the more obscure ones like Displace, Wave, and Lighting Effects. Layer options are explained and we also get into creating duotones, bitmaps, adding textures to images, and other fun things.

Photoshop is great fun! And the more you know, the better time you will have and the easier it will be to turn the images in your mind into reality. We hope *Photoshop Artistry* helps you have more fun than ever before with photography and digital imaging.

Happy Photoshopping!

AN OVERVIEW OF DIGITAL IMAGING

It's the year 2001 and you're on location in the Amazon jungle taking photos of a bambleberry plantation for tonight's issue of *Earth Survival News*. Since the discovery that the rain forest bambleberry cures AIDS and the teetee bush cures cancer, all countries have agreed to stop old-growth forest cutting. You're sitting high on top of a 90 foot bambleberry tree looking at the electronic layout of the article on the screen of your 13" color, 640 by 480, fold-out, wristwatch Mac Decca. From the layout, you can see they need a 5x7 still photo for the cover and a 5 minute movie slot for the rest of the article on screen 10. Now you're taking the photo they will need; gee this is going to look great in the layout! The 20 megabyte file is transmitted directly from your Nikon F10 digital camera into the layout on the Mac Decca. Now you're using Photoshop 9.1 to crop and edit the photos for final transmission. It's now 4:50 PM in Manhattan, so you only have five minutes to finish working with the photo. It is transmitted via satellite from your Mac Decca directly into the page layout. This gives them five minutes to make final approvals and adjustments for the 5:00 PM transmission. Readers around the world now see *Earth Survival News*, and get most of their news and information on their wristwatch Mac Deccas and PC communicators. Think of all the trees this digital transmission technology is now saving. With the street prices for entry level Mac Deccas dropping to $100, newspapers, magazines and catalog advertisers across the world have either gone out of business or converted to digital transmission. Paper is no longer the medium of choice. Aren't you glad you stuck with digital photography when it was so frustrating in the early years?

BACK TO THE FUTURE

Now it's back to reality in 1995. Here I am with my $20,000 Macintosh digital photography system. When I set out on my own in 1990, after 10 years doing software development and imaging research at Apple Computer, I wanted to return to my love for photography. I planned to set up a self sufficient business that could be run from home with my own equipment and without the need for partners or outside investors. It cost me under $10,000 to purchase a 4x5 camera system and a traditional color darkroom that can make professional quality 16x20 color prints. This traditional color darkroom now sits idle most of the time because I'm in front of the computer screen playing with my digital darkroom. With Photoshop on the Mac or PC it is much easier to do anything that a traditional darkroom

For Those of You Who Are New to the Digital World, this Is a Quick Introduction to the Possibilities. More Advanced Users May Find They Are Familiar with Many Things in this Chapter

can do with an image. It is easy and fast to try something or to try twenty different variations and pick the one you like most. With complete personal control and much more creative software on your own computer, you can do anything a high-end Scitex retouching station can do and much more. The possibilities for creativity in a digital darkroom are endless.

I'm sure that many of you have been wondering about digital photography. It is possible today to produce the highest quality digital images using a desktop system. My dream is to make professional quality 20x24 color prints with my personal digital photography system! Although this is possible, there are things about the process that can make it confusing, expensive and in some ways more trouble than a traditional photographic approach.

THE OPTIONS FOR DIGITAL PHOTOGRAPHY

You may be wondering if digital photography is worth the cost and effort. In this introductory discussion, will divide digital photography into three functional areas:
1. Capturing the image
2. Adjusting and manipulating the image
3. Outputting the image

CAPTURING THE IMAGE

In most cases film is still the highest quality medium for image capture. This is especially true if you are talking about short exposures on 4x5 or larger film. Once you capture an image on film, there are various ways to scan it into a digital version for your computer. You can take your original to a traditional color house and have it scanned with a quality drum scanner. This will cost you anywhere from $50 to $150 or more. A second alternative is to take your film to a desktop service bureau and have it scanned with a desktop scanner. With either of these alternatives, you often have little or no personal control over the quality of the scans. This book will help you learn what to look for in a good scan.

SCAN IT YOURSELF

A third alternative for scanning is to rent or purchase a desktop scanner and do the scans yourself. Doing your own scans is a great way to learn about scanning. There are desktop scanners that scan film and there are flatbed scanners to scan prints and artwork. Some flatbed scanners have optional attachments to scan film. Scanning original film gives you the best quality. I did extensive testing with a Leafscan-45 which enabled me to do my own high quality scans on 35mm, 2¼ and 4x5 film. This is a great scanner! If you can afford your own scanner, it makes it much easier to prototype image creations and publishing projects. Before buying a scanner, read the latest articles comparing the newest scanners since they get better and cheaper all the time.

THE KODAK PHOTO CD SYSTEM

An exciting alternative that is now available for scanning is the Kodak Photo CD system. This allows the masses to get high quality scans quickly and in bulk for very little expense—about $1 to $2 per scan in most places. With Photo CD, you bring your film to get it processed and at the same time the images can be scanned and placed on a digital Photo CD disc. You can also send in any 35mm original (positive, negative, color or B&W) that has been previously taken and get it put on Photo CD. The Photo CD discs will hold up to 120 images. The quality of these images is high enough for a majority of publishing output. What I have done is get over 400 of my best photographs put on Photo CD. This allows me to use these images in

brochures, this book, advertising and other promotions. For publication at 150 line screen, Photo CD images are usually good for sizes of about 7x9 or smaller. Sometimes you can go bigger than this; it all depends on the image and the quality of the scan. I have some great looking 11x17 Super-Mac ProofPositive prints from Photo CD scans. The maximum image size for a regular Photo CD scan is 18 megabytes. Photo CD Pro will allow scans of up to 70 megabytes from originals that are 35mm, 2¼ or 4x5. These are a bit more expensive, about $20 each, but are still much cheaper than high-end drum scans. If you give the CD processor a high quality original, the quality of these scans can be excellent. See the Input, Calibration, Correction and Output chapter for more info on how to get great scans from any scanner and also get the most from your Photo CD scans.

THE DIRECT DIGITAL METHOD

For certain applications, it makes sense to capture your images using a direct digital method. This makes your work much simpler since there is no film to process and no scanning to be done. There are several technologies available to do this. One of the earliest offered, still video, uses a 35mm type camera that is loaded with a small, still video disk. You can also get a card for your computer, called a video digitizer, that allows you to get digital still frames from any video camera or player. The problem with video digitizing and still video is that the quality of the digital images is not high enough for most print production.

For significantly better than video quality in a compact filmless camera, you can use the Kodak Digital Camera System (DCS). DCS is a series of digital backs that attach to Nikon, Hasselblad and other cameras. DCS comes in various models and prices. Nikon also makes a high quality digital camera called the Nikon E2. For studio work, there is the Leaf Catchlight Digital Back and the Dicomed Camera Back system. These systems act as digital backs for 2¼ and 4x5 cameras. The quality of the digital files captured with these systems can be very good. Digital cameras make a lot of sense for studio work because, while you are shooting the picture, you can bring the file directly into the Mac or PC and make sure it meets your needs. With digital cameras there is no need for the cost, time and environmental problems associated with film processing. You also don't have the cost or time lag required to get scans done. For studios that do a lot of catalog work, especially with small to medium size images, digital cameras could save a lot of time and money and allow the photographer to shoot the images and provide digital separations. Stephen Johnson, a well known landscape photographer, uses the Dicomed digital camera insert on his 4x5 camera and is very happy with the results he is able to get. This digital back is not able to do fraction of a second exposures but it produces very large accurate files, over 100 megabytes, and is great for still camera work where much detail and dynamic range is required. Steve has mentioned to me that in most lighting situations he can actually capture more detail with this setup than even 4x5 film would get. His Dicomed prints are very beautiful. With this type of camera setup, he actually sees the image on the computer screen of his Mac portable in the field, like on site in Yosemite. Another advantage to direct digital capture with smaller images is that the images are in a form where they can be easily compressed and transmitted over a phone line. Newspapers and magazines use this feature in very time sensitive situations. Pictures can be shot and sent compressed over the phone and be literally on a press a few minutes later. If you use a digital camera and want to learn how to use it to create automatic knock-outs, see the Difference blend mode in the Blend Modes, Calculations and Apply Image chapter.

ADJUSTING AND MANIPULATING THE IMAGE

Once you have converted an image into digital format, you can more easily perform standard darkroom techniques like spotting, cropping, dodging, burning, changing the color balance, contrast, etc. You can use a variety of selection and feather techniques to isolate portions of an image for change without affecting the rest of the image. Layers, masking and other techniques can be used to create knock-outs and combine images in any way you want. You can use the painting tools within Adobe Photoshop and other applications to retouch, colorize, add to and modify your images. In addition to standard darkroom techniques, there are special effects like posterization, rotation, skew, solarization, stretching, perspective, edge effects, sharpening, distortions, image compositing, blending and many others. You will learn how to do all these things using the real world examples in this book. Any manipulation or effect that can be done on a Scitex or other high-end imaging workstation can also be done in Photoshop. Photoshop can actually do far more, and it's fun to use, too.

MAKING COLOR SEPARATIONS

If you are going to output your digital images to film, the digital files need to be in RGB (Red, Green, Blue) format. Most desktop scanners currently scan in this format. If you are going to print your final images on a press, the images need to be converted into CMYK (Cyan, Magenta, Yellow, Black) format. Photoshop and many other desktop applications do the conversions from RGB into CMYK format. This conversion process, called

making color separations, has many variations depending on the type of printer and paper you will be using.

CREATING YOUR OWN BOOKS

One of the advantages of using digital photography is that the computer equipment also gives you the required tools for doing your own publishing. If you want to create a brochure, poster or even a book, you can learn the necessary skills to design and create the entire project yourself. Soon, photographers will be publishing their own books. This entire book—including the design, layout, color correction, compositing and effects as well as the final color separations and the cover—was created by Wendy and me in our home studio in the Santa Cruz mountains using desktop equipment. The scans are mostly Photo CD, which we color corrected and separated using the techniques taught here. A few of the scans were done using the Leafscan-45 and several scans were done on a Howtek drum scanner, also attached to a Mac, at Robyn Color in San Francisco. Using this technology, you can create your own book like we did!

OUTPUTTING THE IMAGE

The choices available for output of your digital image are improving and getting cheaper on a month to month basis. B&W laser printers now cost $\frac{1}{10}$ the price of 10 years ago. This is also happening with color printers. There are many types of digital printers. Here, I am sticking to the ones that make prints of photographic quality or close to it.

DYE SUBLIMATION PRINTERS

My favorite types of digital printers are the dye sublimation printers. On images that are properly color corrected and sharpened, one can make dye sublimation prints that look close to or sometimes better than Cibachrome quality. The Radius/SuperMac ProofPositive Two-Page dye sublimation printer can make prints of sizes up to 11.6x17.1 inches. These prints are beautiful and also big enough to frame and hang on the wall. I have a ProofPositive printer and find that it makes excellent prints. Most people cannot tell the difference between these and color photographs. I like the dye sublimation prints better than photographs because of the amazing control I have over color, effects and sharpness using Photoshop. The ProofPositive printers come with Level 2 PostScript so they can be used to prototype any publishing project up to tabloid size. There are many other companies that make dye sublimation printers including Kodak, Tektronics, Fargo and others. You can usually make dye sub prints at a service bureau for $15 to $50 each. Having a photographic quality digital printer is the final component that really makes a digital darkroom complete. Having it attached to your own computer allows you to work in the iterative way a photographer works in the darkroom. Make a print, tweak the colors and contrast a bit, make another print, etc. until you get exactly what you want. I love it! Having your own printer in your studio allows the control and ease of use that is essential for the artist and high quality image maker. Dye sublimation printers that make prints from 8.5x11 up to tabloid size are in a price range from $1,500 to $15,000. Make sure you check out the market well before purchasing one. There are new products every day. To accurately compare them, you should print the same digital image on each printer you are considering purchasing. Different printers have various resolutions and quality; you need to carefully compare before you buy. For the best quality on most of these printers, you need a 300 dpi original. I use files of about 50 megabytes in size to get the best quality 11x17 prints on my ProofPositive.

Iris Printers and Canon Copiers

There is a series of printers made by Iris that produce art quality work from digital images in sizes up to 30" by 40". These Iris printers can print on many types of standard art paper including parchment. Unfortunately, Iris printers are out of the price range that most individual photographers

can afford. Many specialized service bureaus do quality Iris prints and provide high quality duplication of color and control. Among these service bureaus are Digital Pond in San Francisco and Nash Editions in L.A.

Another set of devices that are very interesting are the Canon full color copiers. With PostScript controllers, like the EFI Fiery, desktop computers can send color images directly to the copier. I have seen some impressive prints from these machines in sizes of up to 11x17. This makes them very useful for prototyping print work. Since the copiers are quite fast, they are also useful for short run color printing. Speaking of short run printing, the bookstore of the future will have many books stored digitally. You will call ahead and let them know what books you want and they will be printed and bound to order. This is another digital development that will make it much easier for individual photographers to publish their own work. You won't have to pay the setup and material costs for large press runs.

Protecting Your Prints

One thing to look into when making digital prints is that they may not have the color permanence of a Cibachrome or C print. I mount my ProofPositive prints behind UV protective True-View glass and also UV protective plastics. They seem to do fine as long as I don't hang them where the sun hits them directly. Still, I've only had these prints for two years. You should contact Henry Willhelm at Preservation Publishing to get the latest independent test results on digital prints. Henry wrote the book, *The Permanence and Care of Color Photographs* and is in the process of testing digital prints.

Output to Film

Various companies make film recorders with a wide variety of prices and quality. These take a digital file and output it back to an original piece of film. You can create original quality film with the best of these. The film recorders I have seen that seem to create the best quality film are the Kodak LVT (Light Valve Technology) and the Symbolic Sciences' Fire 1000 or Light Jet. These are both very expensive devices, so output to film of original quality will probably have to be done at a service bureau for now. If you want to create a piece of film that has the same quality as an original, you will need about 90 megabytes for a 4x5 transparency and much more for an 8x10. Many photographers who do successful commercial work use files in the 30 meg range for 4x5 film output. If you look at this film with a loupe, it won't be quite as sharp as a properly focused original, but it is good for many commercial purposes. You will have to run tests at your service bureau to determine the size file and image quality that works best for you.

POSTSCRIPT IMAGESETTERS

It may be that the imagesetter is the most popular output device for digital systems. Imagesetters make halftone films for B&W and color printing. Imagesetters, and many of the other printers I have been talking about, use a computer language called PostScript. PostScript allows computer graphic data, like text and line drawings, to be represented generically within the computer and output in various sizes at the highest possible resolution that each printer or imagesetter allows. Some imagesetters print at over 3,000 dots per inch. Early PostScript imagesetters could not achieve the same quality halftones as their traditional counterparts. These problems have now been solved, so it is possible for PostScript imagesetters to make halftones and color separations of the best quality. When printing color to a PostScript imagesetter, you will get better results if it has a Level 2 or Emerald PostScript RIP. RIP stands for Raster Image Processor, and RIPping is a computer process that converts a digital CMYK file from computer byte values into halftone screen dots and patterns.

THE DIGITAL DELIVERABLE

The day will come when most deliverables will be digital. The Communications Superhighway that we keep hearing about is actually happening. From our home studio in the Santa Cruz mountains, which is 20 minutes by car from the nearest town, we can get 200 TV channels on a small radio dish pointed up towards a satellite. One day we'll be able to transmit back. Over our phone lines we can get and receive basic rate ISDN digital services. The speeds of digital access to the home or business can be orders of magnitude faster than what we have. The technology exists in some areas to send hundreds of megabits per second over fiber optic phone lines called Broadband ISDN. The technology exists for a photographer to quickly send an entire book digitally over these high speed broadband ISDN lines to a printer or, better yet, to a customer who wants to read and interact with a digital book on their computer screen. Although the technology exists, both the artists and their clients must have easy access to this for it to be used.

For the next few years, it will still be easier for many photographers to output a digital creation to film and deliver that to the client. Art directors are used to film, and with film, the photographer doesn't have to be responsible for color separations and other possible reproduction problems. In creating this book, we sent digital files, mostly from Photo CD scans, to the print shop on removable Bernoulli 230 meg disks. We sent a few JPEG compressed files over the phone line. Maybe your next book or art piece will be sent digitally from your studio to your client or output center. We are entering the digital era.

DIGITAL IMAGING OVERVIEW

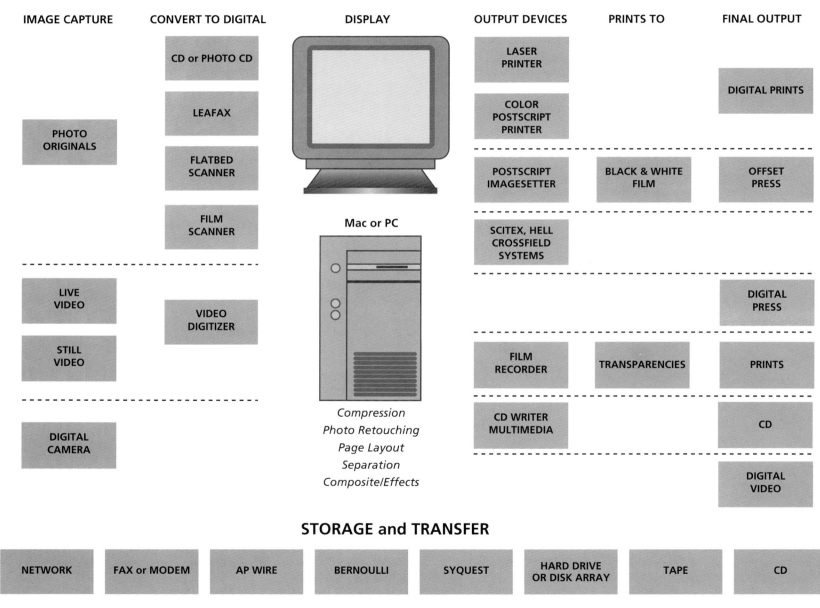

IMAGE CAPTURE	CONVERT TO DIGITAL	DISPLAY	OUTPUT DEVICES	PRINTS TO	FINAL OUTPUT

STORAGE and TRANSFER

| NETWORK | FAX or MODEM | AP WIRE | BERNOULLI | SYQUEST | HARD DRIVE OR DISK ARRAY | TAPE | CD |

THINGS YOU NEED TO KNOW

HOW TO USE THIS BOOK

*This Chapter Gives You a Quick Preview of
What You'll Find in this Book and Gives You Some
Valuable Tips on the Best Way to Use It*

We believe *Photoshop Artistry* will be helpful to both new and advanced Photoshop users. If you read this book from front to back and do the hands-on in order, it is an in-depth self paced course in digital imaging. For those that are new to Photoshop and digital imaging, this may be the best way to proceed. If you are a more advanced Photoshop user, who wants to learn new techniques, you may want to read the sections and do the hands-on that cover the skills you need to learn. The table of contents and index will help advanced users quickly find the areas you want to reference.

The book has two types of chapters: overview chapters, which contain information that everyone should learn, and hands-on chapters where you learn by color correcting and creating images. The chapters are in order starting with the foundation skills and moving on to more advanced skills. All the chapters are in-depth, and we expect most users, even experienced Photoshoppers, to learn something from each chapter. Some of the chapters towards the end of the book are very detailed and assume you already have a lot of Photoshop knowledge. You need to know the foundation skills, taught earlier on, to do the later, more advanced chapters.

The first part of the book, Things You Need to Know, has overview chapters that provide readers with a common base of knowledge. Everyone should read the Setting System and Photoshop Preferences chapter and the Input, Calibration, Correction and Output chapter so you can set up your system and Photoshop correctly, and calibrate your monitor for working with the book and doing color output. The rest of these overview chapters go into a lot of detail. If you are anxious to get your hands into the program, you don't need to read all of them before you start the hands-on. You should come back to these chapters later, however, to learn valuable information about the Zone System, picking colors, all the color correcting tools and other matters. Before doing a hands-on chapter, it's a good idea to read any overview chapter in that part of the book.

All the images you need (including the authors' before and after versions, Levels and Curves settings, masks, etc.) are included on the Photoshop Artistry CD that comes with the book. There are specialized sets of these images on the CD for Mac users and PC users. For the more powerful computers, there is a full size set of images in Photoshop 3.0 and JPEG formats and for teaching situations and smaller computers, there are compressed and smaller versions of the images. Each hands-on chapter has a separate folder on the CD with Essential Files and Extra Info Files subdirectories. The Essential Files are the original scan files you absolutely need to do the hands-on. The Extra Info Files are the authors' versions of the exercise including masks, steps along the way and Levels, Curves, Hue/Saturation and other tool settings. Use these files to compare your results to the authors' and/or to recreate the authors' results. For more information about using the CD, see the chapter on Using the Photoshop Artistry CD.

IMPORTANT DIFFERENCES FOR MAC AND WINDOWS USERS

All Photoshop users, on both the Mac and the PC, will find this book beneficial. That's because everything is exactly the same for Mac and PC users in 99.9% of the cases within Photoshop. The contents of each of Photoshop's tool windows and menu bars is the same whether it is displayed in a Mac window or a Windows window. Adobe has done an excellent job in making Photoshop compatible in every way it can. This book has been tested by Mac and PC users, and both find it valuable and easy to use. We have taught in classrooms where some of the computers are Macs and some are PCs and this works fine.

Here is a list of the few minor differences between Photoshop on the Mac and on the PC. Any important difference is also pointed out within the appropriate chapter.

MODIFIER KEYS

The references in *Photoshop Artistry* to keyboard modifier keys are written using the Option key and Command key, which are the main modifier keys for the Mac. **Windows users need to remember that whenever we mention the Option key, you use the Alt key and whenever we mention the Command key you use the Control key.** In those cases where we actually mention the Control key, which we rarely do, you also use the Control key on the PC.

FUNCTION KEYS

Most PCs only have 12 function keys on their keyboards where the Mac extended keyboards have 15. *Photoshop Artistry* includes a predefined set of function keys, called ArtistKeys, which we reference in the book. We have set these up so the ones used most often are within the first 12 keys. They will work the same for the Mac and the PC. This is discussed further in the chapter on Setting System and Photoshop Preferences.

PHOTOSHOP HELP

Mac users of Photoshop don't have a Help menu, which supplies Windows Photoshop users with the standard Windows on-line help system. This is available to Windows users by pressing the F1 (Help) function key.

STATUS BAR

Windows users also have a Status bar that tells you what tool you are using and gives you additional information about what you are doing.

MEMORY SETUP

For Photoshop to work most efficiently, the computer's application memory needs to be set up correctly. The process for setting up memory on the Mac is a little different than on the PC. Setting up memory for both types of systems is explained in the Setting System and Photoshop Preferences chapter.

GAMMA CALIBRATION

You access the Gamma Monitor Calibration utility from a different place on the Mac than you do on the PC. These differences are explained within the Input, Calibration, Correction and Output chapter.

VIDEO LUT ANIMATION

A few Macs and many more PCs don't have support for Video LUT animation within their 24-bit video boards. If you don't have Video LUT animation support, the way you use certain tools, like Levels and Curves, will change slightly. This is explained in the Setting System and Photoshop Preferences chapter and also both uses are covered throughout the book whenever Video LUT animation becomes a major part of an exercise.

NAVIGATING IN PHOTOSHOP

How to Most Efficiently Use the Tools, Palettes
and Windows that Photoshop Provides;
Make the Most of Big and Small Monitors;
and Use Some General Shortcut
Tips that Make Photoshop More Fun

Each digital image file you open into Photoshop has its own window. At the top of the window is the name of the file as it was last saved to the disk. This is a standard Macintosh window with scroll bars and a grow box in the lower right corner, etc. If windows are covered by others, you can find the one you want by going to the list of open files in the Window menu. Each one of these windows can be viewed in any of three modes denoted by icons at the bottom of the Tool palette. The left icon denotes the standard Mac window mode, which we see here. The middle icon, which we call Full Screen mode, places the active, top, window in the center of the screen in the middle of a field of gray.

WORKING IN FULL SCREEN MODE

There are a lot of advantages to working in Full Screen mode. If you are working on a small monitor, Full Screen mode does not waste the space normally taken up by the scroll bars. Also, in Full Screen mode, if you accidentally click down in the gray area, you won't switch to the Finder or some other application. This gray area is especially useful when making selections that need to include the pixels at the very edge of the window. Using any of the selection tools, you can actually select into the gray area and all this will do is insure that all the pixels along that edge are selected. When using a normal Mac window, the cursor often switches back and forth between the tool you are using and the arrow cursor for the scroll bar if you move the mouse ever so slightly when at the edge of the window.

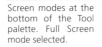

Full Screen mode

Screen modes at the bottom of the Tool palette. Full Screen mode selected.

Here we see the Photoshop desktop with three windows open. The active window, Camden-FogSailBoat, is the window on top with its title bar striped. This window will have a check mark next to it in the Window menu. You can bring any window to the top, even a hidden one, by choosing it from the Window menu.

Here we see the Photoshop desktop in Standard Screen mode and how it can be cluttered by other applications in the background. It is easy to accidentally click outside a window and switch to another application.

4

Here we see Photoshop working in Full Screen mode with various palettes around the active window. We can still get to underlying windows by selecting them with the Window menu. A single click on the Tab key will remove all these palettes and allow you to use the whole screen for your work. A second Tab click and all the same palettes are back in the same positions. This is a great way to see the big picture.

Again in Full Screen mode, here we have used Command-Spacebar-click to zoom in and fill the screen with our image, a more inspiring way to work. Learn to use Command-Spacebar-click to zoom in, Option-Spacebar-click to zoom out and the Spacebar with a mouse drag for scrolling. This is the most efficient way to move around the Photoshop screen, especially when in Full Screen mode or using a dialog box like Levels.

Even if you are not using Full Screen mode, if you are making an edit along the edge of the image, you may want to make the window a little bigger than the image. This will add Photoshop gray space between the edge of the file and the window's scroll bars so you can more easily make these edge edits. As you can tell, I am very fond of Full Screen mode. It removes all other distractions from your Mac screen and allows you to focus on your beautiful image surrounded by nondistracting neutral gray.

The right icon at the bottom of the Tool palette is similar to Full Screen mode but the image is surrounded by black instead of gray, and the menu bar is also removed. If you are a Photoshop power user, you can work without the menu bar by using command and function keys, but I usually just use this mode for presentations.

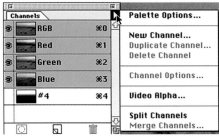

Here we see a typical palette with its Options menu on the top right accessible by clicking on the black triangle icon. The Palette Options item shows you different ways to display the palette. You should check out the Palette Options on all the palettes that have them. Most Palettes have a close box on the top left and a similar box on the right for collapsing or opening the palette. The icons at the bottom of the palette are shortcuts for various functions associated with the palette. The name at the top is the palette's name tab.

CONTROL KEYS FOR ZOOMING AND SCROLLING

There are some control keys that I make everyone learn when I teach Photoshop. IT IS VERY IMPORTANT THAT YOU LEARN THESE THREE CONTROL KEYS! Even if you hate control keys and you don't want to be a power user, you have to learn these or working in Photoshop will be a constant pain. I worked on the Lisa project at Apple. The Lisa was the predecessor to the Mac and a lot of the Mac's user interface was actually designed for the Lisa. Larry Tesler, who was head of applications software for the Lisa project, had a license plate on his car that read, No Modes. A mode is a place within the user interface of a program where you can't access the normal tools you work with. Programs that have a lot of modes can be very confusing, especially for the beginner. Photoshop is less modey than it used to be, but it still has a lot of modes. There are many tools in Photoshop that come up in a modal dialog: for example, Levels, Curves, Color Balance and most of the color correction tools. When using these tools you are in a mode because you can't go to the Tool palette and switch to the Zoom tool, for instance.

ZOOMING IN AND OUT

If you are inside Levels and you want to zoom in to see more detail, which I do all the time, you can't get this tool in the normal manner. You can, however, hold the Command key and the Spacebar down and you will see the Zoom icon. At this point, clicking with the mouse will do a zoom in and you will be looking at your image from closer up. Option-Spacebar-click will do a zoom out. When you zoom in and out with the Zoom tool or by using these control keys, Photoshop zooms by a factor of two. If you are at 1:1, where you see all the pixels, then you will zoom into 2:1 and then 4:1 and then 8:1. Each time you get twice as close. If you have a large file and are trying to get the file to fill the screen exactly, you can use Command-+ to zoom in by one digit. For example, if you are at 1:2 and you do Command-+, you will zoom into 1:3 not 1:4. The same thing works for zooming out with Command-minus (-). The difference is these techniques work in smaller increments and are more obvious with larger files. (Don't forget that, when not in a mode, you can always zoom so the entire image fits within the screen by double-clicking on the Hand tool within the Tool Palette. If you double-click on the Zoom tool the image will resize to 1:1.)

SCROLLING WITH THE HAND ICON

Just holding the Spacebar down will bring up the Hand icon, and clicking and dragging with this icon will scroll your file.

If you are working in Windows on the PC, use the Alt key where we specify the Option key and where we specify the Command key, use the Control key .

PALETTE MANAGEMENT

Photoshop contains a lot of different palettes each of which controls a different set of functions. The Tool palette is the main palette and its functions are discussed in the Tool Palette chapter of this book. The different color picking palettes are discussed in the chapter called Picking and Using Color. There are Channels, Layers and Paths palettes and each of these is discussed in appropriate chapters in this book. What we will discuss here is how to most efficiently use those palettes on the Photoshop screen.

ACCESSING PALETTES

Except for the Tool palette, all palettes are accessed from the Window/Palettes menu. You can use this menu to bring up or close a particular palette. We recommend using the Command palette to define function keys to bring up and close the palettes you use most often. The next chapter, Setting System and Photoshop Preferences, explains how to do this. The Tool palette does not show up in the Window/Palette submenu, instead you use the Tab key to access this palette. Pressing the Tab key again makes the Tool

palette disappear. It also makes any other palettes that are currently open disappear. Pressing Tab again brings all these palettes up in the same locations. Option-Tab opens or closes the Tool palette without changing the status of the other palettes. Option-Tab is a new feature of 3.0 that I use all the time. You can close any of the palettes, except the Tool palette, by clicking on the close box in the top left corner of the palette.

PALETTE OPTIONS

Most palettes also have an Options menu that is accessible by clicking on the Menu icon at the top right of the palette. Palettes can be moved around on the screen by clicking on the title bar at the top and moving the palette to a new location. Photoshop will open with palettes in the same location they were last used unless you turn off the Restore Palette & Dialog Positions option within Photoshop's General Preferences/More.

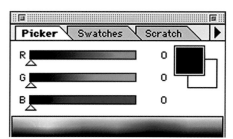

Here we see a group of palettes with the Picker palette currently active. The Palette Options menu would now bring up the Picker palette's options.

GROUPING AND SEPARATING PALETTES

In Photoshop 3.0, several palettes can be grouped within the same palette window. You then switch between palettes in the group by clicking on the name tab of the palette you want or by choosing the palette from the Window/Palettes menu. If you hide any of the palettes within the group, the whole group gets hidden. For this reason, it is better

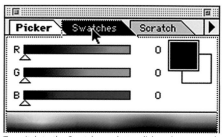

To switch to the Swatches palette, click on its name tab and when you release the mouse, the palette group will look like the group below.

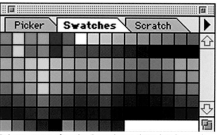

Palette group after the Swatches palette has been chosen. Now the Palette Options menu will show the Swatches palette Options.

6

to only group palettes that are used together. Sometimes you will want to see two palettes at the same time that are usually used within a group. I do this sometimes with Layers and Channels. Usually I use them as a

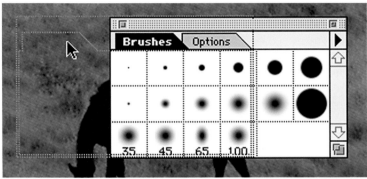

Click on a palette's name tab and drag it outside the group window to put that palette within its own window.

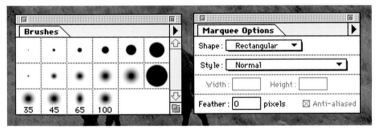

Here we see the Brushes palette after it has been removed from grouping with the Options palette. To regroup these palettes, click on the name tab of one of them and drag it on top of the window of the other. The palette that is within a group window first will have its name tab on the left. New palette tabs are added to the right.

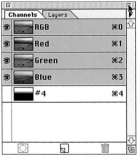

Clicking the first time in the grow box, at the top right, resizes the palette so it will just hold the things within it, like the palette on the right.

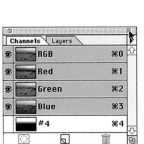

Clicking a second time in the grow box resizes the palette to just show name tabs like the palette on the right.

Clicking again in this palette's grow box will expand it to the size to the immediate left. This compacted size shown here can be left at the bottom of your monitor without taking up a lot a screen real estate until you need it again later.

group, but when I'm working on a complicated layer document that has a lot of mask channels, I separate them to see both at the same time. To do this, click on the name tab of the palette you want to separate and then drag it out of the group window to a new location by itself. To move more palettes into a group, click on the name tab of the palette you want to add and then drag it on top of the group window. New palettes in a group are added to the right. If you have a small monitor, you may want to group more of your palettes together to save screen space. You can also compact and collapse your palettes by clicking in the grow box at the top right.

MORE THAN ONE WINDOW PER FILE

You can have more than one window open at a time for the same Photoshop document. To do this, first open a Photoshop file which will give you your first window. Now go to the Window/New Window command to open a second window of the same file. With this capability, you can, for example, have one window looking at a section of the file up close and the other window looking at the entire file. You can also use this technique to have one window looking at a particular channel or mask of the file while another window looks at the RGB or CMYK version. There are many uses of this feature.

USING THE INFO PALETTE

The Info palette is one of the most useful tools in Photoshop. Not only does it measure colors like a densitometer (which we will do extensively in the color correction exercises in later chapters in this book), it also gives you important measurements any time you are scaling, rotating, making or adjusting a selection. The size of the box you are drawing, the degree of rotation and many other useful measurements are always there in the Info palette. This is a good one to keep up on the screen most of the time.

Here we see two views of the same file. The one on the top-left is a closeup of the inscription on the stone above the door at Tintagel Castle, England, the supposed castle of the Knights of the Round Table.

7

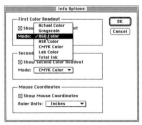

The two sections you see here, at the bottom of the Info palette, only appear while you are in the middle of drawing, sizing or rotating. Here we are using the Scale command.

Check out the many options of the Info palette.

SETTING SYSTEM AND PHOTOSHOP PREFERENCES

Setting Up Your System and
Photoshop's Preferences to
Make Photoshop Run More Efficiently
and Make Your Work Easier

If you are new to computers or Photoshop, some of the discussions and settings here may seem a bit confusing to you. We suggest that you read this chapter anyhow and set up your preferences as we recommend. This will make Photoshop run more efficiently and give you better results with your color corrections and separations. You will gain further understanding as you do the exercises and read the rest of the book, especially the Input, Calibration, Correction and Output chapter.

SETTING UP YOUR MAC

You may want to read this with your Macintosh turned on so you can follow the steps that are described as you refer to your screen. When you are in the System 7 or 7.5 Finder, choose About This Macintosh from the Apple menu. This brings up an information window with the total memory available on your Macintosh and how much memory is being taken up by each application you are running. If you check this when no applications are running, Largest Unused Block tells you the amount of space available for all your applications in multiples of 1024 bytes. An abbreviation for 1024 bytes is the expression One K. One thousand twenty four K, (1024 ° 1024) bytes of memory, is equal to one megabyte (Mb) or 1,048,576 bytes of memory. If you had, like I do, 112 Mb (megabytes) of Total Memory (114688K), and your system software used about 5 Mb (5120K), then the Largest Unused Block would display about 107 Mb (109,568K). This 107 Mb is available to divide between the applications that you want to run concurrently.

If you are only going to use one application at a time, like Photoshop, then you can give most of this remaining memory to Photoshop. You want to leave at least 1-2 Mb of space free for desk accessories to run. I often use Photoshop and Quark at the same time, so I assign 80 Mbs to Photoshop

and 16 Mb to Quark. This still leaves me about 10 Mb for other applications. If I were working on a really large Photoshop project, I would assign all of the available memory to Photoshop. Still, I would leave a megabyte or two for desk accessories. If you don't leave enough room for the desk accessories, sometimes you will get a message that there isn't enough memory to run a particular desk accessory. When there is barely enough room to run a desk accessory, the system can be more prone to crashing.

The way you tell the system how much memory to assign an application is to first select the icon for the application while you are in the Finder. You select an application icon by opening the folder that contains that application and then clicking on the application file only once. This must be done when the application is not currently running, so don't click twice since this will start the application. Now choose Get Info from the File menu in the Finder. An information window about that application will appear. Every application has a suggested size and a preferred size which are displayed at the bottom of the information window. Suggested size is usually the minimum size recommended by the application developer to allow the application to operate efficiently. Preferred size is the amount of memory this application will actually be given when it runs. Some applications will still operate if you set preferred size to less than suggested size and some will not. I would recommend an absolute minimum of at least 8 Mb of memory for Photoshop 3.0. With this 8Mb minimum, some features may still not have room to work depending on your file size. If you have a 68000 Mac, it's better if the preferred size is at least 10 Mb and if you have a Power Mac, you want the preferred size to be at least 12 Mb.

You can always set preferred size to more than suggested size and this will usually make the application perform better. Photoshop usually requires 3 to 5 times the amount of temporary space as the size of the file(s) you currently have open. It is much faster if Photoshop can put all of this temporary space into real memory. If there is not enough real memory for the temp

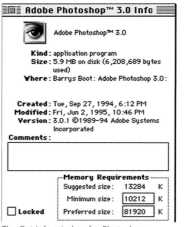

The Get Info window for Photoshop.

The About This Macintosh window with only the System running. The space for System Software and Largest Unused Block don't add up to exactly Total Memory since the system is constantly borrowing small amounts of memory to use for this and that.

About This Macintosh on my Mac with the System, Photoshop and Quark running.

space, Photoshop will allocate a temp file on the disk and use it as virtual memory for its temp space needs. When this happens, Photoshop runs much slower than when everything is in real memory. Photoshop comes with its Preferred size set to a default of 8 Mb. If you are trying to work on large files with this little memory, Photoshop will be very slow. If you increase Photoshop's memory on your Macintosh, you should notice a great improvement in performance.

There are several settings in the Memory control panel (Apple Menu/ Control Panels/Memory) that are important to Photoshop's performance.

DISK CACHE

Photoshop runs faster if you set the Disk Cache size to 32K. Making the Disk Cache larger than this makes Photoshop run slower.

VIRTUAL MEMORY

Photoshop has its own virtual memory system that is much more efficient for Photoshop than System 7's Virtual Memory. Therefore, it is very important that you turn Virtual Memory off in the Memory control panel. Power Mac owners get a message that system RAM requirements decrease by "x" if they use virtual memory. Still, Photoshop will run better on Power Macs with Virtual Memory turned off.

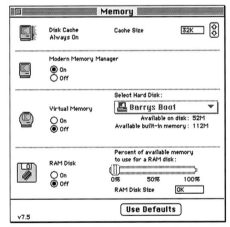

The Memory Control Panel and how it should be set for Photoshop.

32-BIT ADDRESSING

Keep 32-Bit Addressing on.

RAM DISK

Giving more memory to Photoshop using the Get Info procedure we just described makes Photoshop faster than allocating that same memory as a RAM Disk, so keep the RAM Disk off.

SETTING UP YOUR PC

When using Photoshop on a Windows based machine, setting up your Photoshop memory usage is less complicated than on the Mac. Choose File/Preferences/Memory from Photoshop and make sure that the Memory Usage setting is 100%. 100% should be the default setting anyhow. Set your primary scratch disk to your fastest drive that also has the most free space. See the further discussions about scratch disks later within this chapter. For the PC, you set your scratch disk within this Memory dialog instead of within the separate Scratch Disk menu on the Mac. Now click OK within the Memory Preferences setting. You need to quit Photoshop and then restart it for these changes to take effect. When Photoshop starts up, it calculates the amount of available RAM within your system. Photoshop measures this RAM by taking the amount of installed RAM and subtracting any that is used by disk caching software, RAM disks and other software that permanently reserves RAM (including the Windows OS). Photoshop will allocate 100 percent of the available RAM for its own use. 12 Mb of RAM is the minimum you should have available for Photoshop to use on a standard PC. For Pentium based machines, you want to have a minimum of 16 Mb available for Photoshop. Check the Scratch Size and Efficiency box at the bottom left of your open document to see how much RAM is available and how Photoshop is using it. See the Scratch Disk section later in this chapter for more information on these.

SETTING UP THE PHOTOSHOP PREFERENCES

Most of the Photoshop preferences are accessed from the File/Preferences menu. We will go through the preferences in order and will talk about the ones that are important for working efficiently with photographs. For a description of Photoshop preferences that we don't talk about, see the Photoshop 3.0 manual. If you are new to Photoshop, pre-press or photography, some of the concepts or Photoshop functions mentioned in this chapter may be unknown to you. If this is the case, just set the preferences as we recommend now, and then reread this chapter after you have studied the rest of the book.

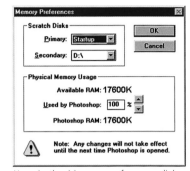

Here is the Memory preferences dialog from the Windows version of Photoshop. Use this to set up how Photoshop will use memory on your PC and also to set up the scratch disk it will use.

GENERAL PREFERENCES

COLOR PICKER

You usually want the Photoshop Color Picker since it gives you more options than the Apple Color Picker.

INTERPOLATION

Bicubic interpolation is the most accurate way to resize images, so you want to select this for the best quality. If you are prototyping ideas and speed is more important than image quality, you might try one of the other choices. Nearest Neighbor is the fastest and poorest quality.

CMYK COMPOSITES

If you are working in CMYK color, you should choose Faster for the CMYK Composites option. Smoother is a little more accurate but it is very hard to see the difference in most cases. However, to see CMYK gradients more accurately, turn on the Smoother option.

COLOR CHANNELS IN COLOR

Turn off Color Channels in Color which displays your Red, Green and Blue, or CMYK channels with a colored overlay that makes it very hard to see detail. Viewing individual channels in grayscale is more accurate.

SYSTEM PALETTE

If you are working in 8-bit color, you don't usually want to use the System palette. You usually want a custom adaptive palette for each image. Having a custom palette for each image makes that image display more accurately, but the screen will flicker when you switch from one image to another in the 8-bit mode.

DIFFUSION DITHER

When working on an 8-bit system, the Diffusion Dither option makes smoother transitions on colors that are not in the current palette. I like the Use Diffusion Dither option to display 24-bit images on an 8-bit screen. I recommend leaving this option on.

VIDEO LUT ANIMATION

Unless you have a very old video board, you want Video LUT Animation to be on. This allows you to see many color and contrast changes instantly by tweaking the monitor display through the video card. A few old or poor video circuits don't support this, and you only want to turn this feature off if you have one of those displays. Video LUT Animation is not available on some PCs, as this feature is not supported by some PC-video cards. PC users should ask their video board supplier if Video LUT Animation is supported and only turn it on if it's there. You can also just turn this option on and then go through the steps in the Grand Canyon exercise, which uses Video LUT Animation, to see if Video LUT Animation is working. If it is, then leave the option on here. If it doesn't work, turn this option off.

TOOL CURSORS

The Tool Cursors settings are important! If you set the Painting Tools to the new 3.0 Brush Size, you will paint with a circle outline the size of your brush. This even takes into account the current zoom factor. I recommend Brush Size. The precise option is like using the Caps Lock key in Photoshop 2.5 in that you will paint with a cross-hair cursor. Standard uses

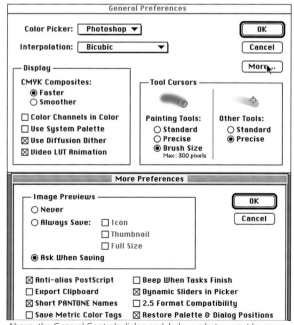

Above, the General Controls dialog and, below, what you get by pressing the More button. These are our recommended settings.

the standard Photoshop cursors, a different cursor for each tool. I find the standard cursors usually get in the way of seeing what you are painting. For the Other Tools option, I recommend the Precise setting.

To get more preferences, press the More button in General Controls.

IMAGE PREVIEWS

I like to decide whether to save an icon or not whenever I save a file. You can also always save an icon or never save one. Icon refers to the icon you see when you are in the Finder. Thumbnail refers to the preview seen in the Open dialog box. Full Size saves a 72dpi full size preview for applications such as Specular Collage. The Image Previews options are not available for the Windows version of Photoshop.

ANTI-ALIAS POSTSCRIPT

Check Anti-alias PostScript if importing PostScript from Illustrator or Freehand, otherwise your PostScript imports will have jaggy diagonal and circular edges.

EXPORT CLIPBOARD

Have you ever seen the message "Converting Clipboard to Pict Format" while you impatiently waited to switch to the Finder or some other application? Turn off Export Clipboard to make switching between Photoshop and other applications much faster. You can still cut and paste inside Photoshop, just not between Photoshop and other applications.

SHORT PANTONE NAMES

Check Short PANTONE Names if you're exporting a Pantone color as a Duotone EPS or in some other way to Quark, PageMaker or Illustrator. Make sure those other applications use the exact same Pantone names as you used in Photoshop.

SAVE METRIC COLOR TAGS

Save Metric Color Tags is not needed unless you are using the EFI color system and you want color information forwarded to Quark or some other application.

BEEP WHEN TASKS FINISH

Beep When Tasks Finish is useful if you have a slow computer or are working on very large files. That way you can go cook dinner while Unsharp Mask is finishing. I used this a lot when I had a Mac IIx. With my Quadra/PowerPC, 112 Mb of memory, DSP accelerator and fast hard disk, I don't need the beeps much anymore.

DYNAMIC SLIDERS IN PICKER

Dynamic Sliders in Picker allows the Picker palette to show you all the possible colors, for future changes, on the fly, as you are changing one color. It is very useful when color correcting to have this on.

2.5 FORMAT COMPATIBILITY

2.5 Format Compatibility allows applications that can read Photoshop 2.5 file format to open Photoshop 3.0 files. If you have layers in your Photoshop 3.0 files, Photoshop 2.5 cannot see the layers but it can open a flattened version of the layers whose Eye icons were on last time the file was saved. There is a space cost for this convenience though. Photoshop 3.0 must save a flattened version of the file in addition to all the layers every time the file is saved. Turning off 2.5 Format Compatibility will save disk space and time when working on files that have more than one layer.

RESTORE PALETTE

Restore Palette & Dialog Positions remembers where you had all the palettes last time you shut down and restores them next time you power up.

FUNCTION KEYS AND THE COMMANDS PALETTE

The function keys that used to be in the Preferences section of Photoshop 2.5 have been replaced by the Commands palette in Photoshop 3.0. If you have an extended keyboard, there are 15 function keys you can define and 15 more with the Shift key down. Most PC users have only 12 function keys on their keyboard so they won't be able to access keys F13 through F15. We didn't assign these keys to anything that is used all the time. Function key F1 is always used for help in Windows systems. The advantage of the Commands palette is that you can have it on your desktop and click on commands even if you don't have an extended keyboard. If you are a Photoshop power user, function keys can be very useful. We have included, in the Photoshop Preferences folder on the CD, a set of predefined commands called ArtistKeys. Candidates for commands are menu items that you use a lot and that don't already have a keyboard alternative. In ArtistKeys we tried

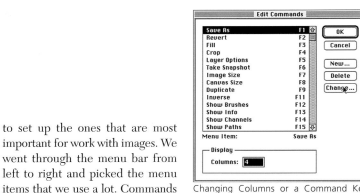

The Commands Palette with ArtistKeys Commands loaded and columns set to 1.

Loading ArtistKeys.

Changing Columns or a Command Key using Edit Commands.

to set up the ones that are most important for work with images. We went through the menu bar from left to right and picked the menu items that we use a lot. Commands can also be chosen from menus that are attached to palettes like the Layers and Channels palettes. To load ArtistKeys, choose Load Commands from the pop-up menu in the Command palette then access it from the Photoshop Preferences folder on the CD.

The Command palette can have more than one column, in which case it may be wider than long. I like to have mine set up as 8 columns wide—a wide skinny window that I can put at the bottom of my screen. To change the number of columns or to create a new function key or edit a function key, choose Edit Commands from the Command palette's pop-up menu. Edit Commands also allows you to delete a command. To create a new command, press the New button and choose the function key number. Only those keys that are not already used show up in the New option. If the function key is already defined, click on that key in the Edit Commands window and choose the Change button. Once you have defined the commands you want, choose Save Commands from the pop-up menu and save them in a file.

PLUG-INS

The Plug-ins preference tells Photoshop where to find its Plug-in filters. Usually these are in a folder called Plug-ins within the Photoshop 3.0 folder. This dialog can easily be interpreted wrongly and you might click on the wrong button. When you find the folder that contains the Plug-ins, you need to click the Select "Plug-Ins" button at the bottom of the dialog box.

Don't click on the Open button at that point like you would for most other uses of this dialog box.

SCRATCH DISK

The Scratch Disk preference on the Mac tells Photoshop where to store temporary files on disk. You set this in the Windows version within the File/Preferences/Memory dialog box. Even if you give Photoshop a lot of memory, it will often also store things on a scratch disk. Use the largest, fastest disk drive for your primary scratch disk. If you purchase a Mac with a built in drive then later go out and purchase a very large high performance external drive, you probably want to specify that external drive as your primary scratch disk since it may be faster than your built in original drive. You can also specify a secondary drive for Photoshop to store temp files when it runs out of space on the primary drive. Try to leave at least 5 times the scratch space on disk as the size of the file you are working on.

Photoshop 3.0.4 has a new scratch disk efficiency indicator. To access it, select the pop-up menu at the bottom left of the image border and choose Efficiency. The efficiency rating changes depending on the amount of time Photoshop spends swapping image data in and out of RAM from the disk. If your efficiency rating is less than 75% for most operations you might want to add more RAM to your system to get better performance. If the "†" character follows the percent display, this means that your primary scratch disk is operating with asynchronous I/O working. That is good for better performance. The Document Sizes option in this same pop-up shows you the flattened image size on the left (if you saved the file with no channels or layers) and the actual size including all the channels and layers on the right. The Scratch Sizes option gives you the amount of image data space

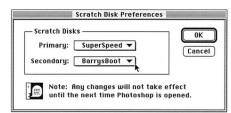

This dialog can be confusing since it looks like the standard Open dialog, but you are supposed to click on Select "Folder Name", not Open, once you find the correct folder containing your Plug-Ins. If this is not set correctly, some of your Photoshop filters will not show up.

Set your primary scratch disk to your largest fastest hard disk. Photoshop will use space on the secondary scratch disk when the primary one is full. You do not need to set a secondary scratch disk.

The Commands palette with Columns set to 8.

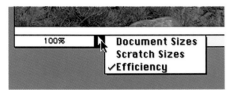

Use these features to find out about your file sizes and Photoshop's use of scratch memory and disk space.

Photoshop is using for all open images on the left and on the right the amount of scratch memory space available to Photoshop. If the number on the left is bigger than the number on the right, you are using the hard disk for scratch space and this may slow Photoshop down. See the ReadMe that comes with Photoshop 3.0.4 for more information about improving scratch disk performance.

RULER UNITS

The Ruler Units setting in the Units Preferences dialog box controls the scale on Photoshop's rulers when you go to Window/Show Rulers (Command-R). It also controls the dimension display settings in the Info palette and the initial dimension display when you enter the Image Size command. If you change the setting in the Info palette, it will also change this setting here. Usually we leave it set at inches but for very detailed measurements, we sometimes change it to pixels.

COLOR SEPARATION SETTINGS

The Photoshop preferences that occur below the line in the Preferences menu are the settings that can affect how Photoshop displays images on the computer screen as well as how Photoshop does color separations. These preferences settings are very important to set up correctly and it is also important that you standardize on these settings if you have several people contributing Photoshop files to the same publication. These settings have been worked out by Jim Rich and myself. Jim Rich is a color separation expert with a masters degree from RIT in Printing Technology and 20 years experience doing color separations and setting up high end scanners and color output systems for companies like National Geographic and Crosfield. Jim co-authored *Photoshop in Black and White* and several other great books about getting high quality scans and purchasing desktop scanners. These color separation preferences give you good quality for web and sheet fed coated stock without a lot of hassle and experimentation. These settings also work well for RGB files to be output to dye sublimation printers and film recorders. We recommend these settings as a starting point and will explain how to change them if you want to develop your own custom settings. These settings were used to create the color separations in this book.

MONITOR SETUP

Choose the selections here that match the monitor you use to display and color correct your Photoshop images. Photoshop 3.0 has built in support for many monitors. If your monitor is not listed when you click down on the Monitor pop-up, you can also use the Other setting along with the monitor manufacturer's suggestions for your monitor. If you don't have a hardware monitor calibration device, set the Gamma and White Point to 1.8 and 6500 and use the Gamma control panel that comes with Photoshop to calibrate your monitor. This control panel allows you to accurately calibrate your monitor to your own standard output proof, but that may not be an accurate measure of a particular gamma and color temperature. 1.8 and 6500 are the Adobe recommended standards under those circumstances.

If you do have a hardware monitor calibration device (one of those suction cup things), you can set your monitor to other accurately measured color temperatures and gammas. In that case, you should enter the values you are using from your hardware calibrator. The phosphors should be set for the type your monitor has. Photoshop sets this for you when you choose one of the Monitors on the list in the Monitor pop-up. The ambient light should be set for the lighting conditions in your room. The Monitor Setup settings effect how Photoshop displays images on the screen in CMYK mode and also the conversion from RGB to CMYK. See the later chapter in this book entitled: Input, Calibration, Correction and Output to calibrate your Monitor before you start the exercises. There is more detail in that chapter about these settings and how they influence what Photoshop does with color.

EYEDROPPER TOOL SETUP

Usually when you measure digital values in Photoshop, you want the Eyedropper set to measure a 3x3 rectangle of pixels. This gives you a more accurate measurement in a continuous tone image since most colors are made up of groups of different

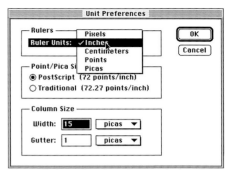

We usually leave the ruler units set to inches. Sometimes we change it to pixels to get very detailed measurements. This also controls the dimension display in the Info palette when selecting or drawing rectangles.

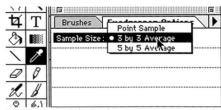

Set the monitor to the type of monitor you have. This will also set the phosphors for you. If your monitor is not listed, ask the monitor manufacturer what settings to use. Unless you have a hardware calibrator to accurately set your gamma and white point, leave them set to 1.8 and 6500. Set the ambient light based on the standard lighting in your room.

Usually you want the Eyedropper set to measure a 3 by 3 average when measuring continuous tone color.

13

colors. If you were to measure a Point Sample, the default, you might accidentally measure the single pixel that was much different in color from those around it. Double-click on the Eyedropper and set its Sample Size to 3x3 Average.

PRINTING INKS SETUP

INK COLORS: The settings for Printing Inks Setup are slightly different than the standard Photoshop settings. When you convert from RGB to CMYK, the actual CMYK values you get for a given RGB color depend on a combination of the preferences settings in Monitor Setup, Printing Inks Setup and Separation Setup along with the highlight and shadow preference values set in Levels or Curves. You want the Ink Colors setting in Printing Inks Setup to be set for the type of output you are doing. For magazine quality output to coated stock, you should start out using the SWOP Coated setting here.

DOT GAIN : The Dot Gain setting adjusts how dark Photoshop displays the CMYK image on the screen as well as how dense Photoshop makes each of the CMYK separation layers. The Dot Gain value represents how much the printing inks will spread when printed on certain papers. If you set the dot gain to 30%, Photoshop will separate each CMYK color with less density and it will display the colors on the screen darker than if the dot gain were set to 20%. The dot gain setting you should start with is 20%.

GRAY BALANCE: The Gray Balance controls the relationship between the amount of cyan, magenta, yellow and black inks when you convert from RGB to CMYK. Our suggested setting is to leave cyan, magenta and yellow all set to 1.0 and set black to .9. This will generate a little less black and more color than normal.

USE DOT GAIN FOR GRAYSCALE IMAGES: We recommend that you leave the Use Dot Gain for Grayscale Images checkbox at the bottom of Printing Inks Setup off. When displaying grayscale images, this setting will adjust your monitor's brightness depending on the dot gain setting. It will also give you the wrong 0..255 values in the Info palette when measuring a grayscale image. We recommend that you leave this setting

To get these settings, first set the Ink Colors to SWOP Coated. Then change the black, K, value in Gray Balance to .9 instead of 1.0. This will generate a little less black ink. Now choose the Save button and save these settings in your Photoshop 3.0 folder. I like to call them C1,M1,Y1,K.9 since that is the modification we are making to the SWOP Coated settings. This will change the Ink Colors pop-up to C1,M1,Y1,K.9 which is an Other setting.

unchecked and create a different monitor calibration setting in Gamma that is calibrated to your grayscale image output device. This way you will get accurate numerical readings in the Info palette.

Since we have changed all these Printing Ink settings, Photoshop will better remember them as defaults if we save them in a file. Click on the Save button and name this file C1,M1,Y1,K.9. Save it in your Photoshop folder.

SEPARATION SETUP

The Separation Setup works in conjunction with Printing Inks Setup and Monitor Setup to control CMYK conversion values. It contains a curve diagram showing how Cyan, Magenta, Yellow and Black are generated as the image goes from highlights on the left to shadows on the right.

There is more ink used in the shadows, and black ink only gets used in the darker half of the color ranges. If you adjust the settings for Black Generation from Light to Medium or Dark, you can see how the black setting effects the Cyan, Magenta and Yellow curves. Changing the Black Ink Limit and Total Ink Limit also effects all the curves. Our recommended settings are GCR (Gray Component Replacement) on; Black Generation, Light; Black Ink Limit, 100%; and Total Ink Limit, 320%. These settings are based on the CMYK values we actually got when separating a standard grayscale stepwedge and from comparing the numbers to known good CMYK values for neutral colors and coated stock.

Here are the Separation Setup settings we recommend for output to coated stock. We are basing these settings more on the actual CMYK values we get when separating a gray stepwedge file. Measuring what you actually get, after influence from Printing Inks Setup and Highlight/Shadow settings, when making a separation is more accurate than just looking at the limits shown in this dialog box.

SEPARATION TABLES

When using Printing Inks Setup and Separation Setup, you want the Separation Tables dialog to have the choices shown here.

These are the settings for getting your separation and printing inks values from Photoshop's Separation Setup and Printing Inks Setup dialogs. Only select Use Table if you are going to apply the techniques explained in Adobe's technical note.

14

HIGHLIGHT AND SHADOW PREFERENCES

The last preferences items that you need to set up for color separations are the Highlight and Shadow settings. You can reach these by choosing either Levels or Curves. Here we show you how to get to them from Levels. Choose Image/Adjust/Levels and double-click on the Highlight Eyedropper which is the rightmost one. This will bring up the Color Picker where you want to set the CMYK values to 5, 3, 3, 0. This is a neutral color for highlights. If all your other preferences were set correctly, after entering 5, 3, 3, 0 for CMYK, you should see 244, 244, 244 as your RGB settings. If this is not the case, double check your Monitor Setup, Printing Inks Setup and Separation Setup. In all cases, even if you are using different settings than ours, make sure the RGB values are all equal to each other which gives you a neutral color. Click OK in the Color Picker to return to Levels and double-click on the Shadow Eyedropper, which is the leftmost one. Set the CMYK values in the Color Picker to 95, 85, 83, 95 and check to make sure the RGB values are 2, 2, 2. If they are not, then double check your Monitor Setup, Printing Inks Setup and Separation Setup. Again, the RGB values should always be neutral. Click OK on the Color Picker and OK on Levels. To learn more about these Highlight and Shadow settings and how you use them, turn to The Grand Canyon chapter, which goes through all the basics of color correction.

You have now set the correct separation settings for coated stock. These settings also work well for RGB digital printer output, like to a dye

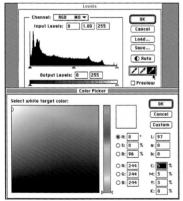 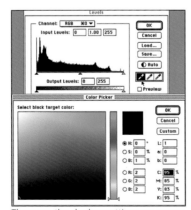

These are the highlight settings we recommend for CMYK coated stock, RGB output to film recorders and digital printers and general overall color correction of a file. Double-click on the Highlight Eyedropper in Levels or Curves to change these settings. The RGB values here should always be all the same, a neutral color.

These are the shadow settings we recommend for CMYK coated stock, RGB output to film recorders and digital printers and general overall color correction of a file. Double-click on the Shadow Eyedropper in Levels or Curves to change these settings. The RGB values here should always be all the same, a neutral color.

sublimation printer, film recorder output and general overall color correction of a file for archiving. Using the technique discussed in the section of this chapter on Creating Custom Separation Settings, you will need to change these values and your other preferences for newsprint and maybe other types of output.

SAVING AND STANDARDIZING YOUR PREFERENCES

After you change your Photoshop preferences, it is a good idea to quit from Photoshop as soon as you are finished making the changes. When you leave Photoshop, its current state (preferences, tool option choices, window locations, etc) is saved in the file named **Adobe Photoshop 3.0 Prefs** on the Mac and **PHOTOS30.PSP** on the PC. Quitting at this point assures your preferences changes are saved in this file. If you crashed before quitting Photoshop, you would loose these latest preferences changes and revert to the preferences you had when you last successfully quit from Photoshop. On the Mac, this file is located in the Preferences folder within the System Folder. It is located in the Windows directory on the PC.

It is a good idea for everyone in your company to standardize on a set of separation preferences, especially for the same publication. You could copy a standard version of this file to the preferences folder on everyone else's machine. This worked fine in version 2.5 and earlier Photoshops. In version 3.0, this only works for other machines that are exactly the same type, like from one Quadra 900 to another Quadra 900. If you take the preferences file from a Quadra 900, for example, and use this as the preferences for a Quadra 650 or Power PC, this could cause problems and even program crashes. This bug has supposedly been fixed in the new 3.0.4 version of Photoshop. It is a very good idea to standardize on separation preferences if you are doing color corrections and separations. The other way to do this is to print up a standards document and have your systems administrator make sure that everyone is using those settings.

CREATING CUSTOM SEPARATION SETTINGS

If you are trying to calibrate Photoshop separation settings for a newspaper, a particular type of Web press or other custom CMYK output, this can be done, although it is tricky. First find out what the correct CMYK values should be for the full range of neutral colors in a stepwedge file, like the one here. Your pressman or printer manufacturer should know this information. Then adjust Monitor Setup, Printing Inks Setup and Separation Setup, as well as the way you set highlights and shadows until you get the CMYK values that are closest to this for neutral colors in the stepwedge file. Using those settings in Photoshop will usually get you very close to the separations that you want. This is basically what we did to get our settings using the following table of desired values for coated stock.

	Neutral RGB 0..255 values			Target CMYK values to print these as neutrals			
	Red	*Green*	*Blue*	*Cyan*	*Magenta*	*Yellow*	*Black*
highlight	250	250	250	5%	3%	3%	0%
1/4 tone	190	190	190	28%	21%	21%	0%
midtone	128	128	128	62%	50%	48%	12%
3/4 tone	68	68	68	78%	68%	66%	45%
shadow	5	5	5	95%	85%	83%	80%

Actual CMYK values when separating the StepWedgeFile using our Photoshop Separation Settings with Highlight set at 2%, Shadow at 98%

	Cyan	*Magenta*	*Yellow*	*Black*
highlight	5%	3%	3%	0%
1/4 tone	32%	22%	22%	0%
midtone	58%	45%	44%	4%
3/4 tone	75%	63%	62%	36%
shadow	80%	69%	69%	98%

The preference settings we chose don't give exactly the values in this table. They give the closest overall to these values, which are also the most useful starting point settings. For more information on calibration, see the chapter entitled: Input, Calibration, Correction and Output.

NEWSPAPERS AND OTHER CUSTOM SETTINGS

Our default values are usually good for most RGB output purposes including output to film recorders and also for CMYK separations to coated stock. If they are not working for you, use this process to change them. Newspaper presses tend to vary much more than web or sheet fed presses for coated stock. If you are doing output for newspapers or some other special process, first get a set of correct values for printing neutral colors from your press person. This should look like the table above but the numbers will be different. For newspapers, start out with the Printing Inks set to SWOP Newsprint with a dot gain of 30%. Set the Separation Setup to: GCR; Black Generation, Medium; Black Ink Limit, 100%; and Total Ink Limit, 300%. Set the highlight (5, 3, 3, 0) and shadow (95, 85, 83, 95) preference values in Levels initially as we have recommended for coated stock. If you want to change your coated stock settings, start with our recommendations earlier in this chapter and then use this same process to adjust them.

Bring up the StepWedgeFile, which starts out as a grayscale, and convert it to RGB. Click with the highlight Eyedropper to set the highlight (using Levels as described in the GrandCanyon chapter) on the 2% gray wedge and set the shadow at the 98% wedge. For Newspapers use the 5% and 95% wedges for Highlight and Shadow Eyedropper clicks. Bring up the Info palette and measure the RGB and CMYK values you get at different density areas along your stepwedge. Compare the CMYK numbers with the ones you got from your press person. Change the Dot Gain and Gray Balance settings in Printing Inks Setup and the Black Ink Limit and Total Ink limit settings in Separation Setup until you get values that are as close as possible to those from your press person. You can also change the Black curve between Light, Medium and Heavy in Separation Setup as well as creating a custom Black curve. Separation Setup doesn't give you direct control over the Cyan, Magenta or Yellow curves but they are affected by the changes you make to the Black curve. You can adjust the weight relationship between cyan, magenta, yellow and black using the Gray Balance settings in Printing Inks Setup.

You will have to play with all these settings until you get a feeling for the relationship they have with each other. The settings we have recommended for coated stock have worked quite well in producing this book and for other projects that Jim Rich and I have done. We don't recommend particular settings for newspapers since they tend to vary from paper to paper. For more help with newspapers you might want to get *Mac Newspaper News*, a monthly newsletter pertaining to Macs and newspaper publishing. The co-editors are Michael Kienitz and Ken Miller. They can be reached at: Michael Kienitz, DLM Imaging, Suite 208, 2002 Atwood Ave. Madison, WI 53704 and Ken Miller c/o the Milwaukee Journal Sentinel, 333 W. State St., Milwaukee, WI 53201. For more information on output to black-and-white halftones, you should get *Photoshop in Black-and-White* by Jim Rich and Sandy Bozek from PeachPit press.

With the Separation Tables preferences settings, you can also load a custom table using the Load button. This custom table would decide for you how to convert from RGB to CMYK. When you load a custom table, Use Table should be selected in both To CMYK and From CMYK. Companies like Electronics For Imaging (EFI) and Kodak (the KEPS system), sell custom separation tables for Photoshop. If you have another color separation system that you would like to import into Photoshop, like from Scitex or some other high-end system, Adobe has a technical note called **SEP TABLES FROM OTHER APPS** explaining how to do this using Load Separation Tables. This very interesting technical note is on the Photoshop 3.0 Deluxe CD ROM within the Photoshop Tech Notes folder in the Technical Library folder. Anyone responsible for color separations should read this technical note. It can be very useful.

A standard grayscale stepwedge file. We use this with the Eyedropper and Info palette to measure what Photoshop actually does when making a separation. As you make changes in the Monitor Setup, Printing Inks Setup and Separation Setup, as well as how you set your highlights and shadows, you can see how those changes effect the separations by measuring this stepwedge with the Eyedropper. This StepWedge file is in the Calibration folder on the CD.

FILE FORMATS AND IMAGE COMPRESSION

OVERVIEW OF FILE FORMAT ISSUES

OPENING AND SAVING FILES

When you read a file into Photoshop, no matter what format it was in when you read it, the file will be in Photoshop's built in format while you are working on it. Photoshop creates a temporary work file in memory and also, depending on the size of the file you are working with, in the free space remaining on your disk. The original file that you opened on the disk remains untouched by Photoshop until you do a File/Save. As you are working on a project within Photoshop, it is a good idea to save along the way. Every time you have done enough work since your last save that you would be upset if your computer crashed and you lost that work, you should do another save. When you choose File/Save (Command-S) to save the file, this saved file will overwrite your original file on the disk. If you have just had a file scanned, or if you want to save the original before you change it in Photoshop, you should choose File/Save As to save the file you are about to modify with a different name. This will leave your original file unchanged. When you do a Save As, you will notice that the name of your window will change from the your original file name to the new name you used in the Save As. If you later do another Save, that save will overwrite the file with the new name. This is often recommended because your original file is still intact under the original name.

PHOTOSHOP 3.0 VS OTHER FORMATS

While you are working on a project, saves should normally be in Photoshop 3.0 format. When you first open a file into Photoshop, the first save will save the file using the same format you opened it with. If you opened it as a TIFF, Photoshop will save it as a TIFF. If you opened it as a JPEG, Photoshop will save it as a JPEG. The first time you do a save, make it a Save As and change the format to Photoshop 3.0. This will make Photoshop more efficient because 3.0 is Photoshop's internal format and also Photoshop 3.0 format supports everything that Photoshop can do including layers, channels and paths. Some of the other file formats don't support some of these features. It is especially important not to resave JPEG files over and over again because every time you save a JPEG file it looses some information; more about this later. If you opened a file that was TIFF format and added a channel to it, Photoshop would still save this in TIFF format because TIFF supports extra channels. If you added a layer to this

When and How to Use Each of the Important File Formats, and Understanding Photoshop, TIFF and JPEG Image Compression

same file, Photoshop would save it in Photoshop 3.0 format because TIFF doesn't support layers. If the format is changed automatically to Photoshop 3.0, this is because you added a feature to the file that isn't supported in the format you were working with before.

DIFFERENCES BETWEEN FILE FORMATS

What are the differences between file formats? Once the file is opened up and inside Photoshop, it always resides there in Photoshop's own internal format. Saving the file into a different format is sort of like translating a book into a different language. In most cases, the raw data for the different formats will be exactly the same, it is just the way the data is stored or what additional information can go with the data that changes. For example, an RGB file in format A may have all the red bytes stored together, then all the greens, then all the blues stored together. In format B the storage might be a red, green and blue byte for pixel 1, then a red, green and blue byte for pixel 2, etc. Some formats may use a simple type of compression called run length encoding. This is a lossless compression where, if there are say 50 bytes in a row that are exactly the same, these 50 bytes will be stored using a special code so they only take up 4 bytes. Another format may specify a space at the beginning of the file where extra information can be stored. The EPS file format, for example, allows you to store clipping paths, preview picts, screen angles and transfer function information within the file. In all these cases, the RGB or CMYK information in the file format will be the same. It is just the packaging of this information that changes from one format to another. If you save the file as a JPEG or PICT file, these formats do a data compression that is lossy. The lossy compression allows these formats to save the file in much less space than in the other formats. The lossy part means that when you read the file back in, or decompress the file, it will be the same size you started with but the actual data won't be identical. You need to be careful when using lossy compression not to loose important image data. We will be talking about this in the second part of this chapter.

INFORMATION ABOUT EACH FORMAT

Now let's discuss each of the formats that most of you will be using and when it might be best to use that format. The file formats you will probably be using most often with Photoshop are Photoshop 3.0, Photoshop 2.0, TIFF, EPS, JPEG, PICT and Scitex CT.

PHOTOSHOP 3.0 AND 2.0

When you are continuing to work on the same file in Photoshop between shutdowns of your computer, you should usually be working on that file in Photoshop 3.0 format. This is the only format that supports all of Photoshop 3.0's features like Layers. If you need to exchange files with others that are using Photoshop 2.0 or 2.5, you can make sure every Photoshopper can open this file by saving it in Photoshop 2.0 format. Photoshop 2.0 and 2.5 formats do not support Layers. If you are working with Photoshop 3.0 and you have the 2.5 Format Compatibility option set from General Preferences/More, then people using 2.5 can open your layered files and see a composite of the layers whose Eye icons were on when you saved the 3.0 file. If the file has multiple Layers, they can't modify the file's different layers and the cost of this 2.5 compatibility is an extra RGB layer the size of your 3.0 canvas. You can save a lot of disk space by turning off the 2.5 Format Compatibility option. Most page layout applications and many other programs can't read any Photoshop format. There are some applications, like Fractal Painter, that read Photoshop 2.5 format.

Photoshop 2.5 and 3.0 file formats do some compression especially on mask channels. Because of this, files saved in this format will be smaller than their corresponding TIFF files especially if they have a lot of mask channels. Photoshop 3.0 does a great job compressing simple masks, they are often in the same size ratio as JPEG. The RGB and CMYK components of Photoshop files are also compressed although this compression does not make the file much smaller unless there are large areas within the file of the same color. The advantage of using Photoshop 3.0 format to compress is that this is a lossless compression.

TIFF

It seems like the most common file format that popular imaging applications support is TIFF. You can save both RGB and CMYK files in TIFF format and TIFF is supported on the Mac and on the PC. I often save grayscale and RGB files in TIFF format to go back and forth between Photoshop and Quark. TIFF

format will also save your mask channels. If you want to save a TIFF file and not save the mask channels, use File/Save a Copy and choose the Don't Include Alpha Channels option.

When working on the Mac, the byte order should be set to Macintosh. If you set the byte order to IBM PC, both Photoshop and Quark on the Mac will still open the TIFF file. There are probably some applications on the PC that won't open the Mac byte order TIFF files.

The TIFF dialog lets you choose LZW compression. LZW compression is a standard TIFF form of compression that typically takes longer to open and close than JPEG or Photoshop 3.0 compression. TIFF LZW compression is a lossless compression so when you reopen the compressed file it will be exactly the same as the original. With LZW, you will usually get a file that is somewhere between ⅓ to ⅔ as large as the original depending on the original. Some applications that use TIFF files do not support LZW compressed TIFF. If you run into problems, resave your TIFF file without compression.

ENCAPSULATED POSTSCRIPT (EPS)

The EPS format is the most versatile format and has many options. This format is especially useful for communicating back and forth between Photoshop, Illustrator and Quark. If you want to save a clipping path from Photoshop, you need to use the EPS format. The Path you choose will show up in the Clipping Path portion of the EPS Format dialog. For more information on saving paths from Photoshop to Quark and Illustrator, see the chapters entitled: Bike Ride in the Sky! and Bob Goes to Vegas.

After converting your file into CMYK with the Mode menu, you can save it into EPS format in several ways. If you leave the DCS, Desktop Color Separation, option off, all four components of your CMYK file will be together. This is less error prone because you place this one CMYK file directly into Quark. The same file that is placed is also printed. The DCS option divides your EPS file into 5 smaller files. There is one file for each of cyan, magenta, yellow and black and the 5th file is a preview file. Before you save any file for final output, make sure the dots per

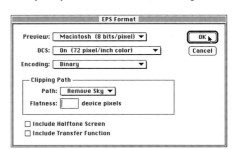

The choices available for saving an EPS image. Here we show you the recommended Mac settings for EPS.DCS 5 file format. If you have chosen a clipping path, it should show up here. Leaving the flatness blank will use the printer's default setting for flatness. Don't check Include Halftone Screens or Transfer Functions unless you are setting these things in Photoshop. Discuss all of these settings with your service bureau before you send them any files.

The normal choices available for saving a TIFF image. To save TIFF without the mask channels, use File/Save a Copy and choose Don't Include Alpha Channels.

Victorians.eps

Victorians.C   Victorians.M

Victorians.Y   Victorians.K

The EPS.DCS option with 72 dpi preview gives you 5 files. The Cyan, Magenta, Yellow and Black files need to be in the same folder as your Quark document when you send the job to the imagesetter. The eps preview file is used for placing and cropping in Quark.

The uncompressed TIFF version of the Victorians image. This file is 6 megabytes.

inch (dpi) setting is correct for that final output. For a 150 line screen, the setting should be 300 dpi. When the dpi is properly set, the 5th preview pict will usually be smaller than the other 4 files and can be very quickly read and placed into Quark.

The big advantage of EPS/DCS is that only the preview pict needs to be transferred over the network, or, on removable media, to the desk of the person who is placing and cropping the pictures within the page layout application. This is much faster than transferring the entire CMYK file, which you would have to do with EPS composite or TIFF format. The tricky thing about EPS/DCS is that you need to make sure the other 4 CMYK files are included in the same folder as your Quark document and preview file when you print your layout to the imagesetter, otherwise you will get a low quality printout. Again, discuss this file format choice with your service bureau. There is more information about the EPS file format in the Photoshop manual.

PICT

Pict format is an Apple standard file format and is supported by automatic compression and decompression within QuickTime. I have found this format to cause some problems when placed in Quark documents. It is, however, the most commonly used multimedia format.

SCITEX CT

Scitex CT format is sometimes used when saving CMYK files that will be processed on a Scitex imaging system. Again, your service bureau will tell you if you need to save in this format.

DISK SPACE AND COMPRESSION FORMATS

In today's world of color page creation, disk space is a commodity that can be used up quite quickly. Color photographs are the items that take up the most disk space. For the best quality, a color photograph has to be scanned at twice the dots per inch (dpi) as the line screen it will be printed. If you are printing your color photographs in a 150 line screen publication, you can calculate the disk space each photograph will need using the following formula:

Byte size of image file = (printed height x TwiceLineScreen) x (printed width x TwiceLineScreen) x (3 for RGB or 4 for CMYK).

For a 5x7 color image in this publication, the required disk space would then be:

(5x300) x (7x300) x 3 = 9,450,000 bytes.

This is over 9 megabytes for just one copy of the file. Usually, by the time you are finished with production, you may need two or three copies of each file. That could be 30 megabytes of storage for just one 5x7 photograph. You might want to consider using compression to reduce the size of your image files.

LZW COMPRESSION

When you save a file in TIFF format from Adobe Photoshop, you can choose LZW compression. This is a lossless compression technique that is built into Photoshop. It saved the 6Mb uncompressed

The JPEG medium compressed version of the Victorians image. This file is 349K.

Victorians file in 4.2Mb. When you look at the amount of time LZW compression takes verses the minimum space savings you get, LZW compression is often not worth the effort.

JPEG COMPRESSION

Using the Joint Photographic Experts Group (JPEG) compression software built into Photoshop with the quality setting on High, the 6Mb Victorians file was compressed to 587K. This is a real savings in data space here since the compressed file is about ¹⁄₁₀ the size of the original! With JPEG compression, you can choose how much you want to compress a

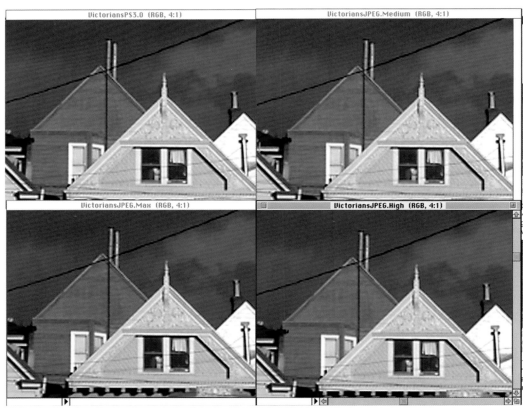

The original Victorians, 6mb, uncompressed is on the top left. Below that is the JPEG compression set to the maximum image quality, 1Mb. On the bottom right is the high quality setting, 587K. Finally on the top right you see the medium quality, 349K. Although you can see some minor degradation on the screen, all these JPEG compressions will work for printing. The worst quality setting, called Low, really degrades the image beyond the point of usefulness for high quality printing on coated stock.

file. Using more compression gives you a smaller file but also more loss of image detail. A smaller amount of compression gives you less loss of image detail but the compressed file will not save as much disk space. Depending on your publication quality requirements, you can choose a compression factor that compresses files without any visible detail loss on the final printed page.

JPEG is an industry standard file format for image compression. There are many companies that sell JPEG software and hardware compression products. The hardware compression boards, which contain DSP chips, can compress and decompress images from 10 to 100 times faster than without the DSP. DSP stands for Digital Signal Processor, which is a chip that speeds up the mathematical operations used in a lot of image processing filters and effects including JPEG compression and decompression. There are also Photoshop plug-ins to speed up JPEG compression if you have an AV Mac with a built in DSP hardware accelerator. These are available from Adobe and often on CompuServe and America Online. America Online has a very useful Photoshop forum you can access with the Keyword: Photoshop. This area has a lot of different discussion groups about Photoshop as well as software upgrades and enhancements like the one for AV Macs.

CHOOSING A COMPRESSION FACTOR

To show you the kinds of problems to look for when choosing your compression factor with JPEG compression, we have printed the same file with different degrees of compression. For coated stock we would recommend not compressing your file at all unless you need to. If you do need to save space, try to use the Maximum quality setting when possible as this will give you the best image quality. If you can't see any data loss in your final printed image, then the loss may not be important to you. On the other hand, if you archive a digital file to be used in future printed pieces, slide productions or multimedia presentations, you need to be sure that compression data loss won't show up in one of those future applications.

Another issue about JPEG compression is that compressed files will take longer to open and process when printing from the service bureau. Before you compress, talk to your service bureau about the decision to use or not use JPEG compressed files. Unless the service bureau owns a Level 2 PostScript imagesetter, they cannot download JPEG files directly. They have to re-open the file in Photoshop and save it to another uncompressed format. They may charge you more for JPEG compressed files if it will take them longer to process them on output. Other options for compressing files, which are lossless compression options, are DiskDoubler and StuffIt. Again, you should discuss these options with your service bureau before choosing one of them.

USING THE PHOTOSHOP ARTISTRY CD

Using the Photoshop Artistry CD to Create
the Examples in this Book; Choosing the Right
CD Images to use for Macintosh vs PC
and for High-End vs Smaller Workstations;
and Using these Images in a Classroom

The Photoshop Artistry CD, which comes with this book, contains all the images to do the examples in the book yourself. You can use this as a self-paced course or you can use it to teach a course at the college or professional level. When you put the CD in a Mac CD player, it will come up with the name Mac Photoshop Artistry, and it will look like a Macintosh directory with folders, files and icons as well as file names that are often longer than 8 characters.

When you put the Photoshop Artistry CD in a PC you will see a DOS directory named PCPSArt with 8 character file names as well as the appropriate 3 character suffixes that the PC requires.

WHAT'S ON THE CD

The directory on the Photoshop Artistry CD opens up to show you a folder for each chapter in the book that is a hands-on exercise. There are also folders with files and images that the reader can use to enhance their knowledge about some of the overview chapters. Green folders are for hands-on exercises and blue folders are for overview sections. The folders are numbered in the order you should go through them if you are using this book as a self-paced course.

When you open each hands-on chapter's folder it will contain two subfolders, Essential Files and Extra Info Files. On the PC, these are called Essntial and ExtrInfo. Essential Files contains the images and other information you will need to complete that hands-on exercise. Extra Info Files contains the authors' intermediary and final versions of the images for that exercise as well as masks, levels and curves settings and other pieces of information that will help you compare your results to the author's. We have tried to make the images printed in this book look as much like those on the CD as possible. The digital files on the disc, however, are a more accurate comparison of the progress that happens on each creation. To get the best results when viewing any of the CD files, it is important that you calibrate your monitor to our course files as explained in the Input, Calibration, Correction and Output chapter.

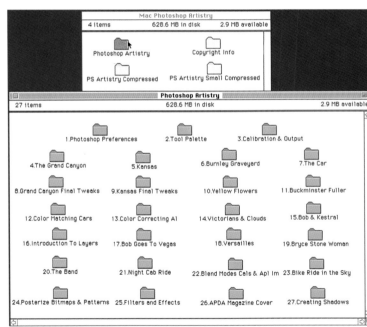

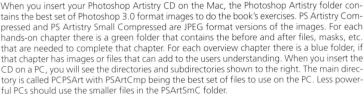

When you insert your Photoshop Artistry CD on the Mac, the Photoshop Artistry folder contains the best set of Photoshop 3.0 format images to do the book's exercises. PS Artistry Compressed and PS Artistry Small Compressed are JPEG format versions of the images. For each hands-on chapter there is a green folder that contains the before and after files, masks, etc. that are needed to complete that chapter. For each overview chapter there is a blue folder, if that chapter has images or files that can add to the users understanding. When you insert the CD on a PC, you will see the directories and subdirectories shown to the right. The main directory is called PCPSArt with PSArtCmp being the best set of files to use on the PC. Less powerful PCs should use the smaller files in the PSArtSmC folder.

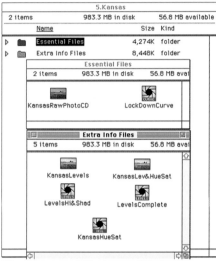

When you open a folder for one of the hands-on sessions, it will contain two sub-folders called Essential Files and Extra Info Files. Essential Files are the images and other files you will need just to complete the hands-on exercise. Extra Info Files will contain things like the intermediate and final versions of the images and masks for that exercise as well as levels and other settings we used along the way. You can compare these with your results if you have any questions about the way you are doing the exercise.

To Teach a Course

We certainly hope that this book will be used by other instructors to teach Photoshop courses around the world. Since 1990, Barry has been using these examples to teach many Photoshop courses at the University of California Santa Cruz Extension, the Palm Beach Photographic Workshops in Florida, Ad Vantage Computers in Des Moines, Photo Metro in San Francisco and many places around the country including the famous, but now defunct, Center for Creative Imaging in Maine. Having a professional course where the students can take home the images and exercises to practice them again later has been a main factor in making Barry's Photoshop courses so well received. Our hope is that you can take advantage of his years developing these exercises by using this book as the text for your Photoshop courses.

Having each student purchase the book will give them a copy of all the images as well as the step by step exercises for each example. The main images on the CD in the Photoshop Artistry folder, along with the extra info files, are in Photoshop 3.0 format and take up about 350 megabytes of information. Most images open to about 4 megabytes in size and can grow from there as the exercise progresses. For a professional course, the author has discovered that it is best to use images that are large enough to see the kinds of details students will be working with when they are doing real projects for magazines, film output and publications. These 4 Mb Photoshop files from the Photoshop Artistry folder are the easiest to use and give the students the most information for doing the course. If your course machines each have CD players, each student should access the images directly from their own CD within the Photoshop Artistry folder.

When to Use the Compressed Images

Many teaching computers are not equipped to handle this much information. Some of the places where the author instructs do not have CD players on all machines. To help out with these situations, we have provided a set of images for both the Mac and the PC that will fit on a single 100 Mb disk. These are JPEG compressed versions of the course images that can be used in a teaching situation where each workstation does not have its own CD player or where distributing 400 Mb of information over a network is too slow. This set of images is on the CD in a folder called PS Artistry Compressed. This is also the set of compressed files that has 8 character file names and PC suffixes for PC users in the directory called PSArtCmp within PCPSArt.

Working with the PS Artistry Compressed or PSArtCmp images in JPEG format is a little different than working with Photoshop 3.0 format images. The exercises assume you are working with the Photoshop 3.0 format images, so these differences need to be explained to the students when using the compressed versions. Although the compressed versions are smaller on the disk, they will open to the same 4 Mb size within Photoshop and their quality is still very good since they were saved using the Maximum JPEG quality setting. Opening JPEG images usually takes a bit longer since many calculations have to be done to decompress them. Once the student opens a JPEG image it should be saved on their hard disk in Photoshop 3.0 format to use while working on the exercise. Continually saving over again in JPEG format will degrade the image quality further for each save and also take up a lot more time.

JPEG images cannot have mask channels built into them like the Photoshop 3.0 versions do. When students are using a JPEG image that references an author-created mask, the JPEG mask channel will be saved in a separate file under the same name that the mask has within the Photoshop 3.0 version of the image. To access this mask, the student will have to open the mask file, switch back to the example image, then do a Select/Load Selection to load the mask that is in the separate mask file. If you are teaching an exercise, you should do a dry run with the same version of the files that the students will use. That way you will be able to explain any differences that the JPEG files bring up. I use these JPEG files all the time and they work fine.

Using the Small Compressed Images

If you are working on Macs that are not Quadras or Power PCs or Windows systems that are less powerful, especially if they only have 8 Mb of memory or small 80 to 100 Mb hard disks, you will want to use the PS

Artistry Small Compressed images. This is a third set of smaller images that comes on the CD and will fit on a single 44 Mb SyQuest disk. For Windows users, this set of images is called PSArtSmC and is located in the PCPSArt directory. These images are also JPEG compressed, like the ones we discussed in the last paragraph, but when you open them they open up to about one megabyte in size instead of four megabytes in size. These are more usable on less powerful computers. They will not show as much detail as the standard Photoshop Artistry, or the PS Artistry Compressed (PSArtCmp for PC) images, which we recommend for users with more powerful computers.

Because they don't show as much detail, only use the PS Artistry Small Compressed images if you have an older less powerful Mac or PC with little memory and/or a small hard disk. If you have a Mac Quadra 650, 700, 900, 950 or faster or any Power PC, with at least 20 megabytes of memory and at least 100 megabytes of free disk space, you should use the standard Photoshop Artistry or the PS Artistry Compressed images. If you have a Mac IIx or IIci or Performa or other older, slower Mac that is not accelerated and also has little memory or free disk space, then you should be using the Photoshop Artistry Small Compressed images. The total set of these small compressed images takes up about 40 megabytes of disk space so they are also easier to distribute over a computer network. If you have a less powerful PC, you can use the PSArtSmC set of images which are a smaller set with PC names and suffixes.

Using these Images without a Copy of the Book

We do not mind if teaching institutions or individual users make use of a copy of the Photoshop Artistry images from their hard disk or over a network as long as they have a copy of the Photoshop Artistry book. If you plan to use Photoshop Artistry to teach a class, please contact SYBEX to find out about school discounts and to also get complete information regarding purchase and distribution of books and images. Each person or student that uses these images to learn about Photoshop should have a copy of the book. If a school, company, institution or person gives out copies of these images to any person who has not purchased the book, that is copyright infringement. If a school, company, institution or person makes copies of the step by step instructions or copies paraphrased step by step instructions and hands either of those out in class, especially when using them with the Photoshop Artistry images, that too, is copyright infringement. Please don't do this as we will prosecute any copyright infringement to the fullest extent of the law. Thanks.

More Info for Windows Users

For all Windows users, we have provided two sets of PC format files (8 characters with 3 character suffix) in the PSArtCmp and PSArtSmC directories. The files in the Photoshop Artistry folder, within the Mac directory, have file names that are often longer than 8 characters. We are hopeful that Windows 95 users will be able to access these longer file names in a similar way as the Mac can access DOS directories and file names. If Windows 95 can see the files, which it could by having an installable file system extension that supports Mac directories, you can copy them to your hard disk and add the suffixes needed for Windows using the Program Manager. If you want to access these larger files with standard Windows, use a Mac with DOS Mounter to copy them to a DOS format hard disk then rename them to the same names and suffixes that you see in the PSArtCmp directory. Now Windows will be able to open them.

THE TOOL PALETTE

An Explanation of Each Tool in the Tool Palette with Tips for Usage

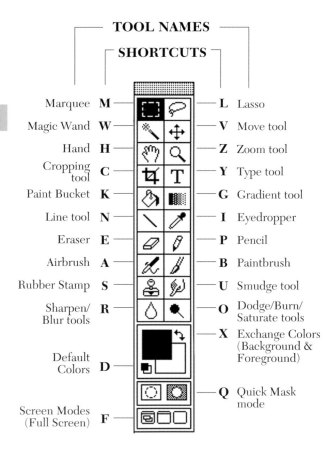

TOOL NAMES

SHORTCUTS

Marquee **M** — **L** Lasso
Magic Wand **W** — **V** Move tool
Hand **H** — **Z** Zoom tool
Cropping tool **C** — **Y** Type tool
Paint Bucket **K** — **G** Gradient tool
Line tool **N** — **I** Eyedropper
Eraser **E** — **P** Pencil
Airbrush **A** — **B** Paintbrush
Rubber Stamp **S** — **U** Smudge tool
Sharpen/ Blur tools **R** — **O** Dodge/Burn/ Saturate tools
— **X** Exchange Colors (Background & Foreground)
Default Colors **D** —
— **Q** Quick Mask mode
Screen Modes (Full Screen) **F** —

The Tool palette with corresponding keyboard commands.

This is not an exhaustive tour of every tool, all its possibilities and applications. There are several other very fine books, including the Photoshop manual, that go into more detail. Here, we will try to give you all the information that you need for working with photographs. This is actually a lot of fun for us and we hope you enjoy and take some time to play with these tools. As you begin to discover how the tools work, you can apply them to the type of images you have been creating and, perhaps, begin to discover new creative impulses. Open the images in the Tool Palette folder and play as you go through this chapter.

All of the tools have changeable options you can access through the menu bar from Window/Palettes/Show Options or by double-clicking on the tool itself. Additionally, some of the tools can have different brush sizes, which are available through the Brushes palette (Window/Palettes/Show Brushes).

THE SELECTION TOOLS

The first three tools in the Tool palette are concerned with making selections. In conjunction with items from the Selection menu and the Pen tool (which we discuss later) you are able to isolate portions of your image for editing.

MARQUEE TOOL

KEYBOARD SHORTCUT: Type the letter M, and if you type M again the tool switches from rectangular to elliptical and back again.

The Marquee tool can be used to make rectangular or oval selections or to select a single row or single column of pixels. You can switch back and forth between the tools in the Options palette as well as being able to set your selection to single row or single column.

CONSTRAINED ASPECT RATIO: The Style pop-up menu allows you to choose a constrained aspect ratio or a fixed size for either the rectangular or oval marquee. You would use a constrained aspect ratio if you were making a selection that you knew needed to have a 4x5 ratio, for example, or a 1 to 1 ratio for a perfect square or circle.

FIXED SIZE: A fixed size is useful when you know exactly the size in pixels of the print you want to make and want to crop to that size. Here, if you click down with the Marquee tool, you get a rectangular selection the size that you specified. By keeping the mouse button down and moving the mouse, you can move the selection around the image to find exactly the crop you desire. Of course, you can also use this option simply

Styles available for Rectangular and Elliptical Marquees. Note that Anti-aliased is not available.

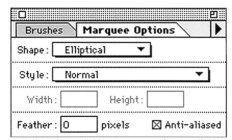

Anti-aliased is available as an option for the Elliptical Marquee.

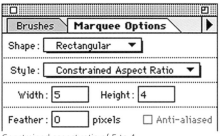

Constrained aspect ratio of 5 to 4.

to select and edit an area of a specific size.

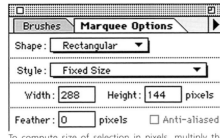

FEATHER: The Feather option allows you to set the amount of blend on the edges of your selection. A larger feather radius will give you more of a vignette effect. The amount of feather is calculated in both directions from your selection border. For example, a 15 pixel feather measures both 15 pixels to the outside of your selection area and 15 pixels to the inside giving you a total feather effect of 30 pixels. We rarely set a feather radius on our Marquee tool, preferring to make a selection and then use Select/Feather from the menu bar to set the feather. This way, we can change our radius if we are unhappy with the effect.

To compute size of selection in pixels, multiply the width or height in inches times the number of pixels per inch of resolution in your image.

ANTI-ALIASED: You may have noticed that the Elliptical Marquee has one other option, Anti-aliased. Anti-aliased subtly blends the edge of your selection with the surrounding area, so you usually want to leave it on. This option is also available on the Lasso tool but is grayed out on the Rectangular, Single Row and Single Column tools. Keep Anti-aliased on when you want your selection edge to blend with the surrounding area. Making your selection with Anti-aliased off will give you a hard edge that will be jagged on diagonal lines and curves.

MODIFIER KEYS: Holding down the Shift key with either of these tools will constrain your selection to 1 to 1. That is, you will get a perfect square or a perfect circle. Make sure you release the mouse button before you release the Shift key. If, however, you already have a selection, the action is different. The Shift key causes a new, unconstrained selection to be added to your original selection.

Holding down the Option key while drawing will force the selection to draw from the center where you first click down. This can be extremely useful, as you will see in the Buckminster Fuller chapter later in this book.

Holding down the Shift and Option keys while dragging will give you a perfect circle or perfect square drawn from the center.

Be careful how you click in a file with an active selection. If you click inside the selection, you may inadvertently move the selection slightly. If you click outside the selection, you lose the selection.

Holding down the Control key will give you the Magic Wand.

SINGLE ROW AND SINGLE COLUMN: Single Row and Single Column are just that. Single Row will give you a selection 1 pixel high all the way across your file, Single Column selects 1 pixel top to bottom. We rarely use this,

but you can use it to draw straight lines or as a sort of guide to make sure things are lined up. Generally, the Line tool is easier to use for both of these purposes. This option is also useful for selecting single row or column artifacts introduced by scanners or bad media and then cloning into that selected area.

LASSO TOOL

KEYBOARD SHORTCUT: Type the letter L.

The Lasso tool is used to make a freehand selection. Although it's a little clunky to draw with a mouse, you'll find yourself using this tool a lot. Clicking and dragging gives you a line that follows the track of your mouse. If you hold down the Option key and click, let go of the mouse button, then click in a new spot, you can draw with straight lines between mouse clicks. Continue clicking this way to make geometric shapes or hold down the mouse button and draw freehand again. When you let go of the mouse and the Option key, a straight line will be drawn connecting the beginning and ending points of your path, so be careful not to let go of the Option key until your path is finished. See the Victorians and Clouds chapter for more information on how to use this feature

Lasso Options.

MAGIC WAND TOOL

KEYBOARD SHORTCUT: Type the letter W.

Where the Marquee and Lasso tools make selections based on physical proximity of pixels, the Magic Wand makes its selections based on color values of adjacent pixels.

TOLERANCE SETTINGS: The tolerance that you set determines how close in value pixels must be to be selected. The lower the tolerance, the more similar the colors must be. A higher tolerance will select a greater range of colors.

Magic Wand Options.

SAMPLE MERGED: The Sample Merged option makes its selection based on a merged version of all the currently visible layers. Whether you want this option on or off depends on the type of image you are working with and the kind of selection you wish to make. If the colors of the object you want to select are affected by another layer, you probably want this option on. If all the colors you want to select are on only one layer, leave it off. But remember, no matter whether your selection is based on one layer or on merged layers, the edits that you make will affect only the currently active layer.

THE GROW AND SIMILAR COMMANDS: The tolerance value that you set on the Magic Wand also affects which pixels get selected when you use the Grow and Similar commands from the Select menu. The Grow command will select adjacent pixels that fall within this tolerance while the Similar command will select pixels throughout the entire image that fall within the tolerance range. You may also change the tolerance setting on the Magic Wand between uses of either of these commands to select a larger or smaller range of colors.

SELECTION TOOL TIPS

ADDING TO YOUR SELECTION: After you've made a selection with any of the selection tools, you can hold down the Shift key and make another selection. Both selections will then be active.

SUBTRACTING FROM A SELECTION: If you hold down the Command key after you've made your initial selection, you can take away portions of the selection.

MOVING A SELECTION MARQUEE: Once you have made a selection you can move the selection marquee without affecting the underlying pixels by using Option-Command-click and drag.

MOVE TOOL

KEYBOARD SHORTCUT: Type the letter V.

The Move tool is the only tool in the tool palette for which there are no options. This tool is used to move a selection or the contents of a layer. Click and drag on a selection or layer to move it to a new location within your document. If you are in a selection tool and click inside the selection border, you will automatically get the Move tool. If you are in any other tool, you can hold down the Command key to access the Move tool. However, the icon for the Move tool when accessed from any other tool will be the selection arrow.

HAND TOOL

KEYBOARD SHORTCUT: Type the letter H.

Use the Hand tool to scroll the image. Scrolling doesn't change your document, it allows you to look at a different part of it. It is more efficient to access the Hand tool using the Spacebar on the keyboard along with a mouse click. This can be done at any time. If you double-click on the Hand tool within the Tool palette, the image will be resized to the largest size that fits completely within the current screen.

Hand Tool Options.

ZOOM TOOL

KEYBOARD SHORTCUT: Type the letter Z.

Use the Zoom tool to magnify the image and with the Option key to shrink the image. The location where you click will be centered within the bigger or smaller image. Think of this tool as moving a photograph you are holding in your hand either closer to your face or farther away. The actual size of the photograph is not changed by this tool, only how closely you are looking at it. It is best to access this tool using Command-Spacebar-click to zoom in closer or Option-Spacebar-click to zoom out farther. These command keys work all the time even when a dialog box, like Levels, is up. If you double-click on the Zoom tool within the Tool palette, the image will be zoomed in or out to the 1 to 1 size. At 1 to 1, the image may be bigger than the screen but you are seeing every pixel of the part of the image you are viewing. Use this for detailed work.

CROPPING TOOL

KEYBOARD SHORTCUT: Type the letter C.

Although we often use the Rectangular Marquee tool and the Crop command to crop an image, the Cropping tool is more powerful. To use the Cropping tool, click and drag a box around the area you want to crop. Click and drag on one of the handles (little boxes in the selection corners) to change the size of the crop area. Finally, move the cursor within that area and click on the scissors to discard the unneeded portion of the image.

THE COMMAND AND OPTION KEYS: Use the Command key on a corner handle of the marquee to move the selection boundary without changing its size. Use the Option key on a corner to rotate the selection boundary. To finish the rotate and crop at the same time, click on the Scissors icon in the center.

FIXED TARGET SIZE: Click on the Front Image button in the Cropping Tool Options to make the crop the exact dimensions and resolution of the image that is currently active, or you can set the width, height and resolution of the crop manually. Whatever crop you make will be constrained to these proportions and it will be resampled to exactly these specs when you click on the scissors. Leave the resolution blank and the specified aspect ratio will be maintained. The file will be resampled if needed. For example, if you ask for your crop in inches, and the dimensions are larger than your current file, the resolution of the file will be sampled down after the crop. However, if you ask for your

Cropping Tool Options.

Cropping tool selection boundary rotated.

After the crop, your image looks like this.

crop in pixels and the crop is larger than the current file, the resolution of the image will be maintained but pixels will be added; in effect, sampling up the image. Make all entries blank, deselect Fixed Target Size or choose Reset Tool from the Options triangle to put the tool back to normal cropping operation.

TYPE TOOL

KEYBOARD SHORTCUT: Type the letter Y.

With the Type tool you enter text by clicking on the image in the location where you want the text. Text looks better if you have Adobe Type Manager installed and have the Anti-Aliased option on except for very small type. Type is added to your image as a floating selection so you can adjust it using Float Controls, Rotate, Effects, Filters and all the other Photoshop commands before it is embedded within your image by dropping the floating selection. For the highest resolution output, text often looks better if it is added using Illustrator or Quark. We show you how to do this in the Bike Ride in the Sky! chapter.

FONT: Font is the name of the face that you will be using. Sometimes the names start with a letter that categorize the weight or cut of the font. In the example here, you have selected B Times Bold. If you're not used to dealing with typeface names this can be confusing. Generally, you look for the name of the typeface such as Times or Garamond, then select the weight of the face that you wish to use, such as light, book, bold or italic. If you are using Adobe Type Reunion, the weights of each face will be grouped together. If you are not using Type Reunion, all the bold fonts will appear in the menu together prefaced by the letter B. All the italic fonts will be grouped together prefaced by the letter I and so forth.

SIZE: The size that text appears depends not only on the size chosen within the Type Tool dialog box, but also on the resolution and dimensions of the image as set using the Image Size command. If the resolution is set to 72dpi, Photoshop will think the image is large, in this case, 5 inches high. 12 point type will look quite small on this file. However, if you change

Type dialog box that appears after you click in your file with the Type tool.

A 760K file at 72 ppi is 5 inches high.

The same file at 300 ppi is 1.2 inches high.

the resolution to 300dpi without changing the file size, Photoshop now states that this image is 1.2 inches high. Your 12 point type will look considerably larger.

LEADING: Leading is the amount of vertical spacing between the baselines of the lines of text. A positive number will give you more space between the lines, a negative number, less space. If you set type in all capitals, a negative number usually gives better spacing between the lines.

SPACING: Spacing refers to the horizontal letter spacing of the text. Use a larger number for more space between the letters. As in leading, a positive number will give you more space between the letters, spreading them out. A negative number will draw the letters tighter together.

STYLE: We rarely use any of the other type style options, preferring to use a typeface that is rendered the way it was designed. If you use Bold or Italic (called machine styling), the type is merely fattened or slanted. It's not beautiful type but you might find some useful effects.

ALIGNMENT: You can change the alignment of your text from flush left to flush right or centered or even align the letters vertically.

SHOW FONT/SIZE: Click on either or both of these options if you want to see what the actual typeface will look like when rendered. Remember that size is relative.

MODIFIER KEYS: When the text is floating, you can take away part of it using Command with the Lasso tool. You can also drop, or make permanent, part of it using Command with the Text tool.

Note that the text will come in as the current foreground color at 100% opacity. This floating selection can be accessed through the Layers palette where the Opacity and Paint mode can be modified. It's best to set your type on a new layer or double-click on the floating selection in the Layers palette to make the type a new layer so you can make changes to the type without disturbing other layers of the file.

PAINT BUCKET TOOL

KEYBOARD SHORTCUT: Type the letter K.

The Paint Bucket tool does the same thing as the Magic Wand but it also fills the selection with the foreground color after the selection is made. We seldom use the Paint Bucket preferring to make

The Paint Bucket Options.

the selection first and then, once we have the right selection, use the Fill command from the Edit menu. The Fill command also has many more options than the Paint Bucket. The Bucket is very useful, and faster than Fill, for colorizing black-and-white line drawings like cartoon drawings or animations.

PAINTING MODES: We will discuss the various painting modes in a later chapter entitled: Blend Modes, Calculations and Apply Image.

OPACITY: Changes the opacity of the fill.

PATTERN: To access the Pattern option, you must first define a pattern. To do this use the Rectangular Marquee with no feather and choose a selection that you'd like to turn into a pattern. Now choose Edit/Define Pattern. You may only have one pattern in the memory buffer at a time, so if you like to have lots of neat patterns available to you, you'll want to save these rectangular selections as separate files or together in one file.

SAMPLE MERGED: If you are using several layers, you can choose which layers the Paint Bucket searches for the color tolerance range. If you click on Sample Merged and have the Eye icon on in more than one layer, Photoshop will sample the data in every layer that is currently visible. The Paint Bucket will fill only the layer that is currently active.

Define Pattern in the Edit menu.

GRADIENT TOOL

KEYBOARD SHORTCUT: Type the letter G.

The Gradient tool is often used in a mask channel to blend two images together seamlessly. We will discuss this technique in the part of this book entitled: Compositing Images with Masks and Channels. The basic function of the Gradi-

The Gradient tool default settings.

ent tool is to make a gradual transition in the selection area from the foreground color to the background color. A blend is accomplished by clicking and dragging a line the length and angle you want the blend to happen. If you'd like to experiment with the tool, open the LeafW/mask file from the Tool palette folder on the CD and the file called GrColOrPur. You can use the Rectangular Marquee tool to make a selection or use Select/Load Selection to apply the Leaf Mask to the file.

THE DEFAULT SETTINGS: When Normal, Linear, Foreground to Background and Midpoint of 50% are selected, everything from the first click on the line to the edge of the selection will be solid foreground color. Everything from the mouse release to the other end of the selection will be solid background color. Along the line there will be a blend from foreground to

Foreground to Background Normal.

Foreground to Background Color Only.

This file called GrColOrPur has an orange foreground and purple background. These are the colors we used to illustrate the Gradient tool. To use the same colors as you experiment, use the Eyedropper tool by itself to click on the orange square and set your foreground color, then hold down the Option key with the Eyedropper and click on the purple square to set your background color.

TheLeafW/mask file. Open this file if you want to play along with the Gradient tool. You can use Select/Load selection to apply the Leaf Mask. See the chapters in Part IV of this book: Compositing Images with Masks and Channels, for more information.

background color, and at a place 50% along the length of the line, the two colors will each be at 50% opacity.

PAINTING MODES: We will discuss the various painting modes in the Blend Modes, Calculations and Apply Image chapter. However, you might want to try some of the modes, Color pictured above) as you explore the Gradient tool. Leaving the Dither option on will result in smoother blends with less banding.

MIDPOINT: If you move the Midpoint to 20%, then you will get more of the background color than the foreground color. 80% would give you more foreground color.

FOREGROUND TO TRANSPARENT / TRANSPARENT TO FOREGROUND: Use this option to blend foreground color to transparent or vice versa.

CLOCKWISE AND COUNTERCLOCKWISE SPECTRUM: The Clockwise Spectrum and Counterclockwise Spectrum options move the colors along the length of the line through

A blend across a selection using 20% as the midpoint options…

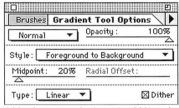

will be 50% of the foreground and background colors at 20% of the blend length.

A blend across the selected area with the default setting…

gives a blend from foreground to background with 50% of each color at the midway point.

A blend that begins or ends before the selection boundaries…

will be 100% of the foreground color before the beginning of the blend and 100% of the background color after the blend line ends. When using the default settings, the midpoint, where color is 50% foreground and 50% background, will still be at the midway point.

A diagonal blend…

using foreground to transparent.

Foreground to Transparent blend inside mask of the leaf.

Transparent to Foreground blend inside mask of the leaf.

A Linear Blend with a 50% midpoint using Clockwise Spectrum and moving from orange to purple.

A Linear Blend with a 50% midpoint using Counterclockwise Spectrum and moving from orange to purple.

the rainbow in one direction or another between the foreground and the background colors.

RADIAL BLENDS: Radial blends are circular with the first click being the center with the foreground color, the line length being the radius and the mouse release being background color. The Radial Offset controls the percent of the line from the center of the circle that is solid foreground color.

A Radial Blend from the center of the leaf...

with no radial offset...

and with a 20% radial offset.

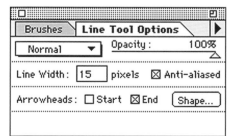

Line Tool Options with Arrowheads selected.

Using the Line tool with a zero pixel width to measure distance with the Info palette.

LINE TOOL

KEYBOARD SHORTCUT: Type the letter N.

The Line tool makes great anti-aliased lines in whatever thickness you specify. To make a line you click where you want the line to start, drag and then release where you want the line to end. You can also have arrows at the beginning or end of a line, and you can edit the width, length and concavity of the arrows. If you set the line width to 0 and turn off the arrows on both ends, you can use the Line tool, in conjunction with the measurements in the Info palette, as a ruler.

Arrow drawn using the preceding options.

EYEDROPPER TOOL

KEYBOARD SHORTCUT: Type the letter I.

The Eyedropper tool is used for choosing the foreground and background color from within an image on the screen. You can click on the Eyedropper tool to use it and then click on the color you want to make the foreground color. You can Option-click to get the background color. You can get to the Eyedropper by holding down the Option key when using any of the painting tools and then clicking where you want to pick up a new foreground color.

Eyedropper Options: Use Point Sample when choosing specific colors, 3 by 3 Average when color correcting.

AUTOMATIC EYE DROPPER: The Eyedropper automatically shows up whenever you are in Levels, Curves, Color Balance or any of the color correction tools and you move the cursor over the image. This allows you to see the color values of any location within the Info palette and Colors palette while you are correcting and changing those values. As a preference setting, for this type of use with continuous tone images, you should double-click on the Eyedropper and set the sample size to 3 by 3 Average rather than the default Point Sample setting.

ERASER TOOL

KEYBOARD SHORTCUT: Type the letter E.

The Eraser tool erases to the background color in the background layer and to transparent in any other layer. The background color is usually white but can be any color. Erasing a layer to transparent allows you to see layers below through the erased area. There are four options for the type of eraser nib that you can use: Paintbrush, Airbrush, Pencil and Block. The first three give you eraser nibs that act exactly like their painting tool counterparts in respect to style, so we will discuss those styles with the individual tools. The Block option is most like the eraser from previous versions of the program. It does not have anti-aliased edges and the size of the

The Eraser Options.

The four different erasers at 50% opacity.

area you erase is determined not by brush size, but rather by the magnification of the image that you are working with. The higher the magnification, the smaller your erased area will be until you reach the point that you are erasing individual pixels.

You usually use the Eraser when you want to completely remove something in a small area. If you hold down the Option key when erasing or click the Erase to Saved option, you get the Magic Eraser, which will erase back to the last saved version of the image. You can also click the Erase Image option to erase your entire image, but don't worry, you get a warning before the big zap! If you hold down the Option key and click on the Eraser icon, or if you continue to type the letter E, you will cycle through the tool's painting options. The Stylus options only work if you have a pen tablet attached instead of a mouse.

THE PAINTING TOOLS

The Pencil, Paintbrush and the Airbrush are the regular painting tools. There are also the Rubber Stamp, Smudge, Blur/Sharpen and Dodge/Burn/Sponge tools which are more specialized painting tools. If you double-click on any of these tools or go to Window/Palettes/Show Options, you get the specific options for that tool. Note also that the way your tool cursor is displayed is controlled by the tool cursor options you set in your General preferences (Command K). We use Brush Size for the painting tools and Precise for other tools. Before we go to each particular tool, we'll discuss the Brushes palette and some of the options that are pretty standard to all the tools.

THE BRUSHES PALETTE

All of the painting tools get their brush information from the Brushes palette. To see this window, choose Window/Palettes/Show Brushes (F12 with ArtistKeys). The set of brushes is the same for all the tools except the Pencil tool which has only hard-edged brushes. Each tool remembers which brush and option set were last used for that tool. You can add and save brushes or groups of brushes using the pop-up menu at the top right of the Brushes palette.

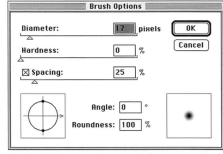
Brushes palette and its options.

SETTING BRUSH OPTIONS: If you double-click on a particular brush, or an area where no brush is currently defined, you get the Brush Options window. This allows you to change the diameter of the brush, up to 999 pixels, the hardness of the brush and also the spacing. When the hardness is set to 100%, there is no, or very little, blending of the color or image you are painting with the background. A hardness of 0 gives maximum blending with the background. Try the same large brush with different hardness settings to see how this can affect the stroke. The spacing effects how closely dabs of the paint tool are placed together on the screen. The default value for this is 25%, which causes a 75% overlap of each dab so it looks like a continuous stroke. To learn about spacing, set it to

Double-clicking on any brush will take you to its Brush Options.

100% and then paint using a big brush with the Paintbrush tool. At 100%, the dabs will be tangent to each other on the canvas. Now try turning the spacing off by unchecking the Spacing box. With spacing off, the spacing is controlled by how fast you move the brush. Try it!

You can change the angle and roundness of the brush by typing in values in the dialog box or by using the handles and arrow on the brush definition area on the lower left of the palette. The lower right portion of the window will illustrate what that brush will look like.

DEFINING A CUSTOM BRUSH: In addition, you can define a custom brush by drawing a rectangle around all or part of an image and pulling down the Brush Options to Define Brush. You can use a color or grayscale rectangular selection to define your brush, but the brush will appear as grayscale in your palette. Consequently, if your brushes are built in grayscale with a white background, your results will be more predictable. When you paint with any brush, it uses the density of the gray in the brush to determine the amount of foreground color laid down.Once you have defined your custom brushes, you can use Save Brushes from the Brushes Menu to give your new brushes a distinctive name. You can save the

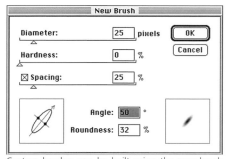

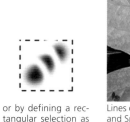

Custom brushes can be built using the new brush option...

or by defining a rectangular selection as a brush shape.

Lines drawn with the brush shape to the left and Spacing turned off.

brushes wherever you like, but if you've hit on something you think you're going to use again, save your brushes in the Photoshop folder inside the Goodies/Brushes and Patterns folder.

Photoshop includes several custom brush palettes inside this folder already. You can load these or any palette you create by using Load

Brushes from the pull-down options, or if you want to add those brushes to the current palette, choose Append Brushes.

Reset Brushes will take you back to the default Brushes palette.

COOL BRUSH TIP: While you are painting, you can change the size of the brush by typing with the right and left bracket symbols, [and]. The right bracket will move you to the next bigger brush and the left bracket to the next smaller brush. If your General Preference Painting Tools is set to Brush Size, then you can be changing the brush size as the brush is sitting over the area you want to paint. You'll see when you've reached the right size.

THE OPTIONS PALETTE

The following options work primarily the same way for all of the painting tools.

OPACITY: You will notice the painting mode and opacity settings at the top of the Options palette. The default painting mode is Normal and the default opacity is 100%. Try out the different painting modes and try painting with different opacities. You can change the opacity by typing in a number from 0–9 while using one of the brush tools. 1 = 10%, 2 = 20%...9 = 90% and 0 = 100%. Also, please note that the tools do not all handle the buildup of paint the same way. The Pencil, Paintbrush and Rubber Stamp tools paint in strokes only. That is, if you lay down a stroke of color or image at a certain opacity, keeping the mouse button down and moving back over that stroke will have no cumulative effect. You must let go of the mouse and paint a new stroke to build up the amount of paint. In contrast, the Smudge tool, Focus tools and Toning tools are cumulative. Holding down the mouse button and moving back and forth over a stroke increases the effect on each pass. Finally, the Airbrush produces a cumulative effect whether stationary or moving. Paint continues to be applied in the mouse location until you let go of the mouse button.

FADE: The Fade distance will cause color painted with the tool to fade to either transparent or the background color over the number of pixels you choose for the distance. If you leave the distance box empty—the normal setting— there will be no fade-out.

STYLUS PRESSURE: The size, color and opacity can be varied by the stylus pressure only if you have a pen tablet attached instead of a mouse.

MODIFIER KEYS: With all the painting tools, you will draw either vertically or horizontally if you hold down the Shift key while painting. Also, if you click once with the tool, let go of the mouse button, then Shift-click somewhere else, a straight line will be drawn between these two points with the current brush.

PENCIL TOOL

KEYBOARD SHORTCUT: Type the letter P.

When you are using the Pencil tool, the edges of your drawing will be jagged since there is no anti-aliasing here. Use the Pencil when you want to be sure to get a solid color even on the edge of the painted area.

Pencil Options.

BRUSHES: Note that when you switch from an anti-aliased paint tool such as the Paintbrush to the Pencil, the brushes in the Brushes palette switch to hard edge brushes.

AUTO ERASE: The Auto Erase option replaces any pixels that are currently the foreground color with the background color. You usually want this option off.

AIRBRUSH TOOL

KEYBOARD SHORTCUT: Type the letter A.

The Airbrush nib looks similar to the Paintbrush except that it continues to add density as you hold down the mouse button and go over the same area again and again. If you click the Airbrush down in one spot and continue to hold down the mouse button, paint will continue to be applied until 100% opacity is reached. Instead of the opacity setting, this tool has a pressure setting that controls how fast the den-

Airbrush Options.

sity is added. Using the Airbrush is like painting with an airbrush or a spraypaint can. For even more of a real airbrush effect, use the brushes options to set the spacing on your brush to 1 and then set the pressure to very, very low, about 5–10% or lower. You might also like the effect of turning the spacing off completely.

PAINTBRUSH TOOL

KEYBOARD SHORTCUT: Type the letter B.

The Paintbrush has anti-aliased edges that make the edge of where you paint blend more evenly with what you are painting over.

When painting with the Pencil or Paintbrush, the opacity setting from the Brushes palette will not be exceeded so long as you hold the mouse button down, even if you paint over the same area again and again.

Paintbrush Options.

WET EDGES: If you turn this option on, more color is laid down on the edges of your brushstroke. It's sort of a watercolor effect.

RUBBER STAMP TOOL

KEYBOARD SHORTCUT: Type the letter S.

The Rubber Stamp tool is one of the most useful tools in Photoshop. There are many different painting options with the Rubber Stamp tool. If you'd like to try some of the options that we show here, open the file MenInBoat in the Tool Palette folder on the CD.

CLONE ALIGNED: Clone (aligned) is the option you will use most often. You use it to remove spots and scratches and also to copy part of an image from one place to another. To use it, pick a brush size from the Brushes palette then hold down the Option key and click at the location where you want to pick up the image. This is the pickup location. Now, without the Option key down, click on the place where you want to clone the new information. This is the putdown location. As long as you hold down the mouse, information will be copied from the pickup location to the putdown location. Both of these move correspondingly when you move the mouse. When you pick up the mouse, move it

Rubber Stamp Options.

33

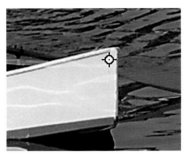

For Clone (aligned), Option-click at the pickup location…

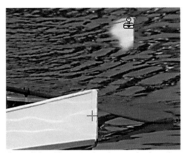

then click with no Option key at the location where you want to put down the clone. Notice the + that shows you where you are picking up from.

Select a rectangular area and define a pattern.

Pattern (aligned) clones the pattern in perfectly abutted regularity.

With Clone (aligned) if you let go of the mouse and move to a new location, the Rubber Stamp remembers the original location of your Option-click and maintains the relative distance.

With Clone (non-aligned) if you let go of the mouse and move to a new location, the rubber stamp begins cloning again from the original location.

and then click down again, the relative distance between the pickup location and the putdown location remains the same, but both will move the offset distance that you moved the mouse. This means that you can clone part of the image, stop for lunch, then come back and finish the job without worrying about misaligning your clone. This makes Clone (aligned) very good for removing spots. You can also clone from one image to another by Option-clicking in the pickup image and then clicking down to clone in the putdown image. See the chapter entitled: The Grand Canyon—Final Tweaks for more information on removing spots and scratches with the Clone (aligned) mode.

CLONE NON-ALIGNED: Clone (non-aligned) is used when you want to copy the same object into various places within the image. With this option, the pickup location remains the same when you move the mouse and click down in a new putdown location. This allows you to copy the same part of the image to multiple places within the image. When you want to change the pickup location, you need to Option-click again.

PATTERN ALIGNED: Patterned cloning uses the current Photoshop pattern and copies it wherever you paint with the mouse. When different painting areas come up against each other, the patterns will line up even if you have released the mouse button and started drawing more than once. This is the tool you want to use if you are painting wallpaper or some pattern that must match. To define a pattern, you select a rectangular area with the Rectangular Marquee then choose Edit/Define Pattern. This will be the current pattern until you define a new one.

PATTERN NON-ALIGNED: Pattern (non-aligned) is the same as Pattern (aligned) except that the patterns will not necessarily match when different painting areas come up against each

other. You would not want to use this option to paint wallpaper.

FROM SNAPSHOT: Clone From Snapshot allows you to clone from the last version of the file that was saved as a Snapshot. To use From Snapshot you would have needed to previously use Take Snapshot from the Edit menu. A Snapshot saves the current version of the image in a special buffer. You can therefore work with three versions of the image at the same time—the saved version, the snapshot version and the current version—in your workspace. Cloning from the Snapshot is faster than from the last saved version.

Pattern (non-aligned) will clone over an existing pattern if you lift the mouse and begin a new clone.

FROM SAVED: You can only clone from the last version of the file that was saved if you have not cropped the file since that last save. From Saved is very useful when compositing images and the need comes up to revert a

A Snapshot taken after Filter/Stylize/Find Edges and Filter/Pixelate/Crystalize were applied.

File reverted to Saved and rubber stamped from the Snapshot in certain areas.

34

small area back to the way it looked before a composite. You can also use it to remove mistakes made with the other painting tools.

IMPRESSIONIST: This is not an option that we have used very often, but it's fun to try some options if you have time. The Impressionist mode uses the brush size and hardness that you choose, as well as the direction and length of the strokes that you make to transform all or part of your image into a soft-focus Impressionist painting.

After more filtering, parts of the image Cloned from Saved at 30% opacity.

Impressionist rubber stamp over original file using a small brush and short strokes.

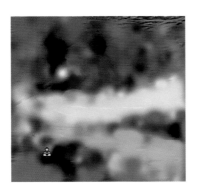
The same file using Impressionist mode with a large brush.

THE EDITING TOOLS

SMUDGE TOOL

KEYBOARD SHORTCUT: Type the letter U.

Open the file CeramicFruit from the CD to follow the next part of this chapter on the Tool palette. The Smudge tool turns your whole image into wet paint. You can click and drag to smear one color area into another. This blends the colors within

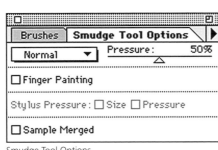
Smudge Tool Options.

Smudge tool in action.

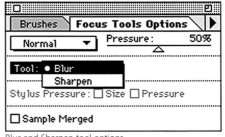
Orange foreground color mixed with the image with Fingerpaint mode.

the brush area, so the size of the blend depends on the size and softness of the brush you use. The pressure controls the amount of paint that gets mixed with each stroke and how far into the stroke the paint is smeared. At 100%, the color that you pick up will be laid down the whole length of the stroke. If you hold the Option key down when you start a paint stroke or click on the Fingerpaint mode, a dab of the foreground color gets mixed in with the rest of the colors that are being smudged.

BLUR/SHARPEN TOOLS

KEYBOARD SHORTCUT: Type the letter R.

The Blur tool can be switched to a Sharpen tool by double-clicking on the tool and using the pop-up option menu. If you Option-click on the tool it will toggle between the Blur and Sharpen tools. You will use the Blur tool to help blend jagged edges between two images that are being composited. You can also use it to remove the jaggies from a diagonal line or

Blur and Sharpen tool options.

35

Blur tool after several applications.

Sharpen tool after several applications. Be careful not to over sharpen.

The original image.

just soften selected parts of an image. The Sharpen tool can be used to locally sharpen an area without making a selection. Both of these tools work best when you try different levels of pressure (opacity) from the Options palette.

DODGE/BURN/SPONGE TOOLS

KEYBOARD SHORTCUT: Type the letter O.

The Dodging tool can be switched to the Burn or Sponge tool by double-clicking on the tool and using the pop-up option menu. If you Option-click on the tool it will toggle between the Dodge, Burn and Sponge tools. You will use the Dodge tool when you want to make local areas of your image lighter. The Burn tool is used to make local areas of your image darker. Both of these tools work best when you try different levels of exposure (opacity) from the Options palette. Start with a low value of about 30%.

With the Burn and Dodge tools, you need to specify the type of image area you are working on. Set Highlights, Midtones or Shadows depending on the part of the image you are dodging or burning.

Other techniques for dodging and burning that we like better are described in the Buckminster Fuller, Grand Canyon Final Tweaks and Blend Modes, Calculations and Apply Image chapters.

The Sponge tool allows you to saturate or desaturate the area you brush over. It is very useful for desaturating out-of-gamut colors (colors that can be seen on screen that are unprintable) to bring them back into gamut (printable colors).

After dodging with the Dodge tool.   After burning with the Burn tool.

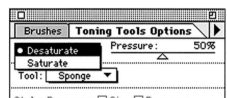
You can dodge or burn in the shadows, midtone or highlight areas.

With the Sponge tool you can saturate or desaturate the colors.

Several applications of the Saturate Sponge.

Several applications of the Desaturate Sponge.

36

PICKING AND USING COLOR

A Look at RGB, CMYK, HSB and LAB Color Spaces, What They Are, When to Use Each and How to Access Them from Photoshop; the Photoshop Color Picker and the Picker, Swatches and Scratch Palettes Explained in Detail

There are different color spaces available in Photoshop that you can use for different purposes at different times. Instead of just working in one color space, like RGB or CMYK, it is a good idea to learn the advantages and disadvantages of the different spaces. There are various tools in Photoshop for picking and saving colors. We will talk about these issues in this chapter. The rest of the book will make the general assumption that you are familiar with these tools and issues.

THE RGB COLOR SPACE

For overall color correction and ease of work there are a lot of advantages to using the Red, Green, Blue (RGB) color space. Red, green and blue are the additive colors of light that occur in nature. White light is made up of wavelengths from the red, green and blue spectrums. All scanners, even high end drum scanners, actually have sensors that originally capture the data in RGB format. You can use RGB for final output to computers, multimedia and TV monitors, color transparency writers, digital video and some digital printers because all of these are native RGB devices. RGB files are smaller than CMYK files because there are only three components of color instead of four.

THE CMYK COLOR SPACE

Cyan, magenta and yellow are the complementary colors to red, green and blue. Red and cyan are opposites, so if you take away all the red from white light, cyan is what you will have left. Cyan is made up by mixing green and blue light. Green and magenta as well as blue and yellow work in similar ways, they are complementary colors. When you print on a printing press, the colors of ink that are used are cyan, magenta and yellow. These are called subtractive colors because when you view something that is printed you are actually seeing the light that is reflected back. When white light, which contains all the colors, hits a surface that is painted cyan, you see cyan because the cyan paint subtracts the red from the white light and only green and blue are reflected back for you to see. To print red using CMY inks, you use magenta and yellow inks. Magenta subtracts the green light and yellow subtracts the blue light so what is reflected back to your eyes is red light. The cyan, magenta and yellow dyes that make up printing inks are not pure, so when you print all three of them at the same time, instead of reflecting no

light and giving you black, you get a muddy gray color. Because of this problem, the printing trade adds black ink (the K in CMYK) to the four color process to force dark areas to be really as dark as possible.

THE AMOUNT OF BLACK

The amount of black ink that is used in the printing process and the way that it is used depends on the type of paper and press that you are using. Newspaper presses typically use a lot of black ink and as little color ink as possible because black ink is cheaper. High quality advertising color for magazines and other coated stock is printed with much more colored ink and less black. A skilled printer can create the same image in CMYK using either a lot of black ink or very little black ink. There are many different ways to combine the colored and black inks to get the final result.

CONVERTING RGB TO CMYK

Because of these different choices, the conversion from RGB to CMYK can be a complicated process. Once an image is converted to CMYK, whether by a high end scanner or by you in Photoshop, there is a relationship between the CMY colors and the black ink that can be tricky to manage. This is one of the reasons that it is better to do your overall color corrections in RGB so that you are taking a correct RGB file and then converting it to CMYK. You then end up with a CMYK file that has the black in the right place in relationship with the final, or close to final, CMY colors. The main reason to use the CMYK color space is that your final output will be on a printing press or a digital printer that uses CMYK inks or dyes. We will be discussing color correction in both RGB and CMYK as we go through the examples in this book.

THE HUE, SATURATION AND LIGHTNESS COLOR SPACE

Another color space that is used in Photoshop is Hue, Saturation and Lightness. You can no longer use the Mode menu to convert an image into HSL mode like you could in some older versions of Photoshop, but there are many color tools that allow you to think about and massage color using this color space. Instead of dividing a color into components of red, green and blue or cyan, magenta and yellow, HSL divides a color into its hue, its saturation and its lightness. The hue is the actual color and can include all the colors of the rainbow. A particular red hue is different from a purple, yellow, orange, or even a different red hue. The saturation is the intensity of that particular hue. Very saturated colors are quite intense and vivid, they almost look florescent. Colors of low saturation are dull and subtle. The lightness of a part of an image determines how light or dark that part is in overall density. Lightness is the value in the image that gives it detail. Imagine taking a black-and-white image and then colorizing it. The black-and-white image originally had different tonal values of gray. The details show up based on how light or dark the black-and-white image is. Removing the lightness value would be similar to taking this black-and-white detail part out of a color image. If you increase the lightness, the image starts to become flat and show less depth. If you increase the lightness all the way, the image will loose all its details and become white. If you decrease the lightness, the image may appear to have more depth and if you decrease it all the way the image will become black. For working with the image using the Hue/Saturation/Lightness model, you use Image/Adjust/Hue/Saturation or Image/Adjust/Replace Color. The different color pickers allow you to work in the HSL color model and there is also an old filter called HSL & HSB that allows you to convert RGB (Red, Green and Blue) into HSL (Hue, Saturation and Lightness) and back.

THE LAB COLOR SPACE

The Lab color space is used internally by Photoshop to convert between RGB and CMYK and can be used for device independent output to Level 2 PostScript devices. The Lab color space is quite useful for some

production tasks. For example, sharpening only the Lightness channel sharpens the image without "popping" the colors. There are also some technical notes about the Lab color space in the Photoshop 3.0 Manual.

USING THE COLOR PICKER

The main tool for picking colors in Photoshop is the Color Picker. You access the Color Picker by clicking on the foreground or background color swatch at the bottom of the Tool palette. You can use this picker in Hue mode, Saturation mode, Lightness mode or Red, Green or Blue mode. See the diagrams here for an explanation of each mode. In addition, you can set a specific color by typing in its Lab, RGB or CMYK values.

The Custom button brings up the Custom Picker for choosing Pantone, Trumatch and other standard colors. These can actually be used as separate color channels within Photoshop's Duotone mode, or they will be automatically converted to RGB or CMYK depending on the color space you are working in.

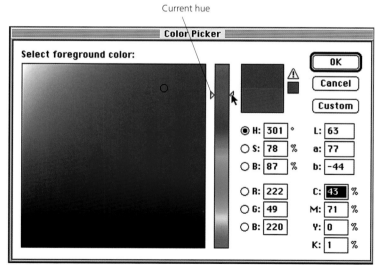

The Color Picker in Hue mode, which is the default. Sliding the color slider (shown with the arrow cursor above) up and down changes the hue in Hue mode. For a particular hue, purple here, click and drag the circle in the color box to the left to pick a particular color. As you move the cursor around in the color box with the mouse button down, left to right movement changes the saturation and up and down movement changes the brightness. You will see the values for saturation and brightness change in the number boxes to the right. You also see the corresponding RGB and CMYK values for each color. Hue is frozen by the color slider position.

Current saturation

Current brightness

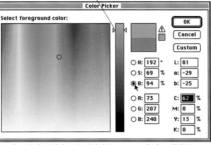

Put the Color Picker in Saturation mode by clicking on the S radio button. Now sliding the color slider up and down changes the saturation. Left to right movement of the cursor circle changes the hue and up and down movement changes the brightness.

Put the Color Picker in Brightness mode by clicking on the B radio button. Now sliding the color slider up and down changes the brightness. Left to right movement of the cursor circle changes the hue and up and down movement changes the saturation. Brightness here is similar to Lightness, mentioned elsewhere in this chapter.

Out-of-gamut warning   New in-gamut color

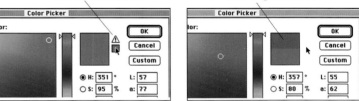

The exclamation sign shows you that the current color may be out-of-gamut (not printable in CMYK). Click on the sign, and the chosen color will be changed to the closest in-gamut color (shown at right). See the Kansas—Final Tweaks chapter for a discussion of out-of-gamut colors.

Red mode

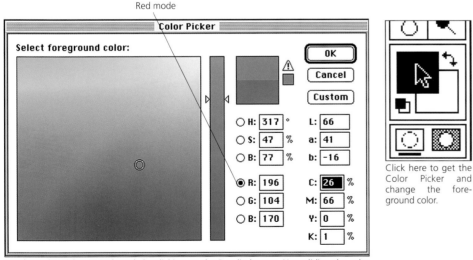

Click here to get the Color Picker and change the foreground color.

Put the Color Picker in Red mode by clicking on the R radio button. Now sliding the color slider up and down changes the amount of red in your color. For particular blue and green values, click and drag the circle in the color box to the left. Left to right movement changes the amount of blue and up and down movement changes the amount of green. You will see the values for red and green change in the number boxes to the right. Red is frozen by the color slider position. The values for cyan, magenta, yellow and black also change as you move around in the color box. This is a great way to see how the RGB and CMYK components change for different colors. If you are not sure how to adjust a certain color, go into the Color Picker and visually see what will happen to it as you add or subtract different component colors from it.

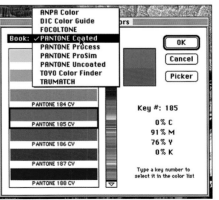

The Custom Colors picker with the different color systems that it makes available within the pop-up menu. Drag the slider or click the up/down arrows to locate a color, click on a color to choose it or type in the number associated with a particular color and that one will be chosen. Saying OK picks that color and returns you to the Color Picker.

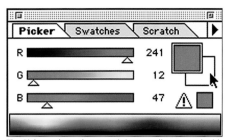

The Picker palette shown as it is normally grouped with the Swatches and Scratch palettes. The foreground and background colors are shown to the right. The foreground color is currently active because the double line is around it. If you move the sliders you will be adjusting the foreground color. The arrow cursor is over the background color. If you click on the background color, it will become the active color and moving the sliders will modify it. This palette also shows you the gamut warning icon.

You can set the display of the Picker palette to RGB, CMYK, HSB, Lab or Grayscale.

The Color Bar choice brings up options for how the color bar at the bottom is displayed. You can choose the foreground color by clicking on a color in the color bar; Option-click for the background color.

You can load and save different sets of swatches to files. If you have certain colors that you use for a particular client, you may want to save these in a file with that client's name. You can append swatches, which adds swatches stored in a file to the ones you already have in the palette. Reset Swatches just goes back to the default set of swatches.

40

USING THE COLOR PALETTES

Besides the Color Picker that you access from the Tool palette, there are also the Picker palette, the Swatches palette and the Scratch palette that you access from the Window/Palettes menu. Normally these are grouped together on the desktop, but you can separate them by clicking on their name tabs and dragging each of them to its own location on the desktop. Since the big Color Picker is a modal dialog and cannot be accessed on the fly with the painting tools, these palettes are very helpful in quickly getting the colors you need.

THE PICKER PALETTE

In the Picker palette you can move the RGB, CMYK, HSB or other color sliders to create a color that you like. You pick this color for either the foreground or background depending on which of these swatches is chosen within the Picker palette. You change the display mode in the Picker palette using its pop-up option menu. You can also pick colors from the color bar along the bottom of the palette. This color bar has different display modes that you can choose from using the Picker palette's options. The Picker palette is also useful to have around while you are in Levels, Curves and the other color correction tools. It remembers the colors at the last location where you clicked the Eyedropper within an image, and it shows you how that location is changing by the color adjustments you are making.

THE SWATCHES PALETTE

The Swatches palette allows you to save and then later access your favorite set of colors. To pick a color from the Swatches palette and make it the foreground color, you just click on the color with the Eyedropper. Option-click picks a new background color. You automatically get the Eyedropper when the cursor moves over the swatches area. To save the current foreground color in the Swatches palette, you Shift-click on the swatch you want to overwrite. If you want to add a new swatch without overwriting the ones that are there,

Option-Shift-click on top of a swatch and it and all the other swatches will shift one to the right making room for the new swatch. The Command key gives you the scissors and clicking with them over a swatch removes it. Using the pop-up options menu, you can load custom swatch sets into the Swatches palette, including sets for the custom colors, like Pantone, that are supplied in the Color Palettes folder that comes with Photoshop.

If you have a continuous tone 24-bit color image that has many colors that you might want to use for other projects, there is a quick way to load 256 of these colors into the Swatches palette. First choose Mode/Indexed Color to convert a copy of your image into Indexed Color mode. Do this to a copy so you don't destroy your original image. Using the 8-bit color, Adaptive Palette and Diffusion Dither settings in the Indexed Color dialog

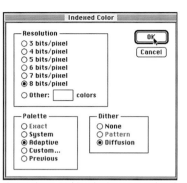

Converting a 24-bit color image to Indexed Color to create a color table for loading into the Swatches palette.

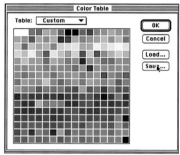

Saving your indexed color table using the Color Table editor. After saving this table, you choose Load Swatches from the Swatches palette pop-up menu to make this the current set of colors in the Swatches palette.

will give you the 256 colors that are most common within this image. After clicking on OK in the Index Color dialog, choose Mode/Color Table to see a table of the 256 colors you have created from this image. Click the Save button in the Color Table to save these colors in a file. You can now use Load Swatches in the Swatches palette to load all these colors from this file. They are now easily available for painting projects in Photoshop.

THE SCRATCH PALETTE

The last tool in Photoshop's color picking set is the Scratch palette. This is actually a little window you can use like a painter's palette to mix colors using the Paintbrush, Airbrush and other painting tools. You can also cut objects and colors from regular image windows and paste them into this window. To copy from or paste to the Scratch palette, you need to use the Copy command from its pop-up menu. The pop-up menu also allows

The Scratch palette is a small Photoshop window where you can mix colors using Photoshop's editing and painting tools. Use this like a painter would mix oil or acrylic colors on a canvas. You can also pick foreground and background colors from here using the Eyedropper tool. Again, you can save and load your favorite Scratch palette color sets.

you to clear the palette to the background color, to lock it so it can't be changed, or to save and load Scratch palettes to and from your hard disk.

A LITTLE MORE ABOUT INDEXED COLOR

When you choose Mode/Indexed Color, you are converting your 24-bit color file into 256 Color mode. When Macintosh first came with built in color support for its computers, only 256 colors were supported. Many new Macs today have built in support for thousands and millions of colors. You really need millions of colors to do accurate 24-bit color correction and output. Indexed Color mode (only 256 colors), will still often be used in multimedia applications when you are placing color images on a interactive CD.

COLOR LOOKUP TABLES

Color is displayed in an indexed color image, and in 256 Color mode on a computer, by using a color lookup table. Since the computer monitor actually needs a 24-bit value to display a color on the screen, a color lookup table with 256 entries is used to convert those 256 values into 24-bit colors. Index color images only store one byte of color information per pixel instead of the 3 bytes used in 24-bit color images. This makes them smaller and faster to load from a CD. That one byte of information, which can have 256 possible values, is used as a lookup into a 256 entry table of 24-bit color values. These 24-bit values are then sent to the monitor to drive the colors on the screen.

THE ADAPTIVE PALETTE

When you use the Indexed Color mode in Photoshop to convert a 24-bit color image, you can choose to create either an Adaptive palette or use the System palette. The Adaptive palette maps the 24-bit values in the image into a special table of the 256 colors that can best represent this image. This way, each 24-bit image could have its own optimal palette. In a multimedia application, displayed on a monitor with only 256 Color mode, there can only be one palette loaded at a time to display all the colors on the screen. If you are using two or more different images on the screen at the same time, each with its own Adaptive palette, only one of these palettes can be loaded into the system at a time to control the monitor colors. The image associated with that palette will look fine, but the other images may look very strange because they will be displayed using another image's palette.

THE SYSTEM PALETTE

Some of you may have noticed images coming up with strange colors when working in 256 Color mode. The problem is usually not having the correct color palette loaded for that image. If you want several images on the screen at the same time, you need to create those images with the Indexed Color mode using the System palette. The System palette is a palette that Apple provides that has colors covering a full range of the spectrum. It can display any image in 256 Color mode and make it look OK. Most images that are converted using the System palette won't look as good as the same image converted using an Adaptive palette.

CUSTOM ADAPTIVE PALETTES

The other choice is to create a special Adaptive palette for just the images that will be on the screen at the same time. You can do this in Photoshop by pasting all of these images into a single bigger canvas and converting that canvas to 256 Color mode using an Adaptive palette. The images can then be redivided again and all saved with this same Adaptive Palette. Or, if it's easier, you can save this Adaptive palette as a Custom palette with the Save button from Mode/Color Table, then convert all of your original files to 256 Color mode using your newly created Custom palette. If you do this a lot, there are special multimedia applications that will create custom Adaptive palettes more easily. For more information about creating and editing indexed color, see the Photoshop 3.0 Manual.

To bias the color table towards particular colors in an image, make a selection of those color areas before the mode conversion to Indexed color.

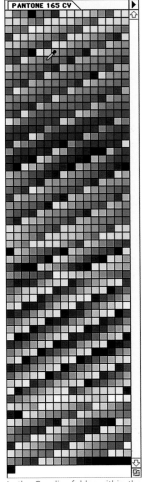

In the Goodies folder within the Photoshop folder there is a Color Palettes folder that contains swatch sets for Pantone, Trumatch and other standard color systems. Here we see all the Pantone colors loaded into the Swatches palette. When the Eyedropper gets over a particular color, the Swatches tab changes to tell you which Pantone you are about to choose. This may be a quicker way for you to find the custom color you want.

COLOR CORRECTION TOOLS

Overview of Photoshop's Many Color Correction and Gamma Adjustment Tools; Which Ones Are Most Useful, for What and Why, and Which Ones Are Fairly Useless for the Professional

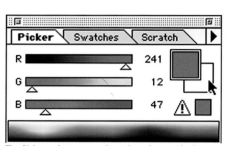

The Picker palette remembers the values at the last location you clicked with the Eyedropper, then shows you how those values change when you make adjustments in a color correction tool.

The Picker palette has a subtle but important difference from the Info palette in that it displays the values of the last place where you clicked with the Eyedropper. This allows you to select a picture tone or color area and see how the pixel values of that particular area will change as you make adjustments with the color tool.

The color correction tools are in the Image/Adjust menu.

There are many tools in Photoshop for adjusting color and modifying image gamma or contrast. This chapter will clear up general confusion about what the different tools do and when to use each tool. The color correction tools are in the Image/Adjust menu. They are, listed in the order we use them most, Levels, Hue/Saturation, Curves, Replace Color, Selective Color, Color Balance, Brightness/Contrast and Variations. In later hands-on chapters, we actually go through the details of each tool's features and how they're used in real world examples.

USING THE INFO AND PICKER PALETTES

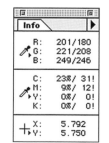

The Info palette with the before values to the left and the after values to the right of the slash.

When using any of these color correction tools, it is very helpful to also have the Info palette and the Picker palette visible on your screen. Use Window/Palettes/Show Info (F9 with ArtistKeys), and Window/Palettes/Show Picker (Shift-F9 with ArtistKeys) to bring up these palettes. While color correcting, it is also important to have the Eyedropper available to measure colors within the image. Photoshop automatically selects the Eyedropper for you when using any of the color correction tools. The Info palette shows you the RGB values and the CYMK values of the pixel, or group of pixels, you are currently over with the Eyedropper tool. It shows you these values both before (left of slash) and after (right of slash) any changes you have made during the current incantation of the color correction tool you are now using.

When adjusting a digital image, it is important to make as few separate file modifications as possible to achieve the desired result. A file modification is when you click on the OK button for any of the color correction tools. With each file modification, the original data is changed and eventually the quality of the data can be degraded by too many of these changes. For this reason, you don't want to be continually going from one color correction tool to the other frantically trying to get the effect you need. You want to use these tools intelligently, knowing what each one is good for and keeping the total number of uses down to the minimum required to do the final adjustments on a particular image.

COMMON COLOR CORRECTION TECHNIQUES

There are some things that all the color correction tools have in common. When using Levels, Curves, Color Balance and Brightness/Contrast on the entire image, you want to have the Preview button turned off. With the Preview button turned off in these tools, Photoshop adjusts the color and brightness output of the video card controlling colors on the monitor. This gives you instant results on the screen when you make changes. This technique of adjusting the video card to preview color and contrast changes is called Video LUT animation. The changes happen over the entire computer screen, not just in the window you are working with. Because of this, you need to work with the Preview button on when you are trying to adjust and compare an image in one window with that in another window. Also, when the Preview button is off, you can click on the title bar of the Tool palette and hold the mouse button down to see the image as it looked before making that adjustment. Click and let go with the mouse on the title bar and you instantly see a before and after view of your image. This is important when making subtle color adjustments, because if you stare at an image on the computer screen for more than a few seconds your eye will tend to adjust to make that image look more correct. This quick before/after toggle stops your eye from having time to do this and you can better decide if you really like the color adjustments you have made. Video LUT Animation, with the Preview button off, gives a quick preview of your results. It is usually fairly accurate and should be used when possible while you are making changes to the overall image in Levels, Curves, Color Balance and Brightness/Contrast. When you are done with your changes, you may want to turn on the Preview button to force Photoshop to calculate all the changes and show you exactly how they will look, not just an approximation with the Video LUT Animation. When using the Hue/Saturation, Replace Color and Selective Color commands, the corrections are too complicated for Photoshop to simulate them by changing the video board, so you will usually want to work with the Preview button turned on. Video LUT Animation will not work with a few Macs and with many PCs and compatibles. If your video board does not support this, just always work with the preview button on.

When working with a selected sub-area or comparing one window to another within Levels, Curves, Color Balance or Brightness/Contrast you will usually work with the Preview button on so you can compare the changes you are making to the selected area with the rest of the image. When the Preview button is on in any tool, clicking on the title bar won't give you the quick before/after toggle. You can never get this quick toggle when using the Hue/Saturation, Replace Color or Selective Color commands.

With all the color correction tools, you can Option-Cancel to stay in the tool but cancel any changes you have made. Many of these tools also let you load and save a collection of settings. This is useful when you have a lot of very similar images within a production situation. You could carefully make your Levels setting for the first image, and then use the Save button to save those settings in a file. With subsequent images in the group, you could use the Load button to automatically run the same settings.

LEVELS AND CURVES

The Levels and Curves tools are the color correction tools that have the broadest range of capabilities. When you are color correcting an image from its original scan, you want to do this color correction process in a particular order. This order is discussed in great detail in the Input, Calibration, Correction and Output chapter of this book. If you haven't read this chapter yet, you should read it first to get a better understanding of this overview. The first step after doing a scan is to do overall color correction.

This is correcting the complete image without any selections. Levels is the best tool for this because you see a histogram of the data within the image. You can use the histogram to judge the quality of the scan and to fix a lot of scanning problems. With Levels you can exactly adjust the highlight and shadow values, the overall brightness and contrast, and the color balance while seeing the results on the screen and in the histogram. You make all these changes in one step and only have to choose OK once for all these improvements. Levels is the color correction tool we use most often.

The Curves command can also be used to do your initial overall color adjustments of the entire image. With Curves you can do all the same adjustments Levels can do. The Curves command has a different user interface than Levels. Instead of seeing the histogram, you see the curve diagram shown here. The horizontal axis of this diagram represents the original image values with black and shadows on the left and white and highlights on the right. The vertical axis represents the modified image values with the shadows at the bottom and the highlights on the top. When the curve is a straight diagonal, as shown here, the image has not been changed. Moving the curve down in the middle will make the image darker, and moving it upwards will make the image lighter. The endpoints of the curve can also be moved to change the highlight and shadow values. Using Curves, it is possible to measure individual colors, see the range of values they represent on the curve and then only change that color range. That is one of the advantages of using Curves instead of Levels. The advantage of Levels is seeing the histogram when making the changes.

Levels and Curves are the most powerful color correction tools. See The Grand Canyon, Kansas and Al chapters for good discussions of using Levels and Curves in the ways they are best suited. Also read the chapter entitled: Digital Imaging and the Zone System to understand how Levels histograms relate to the original photograph.

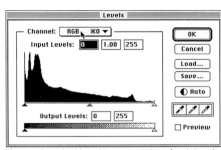

The Levels tool with its histogram is best for doing the overall color correction right after bringing in a scan.

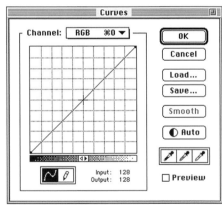

The Curves tool with a curve showing no adjustments to the image. The horizontal axis shows the original image values and the vertical axis shows these values as modified by the curve.

43

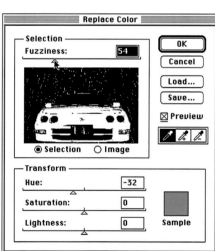

The Hue/Saturation tool. Usually you want the Preview button on when using Hue/Saturation.

The Replace Color command has a selection capability based on object color and has some of the controls from Hue/Saturation built into it. Use it for quickly selecting and changing the color of objects. Use the sample swatch as a quick reference to see how your color will change, then use the Preview button to see the change happen within the file.

THE HUE/SATURATION COMMAND

Hue/Saturation is often used to increase the saturation of all the colors by 10% to 20% after doing the overall color correction using Levels. This change is done with the Master button on. Using the Red, Yellow, Green, Cyan, Blue or Magenta radio buttons, the hue, saturation or lightness of objects within the image that have one of these standard colors as their primary color can be changed without actually making a detailed selection. Hue/Saturation should be used when you want to change the color, saturation or lightness of a particular object or color range without changing its gamma or other characteristics. The first part of the process is to select the object(s) you want to change and use the Eyedropper to get a dab of representative color. This will show changes in the patch to the bottom of the Hue/Saturation window. Unlike Levels and Curves, with this tool you need to use the Preview button to see your changes within a file on a 24-bit color monitor.

The Hue slider looks at hues in a circular fashion sort of like the old Apple Color Picker. The initial hue value, 0, is the degree value where your initial color is found. To change just the color, sliding the Hue slider to the right is like rotating counter clockwise on the Apple Color Picker. If your initial color was red, that would then be 0. A hue change of 90 degrees would make the color green. A Hue change of -90 degrees would make your color purple. A Hue change of 180 or -180 would yield the opposite of red, cyan. Sliding the Saturation slider to the right makes the selected items more saturated and sliding to the left makes them less saturated. This is like moving further from the center or closer to the center on the Apple Color Picker.

The Lightness slider will take away gray values when moved to the right and will add gray values when moved to the left. This is similar to the sliding bar on the right side of the Apple Color Picker. See The Grand Canyon and The Car chapters for more info on the Hue/Saturation tool.

THE REPLACE COLOR COMMAND

The Replace Color command allows you to make a selection based on color and then actually change the color of the selected objects using sliders built into the command's dialog box. The selections are similar to selections made with the Magic Wand, but you have more control over them within this tool. With the Magic Wand you need to make a selection by clicking on a color using a certain tolerance setting. Adjacent areas are selected or not selected depending on whether their colors fall within the tolerance value you set for the Magic Wand. If the selection is incorrect with the Magic Wand, you need to change the tolerance and then remake the selection. This takes a lot of time and iteration. The Replace Color command allows you to change the tolerance on the fly while seeing the actual objects or colors that are being selected.

The tolerance here is called Fuzziness. Increasing it, by moving the slider within the dialog to the right, enlarges your selection, and decreasing the Fuzziness makes the selection smaller. You see a preview of what is happening with the selection in a little mask window within the dialog.

Once the color selection is perfected, you then use the Hue, Saturation and Lightness sliders in the Replace Color dialog to change the color of the selected objects. You can see this color change in the image by clicking the Preview button. This allows you to make further tweaks on the selection while actually seeing how it is affecting the color change. Replace Color selects and changes color on these objects from everywhere within the part of the image that was initially selected when you first entered Replace Color. To learn more about using Replace Color, see the Yellow Flowers chapter.

THE SELECTIVE COLOR TOOL AND CMYK

The Selective Color tool works best when you are working with CMYK images. It is a good tool for making final tweaks to CMYK colors after converting from RGB to CMYK. With this tool you adjust the amount of cyan, magenta, yellow or black ink within the red, green,

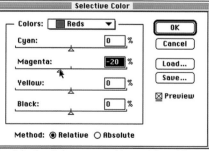

The Selective Color command is used for adding or subtracting the percentage of cyan, magenta, yellow or black inks within the red, green, blue, cyan, magenta, yellow, black, neutral or white colors in the selected area of a CMYK image. These percentages can be relative to the amount of an ink color that is already there or they can be absolute percentages.

blue, cyan, magenta, yellow, black, neutral or white colors in the selected area. This is a great tool for fine control over fixing color areas that fade a bit when converted to CMYK. For more information about using this tool, see the Yellow Flowers and The Color Matching Cars chapters.

COLOR BALANCE, BRIGHTNESS/CONTRAST AND VARIATIONS

You will notice that we don't use Color Balance, Brightness/Contrast and Variations tools much in this book. We consider them less precise than the other five color correction tools previously mentioned. We will explain the advantages and disadvantages of using these three tools within this section. In general, they are more for color beginners and don't offer as much control as the Levels, Curves, Hue/Saturation, Replace Color or Selective Color commands.

THE COLOR BALANCE TOOL

The Color Balance tool shows the the relationship between the additive colors (red, green and blue) on the right, and the subtractive colors (cyan, magenta and yellow) on the left. You move three sliders, the Cyan/Red slider, the Magenta/Green slider and the Yellow/Blue slider, either to the left to get the CMY colors or to the right to get their complementary RGB colors. If you don't understand the relationship between RGB and CMY, this tool makes it a little easier to see. With Color Balance you need to adjust your shadows, midtones and highlights each separately. This can take more time than using Levels or Curves.

In general, the Color Balance tool is much less powerful than Levels or Curves since there is no way to set exact highlight or shadow values, and there is also not much control over brightness and contrast. If you were using Color Balance to do the overall correction of an image, you would probably have to go back and forth between this tool and Brightness/Contrast several

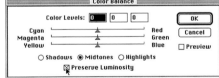

The Color Balance tool. Color levels of 0 mean that no adjustment has been made. Negative values mean adjustments in the CMY direction, and positive values are adjustments in the RGB direction. Preserve Luminosity is the only feature this tool has that can't be done with more precise control using Levels or Curves.

times. This breaks the rule of clicking on OK as little as possible and still gives you less overall control than Levels or Curves. There is also no way to adjust where the breakdown happens between highlights, midtones and shadows. Moreover, if you have a setting that you use all the time in Levels,

Hue/Saturation or Curves, you can save it in a file and load it later to use on a similar image. This is very useful when you want to save time and make a group of images have similar color adjustments. The Color Balance tool also doesn't have this option.

> *Overall, I would say that the Color Balance tool is more of a toy for beginning color correctors and not the recommended tool for imaging professionals. The one exception to this is that you can make adjustments in Color Balance with the Preserve Luminosity button on. This allows you, for example, to radically alter the color balance of a selected object towards red without the object becoming super bright like it would if you made such a radical adjustment in Levels or Curves. There are times when this is very useful.*

THE BRIGHTNESS/CONTRAST TOOL

The Brightness/Contrast tool allows you to adjust the brightness and/or contrast of your image using Brightness and Contrast sliders. Usually we adjust the brightness and contrast using Levels or Curves because those tools allow you to also adjust the color balance and highlight/shadow values at the same time. Like the Color Balance tool, I would say that Brightness/Contrast is more of a toy, entry level tool. Most professionals will use Levels and Curves. The only time you might use Brightness/Contrast is when there is no color adjustment to be made and only a subtle brightness or contrast adjustment is needed. An example of its use can be found in The Band chapter. There we are doing a very subtle adjustment to match the brightness and contrast of two grayscale channels.

When using Color Balance and Brightness/Contrast, you will usually do your initial adjustments with the Preview button off like you would when using Levels and Curves. Again, the exception to this is when you want to see how the changes within a selected area blend with the rest of the image or when you want to compare changes happening in one window with other images that are on the same computer screen.

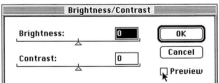

The Brightness/Contrast tool. Moving the sliders to the right increases the brightness or contrast giving positive numbers in the respective boxes. Moving the sliders to the left decreases brightness or contrast and results in negative numbers.

THE VARIATIONS TOOL

The Variations tool is a neat idea, but it has several serious flaws. Variations is useful for the person who is new to color correction and may not know the difference between adding a little cyan and adding a little green to an image. With Variations, you see the current image surrounded by different color correction choices. The main problem with Variations is that you cannot zoom in on the current image or any of its new choices to see the details of what will happen when you make possible changes. If there were a way to zoom in and look closely at the changes, that would be a big improvement to Variations.

Variations works better on a 19" or 21" monitor simply because the small images used to illustrate the changes are a little bigger on a larger monitor. Still, once you make the changes and say OK to Variations, you are often surprised by how certain color areas have been adversely affected by the changes that looked cool in small size inside the Variations dialog box. Like the Color Balance tool, there is also no way to exactly set where the highlight and/or shadow values begin. You have to adjust highlight and shadow values separately using the radio buttons at the top right of the Variations dialog box. You can't set the highlights or shadows to known values like you can in Levels and Curves.

With Variations, you can also adjust the saturation by selecting the Saturation radio button. The saturation, highlight and shadow settings will show you out-of-gamut colors if you have the Show Clipping box checked. When shadows will print as pure black or highlights as pure white, these clipped areas will show up as a bright complementary warning color. In Saturation mode, colors that are too saturated for the CMYK gamut also show up in this way.

If you are not used to doing color corrections, Variations is a good way to prototype the corrections you want to make. Maybe you'll decide to add some yellow, darken the image and increase the saturation a bit. After you have made these decisions with the aid of Variations, you may want to go back to Levels, Curves or Hue/Saturation and try to make the corresponding changes there. Then you can also set the highlights and shadows more exactly and see the details of the changes you are making while you are making them.

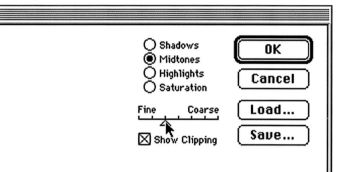

In the top right corner of Variations are the controls which allow you to adjust either shadows, midtones or highlights as well as saturation. The Fine/Coarse adjustment controls how large the variations in different picture choices are in color balance, brightness and saturation. When Show Clipping is turned on, Variations will emphasize shadow, highlight or saturation values that will print as either all black, all white or with out-of-gamut CMYK saturation respectively.

The Variations color correction tool shows you the original and current version of the image up in the top left corner. As you change the current image, you can easily compare it here to the original. The big box in the bottom left corner shows the current image in the middle surrounded by versions with more green, yellow, red, magenta, blue or cyan added to it. You click on one of these surrounding versions of the image if you like it better. It replaces the current image in the middle of this circle (also at the top), and then another round of new color iterations surround this new current image. On the right hand side, the current image is in the middle with a lighter one above and a darker one below. Again you can click on one of these to make it the current image.

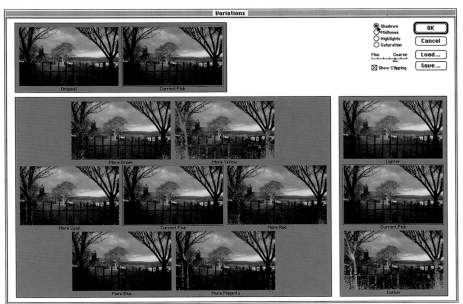

Adjusting the shadows within Variations. The Show Clipping option is on and you can see the clipping display in most of the color modifications. Clipping also shows up in the darker selection at the bottom of the box on the right. If you were to select any of these clipped versions, the contrasty clipped areas would be areas that would print as pure black in the final printed image.

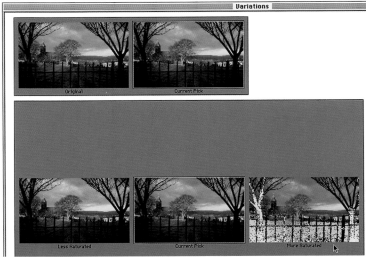

Adjusting the saturation within Variations. The Show Clipping option is on and you can see the clipping display in the image to the right. If you were to select this more saturated version, the contrasty clipped areas would be areas that are out-of-gamut for CMYK printing.

THE AUTO LEVELS AND DESATURATE COMMANDS

The Auto Levels command does an automatic color correction of your image. I would not recommend this for quality color control, but it is OK for a quick color fix to an FPO proof. The Desaturate command completely desaturates your image taking all the hue or color values out of it. You are then left with a black-and-white image in RGB or CMYK mode.

WHERE TO LEARN MORE

To learn more about the color correction tools that are mentioned in this overview, read the chapters entitled: Input, Calibration, Correction and Output, Digital Imaging and the Zone System, Setting System and Photoshop Preferences and do the step by step examples in The Grand Canyon, Kansas and Al chapters as well as their Final Tweaks chapters. The Yellow Flowers, Color Matching Cars, The Band, Versailles and the Bryce Stone Woman chapters also have color correction techniques in them.

RGB to CMY Relationship

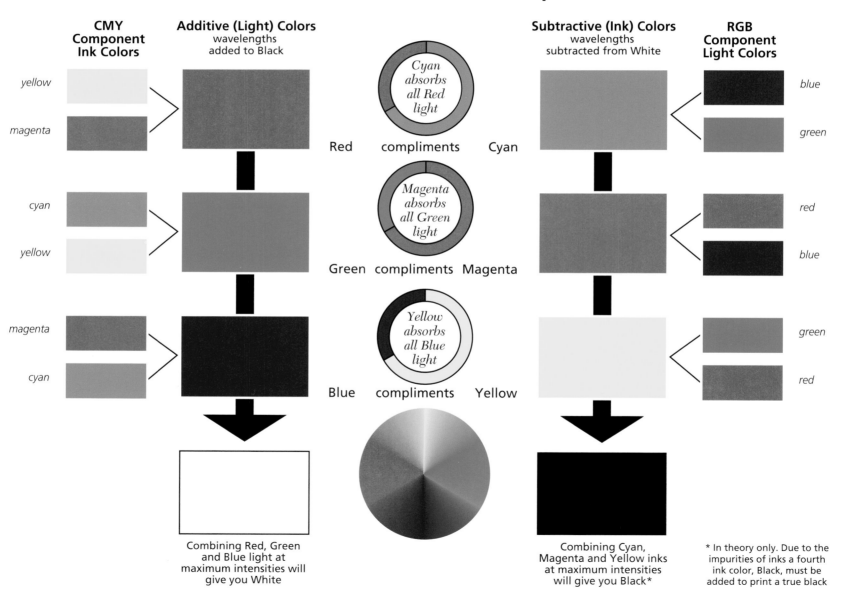

CMY Component Ink Colors

yellow

magenta

cyan

yellow

magenta

cyan

Additive (Light) Colors
wavelengths added to Black

Combining Red, Green and Blue light at maximum intensities will give you White

Cyan absorbs all Red light

Red   compliments   Cyan

Magenta absorbs all Green light

Green   compliments   Magenta

Yellow absorbs all Blue light

Blue   compliments   Yellow

Subtractive (Ink) Colors
wavelengths subtracted from White

Combining Cyan, Magenta and Yellow inks at maximum intensities will give you Black*

RGB Component Light Colors

blue

green

red

blue

green

red

* In theory only. Due to the impurities of inks a fourth ink color, Black, must be added to print a true black

PHOTOGRAPHY AND OVERALL
COLOR CORRECTION

DIGITAL IMAGING AND THE ZONE SYSTEM

Digital Imaging as It Relates to Traditional Photography and the Zone System and How to Create a High Quality Original Photograph

Images in nature, that you see with your eyes, have the greatest beauty because they are usually illuminated by very wonderful light and have depth and texture we can only simulate on a print or computer screen. The range of light, from the darkest black shadow to the brightest sparkling highlight, reflected from reality to our eyes is far greater than we can reproduce with any printed or screen image. Our eyes can adjust as we gaze into a shadow or squint to see a bright detail. When you look at a scene in nature, it will have the best quality and the most detail. The T.V. set, which we watch so much, has the least amount of detail and sharpness. Go out and see the real world!

TRANSITIONS TO THE DIGITAL WORLD

There are many reasons to copy a scene from nature, a pretty face or a product, and reproduce this image so it can be carried around and seen again. How to do this, and get the best quality, is the subject of *Photoshop Artistry*. I give thanks to Ansel Adams, perhaps the most well known nature photographer, and his great series of books: *The Camera*, *The Negative* and *The Print* for my introduction to an understanding of artistic photography. These titles by New York Graphic Society books are a must read for anyone who wants to understand how to take the best quality photographs. *Ansel Adams an Autobiography* is also a wonderful book. Many of Adams' discussions are about black-and-white photography, but the concepts apply to color. The depth and joy of his philosophies are something all people who deal with images should have a feeling for.

Although he died in 1984, before digital imaging became easily available and popular, Ansel Adams was ahead of his time and says in his book *The Negative* "I eagerly await new concepts and processes. I believe that the electronic image will be the next major advance. Such systems will have their own inherent and inescapable structural characteristics, and the artist and functional practitioner will again strive to comprehend and control them." This chapter should help you to understand the nature of an original image and then how to control and improve it in the digital world.

ACHIEVING YOUR VISUALIZATION

The Zone System, developed by Ansel Adams in 1940, gives photographers a way to measure an image in nature and then capture it on film so it can be reproduced with the photographer's intentions in mind. Adams uses the term "Visualization" to explain a technique where photographers imagine what they want a photo to look like as a print before the photo is taken. Once this image, the visualization, is in the photographer's mind, the Zone System is used to get the correct data on the film so the photographer can achieve that visualization in the darkroom. Getting the right data on the film or into a digital camera is very important in the process of creating a digital image too. We will use the Zone System to explain what the right data is, and then we will discuss how to get that data onto film or into a digital camera. If you get the right data into a digital camera, you can transfer it directly into your computer. When the image is captured on film, you need to correctly scan it to make sure all the information gets into your computer.

CAPTURING THE DYNAMIC RANGE

When you look at an image in nature, or in a photography studio, you can use a photographic light meter to measure the range of brightness within the image. If it is a very sunny day and you are out in the bright sun, there may be a very large range of brightness between the brightest part of your image area and the darkest part of your image area. We will call this range, from the brightest to the darkest part of an image, the dynamic range of that image. Each photographic film, and also each digital camera, has its own dynamic range, called its exposure latitude, which is the range of values from brightest to darkest that the particular film or camera can capture. Many photographic films and digital cameras are not able to capture the full dynamic range of brightness that is in the original scene especially on a bright contrasty day. I'm sure you have all taken photographs where the prints don't show any details in the shadows or where a bright spot on a person's forehead is totally washed out. The objective of the Zone System is to measure, using a light meter, the brightness range in the original scene and then adjust your camera so the parts of that brightness range that you want to capture actually get onto the film or into the digital camera.

DIVIDING AN IMAGE INTO ZONES

The Zone System divides an image into 11 zones from the brightest to the darkest. Ansel Adams uses Roman numerals to denote the zones from 0 to X. (Counting from 0 to 10 in Roman numerals is: 0, I, II, III, IV, V, VI, VII, VIII, IX, X.) These zones in the printed image reference how light or dark each area will be. Zone 0 is pure black where there is no detail showing whatsoever. In a photograph, a Zone 0 area would be solid black; in a halftone you would see no white dots within the solid black ink. Zone I is still a very dark black but it is not pure black and there is no real measurable detail. If you looked at a Zone I halftone with the naked eye it would still look black without detail but with a loupe or other magnifier you would see very small white dots in a sea of black ink.

On the other end of the scale, Zone X is solid white, so in a print this would be the color of the paper; in a halftone there would be no dots in a Zone X area. You would use Zone X to represent a specular highlight like the reflection of the sun on a chrome bumper. Zone IX is a very bright white without detail but again you would see some very small halftone dots with a loupe. The range of image brightness areas that will have obvious detail in the printed image include Zone II through Zone VIII. Zone VIII will be very bright detail and Zone II will be very dark detail. In the middle of this area of print detail is Zone V. In a black-and-white print, Zone V would print as middle gray, halfway between pure black and pure white. In a color print, a Zone V area would print as normal color and brightness for that area if you were looking at it in normal lighting conditions with your eyes adjusted to it. When you set the exposure setting on your camera, areas in the image that have a brightness equal to that exposure setting are getting a Zone V exposure. We will explain this further.

GETTING A GOOD EXPOSURE

Let's talk for a moment about how you take a picture with a camera. We will use black-and-white negative and color positive transparency as examples in this discussion. Normally, when you take a transparency picture with a camera, you measure the range of brightness in the original scene and set the exposure on your camera so that range of brightness will be reproduced on the film looking the same way it did in the original scene. When you use an automatic exposure camera, the camera does this for you.

When you use a manual camera with a hand-held light meter, you need to do it manually. Even though a lot of you probably have automatic cameras as I do, let's describe the manual camera process so we all understand what needs to happen to take a good picture. The automatic cameras of today have computerized light meters that do all this for you although you sometimes still need to do it manually to get exactly what you want. This discussion also applies to getting a good exposure with a digital camera.

MEASURING THE BRIGHTNESS

To get a good exposure, you need to measure the brightness range of different subjects within the photograph. Let's say you were taking a photograph of a Spanish home in Costa Rica. You will want to set the exposure somewhere in the middle of the brightness range that occurs naturally in the setting. That middle position, wherever you set it, will then become Zone V. A hand-held spot light meter allows you to point at any very small area within a scene and measure the amount of light reflected from that area. The light meter will measure the brightness of light, the luminance, reflected from the metered part of the image. This is all you really need to measure whether you are taking a black-and-white or color photo.

In the Spanish home picture, the brightest areas are the little bit of sky at the top and the reflection of the sun in the right side of the window frame at the bottom. The darkest areas are the shadows in the bottom right corner. Measuring

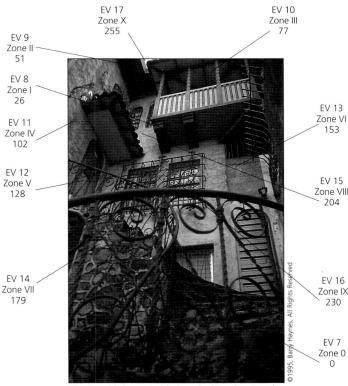

The Spanish home in black-and-white showing, for each zone, the exposure value (EV) read by an exposure meter, the corresponding zone and lastly the 0 to 255 digital value based on placing Zone V at exposure value 12 on the door.

51

these with a light meter that allows spot readings might produce readings like exposure value 17 for the bright section of sky at the top and exposure value 7 for the dark shadow at the bottom. Each change in the exposure value settings on a professional light meter is equal to a difference of two in the amount of light measured.

In the building picture, if we have exposure value readings from 7 in the darkest area to 17 in the brightest area, there is a difference of 1024 times the brightness from the darkest amount of light to the brightest amount of light. This is because each jump in the exposure value represents twice as much light. Here's how we get 1024 times as much light: exposure value 7 = 1 (the lowest amount of light), EV 8 = 2 (twice as much light), EV 9 = 4, EV 10 = 8, EV 11 = 16, EV 12 = 32, EV 13 = 64, EV 14 = 128, EV 15 = 256, EV 16 = 512, EV 17 (the brightest reading) = 1024. This is 1024 times as much light from the darkest area to the brightest.

PLACING THE ZONE V EXPOSURE

After measuring the range of exposure values within a scene that you want to photograph, you usually set the camera's exposure to a value in the middle of that range. The value that you set your exposure to will cause the areas that have that exposure value within the scene to show up as a middle gray value on the film and print in black-and-white or as a normal middle detail exposure in color. Where you set your exposure on the camera is called "where you are placing your Zone V exposure." Here we are placing our Zone V exposure at exposure value 12, the reading we got from the door. Usually you set your exposure to the area within the image that you want to look best or most normal. If there were a person standing on the steps in this photo, you might set the exposure to a reading that you would take off the person's face.

When you decide where to set the exposure, you affect what happens to each of the zones within the image area, not just Zone V. If the Spanish home image were a transparency, it would reflect an exposure where you set Zone V based on the reading taken from the middle of the door. If the film is then processed correctly, the middle of the door in the transparency would look

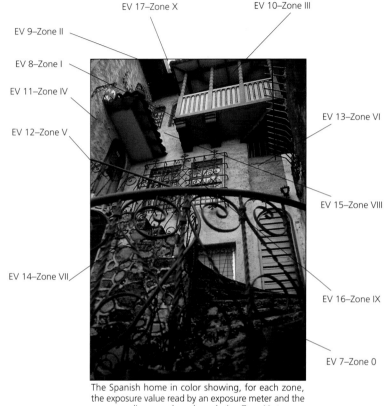

The Spanish home in color showing, for each zone, the exposure value read by an exposure meter and the corresponding zone based on placing Zone V at exposure value 12 on the door. For the color image, the RGB digital values will vary for each color channel depending on the color of the area.

correct, as though you were looking straight at it with your eyes adjusted to it. When you set the exposure to the middle of the door, the areas that are lighter or darker around it, the zones above and below Zone V, become correspondingly lighter or darker on the film. The bright window, which is exposure value 16, will then be placed at Zone IX and will show up as very bright and with almost no detail on the film. This is because it is 4 zones above, 16 times brighter, than where we set our exposure at exposure value 12.

If we were to set the exposure on the camera to exposure value 16, the exposure value for the bright window, this would do to the camera and film what happens to your eye when you move up very close to an area in the bright part of a contrasty scene. The iris on your eye closes and you start to see a lot of detail in that bright area. It is no longer a white area with no detail, because the focus of your field of vision has moved up and your eyes

52

have adjusted to encompass just that area. If you set the exposure on your camera to exposure value 16, that bright window area in the picture would now show up as a middle gray for black-and-white or a normal color in a transparency. By changing this exposure, you would then be placing Zone V at exposure value 16. Now the door would be at Zone I, 16 times darker, and everything darker than the door would be in Zone 0, totally black. This would give you details in the highlights, but you would lose the details in the darker parts of the scene. By measuring the scene and noticing that the bottom of the stairs has exposure value 7 and the sky has exposure value 17, then setting the exposure on your camera in the middle at exposure value 12, you will be placing Zone V there and able to get the full range of these values on the film.

UTILIZING YOUR EXPOSURE LATITUDE

Different films have different exposure latitudes. The exposure latitude of a film is the number of different exposure values it can record at once. The Zone System covers a range of 11 exposure values which is a brightness going from 1 to 1024 times as bright. Most films cannot capture detail in so broad a range of lighting situations. This is a contrasty scene on a sunny day with the sun shining directly on it. Some films can capture detail over a range of 7 exposure values and some over a larger range. In Adams' description of his zones, detail is captured only from Zone II through Zone VIII or over a 7 zone range. Things in Zones 0, I, IX and X are pretty much void of detail and either black or white. Some films will have a lesser exposure latitude and others a greater one. If you know the exposure latitude of your film or digital camera when taking a picture, then you can determine which parts of the picture will have detail and which will be black or white by measuring the range of your image area and setting your exposure, your Zone V area, so the other zones, or brightness ranges, fall where you want them.

We could have gotten more details in the highlights in this picture by placing Zone V, our exposure setting, at exposure value 13 or 14 instead of 12, but then the shadow areas at exposure values 8 or 9, the areas underneath the roof and balcony overhangs, would have shown up as totally black. Some pictures will not be very contrasty, and you will know, by taking light measurements, that the exposure latitude of your film, or digital camera, can handle the total number of zones in the image. All you need to make sure of then, is that you set the exposure in the middle of that range so all the areas of different exposure values are within the latitude of the film or digital camera and their detail is thus captured.

The measurements and diagrams in this chapter don't accurately measure any particular film. They are there to illustrate how the process works.

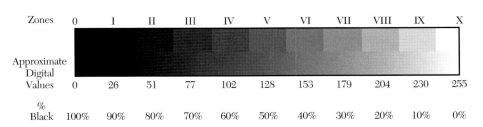

A stepwedge file of the 11 zones in the Zone System with the approximate corresponding digital values and percentage of black ink. The digital values shown here fall somewhere in the center of each zone. Where the actual zone values and digital values appear for each image will be dependent on the type of output you choose. You will have more latitude of where the Zone I detail begins and Zone IX details end when you print at a higher resolution and line screen. If you are printing to newsprint, all of Zone I may print as 100% black and all of Zone IX as 100% white.

If you want to know more about the Zone System and how to take the best photographs, you should read Ansel Adams' book, The Negative. *It is very useful information. His book also shows you some very good techniques for extending or shortening the exposure latitude of your film by under or over developing. Another great book on the Zone System is,* The New Zone System Manual *by White, Zakia and Lorenz from Morgan Press, Inc.*

THE ADVANTAGES OF A DIGITAL IMAGE

Once you have captured all the information you need on the film, you want to move it into your computer by doing the best possible scan. With a digital camera, no scanning is needed; the image is digitally transferred from the camera to the computer. Your objective is to make sure all the zone detail you have captured is there for you to play with. For more information on scanning and bringing images into the computer from Photo CD, see the Input, Calibration, Correction and Output chapter.

When you look at the histogram of a digital image using the Levels or Curves commands in Photoshop, you see all those values, all those zones, and you can move them around and adjust them with much more precision than you would have in the darkroom.

If you are not familiar with Levels and Curves, read The Grand Canyon and the Input, Calibration, Correction and Output chapters.

53

Channel Selector

Curve Graph of Image Value Adjustments

Original Values on Horizontal Axis

Adjusted Values on the Vertical Axis

Highlight values at this end starting at 255

Shadow values at this end starting at 0

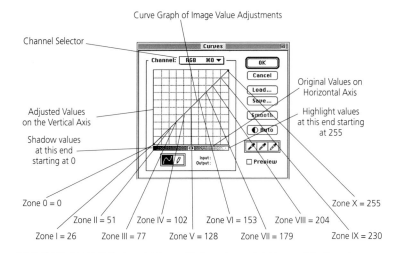

Zone 0 = 0

Zone I = 26   Zone II = 51   Zone III = 77   Zone IV = 102   Zone V = 128   Zone VI = 153   Zone VII = 179   Zone VIII = 204   Zone IX = 230   Zone X = 255

Using the Curves tool, if you want to modify the colors or brightness of the items in a certain zone or zone range of the image, this diagram points out the part of the curve you would modify to change those zones. Using the Eyedropper tool with Curves, you can measure any part of the image and the location of its values will show up on the curve as a small circle. This makes it very easy to adjust any range of values or colors using Curves.

Brightness/Contrast slider

Histogram bar graph of image values

Input Highlight slider

Channel Selector

Input Shadow slider

Shadow values at this end starting at 0

Highlight values at this end starting at 255

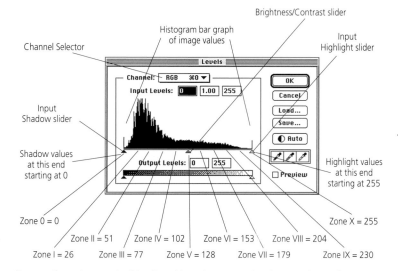

Zone 0 = 0

Zone I = 26   Zone II = 51   Zone III = 77   Zone IV = 102   Zone V = 128   Zone VI = 153   Zone VII = 179   Zone VIII = 204   Zone IX = 230   Zone X = 255

Here are the main controls of Levels and how the zones pointed out on the previous pages show up in the histogram of the Spanish home. The approximate digital value, in the 0 to 255 range, is also shown for each zone.

EV 17–Zone X   EV 10–Zone III

EV 9–Zone II

EV 8–Zone I

EV 11–Zone IV

EV 13–Zone VI

EV 12–Zone V

EV 15–Zone VIII

EV 14–Zone VII

EV 16–Zone IX

EV 7–Zone 0

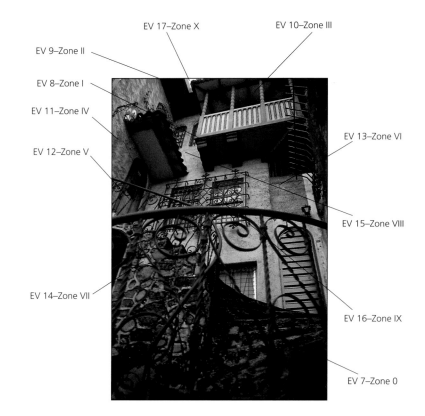

Looking at a scan of the Spanish home image in Levels, we can actually see how many values in the image fall within each zone. Notice that in this image there are a lot of values that fall in Zones I, II and III. That is because this image has a lot of dark areas in it. There are not many values in Zones IX and X since this image does not have a lot of very bright areas. To move the values that are in Zone V towards Zone IV, making the image brighter, or towards Zone VI, making the image darker, you can use the Brightness/Contrast slider in Levels. To move the values in Zones I and II over to Zone 0, making the shadows darker, you can use the Input Shadow slider. In later chapters, you will learn how to use these techniques with the Levels command to give you more control over the different brightness and color zones within your images. You will also learn similar methods and how to do pretty much anything you want with your image data using Curves.

INPUT, CALIBRATION, CORRECTION AND OUTPUT

This Very Important Foundation Section Describes Scanning & Resolution, Monitor & System Calibration, Photo CD Access, Evaluation of Levels Histograms, the Color Correction Process, Sharpening, and Converting from RGB to CMYK

AN OVERVIEW OF THE PROCESS

Many issues arise in attempting to get quality output to a digital printer, film recorder or imagesetter. First, are calibration issues. The output device itself must be calibrated and kept calibrated. If the output device is not calibrated, whatever calibration and correction you do on your computer is not as useful. Next you need to send some known, good output to your output device, make a proof of that output, then compare that proof to the image that made the proof on your monitor. You adjust your monitor so the image on your monitor looks like your proof when both are viewed under your standard lighting conditions.

Second, are information issues. When you scan an image or have it scanned or put onto Photo CD, you need to know how to get the best scan. If you are not doing the scanning yourself, you need to know how to check the scans that others have done to make sure that the maximum amount of information is available for you to work with. And, you need to understand how to make the most of the information that you have.

Finally, you have color correction issues. Once you have the best possible scan from your input device, you need to color-correct the scan that you got. For this discussion, we will assume that your original scan is in RGB format, the format that most desktop scanners and Photo CDs use. The first step in color correcting the scan is overall color correction, after which you correct specific areas that need special adjustments. At this point, you would apply any compositing or special effects to your corrected image or images. The last step in the process is to sharpen the image. If your output is to an RGB device, you are now done. If you are going to a CMYK device, you will need to convert to CMYK and perhaps make final color adjustments in CMYK.

If your scan was done at a high-end color house in CMYK, you may not need to color adjust it at all. High-end drum scanners often also sharpen the image. In that case, you would simply do any compositing or effects that were necessary and then output the CMYK file to your device. If you know that you are not adjusting the color or contrast of the file because it was done by the scanner operator, it is not so important that the image on your screen look exactly like your output. This is only crucial when you are adjusting the color and contrast of the file.

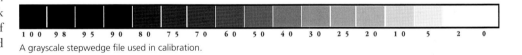

| 100 | 98 | 95 | 90 | 80 | 75 | 70 | 60 | 50 | 40 | 30 | 25 | 20 | 10 | 5 | 2 | 0 |

A grayscale stepwedge file used in calibration.

CALIBRATING YOUR OUTPUT DEVICE

It doesn't do any good to try to calibrate your monitor or try to perfect your process of doing color corrections unless the output device you are sending to (imagesetter, color printer, film recorder, etc.) is first calibrated. A good test for calibration is to send a group of neutral colors to your output device. I have created this file called the StepWedgeFile to be used as a test file for calibrating your output device. The StepWedgeFile consists of wedges of neutral gray that have a known value. There are two issues involved in calibrating your output device. First, will the device print the correct density? If you send a 50% density value (numerically 128) to the device, it should measure and look like 50% when it prints. All densities should print as they are expected. The second issue is getting colors to print correctly. If you get the output device to print these neutral gray values correctly, that is a good sign that it will also print colors correctly. You want the densities on the gray wedges to be correct and you also want each wedge to continue to look gray.

To calibrate an imagesetter, send a grayscale version of the Step-WedgeFile to the imagesetter and output it as one piece of film. Using a densitometer, measure the densities of the swatches on the film and they should match, within plus or minus 1%, the densities that you sent from the file. Make sure the imagesetter is calibrated for density before worrying about color.

PRINT KNOWN COLOR OUTPUT TO MAKE A TEST PRINT

Once you know that your output device is calibrated for density, you should also check it for color. For CMYK output, you need a CMYK file that you know is made up of good color separation values and images. For RGB output, you need a known quality RGB original. On the following pages, we have examples of the type of file you should create for your test. This file, called the Known Output Test, contains known CMYK values at the top in the neutral grays and also various colors to test how known CMYK colors print on your output device.

The CMYK makeup of the colored swatch values we used here is printed at the back of Chapter 6 in the Adobe Press Book, *Imaging Essentials*. Create these swatches in a CMYK file by selecting the area of each swatch then going into the Photoshop Color Picker and typing in the CMYK values that make up that swatch's color. Use Edit/Fill to fill the selection with the color you just created. The Known Output Test file also contains photographs that were separated using known color separation techniques. We have a bigger version of the Ole No Moiré image from Adobe, the Bryce Canyon and Santa Cruz images are mine, the flying books is an Apple magazine cover shot by Marc Simon with effects by me and the fourth image is by one of my students, Will Croft. All these images and these separations have been previously printed on a press with very good results.

For your test image, you should create grayscale bars and color bars like the ones shown here (get the CMYK values from *Imaging Essentials*) and then include several images that you know are good separations of work that is typical of the type of image you normally separate. You can also include the Ole No Moiré image which you can get from the Goodies/Calibration/Separation Sources folder that comes with Photoshop 3.0. Once this file has been output and proofed, in the way you would normally work, you can bring the file that created the proof up onto your screen and adjust your monitor so the image on the screen matches the proof as closely as possible. We will show you how to do that shortly. Our Known Output Test is included in the Calibration folder on the Photoshop Artistry CD and also printed full-size on the next page. For calibrating an RGB output device, use similar images that you know have worked well when output to that type of device is RGB.

CHECK PHOTOSHOP SEPARATIONS ON THIS DEVICE.

To see if your Photoshop color separation preference settings are working well, we will create your Photoshop Separation Test. Before you do this, make sure you read through the Setting System and Photoshop Preferences chapter and set up your Photoshop separation preferences correctly. If you already have Photoshop separation preferences that work well for you, just continue to use those. Create an 8.5 x 11 canvas in RGB mode and fill it with a neutral gray background. Save this as Photoshop Separation Test. Now convert the grayscale StepWedgeFile, in the Calibration folder, to RGB and paste it into Photoshop Separation Test.

Now find some RGB images that are typical of your normal work. Copy these images and paste them into your test file. (We have created a Photoshop Separation Test file from some of the images in this book. It is included in the Calibration & Output folder on the Photoshop Artistry CD and also printed in this chapter.) Save the final RGB version of this file. Use your Photoshop Separation Test (you can try ours if you don't have one), to output all four of the cyan, magenta, yellow, and black pieces of film in the same way you do your normal production. If you normally use the Photoshop Mode menu to convert from RGB to CMYK, then do this on the Photoshop Separation Test. If you use EFI Color, then do it that way. If you normally save your files as EPS/DCS from Photoshop and then put the file into Quark, do the same thing in your test. Save your final CMYK version of the file under a different name than the RGB version.

Print the Photoshop Separation Test to film on your normal imagesetter and make a laminated proof. The densities should look correct in the stepwedge on the proof and they should also look gray. If the stepwedge densities are not right or if they have a cyan, magenta or some combination of color casts, then this is a sign that either the imagesetter is not calibrated or there is a problem in the way you are making separations. You did not alter or color correct the stepwedge file using your monitor so it should be

Here is our KnownOutputTest CMYK file. This file should use known CMYK values and separations. Use this to make a test proof and to calibrate your monitor to that proof.

gray. If it doesn't look gray or the densities are not correct, refer to the separation section and try to adjust your separation values to solve this problem. If the stepwedge looks good but your images have a color cast in the proof, the problem might be the calibration of your monitor. If this test prints with the correct densities and there are no color casts, then you know that you are at a good point to calibrate the rest of your system.

CALIBRATING YOUR MONITOR

Now we are going to take your Known Output Test and your Photoshop Separation Test and use these files along with their proofs to calibrate your monitor. It is important to be sure you can always set up consistent lighting in your office for color correcting images. If you have an office with a large window right next to your screen, you will never have consistent lighting on the screen. The ideal circumstance is to have a color correct, 5000° Kelvin viewing box next to your monitor where you place your proofs for consistent viewing. You want a room where the lighting on your monitor is always the same. You can then adjust the monitor, using the Gamma tool that comes with Photoshop or using a hardware monitor calibrator, so the color and contrast of the image on your screen looks as close as possible to the proof.

SETTING THE BACKGROUND

First, make sure the background on your monitor is neutral gray. To do this on the Mac, go to Control Panels on the Apple menu and locate the General controls. Click on the arrows above the desktop image until you find a neutral gray, then click on the Desktop icon to invoke the change. To do this in Windows, double-click the Control Panel icon in the Program Manager's Main group, then double-click on the Color icon. Choose Windows Default from the Color Schemes menu then click Color Palette and choose Application Workspace from the Screen Elements menu. Now select the lightest gray in the palette and then click on OK. Now return to Photoshop by double-clicking the Photoshop icon.

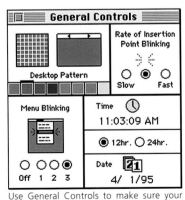
Use General Controls to make sure your background is neutral gray.

SETTING THE GAMMA

To calibrate your monitor using the Gamma control panel, locate Gamma in your Photoshop folder within the Goodies/Calibration folder and move it to the Control Panels folder within your System Folder. That will cause the adjustments you make to your monitor to come up every time you reboot your system. PC users access the Gamma utility by clicking the Calibrate button within File/Preferences/Monitor Setup. This utility is called Calibrate in the PC version of Photoshop. Now, you want to create what we'll call your basic gamma. This will give you a gamma and color balance that is close to the 1.8 and 6500 that you set in your monitor preferences. The gamma of your monitor is similar to the amount of contrast it has. The color balance of the monitor will change how various colors appear on the screen. Bring up the Gamma control panel (Calibrate for PC) against the standard gray background.

Before setting the gamma, make sure the brightness and contrast knobs on your monitor are set where you like them. After the monitor has been calibrated, you should make sure these are not moved as that will throw your calibration out of whack. If there is more than one person using your computer, tape these knobs down and put a Do Not Disturb sign on them. Put the Gamma control panel in the middle of the screen and set the Target Gamma to 1.8. There is no Target Gamma setting on the PC Calibrate so PC users skip this. Make sure the Black Point, Balance and White Point settings are all in the non-adjusted positions. Move the Gamma Adjustment slider quickly and radically back and forth and you will notice that the two lines of vertical bars sometimes look similar and sometimes look quite different. Sit way back and squint, and then move this slider until the two sets of gray bars look as similar as possible. This should give you gamma 1.8. If your final output device will be an RGB film recorder or a video monitor for multimedia, you may find that you want to use the 2.2 radio button, which will give you a 2.2 gamma with this procedure. If you do that, you will need to change the Gamma value in Monitor Setup to 2.2 also. I usually just leave all my gamma settings at 1.8 all the time and that works well for me.

ADJUSTING THE WHITE POINT

Get some paper that is typical to the paper you will normally print on or use the background color of your normal proofing paper. Now click on the White Pt. adjustment and move the Red, Green and Blue sliders to try to get the whites in this dialog box to look more like the whites on your print or proof paper. Remember, you are viewing that paper within your

The Gamma control panel that comes with Photoshop can be used to calibrate your monitor.

58

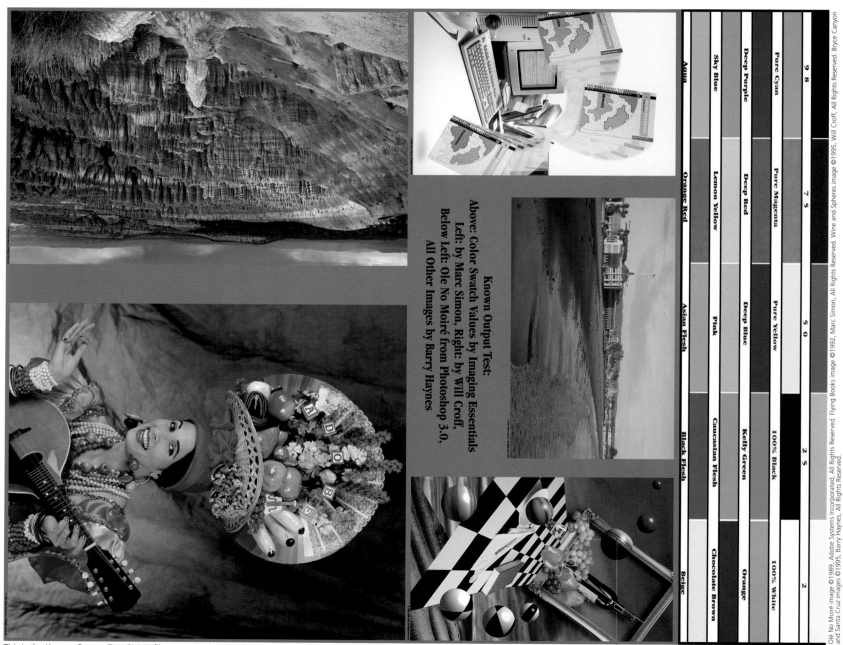

Known Output Test:
Above: Color Swatch Values by Imaging Essentials
Left: by Marc Simon, Right: by Will Croft,
Below Left: Ole No Moiré from Photoshop 3.0,
All Other Images by Barry Haynes

This is the Known Output Test CMYK file as we think it should look when proofed with the Kodak Approval system. Your proof may look slightly different depending on the type of proofing system you use. If your proof of this test looks a lot different, you may want to check the calibration of your imagesetter.

59

This is our Photoshop Separation Test file converted to CMYK with our preferences settings as we think it should look when proofed with the Kodak Approval system. Use Gamma and the techniques in this section to calibrate this file on your screen so it looks like this. Then use Load Settings in the Gamma tool to load these calibration settings when working on the color correction exercises in this book. That way the book's images on your screen will look as close as possible to how they looked on the authors' screen when the exercises were written. It will then be a better comparison when comparing your results to the authors'.

standard viewing light box or lighting conditions. You also have your standard lighting conditions set in the room to view your monitor. Moving the Blue slider to the left will add more yellow to your whites. Moving the Red or Green slider to the left will add cyan or magenta respectively. If you want to add the color of one of these sliders, say green, you would have to move both the Red and the Blue sliders the same amount to the left.

Don't get too detailed about trying to get the whites on the monitor to exactly match the whites on your standard paper. YOU WILL NEVER BE ABLE TO DO THIS! Calibrating your monitor is a process whereby you get the monitor to more closely resemble your output. It will never look exactly the same and getting whites to look the same is probably the hardest part. If the whites on the monitor look a little blue, for example, just move the Blue slider a little to the left and some of the blue cast will go away. Don't move these highlight sliders very far or the calibration process will be thrown off. I have my Blue slider moved over to 235, for example.

SETTING THE COLOR BALANCE

Click on the Balance adjustment button in the middle and adjust the Red, Green and Blue sliders either left or right until the middle values in the grayscale in the bottom part of the Gamma tool look as close to gray as possible. If you have trouble judging gray, placing a standard Kodak Color Separation Guide and Grayscale (Q13 and Q14) in your proof viewing box and compare the grays in the Gamma tool to those on the printed chart. You can also use a MacBeth Color Checker color rendition chart for this. Moving each of the Red, Green or Blue sliders to the right will add more Red, Green or Blue to the color balance of the middle values displayed on your monitor. Moving any of these to the left will add the complementary color, like magenta for the Green slider, to the monitor's balance.

SETTING THE BLACK POINT

Finally, click on the Black Pt. button to adjust the dark parts of Gamma's grayscale wedge. Moving the Blue slider to the right will add blue to the shadows. To add yellow to the shadows, you will need to move Red and Green equally to the right.

FINE TUNING THE ADJUSTMENTS

After adjusting the White Pt., Balance and Black Pt., you may want to go back to the Gamma slider and fine tune it so the two rows of gray bars are still the same. Now you have adjusted your monitor so the gamma, which is similar to the amount of contrast, is close to 1.8 and the color balance is close to neutral. I preface these with "close to" because this is a subjective procedure. Click on the Save Settings button and save this within the Calibration folder of your Photoshop folder and call it Standard

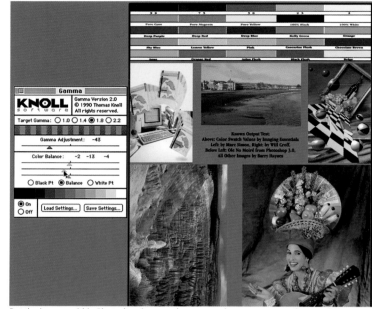

Put the images within Photoshop in normal screen mode so you can see them and Gamma at the same time.

Gamma 1.8. PC users need the .AGP suffix on the file name. When you are working with grayscale images, this may be a good monitor setting to use. We are going to make a different monitor setting that is calibrated to each different output device you work with. Whenever you are starting to calibrate to a new output device, first use Load Settings in Gamma to reload this Standard Gamma 1.8. PC users need to click on the Preview button to see the Gamma change on the entire screen and then click OK in the Calibrate dialog box and OK in Monitor Setup to apply these changes. For Mac users, just leave Gamma on and in the Controls Panels folder.

When you are doing the color correction exercises in this book, you will find the directions most accurate if the book's images on your screen look close to the way they looked to the authors on their screens. For this to happen you will need to use the following monitor calibration method to calibrate the Photoshop Separation Test file on your screen to the full page print of this file earlier in this chapter. The Photoshop Separation Test file can be found in the Calibration & Output folder on the Photoshop Artistry CD.

CALIBRATING YOUR MONITOR TO YOUR OUTPUT DEVICE

Now bring up the digital files that created your Known Output Test and Photoshop Separation Test. You can use our Known Output Test and Photoshop Separation Test within the Calibration folder on the Photoshop Artistry CD if you haven't made your own test files yet. These will get you within the ball park. You will need to calibrate your monitor to your own output device(s) to be the most accurate!

Have these two CMYK digital files on the screen within Photoshop. You always want to do your final critical color corrections in Photoshop since Photoshop will alter the display of CMYK images to match as closely as possible your output device. Make sure the monitor contrast and brightness knobs are set and taped down. Bring up Gamma and do a Load Settings on the Standard Gamma 1.8 settings you did above. This will be your starting point. Place the proofs of the two images in your color correct lightbox or in the standard location you use for viewing proofs. Make sure the lighting on the screen and on the proofs is your standard lighting and that you can see the screen and proofs well. Put the images within Photoshop in Normal Screen mode so you can see them and the Gamma settings at the same time. You will be making changes to Gamma so the images on this screen look as close as possible to the images in the proofs.When you do this adjustment, it will be a compromise. You won't be able to get the images on the screen to look exactly like your proofs. Also, if you move the image to a different computer, its screen will also have to be calibrated using these same steps. If your final output is to an RGB device, like a film recorder, your test file should be in RGB format on the screen when calibrating your Monitor since that is the format where you did your final color correction and output.

CONTRAST AND BRIGHTNESS

First adjust the Gamma Adjustment slider so the contrast and brightness of the images on the screen look like your proofs. Don't worry about the gray stripes in the Gamma control panel this time, get the screen image to match the proof. Pay particular attention to the shadow areas, like the gray background behind the woman in the Ole No Moiré image. Also look at the stepwedge file and try to get the different gray steps on screen to look similar to the proof. This should get your screen as close as possible to the overall brightness and contrast that you have in your proofs.

COLOR BALANCE

Now click on the Balance adjustment and adjust the color balance of the midtones by moving the Red, Green and Blue sliders to the right for more red, green or blue and to the left for more cyan, magenta or yellow. It takes some practice to get your monitor as close as possible to your proofs. Small adjustments in balance can make a bigger difference than you might think. Take it slow and keep an eye on your neutral colors and also any flesh tones you might have. If you get the neutral colors—like the gray background and stepwedge file—to look correct, the other colors will come pretty close. You will find that it is hard to get an exact match on bright saturated colors. Bright reds and saturated blues are especially hard. Don't throw your neutrals out of whack trying to get a bright color to look just right.

FINE TUNE THE ADJUSTMENTS

After adjusting the balance, you may want to readjust the gamma. Now tweak the White Pt. and Black Pt. adjustments to get your bright whites and dark shadows to match your proof as closely as possible. You may find it impossible to get bright whites to match. Again go back and tweak the gamma and balance. You may find that one picture in your proof set will match really well but another won't get as close. Calibrating phosphors on a monitor to reflected light from a print is difficult and will be a compromise. Just get the screen as close as possible.

SAVING YOUR SETTINGS

At this point, choose the Save Settings button and save these settings with the appropriate name. Call it Photoshop Artistry Gamma if you are calibrating to the calibration photos printed in the book. Use a name that refers to the type of proofs that you or your service bureau uses. You will want to create a different calibration setting for each type of output that you do and maybe, for each service bureau that you work with. If you output to color transparency film, you should put the transparency on a color correct light table that is next to your monitor, and then, in Photoshop, calibrate the RGB digital file that created that transparency to the actual transparency on the light table. You can get color correct viewing boxes that allow for both transparency and proof viewing.

CHECKING THE RESULTS

Now turn off the Gamma tool using the button at the bottom left. With Gamma off you see the screen without any calibration. Hopefully the Gamma on position will be much closer to your proof. This will show you that you are better off with the Gamma control panel settings than with no

Why Is It So Difficult to Get Predictible Color?

START ➡️ **FINISH**

Steps in Process	Nature	Photo Original	Scan	Digital Storage	Display	Output Master	Proof	Offset Print
Media	Reflected Light	Photo Dyes & Silver	Magnetic or Optical Data Recording	Magnetic or Optical Data Recording	Phosphor Emission	Halftone Film	Proof Pigments	Cyan Magenta Yellow & Black Inks
Applicable Color Theory	CIE Chromaticity	Photo RGB (CMY)	Photo Separation RGB	CMYK RGB HSV LAB	Video RGB	CMYK	CMYK	CMYK
Form and Range	Analog ∞ range	Analog 3.0 – 1.7 optical density	Digital 24-bit	Digital 24-bit	Analog variable gamma	Digital Halftone	Analog 2.0 optical density	Analog 2.0 or less optical density

When you transfer an image from nature onto film, scan it into the computer, output to proofs and film, then finally print it on a press, the image goes through many changes along the way. Each of these changes can affect the colors in the image within that particular media and how you see those colors. Managing all these changes and ending up with an image that looks like the original nature scene when you're done is a difficult process. This diagram shows you all the steps in the process, the media used for each step, the color theory associated with that media and the form and range of that color theory.

monitor calibration at all. You will get used to the differences between the way an image looks on the screen and the way it looks on a proof or transparency. Certain colors and brightness values will never look exactly the same and you will learn how to deal with these subtle differences. The purpose of calibrating your monitor is to get things as close as possible and noticeably better than no calibration at all.

To adjust your monitor using a hardware calibrator, use the directions that come with that calibrator. With the gamma utility or with a hardware calibrator, you will never be able to get the image on the screen to look exactly like the proof, but you can make it much closer than it would be if you didn't do this calibration. If you don't have a color correct lightbox next to your monitor, just make sure that you always view the proof in the same lighting conditions and that you can see it well with that light. Also, make sure that the light on the monitor is always the same.

A Custom Setting for Each Type of Output

If you work with several different service bureaus to do different types of output, you may need to have a different monitor setting for each type of output at each service bureau. When I output 4x5 transparency film to Robyn Color in San Francisco, I use different monitor calibration settings than when I output to my SuperMac ProofPositive color printer. Whenever I am working on a job for Robyn Color, I load the Robyn Color Monitor settings; this way I know the colors on my screen will be very close to the final output on their RGB film recorder. You may want to have a different monitor calibration setting for printing grayscale images and maybe even duotones rather than the ones you use for working with CMYK. Experiment and see what works for you. To do the separations for this book, we asked the printer to use their Kodak Approval digital proofing system to make proofs on the exact same paper the book would be printed on. We then calibrated our monitor to the Known Output Test and Photoshop Separation Test proofed on that paper. The advantage of the system of calibration described here is that you can do it yourself with the tools that come with Photoshop, so you have complete control over it.

Color Management Systems: What They Do

Color management systems take a standard image that you have corrected on your computer screen and remap that image to the different color gamut of the particular output device it is being printed on. The color gamut of an output device is the set of colors and brightness ranges that the output device can print. Each different output device, such as digital printers, CMYK proofing systems, transparency writers, etc. will have its own specific gamut. If you take the same digital file and print it,

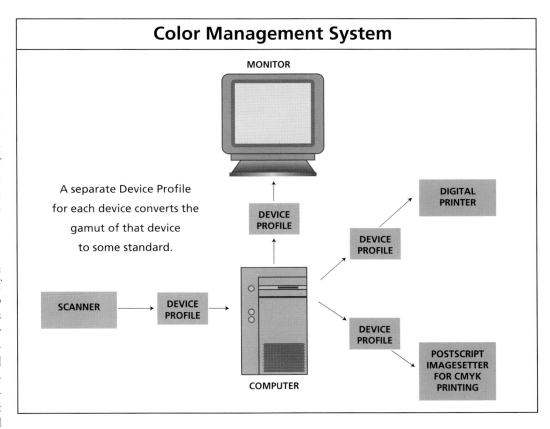

unmodified, on a number of different output devices, each of these prints will look different—different from each other and also probably different from the image on your computer screen.

The monitor calibration technique we just went through in the last section shows you how to calibrate your monitor so it looks as close as possible to one particular output device. But you will have to do this calibration routine separately for each output device you are working with. A color management system has measured the difference between different types of output devices and has a color gamut table for each device. As an image is being sent to a particular device, the color management system changes the image, on the fly, to try to make it print in a standard way on that device. This way, if you print the same picture on a lot of devices, the color management system will try its best to make all those pictures look as close as possible to each other.

Some examples of color management systems are the Kodak KEPS, Electronics For Imaging (EFI), Agfa's FotoTune and Apple's Color Sync systems. Apple's system is a generic one that allows many other 3rd party companies to contribute color gamut tables for their specific products. Color management systems are a step in the right direction to standardizing color. The problem with them so far is that there hasn't been a good way to deal with the subtle differences between each instance of a particular device. I have, for example, a Radius/SuperMac ProofPositive dye sublimation printer. I love the photographic quality prints I can get from this printer. If I took the digital file that produced a print on my ProofPositive printer, even using a color management system, and printed the same file on someone else's ProofPositive printer, there would be subtle differences between the two prints. The other printer may have a different batch number on its ribbon, it may be slightly out of alignment, the temperature and humidity at the other location might be different, and for whatever reason there would be other subtle differences. These are the things that color managements systems have not been able to deal with so far.

Some new products that are coming on the market, like the Colortron color Spectrophotometer from Lightsource, will eventually help users to work with newer versions of color management systems and improve their performance. Color management systems can also characterize different types of scanners and film input types, different types of monitors and other factors that will affect color production along the way to final output. The "Why Is It So Difficult to Get Predictable Color?" chart on the previous page shows you the types of color systems and contortions that a color image can go through in the process of being transferred from a scene in nature to a photograph in a magazine, transparency or other final output format. There are so many variations in what can happen to the colors, no wonder color calibration and correction can be a difficult process.

Color Management systems can help in dealing with the differences in the gamut and characteristics of different types of input and output devices. They are improving all the time. Some of their marketing implies that the color management system will automatically scan, correct and output an image so it prints like the original. This may be possible for medium to poor quality catalog images. To do art and advertising quality photographic output, the photographer and artist will always want to tweak the image and have as much control as possible over the results. We want prints that look better than the original based on our visualization

and digital skills. We hope to help you to understand the things you need to know to work with color in the real world and produce beautiful output.

WHAT ARE BYTES, BITS AND DPI?

To learn how to make a good scan, we need to understand resolution and the issues involved in how big to make the scan. Since we are going to be talking about size in bytes, let's just take a minute to talk about bytes, bits and dpi. A byte is the most common element used to measure an amount of computer memory. A byte actually consists of 8 bits. All computer functionality is based on switches that can be either turned on or off. A single one of these switches is called a bit. When a bit is off, it has a value of 0. When a bit is on, it has a value of one. With a single bit, we can therefore count from 0 to 1. With two bits lined up next to each other, we can count from 0 to 3 since there are four possibilities: (00=0, 01=1, 10=2 and 11=3). If we add a third bit we can count from 0 to 7: (000=0, 001=1, 010=2, 011=3, 100=4, 101=5, 110=6 and 111=7). When there are 8 bits, or a byte, we can count from 0 to 255. This gives us 256 possible values.

With a grayscale digital image, there is one byte of information for each value scanned from the film. A value of 0 is the darkest possible value, black, and a value of 255 is the brightest possible value, white. Values in between are at different levels of gray with the lower numbers being darker and the higher numbers being lighter. Think of these values like you would think of individual pieces of grain within a piece of film. The more of these values that you have per inch, the smaller the grain in your digital file. The more of these values that you have per inch, the higher the resolution (alias dpi [dots per inch] or samples per inch) within your file. In an RGB color digital image, there are three bytes of information (24 bits, one byte for each of red, green, or blue) for each value scanned from the film. CMYK files have four bytes per pixel.

With an enlarger in the traditional darkroom, you can make a 20x24 print from a 35mm original. The quality of this will not be as good as a 20x24 print on the same paper from a 4x5 original of the same type of film since the 4x5 will have more film grain with which to define the image. If we were printing on different types of paper, the grain in the paper would also affect the look of the final print. It is the amount of grain in the original film that is going to make the difference when you project this on the same paper to make a traditional darkroom print.

When you make a print on a printing press, the grain in the photographic paper is analogous to the line screen of the halftone. When you make a print on a digital printer, the grain in the photographic paper is analogous to the dpi (dots per inch) of the printer. The dpi of a digital printer is the number of individual sensors, or ink jets, or laser spots that the particular printer can put down per inch. Each digital printer will have its own maximum possible dpi and this represents a physical limitation of the printer. The relationship between the dpi of a scan and the line screen or dpi of a digital printer is analogous to the relationship between the grain size of film in the enlarger and the grain size of the paper you are printing on in a traditional darkroom. A scan of 100 dpi will print on a digital printer that can output at 300 dpi but it won't look as good as a 300 dpi scan for the same printer. In a similar way, a print on photographic paper from ASA 1600 film won't look as good as a print on the same paper from ASA 25 film.

HOW BIG SHOULD I MAKE A SCAN?

When you are having an image scanned, it is best to know ahead of time what you will be using the scan for.

> *If the image is to be published as a halftone on a printing press and you want the best quality, then you need to scan it with a dpi (dots per inch or scan samples per inch) of twice the line screen of the publication. For example, if you are printing a 6 inch by 7 inch photograph in a 150 line screen publication, this should be scanned at 300 dpi for the number of inches it will be printed.*

The formula to calculate the optimal byte size for a scan of this 6x7 image is: (6x300 dpi) x (7x300 dpi) x 3. This file would be 11,340,000 bytes in size. The final factor of 3 is for a 24-bit RGB color image since there are 3 bytes for each pixel in the image. For a CMYK scan, the factor is 4 instead of 3 since there are 4 bytes for each pixel in the image. Remove this factor if you are doing a black-and-white scan since that only requires one byte per pixel. When scanning for publication it is often best to scan an extra ¼ inch in each dimension so the stripper (electronic or manual) has a little extra space for fine adjustment. The general formula for the required byte size of final publication scans is:

Scan Size=((height of image + ¼") x (2 x line screen dpi)) x ((width of image + ¼") x (2 x line screen dpi)) x 3 (for RGB)

If you are scanning a file for output to a digital printer, like the Radius/SuperMac ProofPositive or the Tektronix Phaser SDX, then you need to do the scan at the same dpi as the resolution of the printer you will use. For output to the Radius/SuperMac ProofPositive, which has a resolution of 300 dpi, the formula and byte size would be (6x300 dpi) x (7x300

dpi) x 3 = 11,340,000 bytes. Most of the other dye sublimation digital printers (RasterOps, Radius/SuperMac, Mitsubishi, GCC, etc.) and the IRIS ink jet printer have a printed dpi of 300. You should check with your service bureau to find out the resolution of the printer you are using there and do your scans accordingly.

If you are scanning a file for output to a film recorder, like the Kodak LVT (Light Valve Technology), or Symbolic Sciences' Fire 1000 or Light Jet, those require a very high dpi. If you want the output to have the same quality as original film, the dpi can be around 1200 or more. To output a 4x5 RGB transparency at 1200 dpi this would be: (4x1200) x (5x1200) x 3, or 86,400,000 bytes. For film recorders the dpi of the file needs to be the same as the maximum dpi of the film recorder to get the best quality.

If you have trouble remembering formulas and don't want to bother with a calculator, there is an easy way to calculate the file size you will need using the New command in Photoshop. Choose File/New then enter the width and height dimensions in inches for the largest size you will want to print the image you are scanning. Based on the above discussion, set the resolution in pixels/inch to the one you will need for your line screen or printer resolution. Now set the mode to Grayscale, RGB or CMYK depending on the type of scan you will be doing. The image size that shows up at the top of the dialog is the size in megabytes you should make your scan. Now you can cancel from this dialog; Photoshop has done the calculation for you.

Use File/New to calculate the size of the scan you will need.

The formulas for file size presented here are the ones you would use to get the best quality. If you make scans that are even larger than these, your quality will be unlikely to improve but the time it will take to work with and output the files will be longer. If you make scans that are smaller than these, your quality will likely suffer, but the time it will take to work with and output the files will be less.

If you need some digital files to prototype a project, there is no need to start with the large scans described here. I find that RGB scans of about one megabyte usually provide plenty of screen detail for any prototyping I might be doing. If you JPEG compress these scans you should be able to get 10 or so on a 1.4 Mb disk. When the final dimensions are decided for the images in your printed piece, a final scan should be done for the intended output device at those final dimensions. When you get a scan, archive the original digital file as it was scanned and use copies of it to do color corrections, color separations and crops. That way you can go back to the original if you make a mistake and need to start over. Happy scanning!

EVALUATING HISTOGRAMS TO MAKE THE BEST SCAN FROM ANY SCANNER

Now that you know how big to make the scan, the next issue is knowing how to make a good scan and also how to do a good job of bringing an image into Photoshop from Photo CD. The key to these techniques is learning how to use the histogram within Levels to evaluate scans. Lets take a look at a few histograms and talk about what they show us about the images they are describing.

A histogram is a bar graph of how many samples of each of the possible settings in the 0 to 255 range there are within the entire image.

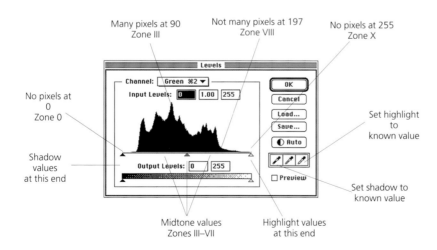

A histogram, like the one above, is the graph you get of an image when you are looking at it within Levels. For more information on levels and histograms, turn to The Grand Canyon chapter where we have a detailed intro to levels. Also refer to Digital Imaging and the Zone System to see how histograms relate to traditional photography and light.

The diagram shown here tells us some of the information that we can learn from a histogram. With normal subject material, the best possible circumstance is to have an original image, transparency or negative, that has a good exposure of the subject matter. This needs to show a full range of values from

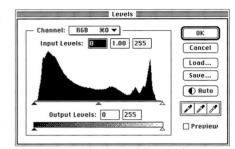

A Histogram that does have a full range of values.

very dark to very bright but have some detail in all areas. The previous chapter on Digital Imaging and the Zone System tells you how to create a high quality exposure with a camera. With a high quality image containing values in all zones that has been scanned correctly, you would see a histogram like the one here.

When you are scanning an image, your goal should be to get a scan that has a full range of values that are present in the original. For most common commercial uses of photography, you want a histogram that looks like the one shown here.

You may not want the shadow values to go right down to 0 and you may not want the highlight values to go right up to 255, depending on the range of values in the original image and also on the intended output device.

SCANNING SHADOWS AND HIGHLIGHTS

When you are scanning an image, there are several areas where you need to be careful what values you obtain. There can be places within the scanned image that are totally black. These should only occur if the original has areas that are totally black. We will call these black shadows; they are in Zone 0. Then there are the regular shadows, which are the darkest places in the image that will still show texture or detail when printed, Zones I and II. On the other end of the spectrum are specular highlights, areas in the original that are totally white, like the reflection of the sun in the chrome bumper of a car. These are Zone X. We next have regular highlights, the brightest areas of the image where we still want to see some texture or detail, Zones VIII and IX.

To some extent, we can call everything between the regular highlights and the regular shadow areas midtones. At the dark end of the midtones we will define the three-quartertones and at the bright end of the midtones, the quartertones. Three-quartertones are shadow areas where you should be able to see a fair amount of detail. Quartertones are highlight areas where you should also be able to see a fair amount of detail.

ADJUSTING THE SCANNER TO GET THE RIGHT VALUES

When you do a scan, the values that you want to obtain for the shadows and the highlights will depend on the type of output device you are directing the final image towards. If you are not sure of the output device or if there might be different output devices, then the highlights (Zone IX) should have a value in the range of 245-250 and the shadows (Zone I) should have a value in the range of 5-10. With an original image that has a full range of colors in each of red, green and blue, it is important that you adjust the scanner to get these types of highlight and shadow values. If you get the highlight and shadow values correct, the values of the quartertones, midtones and three-quartertones will usually fall in between these endpoint shadow and highlight values. When you get this type of scan, the histogram will start out looking like the good histogram mentioned earlier. With this complete scan, you can always adjust the image in Photoshop to get different highlight, midtone and shadow values as well as different contrast, and you will know that you started with all the information from the scanner. I usually do my scans with the normal setting. Some scanners allow you to add a curve that will adjust the image as it is scanned. I generally don't use a preset curve in the scanner because I'd rather do the adjustment myself in Photoshop.

SCANNING STEP BY STEP

Whenever I scan in Photoshop, using any scanner, I always use the same simple technique. First I set up the default brightness, contrast and color balance controls on the scanner. I remove any preset curves in the scanner setting that would change the contrast of the scan. I make sure the scanner is set for the correct type of film. I then do a prescan, which will show me the image in the scanner's preview window. I crop the image to scan the area I want to scan. In the Nikon dialog here, the prescan and crop are shown on the right. Next I set the scanner to do about a one megabyte scan. I usually don't tell desktop scanners to sharpen the image since I'm not sure how good their sharpening software is. If I get a good focused raw scan from the scanner, I know Photoshop sharpening can do a great job. The next step is to do the one Mb scan at the default settings. I would only buy a scanner that had a Photoshop plug-in allowing it to scan directly into Photoshop. This saves a lot of time over scanning into another package, saving the file and then having to reopen it in Photoshop.

Next, I evaluate the one megabyte scan for correctness by first cropping any extra information from around the edges of the scan and then

looking at the image using Levels in Photoshop. You want to crop any black or white borders before you look at the histogram because these borders will throw off the accuracy of the histogram. On the following pages are some sample histograms with explanations of their problems and how to correct them by adjusting the scanner.

Keep on doing one Mb scans and adjust scanner settings until the histogram looks the best. Once you get the levels to look correct on the small one meg scan, use the same scanner settings for exposure and color balance and increase the size of the scan to give you the final number of megabytes that you will need. It is always best to get a good looking histogram from the scanner before you make corrections to the histogram in Photoshop. If you are not the person doing the scan, then at least you now know how to evaluate the scan you got. When there is no way to improve the scan with the scanner (you didn't do the scan, you don't have the scanner, you already did the best that the scanner can do), the next step is to get the histogram correct using the color correction utilities within Photoshop. This will be covered after the next section.

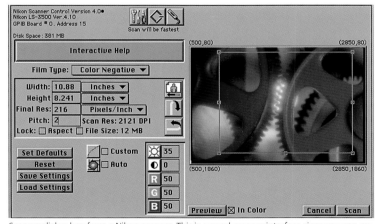

Scanner dialog box from a Nikon scanner. This is a good scanner interface since you can create the cropping box in the prescan window to the right, set its dimensions and its dpi each independently of the other. Nikon scanners also have good controls for brightness in each of the Red, Green and Blue channels as well as overall brightness and shadow settings.

67

Midtones

Highlights

Three-quartertones

Quartertones

Specular highlights

Shadows

Black shadows

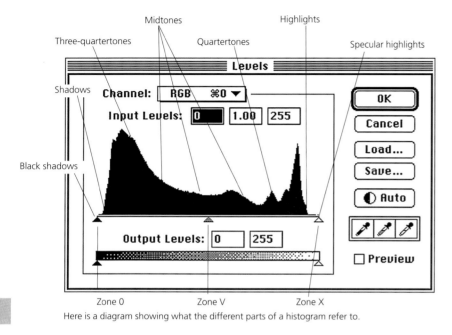

Zone 0   Zone V   Zone X

Here is a diagram showing what the different parts of a histogram refer to.

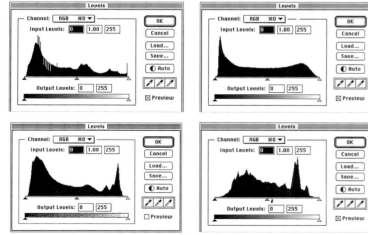

These could all be good normal histograms. Generally, the important issue in a good histogram of a typical photograph is to have values that go all the way from one end of the histogram to the other. This would represent an image that has values from Zone 0, black, all the way to Zone X, white. The way the graph actually looks in between these two end-point areas will be different depending on the particular image. **For some images, like soft fog on a mountain lake after sunset or a subtle snow scene, there may not be bright highlights or dark shadows, and in that case there wouldn't be values that go all the way from one end of the histogram to the other.**

Histograms of different scanning problems and how to fix them.

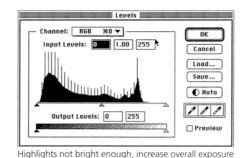

Highlights not bright enough, increase overall exposure on scanner.

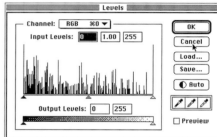

Highlights too bright, decrease overall exposure on scanner.

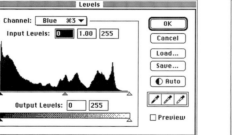

Blacks too dark in the Blue channel, lost shadow detail. Make sure original has detail in the shadows, and if it does, then change black setting in the scan for less black or lighter shadows.

Original is posterized or this is a bad, gappy scan.

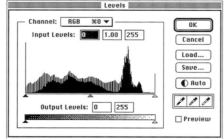

This type of look may indicate one channel was scanned badly. See the Red channel in the histogram to the right.

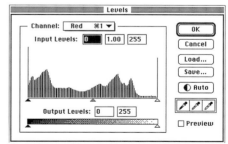

The Red channel from the histogram to the left. Need to lower exposure on red and also lighten black setting.

If the scanner allows you to make separate adjustments for each of the Red, Green and Blue channels, look at the histogram from each channel and adjust the red, green and blue scanner settings separately to get the best histogram in each color.

GETTING THE RIGHT HISTOGRAM

Time and again we are asked in classes, what is a good histogram? Let us ask this in response. If you have three different photographers take a picture of a basket of apples, which would be the "good" photograph: the one that is dark, moody and mysterious; the one that is light, delicate and ethereal; or the one that is an accurate representation of a basket of apples in the sunshine? In actuality any or all of the three may be excellent photographs. Histograms are similar in that there are many different histograms that could be the "right" histogram for a particular photograph depending on the artist's interpretation of the subject.

COMPARING THE HISTOGRAM TO THE ORIGINAL

The histogram can not be viewed separately from the original slide or photo. A good histogram of the original is one that accurately reflects the amount of information in the original. A good histogram of the final output is one that accurately represents the artist's visualization. And never did the adage, "garbage in, garbage out" apply more fully than in digital imaging. If you have an original with no highlight detail, there is absolutely zero possibility that even a high-end scanner can give you something to work with. A good scan of a good original, however, gives you a full range of information that can be manipulated digitally, just as you would manipulate information traditionally in the darkroom.

If you start with a very low contrast original, your histogram will have a shortened value scale, that is, the representation of the pixel values will not stretch across all the values from 0 to 255. In general, as you color correct this scan, you will be forcing the values of the pixels in the scan to spread out along the luminosity axis all the way from deep shadows (between about 3 and 10) to bright highlights (around 245). But notice, we say in general. If the effect that you wish to achieve is a very low contrast image, say, a photo that will appear ghosted back, you may need to do very little adjustment to the histogram. It all depends on what you are visualizing for the final output. Just as you use the Zone System to set where the values of the actual subject matter will fall on the film, in digital imaging you chose (through manipulation of the histogram) where the values of the scan will fall in the final output. Therefore, the histogram must be viewed in context with the original input and the desired output. You must ask yourself, "What is actually there?" and "What do I want the audience to see?"

MODIFYING WITH LEVELS AND CURVES

Once you get a good scan with a good histogram you can modify it with Levels and Curves to get your visualization of that image for your final print. If you move the Levels Input Highlight slider to the left, you are

moving your Zone VIII and IX values towards Zone X and making the highlights brighter. If you move the Output Highlight slider to the left, you are moving your Zone X, IX and VIII values towards Zone IX, VIII and VII, respectively and making the highlights duller. You can use the Shadow sliders to similarly move the zone values around in the shadow parts of the histogram. If you move the Input Brightness/Contrast slider to the right, you are moving Zone V values towards Zone IV or III, making the midtones darker and more contrasty. If you move the slider to the left, you are moving Zone V values towards Zone VI or VII and making the image lighter and brighter.

The Curves tool allows you even finer adjustment to values within specific zones. Read through all of The Grand Canyon, Kansas and Al chapters to try out these techniques and see how digital imaging gives you more power to realize your vision. As Ansel Adams says in his book, *The Negative* "Much of the creativity in photography lies in the infinite range of choices open to the photographer between attempting a nearly literal representation of the subject and freely interpreting it in highly subjective 'departures from reality'." Many people think of Adams' prints as straight photos from nature. Actually, Adams did a lot of adjusting with both his view camera and in the darkroom to create the visualization of the image that would bring forth his feelings and impressions from the original scene. I believe he would enjoy digital imaging.

WORKING WITH PHOTO CD IMAGES

The best way that I've found to open images that are on Photo CD discs is to use the Kodak Photo CD Acquire module. When you get an image scanned onto Photo CD there are two possible formats, Regular and Pro Photo CD. Regular Photo CDs have five scans of different sizes of each image. The five sizes are: 192x128, 384x256, 768x512, 1536x1024 and 3072x2048 pixels. For about $1 to $2 a photograph you get all five sizes of scans of each photograph. The largest of these is an 18 megabyte file, which is useful for a 10"x6.8" separation at 300 dpi (i.e. for a 150 line screen separation). With these 18 Mb files, I have actually made some

Corrected Photographs and Their Good Histograms
(Values in the middle of a histogram look different for each photo)

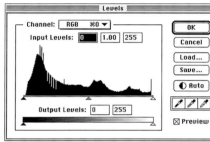

This histogram has lots of dark shadows in the trees and the fence. The spike at the far right is the white buildings.

The Burnley church.

Notice the small spike for the dark shadow areas that are small but so important in the photograph.

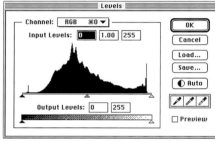

Man on the beach at sunset.

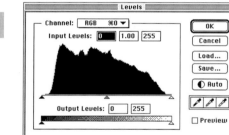

Lots of values everywhere across the full brightness range.

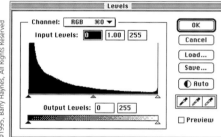

Young Lakes.

Lots of very dark areas and very bright areas, even totally black and white are OK in this photo.

The Paris Cafe.

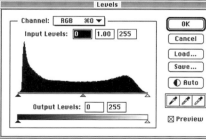

This histogram is probably so smooth because all the objects have a similar range of colors and subtle tones.

Shells in Costa Rica.

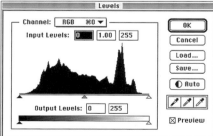

Lots of ¾ tones on the dark parts of the beach. The large number of ¼ tones are probably in the sky and the waves.

Santa Cruz sunset from the boardwalk.

70

Poor Scans and Their Problem Histograms

(Different types of problems require different scanner adjustments)

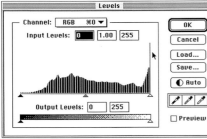

No highlight detail. Rescan with a lower exposure setting.

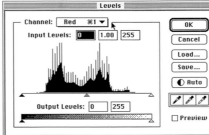

The image is too bright and the detail in the clouds and other highlights is lost.

The Red channel for the scan to the right. Rescan with more exposure on red and different black value.

This scan has quite different ranges for each of the Red, Green and Blue channels. Best to rescan and adjust each channel separately.

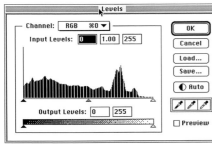

No shadow detail. Rescan and change the shadow setting on the scanner.

No matter what we do in Photoshop, we won't be able to bring out shadow detail because it was lost in the scan.

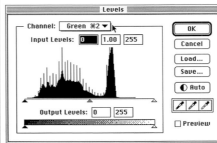

The Green channel for above right. Rescan with larger exposure for green, black is OK here.

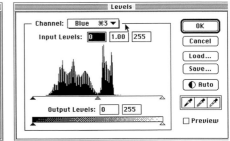

The Blue channel for above image. Rescan with much larger exposure and possible black adjustment.

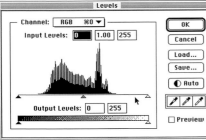

Not a broad enough range on the scan. We could correct this in Photoshop by bringing in the highlight and shadow sliders but then we will end up with the gappy scan to the right. We are better off rescanning with more exposure and a different shadow setting.

The highlights and shadows are way too dull.

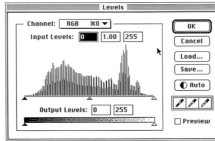

The histogram of the image to the left after fixing in Photoshop now has a bunch of gaps in it that represent lost tonal values. You will get more detail in the printed result by rescanning.

The corrected image with the gappy histogram still prints better than the uncorrected histogram.

71

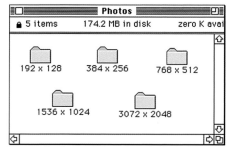

Here are the five resolutions of regular Photo CD scans.

very high quality 11x17 prints by using a SuperMac ProofPositive dye sublimation printer, resampling up the images and sharpening them.

Kodak also offers Pro Photo CD scans. These scans have the same five resolutions as above plus a sixth resolution that is 4096x6144 or up to 72 megabytes in size. This is big enough for 11x17 by 300 dpi without resampling up the scans. The Pro scans cost about $15 to $20 each and they seem to be very good as long as you give them a proper original exposure. I have been getting my Photo CD and Pro Photo CD scans done at Palmer Photographic in Sacramento and have been quite happy with the results. They take jobs from Federal Express and give you 48-hour turnaround.

If you have a difficult negative, one that is improperly exposed, too dark or too light, and you want to get the absolute most out of the scan, you may do better with a high-end drum scan. On the other hand, if the original is a good exposure with a full range of data and you make sure you tell the people doing the Photo CD scans the type of film you are sending them, you should be able to get very usable scans. Like any scan, however, the operator of the scanner and the quality control of the service bureau doing the scans is going to affect the results. If you are not happy with the results at your service bureau, try a different Photo CD scanning location.

The Photo CD scan puts your image onto a CD. A CD, whether it be an audio CD, multimedia CD, etc. can hold up to 650 megabytes of digital information. The Photo CD scans are compressed so even though a file is 18 meg when it is opened, it will only take 4 to 6 megabytes of storage on the disk. This means that you can get about 100 to 120 regular Photo CD scans on a single CD. The Pro format takes much more disk space so you will only be able to get about 30 of these on a single CD.

BRINGING PHOTO CD INTO PHOTOSHOP

There are various options for bringing a Photo CD image into Photoshop. Depending on how you open the image, you should be able to get a better Photoshop histogram of it. When I first started to use Photo CD, I thought that the quality was not very good. The main problem seemed to be loss of highlight detail in bright clouds and other areas. I tend to take very contrasty photographs and require that the full range of contrast be

maintained in a scan. I later learned how to use the Kodak Photo CD Acquire module to get a full range of data from the same CDs that were earlier giving me problems.

USING THE KODAK ACQUIRE MODULE

The process of evaluating the histograms is the same as described earlier when talking about scanning. We just use a different tool, the Kodak Acquire module. When you first enter the Acquire module, you choose the particular scan that you want by looking at the image glossary that comes with the CD. This will show you a tiny picture of each image along with the number that represents that image on the CD. Since a CD is a write once device, the images are always stored by a number and you can't write a name on the CD.

In the picture here, you see us selecting image number 38 from a Photo CD. Once you select an image, you get a little preview picture of the image. If you click on the Edit Image button, you get the more detailed dialog. The Edit Image dialog allows you to see a bigger picture of the image, which is fairly easy to crop. If you crop the image before you open it, opening becomes a much faster process since less data needs to be read from the Photo CD. You can also choose the size (one of 5 or 6) of the scan you want to open. However, the best part of the Kodak Acquire module is that it allows you to choose the gamma and color temperature that you want to use when opening the image.

Choose Edit Image after picking the particular Photo CD image that you want to work on.

What I usually do is open the one Mb version at a gamma of 1.4 and color temperature of 5000. This seem to maintain the most information in the histogram especially in the highlights on contrasty images. After making sure that any black borders have been cropped, I look at the histogram of this scan. I measure the highlight values and make sure detail has not been lost. This is not usually a problem when opening using gamma 1.4 but can be a problem at higher gammas. If the image is really dark, I may reopen it using gamma 1.8 or 2.2. I can usually get a good looking histogram using this technique. When I have decided which setting to use, I use that same setting to open one of the bigger versions of the image (4 Mb, 18 Mb or 72 Mb) for the final usage. The end points of the histogram on the bigger file will be about the same as in the smaller test file but you will notice that histograms of the bigger files are less likely to have gaps in them, which indicates that they have a full range of 256 shades of color for each channel.

The Edit Image dialog allows you to sharpen the image as well as adjust Saturation, Cyan/Red, Magenta/Green, Yellow/Blue and Dark/Light balances as you are opening the image. I usually leave these controls alone and just try to get the best histogram by changing the gamma and color temperature settings. The other adjustments can be done more accurately in Photoshop after you get the best raw information from the Photo CD.

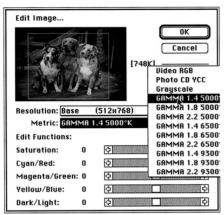

We can choose the gamma and color temperature of the Photo CD image upon opening. I usually use Gamma 1.4 and 5000.

Here are the other controls in the Edit Image dialog. You will have more control if you just get the raw data from the Photo CD and do these kinds of edits within Photoshop.

You can purchase the Acquire module from Kodak by calling 800-235-6325. Make sure you get version 2.03 or later that can open both regular and Pro Photo CDs. For great Photo CD scans, call Palmer Photographic in Sacramento California at: 800-735-1950. We usually ship to them using Federal Express.

COLOR CORRECTING YOUR SCAN OR PHOTO CD

Once you get the best possible histogram from the scanner or from the Photo CD, there is usually some color correction work that has to be done. The first step in color correction is to further work on the histograms until they are as close to perfect as possible with the data you have been given. Before you start the color correction process, it is important to make sure that the Photoshop preferences are set up correctly. The parts of the preferences that affect color correction are:

- Monitor Setup
- Printing Inks Setup
- Separation Setup
- Setting the Eyedropper
- The Highlight and Shadow settings within Levels and Curves

Look at the Setting System and Photoshop Preferences chapter at the beginning of this book and make sure these are set up as recommended. The preferences settings recommended there are default settings for doing color separations for coated stock on a sheet fed press with about 20% dot gain. The settings would be different for newspaper and possibly for other presses. Color correction should be done in a specific order. This part of *Photoshop Artistry* is an overview of the order and steps you should use in making color corrections. There is a much more detailed discussion of this process in The Grand Canyon chapter.

THE STEPS FOR COLOR CORRECTING

The first step is to bring up the Info palette and the Picker palette by choosing Windows/Palettes/Show Info and Windows/Palettes/Show Picker. The Info palette shows you the RGB and CMYK values of the current location of the Eyedropper while in Curves, Levels or Hue/Saturation. It also shows you how these values are being modified during color correction by showing you before values on the left and after values on the right. When you move the cursor into the Levels or Curves dialogs, the values in the Info palette go away but you can use the Picker palette to remember values at the last location you clicked with the Eyedropper. When you click down in a particular location, the values in that location will show

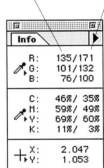

Before values   After values

The Info palette shows you the original values, upon entering the tool, on the left. On the right after the slash, are the values resulting from the tool's adjustments since you entered it this time.

The Picker palette shows values at the last place you clicked. You can see how the values at that location change when you make an adjustment using one of the color correction tools.

up in the Picker palette. These values only change when you click in a new location or make a color adjustment using Levels, Curves or Hue/Saturation that affects the location where you last clicked. It is useful to always have the Info palette showing and sometimes also the Picker palette when you are making color corrections.

Before you start any color correcting, make a copy of the original scan and color correct the copy. This way you can go back to that original if you make any mistakes while color correcting. The basic order for color correction when starting with an RGB scan is:

1. Go into Levels
2. Set the Highlight
3. Set the Shadow
4. Adjust the overall brightness and contrast of the image

The first three steps are done in RGB mode using Levels or Curves but Levels is better since you see a histogram.

5. Go into the Red, Green or Blue channel and remove color casts being especially careful that neutral colors are neutral and don't have a cast.
6. Click on OK in Levels or Curves.
7. Go into Hue/Saturation and increase or decrease overall saturation. Make adjustments to the hue, saturation and lightness of specific color areas.
8. Make color changes to isolated image areas using Selections along with Levels, Curves and Hue/Saturation.
9. Sharpen the image.

At this point, you have a color corrected and sharpened RGB image. This can be printed directly to an RGB printer or output to a RGB film recorder to make a transparency. It is also the final file if you are using EFI color or some other method to convert your images to CMYK on the fly from Photoshop or Quark. If you are going to convert the image to CMYK using Photoshop for separations, first save the final corrected RGB image in case you need to go back to it later.

10. Convert to CMYK using the Mode menu.
11. Make minor color adjustments to specific color areas using Hue/Saturation, Curves and Selective Color with or without selections.

Now let's go through these steps in more detail.

SET HIGHLIGHT

Go to Image/Adjust/Levels (Command-L). You will work in Channel zero, the composite channel, to set the highlight and shadow. The highlight is the brightest point in the image where you still want to have texture. Everything brighter than this will print totally white with no dots. The RGB values here should read somewhere in the range of 240 to 250. Remember that after you set the highlight, everything that is brighter than the highlight location will be totally white. Setting the highlight will also remove color casts from the whole highlight part of your image. Where you set the high-

light needs to be a place that you want to be white when you are finished. It should be at a location you want to print as a neutral value. You want to pick a spot where the detail or texture is just fading but not completely gone. This would usually be the brighter end of Zone IX in the Zone System. Using the highlight Eyedropper, click down at the location where you want to set the highlight. Do this while watching how the Info palette shows the values (before and after in RGB and CMYK), and when you click, the after values should change to the default preference white point values.

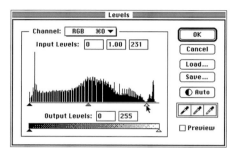

It is often hard to distinguish what point is the brightest on the computer screen. You can find the highlight by holding down the Option key while moving the RGB highlight slider to the left. The first area to turn white on the screen is where you want to look for the highlight. Make sure you move the slider back to 255 once you see where the highlight is.

SET SHADOW

Now pick the point where you want to set the shadow. The RGB values here should read about 5 or less. It should be at a location you want to print with a neutral shadow value. This would be at the darker end of Zone I in the Zone System. Everything that is darker than this point will print as totally black after you set the Shadow. If you

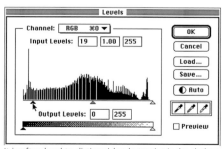

It is often hard to distinguish what point is the darkest on the computer screen. You can find the shadow by holding down the Option key while moving the RGB Shadow slider to the right. The first area to turn black on the screen is where you want to look for the shadow. Make sure you move the slider back to 0 once you see where the shadow is.

want a lot of totally black places in your image, then set the shadow at a location that isn't very dark, say 15, 15, 15. This will make everything that is darker than that location black. If you want a lot of shadow detail in your image, then set the Shadow at a location that is as close as possible to 0, 0, 0 in RGB. These initial RGB highlight and shadow values will vary somewhat from image to image. The purpose of setting the white and black is to normalize these values to neutral grays and also to set the endpoints of detail in the reproduction.

ADJUST FOR OVERALL BRIGHTNESS AND CONTRAST

This step is also done using Channel 0 of Levels. Move the middle slider to the right to make the image darker and more contrasty. Move it to the left to make the image brighter and less contrasty. Adjust this until the image has the level of brightness and contrast that you want.

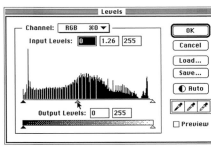
Adjust the overall brightness and contrast by moving the middle slider using Channel 0.

ADJUST FOR OVERALL COLOR CASTS

If the overall image seems too green, go to the Green channel in Levels and move the middle slider to the right. This will add magenta to the image and remove the green cast. If the image is too blue, go to the Blue channel and move the middle slider to the right to add yellow to the image. You just need to remember that the Red channel controls red and its complement, cyan. The Green channel controls green and magenta and the Blue channel controls blue and yellow. The middle sliders of each channel are going to mostly effect the midtones as well as the quartertones and the three-quartertones. The Highlight and Shadow sliders should have been adjusted correctly when you set the highlight and shadow at the beginning.

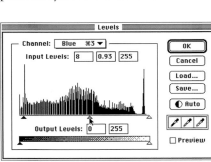
Now deal with color casts by adjusting the middle slider in the color channel that effects the color cast.

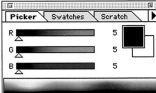
Here we can see the unbalanced values in the Picker palette. The green value is less than red or blue.

Sometimes there can be a color cast in the highlight or the shadow if the point at which you set the highlight was not a neutral location. Some images do not have a neutral location. In these cases, while in Levels, click with the normal Eyedropper at a highlight or shadow location and look at the values for that location within the Colors palette. The values in the Colors palette only change when you click down on the mouse. The Colors palette remembers the last place you clicked. If the numbers are not neutral, (for coated stock, the highlights should be around 244, 244, 244 and the shadows should be around 5, 5, 5) use the Highlight or Shadow sliders for the color channel(s) that are out of adjustment to correct the numbers in the Colors palette. After you do this, you may have to go back and readjust the midtone sliders to slightly adjust the midtone color cast again.

You should modify all these corrections within the Levels dialog as one step. You don't want to say OK until you have completed all of the above steps. If you say OK too many times in the color adjustment dialogs, you will be degrading the image. You don't want to be going into Levels or Curves over and over again. Do it all in one step if possible. Now you have finished the overall color correction with Levels, so you want to say OK to the Levels dialog. For hands-on examples using these techniques, see The Grand Canyon, Kansas and Color Correcting Al chapters.

OVERALL AND SELECTED CHANGES TO HUE, SATURATION AND LIGHTNESS

With the Hue/Saturation tool from the Image menu (Image/Adjust/Hue/Saturation), you may want to increase the overall saturation if you had to brighten the image in Curves or Levels. To increase the overall saturation, move the Saturation slider to the right with the Master button selected. You can also selectively correct color if a certain color range in the image is off. For example, if the reds in the image were too orange you could make them redder by first selecting the Red radio button, then

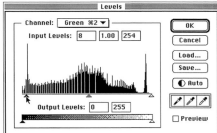
Make the change using the Shadow slider from the Green channel while looking at the values in the Picker palette.

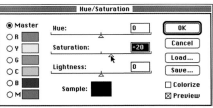
Now the Picker palette shows the correction to neutralize the shadow value in green.

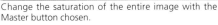
Change the saturation of the entire image with the Master button chosen.

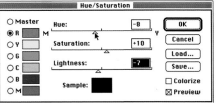
Change the hue, saturation and lightness of just the red colors in the image with the Red button chosen.

75

76

moving the Hue slider towards the M direction. This will add magenta to only the red areas of the image. This is different from adding magenta using Levels or Curves since adding magenta there will usually add magenta to everything in the image.

When the Red radio button is selected, only the items in the image that are red will have magenta added to them. If these items were unsaturated, you could add saturation to just the red items by moving the Saturation slider while red is selected. In the same way you could add or subtract lightness in the reds. If there are different tones of red within your image and you only want to adjust some of them, you should select those areas before making the red adjustment.

Color Changes to Isolated Areas Using Selections, Levels, Curves and Hue/Saturation

The color corrections we have been talking about so far have been global color corrections to the entire image. If a particular area is the wrong color or too light or too dark we may now want to make a selection of that area, using Photoshop's selection tools, and then adjust the colors in that area using Levels, Curves or Hue/Saturation.

Go through The Grand Canyon—Final Tweaks, Kansas—Final Tweaks and AI chapters for a complete description and some hands-on practice showing you how to change isolated areas using selection masks and other techniques.

Sharpen the Image

As a final step, you will often want to use the Unsharp Mask filter or one of the other sharpening filters to sharpen the image. You will have to run some tests to determine the type and amount of sharpening that works best for your different categories of images. Since sharpening can take a lot of time, it is often useful to run tests on a small area of an image. Select a small section that represents the entire image using the Rectangular Selection tool and make a copy of it. Now choose File/New and create a new file. Since you just made a copy, the new file will be the size of the copied section. Say OK to the New dialog and then do an Edit/Paste followed by Select/None. You can repeat this until you have several small files that can be placed next to each other on the screen to compare different parameters of the Unsharp Mask filter.

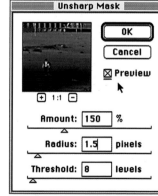

I usually use an Unsharp Mask value similar to this for sharpening 18 meg Photo CD scans.

Let me explain the three parameters of this filter.

AMOUNT: controls the overall amount of sharpening. When you are comparing sharpening effects, you want to zoom into the image to at least 1:1 to be able to see all the detail. Compare different copies of the same image area using different settings for Amount.

RADIUS: Sharpening an image is done by looking for edges within the photograph and enhancing those edges by making one side of the edge darker and the other side lighter. Edges are sharp color or contrast changes within an image. The Radius setting in the Unsharp Mask filter controls the width of pixels along an edge that are modified when the image is sharpened. Again, try running the filter with different settings and comparing two copies of the same image side to side.

THRESHOLD: When you set the Threshold to 0, everything in the image is a candidate for being an edge and getting sharpened. If you set the Threshold to 10, an edge will only be found and sharpened if there is a difference of at least 10 points (in the range from 0 to 255) in the pixel values along that edge. The larger value you give to the Threshold setting, the more contrasty an edge needs to be before it is sharpened and the more you are doing just a sharpen of the edges. When you find the correct Unsharp Mask values, use those to sharpen the entire file. See the Kansas—Final Tweaks chapter for a detailed hands-on example of this.

Converting from RGB to CMYK

If you are printing the file to an RGB digital printer or sending it to an RGB film recorder, then you don't want to convert the file to CMYK format. In all cases, save the final RGB version of the file before converting it to CMYK and then save the CMYK version using a different name. This way you will have the color corrected RGB version to go back to if you are not happy with the way the separations worked on your CMYK version. If you want to save the masks and layers you made while working on the image, it is best to save it in Photoshop 3.0 format. If you want to place the RGB image into Quark, then you probably want to save it in TIFF format. Every time you convert from RGB to CMYK or from CMYK to RGB, you lose some

Converting from RGB to CMYK using the Mode menu.

information. Because of this, if you convert from RGB to CMYK and then back to RGB again, you will not have as good an RGB file as you started with. This is why you always want to save your final RGB file.

After making sure that your preferences are set up correctly for Monitor Setup, Printing Inks Setup and Separation Setup, go to the Mode menu and choose CMYK Color. This will convert the image from RGB into CMYK. Now use File/Save As to save this file under a different name. If you don't correct the RGB before converting to CMYK, the Black channel on your CMYK file will be incorrectly created. Unless your scans are done by the scanner directly into CMYK, you should do overall correction on the RGB file first before converting to CMYK. Scans made by high-end scanners in CMYK should already have had overall color correction done for you by the trained scanner operator. If they don't, correct them in CMYK using a similar procedure as that described here for RGB.

All scanners actually scan in RGB. The high-end drum scanners have a knowledgeable scanner operator and built in software to do the conversion and give you CMYK files that are overall color corrected right from the scanner. You can usually get just as good results from a desktop scanner or even Photo CD using this book's techniques.

FINAL SUBTLE COLOR ADJUSTMENTS IN CMYK

When you are comparing the image on your screen to a proof made from CMYK film, you want to compare the CMYK version of the image on the screen to the proof. When Photoshop displays a CMYK image on the screen, it adjusts the colors to try to give you an accurate representation of how the colors will actually print on a press. There are colors that will show up on an RGB monitor, and in an RGB image, that can't be printed with printing inks on a press. Photoshop tries to adjust your CMYK display to show you those colors as they would appear on a press. It changes this adjustment based on the settings in Monitor Setup, Printing Inks Setup and Separation Setup, so you need to be sure that the preferences values that were used to convert from RGB to CMYK are the same values that you use when displaying the CMYK image.

Since the CMYK image on the screen will more closely match the image on a press, you may need to do final subtle color corrections in CMYK mode. For some images, the CMYK version will look the same on the screen as the RGB version. It depends on the colors that are within the image. Certain colors, for example bright saturated red or deep blue, may get duller or change when you convert to CMYK. Also, the shadow areas may require a slight modification to be sure the correct balance is achieved in the neutral areas. To add contrast, you may want to increase the black middletone. These final color adjustments can be made with Curves, Levels or Selective Color.

SAVING THE CMYK IMAGE

Before you save the image, you should go into Image Size in the Image menu and make sure that the resolution and dimensions are set correctly for the box size the file will be placed into in Quark or PageMaker. If you are printing directly from Photoshop, the file should be the size you want to print. Making these settings in Photoshop, then placing the images at 100% into Quark or PageMaker, will give you the best quality. You may also need to go into Page Setup in the File menu and adjust some of the settings there. You will want to talk to the service bureau doing the output and ask them if you need to set Negative and Emulsion Down. Also, ask the service bureau how to set the Halftone Screens. Often, they will want you not to set either of these values in Photoshop because they will set them using Quark or using the imagesetter. It is very important that you coordinate where these things are going to be set with the service bureau. Also ask the service bureau whether they want the images saved as EPS/DCS, the most common format for CMYK, CMYK TIFF or in some other format. This may change depending on the type of output device they are using.

If you are saving the image in EPS/DCS format for input into Quark, you would probably use the settings in the dialog here. You would only check the Include Halftone Screen box if you set up the screen angles and frequencies using the Screens dialog within the Page Setup dialog. If the screens are to be set in Quark, leave the Include Halftone Screen checkbox unchecked. Good luck with your color. If you have any questions or comments about these techniques, please write us at our address listed at the back of the book.

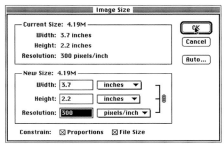

Make sure the image Width, Height and Resolution are set correctly for your layout dimensions and line screen.

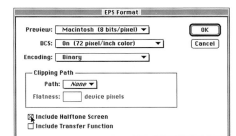

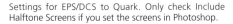

Settings for EPS/DCS to Quark. Only check Include Halftone Screens if you set the screens in Photoshop.

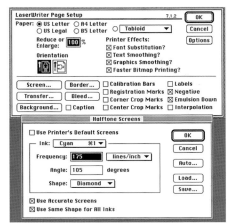

The Page Setup dialog and the Halftone Screens dialog within it. Check with your service bureau for how to set the screens and other settings here. They might want you to leave these unset in Photoshop since they will set them in Quark.

HANDS-ON SESSION: THE GRAND CANYON

Introduction to Levels, Using Levels and Hue/Saturation for Overall Color Correction, Introduction to Curves, Using Curves to Change Specific Color Ranges

The initial uncorrected GrandCanyon image. Notice the green tint in the clouds and the overall flatness.

When an image is originally scanned or brought in from Photo CD, the first thing you should do is check and adjust the overall color correction and saturation. When you are scanning with most desktop scanners or reading images from Photo CD, you usually start out with an RGB image. At this point, it is important to correct overall color and saturation before converting to CMYK. A corrected RGB file will convert to CMYK much better than a non-corrected RGB file. This chapter begins with an RGB image. If you normally begin work with CMYK images, see the note in step 21.

In the Setting System and Photoshop Preferences chapter, we showed you how to set the default highlight (C=5, M=3, Y=3, K=0 or R=244, G=244, B=244) and shadow (C=95, M=85, Y=83, K=95 or R=2, G=2, B=2) values for printing on a sheet-fed press to coated stock. These default values also work pretty well for output to most digital printers, film recorders and for video. If you didn't already do so, go through the Setting System and Photoshop Preferences chapter before doing this exercise. If this setup information is not set correctly, you may not get the expected results from this chapter. If your output will be to a newspaper press or a film recorder, you may want to double-check with the technical specialist at your printer or service bureau to find out the recommended highlight and shadow settings for that particular device. Before you proceed, also read the chapter called Input, Calibration, Correction and Output. This chapter gives you an overview of the entire reproduction process, shows you how to calibrate your monitor and gives you a further understanding of histograms within the Levels tool.

INTRODUCTION TO LEVELS

Before we start actually color correcting the GrandCanyon image, let's take a tour of the Levels tool and explain its different parts and functions.

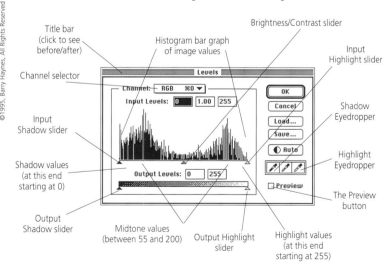

Study this diagram to learn the various controls of the Levels tool.

Levels contains two sets of controls, Input and Output, which can make the image lighter or darker as well as change its contrast. The Input controls on top include the histogram, the Input Levels numbers and three sliders. The Input Shadow slider darkens shadows, the Input Highlight slider lightens highlights, and the Brightness/Contrast slider in the middle, controls brightness, contrast and color balance. The output controls on the bottom of this dialog box contain the Output Levels numbers, the Output Shadow slider for making shadows lighter, and the Output Highlight slider for making highlights darker or duller. The names "Input" and "Output" are chosen by comparing what happens with the Levels Highlight and Shadow sliders to what happens when you move the endpoints of a straight curve in Curves either along the horizontal, Input, axis or along the vertical, Output, axis of Curves. This is a bit obscure to explain at this point but maybe it will make more sense to you after reading this whole chapter then looking again at the Curve diagrams and their captions at step 23.

STEP 1: From the Grand Canyon folder on the CD, open the GrandCanyon file into Photoshop. Crop any white or black borders that are not going to be printed. File/Save As GrandCanyon PS in Photoshop 3.0 format on your hard disk. It is always good to save things in Photoshop 3.0 format while you are working on them, since all your channels and layers also get saved.

STEP 2: Bring up the Info palette from the Window/Palettes menu. If you loaded ArtistKeys, the predefined set of function keys explained in the Setting System and Photoshop Preferences chapter, just hit F9 to bring up the Info palette. Make sure the Info palette is set up to show you both RGB and CMYK values. If not, use the Info palette options to change the settings. Also, use the Picker palette (Shift-F9). With Photoshop 3.0 you can bring up or hide these tool palettes with function keys even after the Levels dialog has been opened.

STEP 3: Choose Image/Adjust/Levels and move the Levels dialog out of the way as much as possible. You want to be able to see as much of the image as you can while color correcting it. You will be using the levels diagram at the beginning of

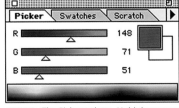

STEP 2: Info palette with before values on the left and after values on the right.

STEP 2: The Picker palette. Hold the mouse button down and measure an image color area to change the values in this window.

this chapter as you review or learn the basic functions in steps 4 through 9. Make sure the Preview button is turned off.

STEP 4: Move the Input Highlight slider to the left and notice that the highlight areas in the clouds get brighter; also the Input Levels number on the right decreases from 255 as you move the slider to the left. Move this slider to the left until the number reads about 220. Let go of the slider and move the cursor over the image—on top of an area where the clouds have turned completely white. While using any of the color correction tools, you automatically get the Eyedropper tool when you move the cursor over an area of the image. Notice that the Info palette shows you two sets of values for this white area. The values to the left of the slash are the original values at the Eyedropper location when you first entered Levels. The values to the right of the slash show you what your levels changes have done to the digital values at the Eyedropper location. You can now see that moving the Input Highlight slider to the left makes the highlights brighter but also causes you to lose detail in the highlights if you move it too far. The original RGB numerical values that were in the range of 230 to 250 have now all changed to 255. This is pure white and will print with no color or detail. You don't want that.

STEP 5: Move the Input Shadow slider to the right so the Input Levels number on the left goes from 0 to about 30 and you will notice the shadow areas of the image turning darker. Move the Eyedropper over a dark area and measure the changes in the Info palette. The RGB values that were originally in the range of 0 to 20 have all moved to 0 now. They have become totally black.

STEP 6: Move the cursor to the title bar at the top of the Levels dialog. When you click on the title bar and hold the mouse button down, notice that the image returns to the way it looked before you changed anything in Levels. When you let go of the mouse button, the image returns to the changed state with no highlight and shadow details. This quick preview feature is very useful for toggling quickly between before and after versions of an image to see if you really like the changes you have made. It only works when the Levels Preview button is turned off. If this toggle is not working for you, your video card may not support Video LUT Animation

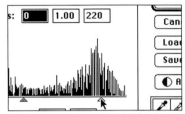

STEP 4: Move the Input Highlight slider to the left so the right Input Level reads about 220.

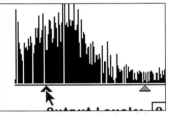

STEP 5: Move the Input Shadow slider to the right so the left Input Level reads about 30.

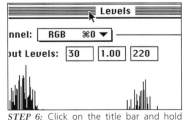

STEP 6: Click on the title bar and hold down the mouse to see before; let go to see after.

STEP 7: Use the Eyedropper to click on the red rocks. In Levels, you are automatically in the Eyedropper.

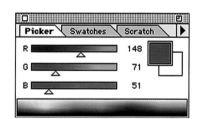

STEP 7: The Picker palette. These values will change as you move the Input Brightness/Contrast slider.

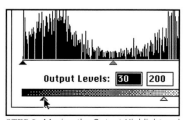

STEP 8: Moving the Output Highlight and Shadow sliders and looking at the Output Levels numbers.

and you will need to work with the Preview button on all the time. See Video LUT Animation in the System and Photoshop Preferences chapter for more information. Now, hold down on the Option key then click the Cancel button. The Cancel button changes to Reset, and when you click it, the levels go back to where they were when you entered Levels this time. All your changes are removed but you don't leave Levels. This saves a lot of time when you are working on large files since it can take a while to calculate the Levels histogram. Notice that the values in the Info palette go away when you move the cursor back into the Levels dialog box. By using the Picker palette, you can remember values at a certain location and see how a change in Levels modifies those values.

STEP 7: Use the Eyedropper to click on a midtone value within the Grand-Canyon image; the orange/red rocks in the foreground will work. When you press down on the mouse button, the values in the Picker palette change. Now go back to Levels and notice that these values don't go away even when you are within the dialog box. Press down on the Input Brightness/Contrast slider and move it to the left. The image gets brighter and less contrasty and the numbers in the Picker palette get larger. Move it to the right and the image gets darker and more contrasty while the numbers in the Picker palette get smaller. Also notice that the middle number in the Input Levels numbers boxes, called the gamma, is changing. When you move the slider to the left, the gamma goes above 1.0, and when you move it to the right, the gamma goes below 1.0. When the Input Levels numbers read 0, 1.0, 255, then you know you haven't changed the Input Levels.

STEP 8: Move the Output Highlight slider to the left until the Output Levels number on the right reaches 200. Now measure the brightest cloud values, and you will notice that values originally in the 230 to 250 range have now all moved to below 200. We changed the Output Levels number from 255 to 200 and the difference of 55, or close to it, has been subtracted from all these highlight values. This has made your highlights darker and duller.

STEP 9: Move the Output Shadow slider to the right and notice how this makes the shadows lighter and duller. If you measure the changes with the Eyedropper and Info palette, you will notice that moving this slider increases the shadow's numerical values, which will make the shadows lighter.

SETTING THE HIGHLIGHT AND SHADOW VALUES

STEP 10: Steps 4 through 9 show you the basic functions of the different parts of the Levels tool. It is important to use those functions in the right order and while taking careful measurements of your progress using the Info palette and Picker palette. We will start out working with the Highlight and Shadow Eyedroppers to set the highlights and shadows on this image—a very important part of this process. All reproduction or printing processes including sheet-fed presses, web presses, newspaper presses, digital printers and film recorders will have certain endpoints to their reproduction process defined by the highlights and shadows. Many newspaper presses can't show detail for shadow values that are more than 85% to 90% black. Some newspapers are even worse than this. Sheet-fed presses, on the other hand, can sometimes show detail in areas with more than 95% black. With a digital file, these percentages are represented by numerical values ranging from 0 (100% black) to 255 (white or 0% black).

When you color correct an image, you don't want that image to contain areas that can't be reproduced by the output medium you are using. Setting the highlight and shadow values correctly for your output device ensures that this won't happen. You also want the white parts of your image to print as white (not with a color cast of yellow, cyan, or magenta) and the black parts of your image to print as black (not dark grey with a green cast). This is also controlled by setting your highlights and shadows correctly. When you set the highlight, you are setting the brightest point within the image that is both a neutral color, white, and will still have a dot pattern. The highlight would be the brightest part of Zone IX in the Zone System. Any point that is brighter than the highlight will print as totally empty paper with no dots. When you set the shadow, you are setting the darkest point within the image that is both a neutral color, black, and will still have a dot pattern. This is the darkest part of Zone I in the Zone System. Any point that is darker than the shadow will print as totally black ink covering the paper with no white holes in the ink to give detail.

STEP 11: Photoshop allows you to decide where you want the highlight to be set. The highlight should be the brightest neutral point that still has detail. Double-click on the Highlight Eyedropper button and make sure the CMYK values in the Color Picker are 5, 3, 3, 0 and the RGB values are 244, 244, 244. These are the neutral values you would want your highlight to have for a sheet-fed press on coated paper. Due to the impurities in printing inks, you get a neutral color by having more cyan than magenta or yellow. Since this is a highlight, there is no black. Click the OK button if you needed to change any of the values.

STEP 12: Now double-click the Shadow Eyedropper and make sure the shadow values are 95, 85, 83, 95 in CMYK and 2, 2, 2 in RGB. If both these shadow values are not correct, fix the CMYK values and the RGB values should change to 2, 2, 2. If they don't, you need to return to the chapter on Setting System and Photoshop Preferences and check the preferences for monitor setup, printing inks setup and separation setup. Click the OK button if you needed to change any of the values.

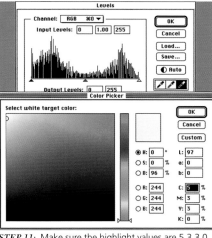

STEP 11: Make sure the highlight values are 5,3,3,0.

SETTING THE HIGHLIGHT

STEP 13: Now we will use the Highlight Eyedropper to click on a highlight, which should be the brightest area of the clouds. You want the highlight to be a neutral white area—the last possible place where you can see a little texture. The RGB values in the Info palette should be in the 240 to 255 range. The CMYK values in the Info palette will be in the 0 to 10 range. If you have specular highlights (the sun reflected off of a chrome bumper, for example) these will not have detail and should have values of 255. You want something just a hair less intense than that. Move the Levels dialog out of the way so you can see the entire clouds area of this image. To find the correct area for setting the highlight, hold the Option key down while moving the Input Highlight slider to the left. The whole image area will first turn black

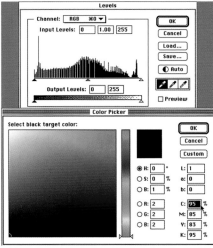

STEP 12: Make sure the shadow values are 95, 85, 83, 95.

and then as you move the slider to the left, white areas will appear. Since this image has no specular highlights, the first white area to appear in the clouds is the place where you should set the highlight. Remember where that location is within the window. Now move the Input Highlight slider back to 255 since you were only using it to locate the brightest point. Click on the Highlight Eyedropper within the Levels dialog. Now move this Eyedropper up to that bright place in the clouds and and move it around in the area while looking at the RGB values in the Info palette for the highest set of numbers. When you find those numbers, (I chose 206, 222, 220), click once, release the mouse button and don't move the mouse after the click. The righthand numbers for RGB in the Info palette should now display 244, 244, 244 for that exact spot where you clicked. Now go up to the Levels title bar and click on it. When the mouse button is down, you are seeing the original image. When the mouse button is up, you are seeing the image after this highlight change. Notice that a subtle green cast in the entire clouds area has been removed by this process of setting the highlight. The clouds should look more white when you are not clicked down on the title bar. If you computer doesn't support Video LUT Animation, you will have to find the highlight point by measuring the areas that seem the brightest and setting the highlight where the largest numbers are. Then turn the Preview button on and off to see how the image looks before and after the change.

SETTING THE SHADOW

STEP 14: Now use the shadow Eyedropper to click on a shadow, which should be the darkest neutral area where you still want a little detail. The RGB values in the Info palette should be in the 1 to 10 range.The CMYK values in the Info palette will be in the 60% to 100% range. Move the Levels dialog to the top so you can see the entire bottom half of this image. To find the correct area for setting the shadow, hold the Option key down while moving the Input Shadow slider to the right. The whole image area will first turn white, and then as you move the slider to the right, black areas will appear. The first black area to appear, in the rocks to the lower right or in the tree, is the place where you should set the shadow. If you set the shadow at a location that has a value of about 1, 1, 1, then you are setting up your image so there will be almost no areas that are totally black when it is printed. If you set your shadow at a location that is around 10, 10, 10, then you are saying that you want everything that is darker than this to be totally black, and

STEP 13: The before and after values for the highlight. Notice how the green color cast was removed and the default neutral 5, 3, 3, 0 values were inserted.

STEP 14: The before and after values for the shadow. Notice that the shadow CMYK values to the right are not the same as the 95, 85, 83, 95 default values you entered, but you should get exactly 2, 2, 2 in RGB.

you will get lots of totally black areas. Now move the Input Shadow slider back to 0 since you were only using it to locate the darkest point. Click on the Shadow Eyedropper within the Levels dialog. Now move this Eyedropper up to that darkest place and move it around in the area while looking at the RGB values in the Info palette. Try clicking at a spot around 10, 10, 10 and see how dark this makes all your shadows. I clicked at a spot around 9, 6, 4, one of the darkest spots under the rock, where I set the shadows for this image. When you find the right spot, click once, release the mouse button and don't move the mouse after the click. The righthand numbers for RGB in the Info palette should now display 2, 2, 2 for that exact spot where you clicked. Now go up to the Levels title bar and click on it. When the mouse button is down, you are seeing the original image. When the mouse button is up, you are seeing the image after the highlight and shadow change.

SETTING OVERALL BRIGHTNESS AND CONTRAST

STEP 15: As you look at this image, you may notice that it is sort of flat. Move the Input Brightness/Contrast slider to the right until the middle Input Levels number reads about .90. Now you will notice more depth and contrast. If you think back to our discussion of the Zone System, you could equate the initial location of the Brightness/Contrast slider with Zone V, the middle gray values. Moving the slider to the right moves Zone V up towards Zone VI or VII depending on how far you move it. What was a Zone VI value now becomes a Zone V value, darker and with more depth. This is similar to the effect you would get by setting the original camera exposure at Zone VI or more, except moving the Brightness/Contrast slider by a zone or two wouldn't change Zone I and IX as much. If you moved this slider to the left, the image would look even more flat. Leave this slider at about .90, and in a few steps we will show you how to saturate your colors to add contrast and drama without sacrificing shadow detail.

CORRECTING FOR COLOR CASTS

STEP 16: All the adjustments we have made so far have been done while the Levels Channel selector was set to RGB (Channel 0). You can now use the Channel selector in Red (Channel 1), Green (Channel 2) and Blue (Channel 3) modes to control the color balance of the image and correct

for color casts. You can switch between channels by a click and drag on the pop-up menu or by using the Command-0 through Command-3 key combinations. The Red channel controls red and its complement, cyan. The Green channel controls green and its complement magenta. The Blue channel controls blue and its complement yellow. You will need to learn this set of complementary colors. To learn more about the complementary colors, refer to the RGB/CMYK table at the end of the Color Correction Tools chapter. This image has a slightly blue color balance, which makes it seem a little cold. Use the Channel selector or Command-3 to move to the Blue channel. Move the Input Brightness/Contrast slider far to the right until the middle Input Levels number reads about .5 and notice how yellow the image is. Now move the same slider far to the left to about 1.5 and notice how blue the image is. You can use this middle slider to control the color balance of the midtones. Move it back to the right until it reads about .92 and notice the difference in the color of the green grass and bushes in the foreground as well as the overall warmer tone of the image compared to when the slider was at the initial value of 1.0. You have added yellow to remove the blue cast in this image.

STEP 17: Press Command-2 to switch to the Green channel. As you move the middle slider to the left, you are adding green, and to the right, you are adding magenta. I moved it slightly to the right to .92, which adds a little magenta to the whole image. Press Command-1 and you can now use this middle slider to move between red and cyan. Again I moved it slightly to the right to .97 and added just a little cyan by removing just a little red. You may make these adjustments slightly differently depending on your likes and dislikes for color and also depending on your monitor. So long as you have calibrated your monitor to your output device, you should be able to get results you are happy with. If you made major cast changes to any particular channel, then go back to RGB (Command-0) and double check your Brightness/Contrast adjustments. Before leaving Levels, click on the title bar to see how the image looked before making any of these changes, and release the mouse to see the new improved image. You should be able to see the improvements on your monitor. When the Preview button is off, Video LUT Animation on the video board is used to instantly simulate the calculated changes you will see based on your levels adjustments. We have been doing these changes in Levels assuming the Preview button is off.

A lot of PC systems and compatibles and a few Macs don't support Video LUT Animation in their video boards. If you don't have Video LUT animation, just work with the Preview button on to be seeing the changes you are making, then turn it off to see the original, unmodified, image. You can't use the title bar as a before/after toggle without Video LUT animation.

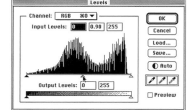

STEP 15: Move the Input Brightness/Contrast slider to the right to make the image show more depth and contrast.

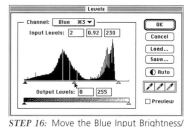

STEP 16: Move the Blue Input Brightness/Contrast slider to the right to add yellow to the image.

Also, on all machines, you may want to turn the Preview button on before leaving Levels and Curves just to check on the screen to be sure the calculated changes, with the Preview button on, actually match the Video LUT Animation simulated changes. Click on the OK button to complete all the changes you have made with Levels. At this point you should do File/Save in case you want to later revert to this version of the image.

STEP 17: The GrandCanyon image after the Levels corrections.

ENHANCING COLOR WITH HUE/SATURATION

STEP 18: In step 15, when you moved the Brightness/Contrast slider to the right to increase contrast, you may have had the urge to go even further for a more dramatic effect. Going to far to the right would have lost too much shadow detail. We can add contrast and drama without losing shadow detail by choosing Image/Adjust Hue/Saturation and moving the Saturation slider to the right to about plus 17%. It may take a few seconds for the screen to update, but you will notice all your colors become more saturated, and this will build some more contrast into the image. When you saturate all the colors, only the midtones get changed; the highlights and shadows are left the same. When using the Hue/Saturation tool, you want the Preview button to be on since Photoshop can't calculate these more complex changes using the monitor on the fly like it can in Levels and Curves. When using Levels and Curves to correct the entire image, you usually want the Preview button off unless you don't have Video LUT animation.

STEP 19: Besides saturating or desaturating all the colors, which you do with the Master radio button selected, you can also use the Hue/Saturation tool to change particular color areas within the entire photo. Click on the radio button next to the red color swatch. Move the Hue slider a little to the left towards the M to about -5. This adds magenta to the red areas of the image. Notice that all the red rocks become a richer darker red color. Now move this slider in the other direction to +5 towards the Y. This takes away magenta and adds yellow to the red parts of the image. Now look at the rocks and they will appear more of a brown color. The reason you can either add magenta or yellow to your reds is that when you print in CMYK, red is made up of magenta and yellow inks. When you use channel 2 or 3 to add magenta or yellow in Levels, you are adding magenta or yellow to everything in the image. With the Red button in Hue/Saturation, you are only changing things in the image that are already red.

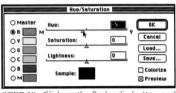

STEP 19: Click on the Red radio button and notice how the red rocks change as you move the slider between -5 and +5.

STEP 20: Click on the Blue button and you can now change blue objects between cyan to the left and magenta to the right. Move the Hue slider between -10 and +10 and notice how the colors in the sky change. You might combine this with adding or subtracting saturation from the blue colors in this image. Remember that changing the blue values not only changes blues in the sky but will also change any other blues that are in an image. Keep an eye on the entire image as you make these adjustments. I moved the blues -5 towards cyan and the cyans +5 towards blue to try to even out the sky. I also desaturated both blue and cyan by -5. Click on the OK button when you have finished the Hue/Saturation changes. Since these changes did not happen instantly, like the ones in Levels do, it may have not been as easy to compare before and after versions. If you choose Undo from the Edit menu and quickly choose Redo from the Edit menu, you can quickly see the before and after version of the Hue/Saturation changes. Get used to using Command-Z to toggle between the Undo and Redo version. We will soon learn how to completely isolate a portion of the image using selections for very fine color control of that area.

STEP 21: Save this color corrected version of the GrandCanyon image in Photoshop 3.0 format so we can use it in future steps.

83

If your initial scan was done in CMYK, then it probably scanned on a high-end scanner, and these overall color corrections should have already been done by the scanner operator. If you started with a CMYK scan, you should check out the image in CMYK mode to make sure it is already Overall corrected; do not convert it to RGB to do these corrections since information can be lost in the CMYK to RGB to CMYK conversion. If you are paying the extra cost to get CMYK scans and they are not already Overall color correct, you should get the scans done elsewhere or just do them in RGB.

INTRODUCTION TO CURVES

Now we will see how to adjust specific color ranges using Curves. Before we start making further adjustments to the GrandCanyon image, let's take a tour of the Curves tool and explain its different parts and functions.

Curves is a graph of input and output values with the input values at the bottom on the horizontal axis and the output values to the left side of the graph on the vertical axis. With Curves, the input values are the original unadjusted values before this invocation of Curves. The output values are the adjusted values which depend on the shape of the curve graph.

In Levels, the histogram is a picture of the actual data that makes up this particular image. In Curves, you see a graph of how any image data

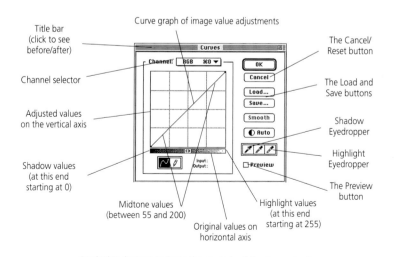

STEP 21: The GrandCanyon image after the Levels and Hue/Saturation corrections.

Title bar
(click to see
before/after)

Curve graph of image value adjustments

The Cancel/
Reset button

Channel selector

The Load and
Save buttons

Adjusted values
on the vertical axis

Shadow
Eyedropper

Highlight
Eyedropper

Shadow values
(at this end
starting at 0)

The Preview
button

Midtone values
(between 55 and 200)

Highlight values
(at this end
starting at 255)

Original values on
horizontal axis

Study this diagram to learn the controls of the Curves tool.

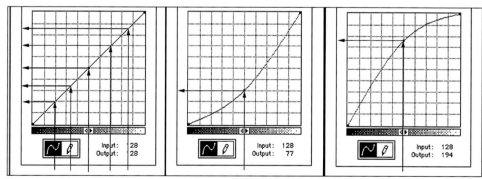

To understand the curve graphs, let's look at these three diagrams. Along the horizontal axis are the original values, called Input, with 0, black, on the left side and 255, white, on the right side. On the vertical axis of the curve, to the lefthand side, are the modified values, called Output, with 0, black, on the bottom and 255, white, at the top. Imagine that the original values are light rays that travel straight up from the bottom of the diagram. When they hit the curve graph, they make an immediate left and exit the diagram on the left side. When the curve is the straight default curve, the values go out the same as they come in, as you can see by the leftmost curve above. When the curve is dragged downwards, like the middle curve, a value that comes in at 128 hits the curve sooner so it will go out at 77. Since lower values represent darker numbers, pulling the curve down makes the image darker. When the curve is dragged upwards, as in the right-hand curve, the input value of 128 doesn't hit the curve until it gets to 194, and that is the brighter output value.

would be modified by this curve but you don't actually see the data that is part of this image. That is why I recommend using Levels first after you do a scan; you can see how the scan worked. Many of the controls in Curves are the same as those in Levels. In both tools, there is the OK button, which you press when you want the changes to become permanent, and the Cancel button, which you press when you want to leave the tool without doing anything. If you hold the Option key down then press Reset, you stay in the tool, all your changes are removed, and the curve goes back to the default straight curve. Both Levels and Curves have Load and Save buttons that load or save settings to the disk.

If you like a curve that corrected one image, you can click Save to save this curve, go into Curves while working on another image and click Load to run this same curve on the other image. Curves also has Highlight and Shadow Eyedropper tools to set the highlight and shadow in the same way you do in Levels. In fact, Curves uses the same preferences values for the highlight and shadow numbers as you set in Levels. These are system-wide preferences. The curve graph is just a picture of what will happen to all the values from 0 to 255. To move the curve, you click on it and drag it to a new position. When you let go, a point will be left along the curve graph. This point has caused the entire curve to move. To get rid of a point, you click on it and drag it outside of the Curves window. When you do this, the curve will bounce back to where it was without that point. Let's experiment a bit now with Curves before we make final adjustments to the Grand-Canyon image.

STEP 22: Using the same image you saved at the end of step 21, choose Image/Adjust/Curves (Command-M) and look at the Curves dialog box. If the curves graph area is only divided into four sections both horizontally and vertically, the default, you can get a more precise grid. Move the cursor to the middle of the graph, Input and Output will both say 128, and Option-click on this center point. Now the curves graph will have 10 sections in each direction. Make sure the Preview button is off.

The default for Curves is that the horizontal axis shows the shadows on the left. The grayscale on this axis is a hint at this. This is easiest to remember since Levels does the same thing. Some curve diagrams show the shadows on the right. If you click on the arrow in the middle of the grayscale, you can flip this curve to put shadows on the right. Doing this makes everything else in the curve adjustment be opposite, a mirror image. Because of this, we recommend leaving shadows on the left. When you set the shadows on the right, the Input and

Output values read as percentages between 0% and 100%. If you are more comfortable reading percentage values than the 0..255 values, you can make your Curves tool work this way. Just remember though, that the curves in this book will be opposite to yours if you flip your curve orientation.

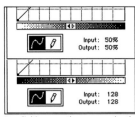

By clicking on the arrows in the middle, the horizontal axis can have shadows on the left or the right. Leave shadows on the left for working with this book.

STEP 23: Now click down in the middle of the curve and move the mouse up and down, left and right, and notice how the curve shape changes and the corresponding changes to the image. Try out all the curves in the diagram below. Option-Cancel between each one to reset the curve to straight. Make sure you understand why each curve changes the image the

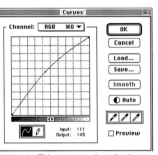
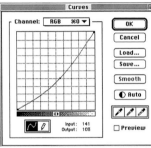
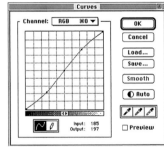

STEP 23: This curve makes the image lighter and brighter. To do this in Levels you would move the Input Brightness/Contrast slider to the left.

This makes the image darker. To do this in Levels you would move the Input Brightness/Contrast slider to the right.

This S-curve makes the midtones more contrasty and the shadows and highlights less contrasty. Overall the image is more contrasty. You can't do exactly the same in Levels.

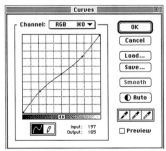
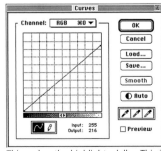

STEP 23: This backwards S-curve makes the midtones more flat and increases contrast in the highlights and shadows. You can't do exactly this in Levels.

This makes the highlights brighter. This is similar to moving the Input Highlight slider in Levels to the left.

This makes the highlights duller. This is similar to moving the Output Highlight slider in Levels to the left.

85

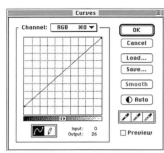

STEP 23: This curve makes the shadows brighter. This is like moving the Output Shadow slider in Levels to the right.

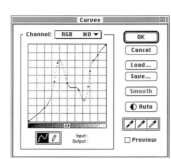

This makes the shadows darker. This is like moving the Input Shadow slider in Levels to the right.

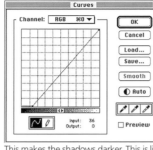

Try this curve to see a prehistoric Grand Canyon! You can't do this kind of adjustment in Levels.

dialog. Click on the curve in that location and move the curve diagonally either up and to the left, more green, or down and to the right, more magenta. We would like to brighten these greens in the field. Notice, however, that the rest of the curve also moves, and because of this, you are adding green, or magenta, to the entire image. What you want to do is add green to just the greens that have the same green color range as this field.

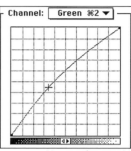

STEP 24: This type of curve adds green to everywhere in the image.

STEP 25: Option-Cancel to return the curve to the default. You will now create what we call a lock-down curve. Click at each intersection of the vertical and horizontal lines in the green curve to leave a point that locks the curve at this location. Make sure the Input and Output numbers are equal before you click. Now you have a lock-down curve in the Green channel. Remeasure the green field and see where the measurements fall between the points on the lock-down curve. Move the points on either side of this range so only this range is open and there are lock-down points at either end. Now click down in the middle of the range, and again, make the movements up and left for more green or down and right for more magenta. I added green for my example. Notice now that only the greens in this valley, and in other parts of the image that had the same range of greens, changed. To save time in the future when doing lock-down curves, we have pre-saved a curve called LockDownCurve that has locked points on all four channels. When you want to tweak a particular color area, just enter Curves, load the LockDownCurve with the Load button and then you can change whatever part of any channel you want without the rest of that color changing. There is a copy of LockDownCurve in the Preferences Folder on the CD.

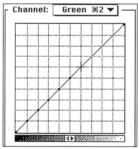

STEP 25: Creating a lock-down curve.

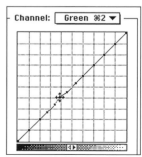

STEP 25: Modify greens in valley color range.

way it does. Remember that each input value has to turn instantly to the left and become an output value as soon as it meets the curve. Trace some values for each of these examples, and I think you will understand how the curve graphs work. It is important that you understand these curve graphs because they come up all over the place in Photoshop (in Curves, Duotones, Separation Setup and Transfer functions) as well as in many books and other applications dealing with color.

CHANGING COLOR RANGES WITH CURVES

STEP 24: Cancel all the different things you tried with Curves and let's go back to the image we ended up with at the end of step 21. Choose File/Revert if you somehow destroyed this image while playing with Curves. We will now use what I call the LockDownCurve to do fine adjustments to the greens in the valley of the Grand Canyon. Enter Curves (Command-M) and move the Curves dialog so it is not covering the green field in the middle of the GrandCanyon image. Since we want to change the greens within the field, select the Green channel from the Channel selector. If you move the cursor out over the field, you will notice that it changes to the Eyedropper. You are automatically in the Eyedropper whenever you are using any of the color correction tools. If you click on the Eyedropper and hold the mouse button down as you move it around over the green field, you will notice that a circle appears on the curve showing you where the values you are measuring occur within the curve. Visually remember where those values are in the curve as you move the mouse back within the Curves

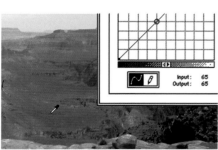

STEP 24: Click on the Eyedropper while over the green field and hold it down while moving around to measure the range of greens in the field. The circle appears to show you where these values are on the curve graph.

STEP 26: Save this image as GrandCanyonPart1. You will work on it again in the Grand Canyon Final Tweaks chapter, where you will lighten the dark tree and rock areas, remove the scratch and spot the image to make it ready for final reproduction.

STEP 26: The GrandCanyon image after popping the greens in the valley with Curves.

HANDS-ON SESSION: KANSAS

Overall Color Correction on a Problem Scan
without Good White or Black Points

The initial Kansas Photo CD scan.

In this example, we will do overall color correction but use some different techniques than with the Grand Canyon—since this image looks different when we view its histogram. We assume you have done the Grand Canyon example.

SETTING HIGHLIGHTS WITH CHANNELS

STEP 1: Open the file KansasRawPhotoCD. This is a 4 meg Photo CD scan of a picture I took while driving through Kansas on a summer vacation during college. Choose File/Save As and save this as KansasLevels. Put the image in Full Screen mode by clicking on the middle icon at the bottom of the Tool palette. Bring up the Info palette (F9 with ArtistKeys), the Picker palette (Shift-F9 with ArtistKeys) and then choose Image/Adjust/Levels (Command-L) to enter Levels.

STEP 2: Look at the RGB histogram and notice that the values don't go all the way to the right, highlight, side. This is what makes the picture look

dull. Type Command-1, -2 and -3 to look at each of the Red, Green and Blue channels. I always do this when I first look at a scan to see if there is a potential problem. In this image, all the channels have dull highlights but each of them has highlight detail that ends at a different point on the histogram. Type Command-0 to go back to RGB, and then hold down the Option key while dragging the Input Highlight slider to the left. The first area to turn white is where you would normally set the highlight. Notice that the "white" buildings are not really that white and the brightest area is actually in the blue clouds somewhere. This is a sign that the Eyedropper may not be the best way to set the highlights. In this photo, there is no good place to set a highlight, which should be pure white after that setting. Type Command-1 again and move the Red Input Highlight slider to the left until it reaches the first real histogram data at about 213. Do the same things for the Green (189) and Blue (171) channels, and then do Command-0 to go back to RGB. Notice how much brighter the image is now and also how much more complete the RGB histogram looks. We have set our highlight for this image.

STEP 3: Notice that the shadow values in the Blue channel suddenly drop off a cliff on the left side unlike those in the Red and Green channels, which taper off like they should. This is a sign that the scanner did not get all the shadow detail in the Blue channel.

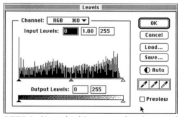

STEP 2: Move the Input Highlight sliders of the Red, Green and Blue histograms to the left until they touch the beginning of the data. This will move all the data to the left of that point all the way to the right spreading out the values in each histogram.

STEP 2: Now the histogram data is spread from 0 to 255.

STEP 2: Original RGB histogram with lack of highlight values.

88

Since this is a Photo CD scan, we have to live with it or buy our own scanner. When this happens to you, look at the original transparency and see if there was actually detail in this area. If there was, you might be able to get better results by rescanning with a high-end drum scanner. However, in the real world, we often have to correct problem images and scans, so hold the Option key down and move the Input Shadow slider to the right to test for a shadow point. There are some good shadow locations on the righthand side of the wheat in the front and also within the big green tree by the house. Click on the Shadow Eyedropper and measure these until you find the darkest spot that is also neutral. I found a few at 5, 5, 5. Click on that spot with the Shadow Eyedropper. The new value for that spot should be around 2, 2, 2 on the right side of the Info palette and your black shadows should look neutral. If this is not the case, click on a new neutral darkest spot until your shadows look and measure neutral. Now you have set your shadow.

BRIGHTNESS, CONTRAST AND COLOR CAST

STEP 4: Move the Input Brightness/Contrast slider in RGB until the overall brightness of the image looks correct. I moved it to the left to bring out a little more shadow detail in the foreground wheat and the dark trees around the house. You can't bring out more detail in an area that is totally black so don't go too far on this shadow detail thing.

STEP 5: Since we moved the highlight sliders on each of the color channels differently, we need to go into each channel and correct for color casts. This is easiest to do if you try to fix the most annoying cast

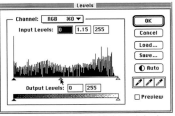

STEP 4: After setting highlight and shadow, set overall brightness and contrast. Move middle slider to left in RGB.

first, and then fine tune the other colors and other casts that appear along the way. The wheat in the foreground seems to have a greenish cast. I often have a hard time with these greenish casts because they are often part green and part cyan. This looks more green, so let's go to the Green channel (Command-2) and move the middle slider to the right to add magenta. This improves the situation and makes the wheat look more golden. Move the slider until the wheat looks too magenta, move it back until you start to see the green again, and then just add a little magenta. If there is still a greenish tinge, it might be more a cyan problem, so move to the Red channel (Command-1) and add a little red by moving the middle slider to the left. Finally, I added a little yellow by moving the middle slider in the Blue channel a little to the right. At this point, before leaving Levels, you might

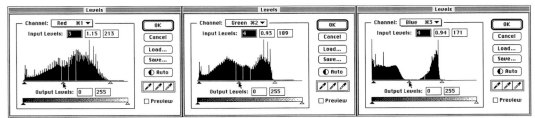

STEP 5: Here are the adjustments I made to the middle sliders of the Red, Green and Blue channels to adjust for color casts in this image. Since the wheat is the major component here, getting that to look good was the main goal. Other parts of the image can be fine tuned later.

want to click on the Preview button just to be sure the video simulation of your corrections matches the calculated changes that happen when you click Preview. They usually match really well on my system. When you're happy, click OK and do a save. Now you have done your initial Levels adjustment on this difficult image.

STEP 5: Kansas after all the Levels adjustments.

SATURATING COLORS

STEP 6: Now that we have done the initial overall histogram correction with Levels, let's use the Hue/Saturation tool to saturate and enhance the colors that are most important to this image. Choose Image/Adjust/Hue/Saturation and make sure the Preview button is on. When you are using Levels or Curves on the whole image, you want to work with the Preview

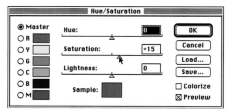

STEP 6: In Master, saturate all the colors by 15.

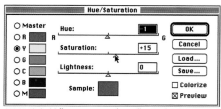

STEP 7: In Yellow, saturate the yellow colors by 15 and move yellows slightly towards red.

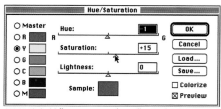

STEP 8: Red Hue/Saturation changes.

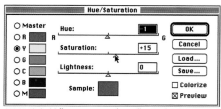

STEP 8: Blue Hue/Saturation changes.

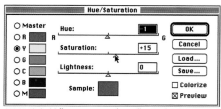

STEP 8: Cyan Hue/Saturation changes.

button off. In that case Photoshop gives you an instant preview using Video LUT Animation, a technique that instantly changes the internal adjustments on the monitor. The calculations done to your image in Hue/Saturation are too complicated to preview in this way, so in this tool, you need the Preview button on. Depending on the speed of your computer, you may need to wait after every change for the screen to update starting in the top left corner working down to the bottom right in rectangular increments. When you first enter Hue/Saturation, the Master button is selected. When you make master changes they happen to all the colors at the same time. Move the Saturation slider to the right to about 15. This will make all colors more vivid.

STEP 7: Click on the Yellow radio button, which restricts the changes you are making to only the parts of the image that are yellow. Since the wheat is mostly composed of yellow, this is an important color to tweak. Move the Saturation slider to the right by 15 and move the Hue slider a little towards red, -1. This will make the yellows a little warmer and also more intense. The changes you make may be a little different depending on your personal taste and exactly how

you have adjusted your version of this image so far. Here are the other changes I made to this image.

STEP 8: Click on the Red radio button and move the reds towards yellow by 5 and saturate reds also by 5. Click on the Blue radio button and saturate the blues by 10 points. This will make the sky blue deeper. Click on the Cyan radio button and move the cyans towards blue by 5 and also saturate them by 10. The cyan changes are also affecting the sky.

STEP 9: In color correcting this image, we have made all the corrections we can make without creating selections. Save this image as KansasCorrected and we will do some final color tweaks in the Kansas—Final Tweaks chapter using selections along with Curves and Hue/Saturation.

STEP 9: Kansas after Levels and Hue/Saturation adjustments.

HANDS-ON SESSION: BURNLEY GRAVEYARD

How to Work with Duotones, How and Why to Adjust Duotone Curves, and How to Save and Calibrate Your Duotone Output

Duotones are used to print black-and-white photos on a press and get more tonal range. If you print black-and-white (B&W) digital images, which can have up to 256 tones in digital format, it is not possible to get those 256 tones on a printing press with just the single black ink. If you use two or more inks to print B&W images, part of the tonal range can be printed by the first ink and part of it by the second ink. Many of Ansel Adams' well known B&W posters are actually duotones. Besides giving you a larger tonal range, duotones allow you to add rich and subtle color to your B&W images.

Typically black ink is used for the dark shadows and a second color, maybe a brown or a gray, is used for the midtones. A third and even a fourth color can be added to enhance the highlights or some other part of the tonal range. Many books are printed with two colors, black for the text and a second color like red or blue for text section titles, underline and other special colored areas. If this type of book has photographs, they can often be made more interesting using duotones instead of just B&W.

CREATING A DUOTONE

STEP 1: Open the BurnleyGraveyard image from the Burnley Graveyard folder on the CD. Choose Mode/Duotone to start working with the Duotone Options. Start out with the Type set to Monotone and the curve for Ink 1 being straight. If the curve is not already straight, click on the Curve box, the leftmost one, for Ink 1 and bring up the curve. Click and drag any extra points in the middle of the curve outside the dialog box to remove them. The horizontal axis of the curve diagrams in Duotone Options has the highlights on the left and the shadows on the right. This is the opposite of the default for Levels and Curves. The numbers in the boxes represent percentage of black. Box 0 is for the brightest highlight and it should read 0, box 100 is for the darkest shadow and it should read 100. All the other boxes should be blank in a straight curve. Click on OK in the Duotone Curve dialog. The Ink box for Ink 1 should be black and Black should be its name. Change the Type to Duotone and Ink 2 will now be activated with a straight curve. To pick the color of Ink 2, click in the Color box, the rightmost one, for Ink 2. This will bring up the Custom Colors picker and allow you to select a Pantone, Focoltone, Toyo, Trumatch or other color from one of the Custom Color Systems. If you were going to print your duotone on a two color book job or a job with a spot color, one of these

STEP 1: The BurnleyGraveyard image printed as black-and-white using only black ink.

color systems would probably be used. We selected PANTONE 10 C for Ink 2. You now have a black ink and a medium gray ink both with straight curves. Click OK on the Custom Colors palette and click OK on the Duotone Options dialog. When you leave the Duotone Options dialog, Photoshop will adjust the image on the screen to give you a preview of what it should look like with the current inks and curves. Printing two inks both with straight curves is like printing the image in

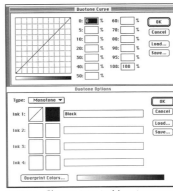

STEP 1: Change type to Monotone mode and start with a straight curve.

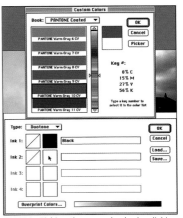

STEP 1: Picking the second color by clicking on the rightmost color square for Ink 2.

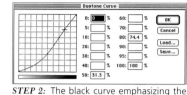

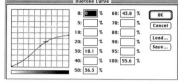

STEP 2: The black curve emphasizing the shadows.

STEP 2: The midtone curve for Ink 2, lowering this color in the shadow areas.

STEP 1: The BurnleyGraveyard image created in Duotone mode as a duotone with black and PANTONE 10 C inks both having straight curves. It was later converted to CMYK for this final output.

STEP 2: The BurnleyGraveyard image created in Duotone mode as a duotone with black for the shadows and PANTONE 10 C for the midtones and highlights. This is after adjusting the curves for those two colors. It was later converted to CMYK for this final output.

black and then printing the exact same image again with the second colored ink. When printing with halftone screens, the second ink will be printed with a different screen angle and this will add some additional tonality over just using one ink. The image will seem very dark because it has too much density. Printing the two inks using the same curve is not taking advantage of the real possibilities for duotone improvements.

ADJUSTING YOUR DUOTONE CURVES

STEP 2: Go back into Mode/Duotone and click on the Curve box, the leftmost box, for Ink 1. You want to adjust the black ink so it is prevalent in the shadows but less prevalent in the midtones and highlights. To do this, click on a point in the middle of the curve and drag that point downwards. This removes black from the midtones and highlights. Now click on the shadow end of the curve, to the middle right and drag this up to add a little more black to this area of the image. Click on the OK button for black and then click on the Curve button for Ink 2, middle gray, so we can work on its

curve. Since we want the dark areas of the image to be represented mostly by black, we need to remove the gray from the shadows. Click at the top right of the curve and drag it down to about 55. Now you need to put the gray back into the highlights and midtones so click a couple of points in the middle of the curve to pull it up so it looks like the curve here. To see these changes, click OK on the Curve dialog and then on the Duotone dialog. You have made the basic adjustments for your duotone curves. Now change each curve just a little bit, one curve at a time. Tweak these curves and after each change click OK to leave the Duotone Options dialog so you can see what that change did to your image. When you are happy with your duotone, save this as BurnleyGraveyardDuo.

CREATING A TRITONE

STEP 3: If we want to further enhance this image, we can add a third ink for the highlight areas. Before we do this though, let's make a copy of the two ink version of the image so you can compare them on the screen. Choose Image/Duplicate and name the copy Burn-leyGraveyardTri. Choose Mode/Duotone and select Tritone from the Type menu in Duotone Options so a choice for Ink 3 will be added. Click on the ink color box and choose a lighter gray for the highlights. We chose PAN-TONE 422 CV. Adjust the curve for this highlight color so it just has ink in the brightest part of the image. Here is the curve we chose for the third ink. Notice how we moved the 0 position of the curve up to 6.3 instead of leaving it at 0. This actually adds some density to the brightest parts of the image in the clouds and where the sun reflects off the gravestones. These areas previously were pure white. Click on OK so you can see the results of adding this third color.

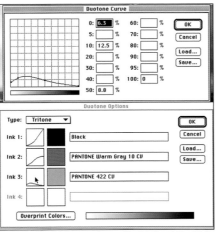

STEP 3: Final tritone values with details of the highlight curve. Notice how this curve actually starts above 0 on the Y axis. This adds density in the very brightest areas.

STEP 4: You may want to measure some values on the screen using the Eyedropper. When working with duotones, you want the Eyedropper set to Actual Color. This will give you measurements of the ink density percentage of each color. If we measure one of those highlight areas in the clouds, we can see that there is no density there from Inks 1 and 2 but Ink 3 has 6% density in that area. If you measure a shadow area, the maximum density there will be from Ink 1, black. There will be some density from Ink 2 and there will be no density from Ink 3 since its curve specifies no ink in the shadow areas.

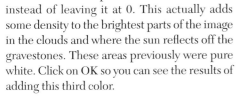

STEP 4: Set the Info palette to Actual Color for duotones.

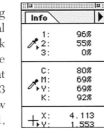

STEP 4: The Info palette measuring a shadow in Tritone mode.

STEP 5: Since you have added a third color specifically for the highlights, you may want to go back to Ink 2 and remove some of the midtone ink from the highlight areas. Click on the Curve box for Ink 2 and lower its curve in the highlight areas by clicking a point there and dragging that point downwards. Here is the final curve we used for Ink 2 in the tritone. Our final tritone image is displayed at the end of this exercise.

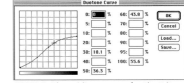

STEP 5: The midtone curve for the tritone with a small dip in the highlight area and a bigger dip in the shadows.

STEP 6: Go back and try some different colors and different curves for this duotone or tritone. Try some blues, greens, purples, magentas, yellows—lots of wild things. Experiment and try some radical curves to discover the great range of effects you can achieve with the Duotone Options.

CALIBRATING AND OUTPUTTING YOUR DUOTONES

You may find that you need to calibrate your monitor differently for duotone output than for CMYK output. If duotones are not matching between your monitor and final output, redo the monitor calibration steps with Gamma for duotones and make a duotone proof to create a separate Gamma setting for working with duotones. We recommend that you leave your preferences set up the same as those for CMYK output in the Setting System and Photoshop Preferences chapter. When you output your duotones, there are several choices. If you are actually printing with Pantone or some other custom spot color, you will need to save the file as a duotone in EPS format. You can set your screen angles for the duotone in Photoshop using the File/Page Setup/Screen button or you can set your screen angles in Quark if you are placing your duotone into that page layout application. Talk to your service bureau about how and where to set your screens and what screen angles and frequencies to use. They may be different depending on the type of imagesetter your service bureau uses. Make sure the Short PANTONE Names option is chosen in the General Preferences/More section. This makes the Pantone names chosen in Photoshop more compatible with those specified in Quark, Illustrator and other layout applications. Make sure the name of each color is exactly the same (including upper and lower case letters) in your page layout application otherwise your duotone

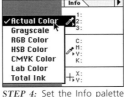

The dialog and settings for saving the file as CMYK EPS/DCS 5 file format. The dialog and settings for saving EPS Duotone are the same but there is no DCS menu.

the particular tritone color is used to modify it before it goes to the printer. If you want to see each of these three color tritone channels as they will look after the curves are applied, switch the Mode menu to Multichannel. The Channels palette will now show you 3 channels: Channel 1 for black, Channel 2 for Pantone 10 and Channel 3 for Pantone 422. You can then click on each channel in the Channels palette and see how that channel will look on film on the press. If you wanted to edit each of these channels separately you could do so now, but then you could not convert them back to Duotone mode. They would have to be output as three separate black-and-white files. Normally you would choose Edit/Undo to undo the mode change and put things back into Duotone mode.

Mode
- Bitmap...
- Grayscale
- ✓ Duotone...
- Indexed Color
- RGB Color
- CMYK Color
- Lab Color
- Multichannel

Color Table...

CMYK Preview
Gamut Warning

Converting a file from Duotone to CMYK format for output to process colors.

may be output as CMYK. To save from Photoshop as a duotone, leave the Mode menu set to Duotone, choose File/Save As and then set the Format to EPS. In the EPS dialog, set the Preview to Macintosh (8 bits/pixel), the Encoding to Binary and click on the Include Halftone Screen checkbox only if you have set your screens and frequencies in Photoshop.

If you want to convert the duotone to CMYK to output it with process colors, use the Mode menu to convert the image to CMYK color. You will still probably save the file as an EPS, but this time there will be an additional option for DCS. Set this to On (72 pixel/inch color) to get the 5 file format with a color preview. For more information on the options for saving CMYK files, see the chapter on Input, Calibration, Correction and Output.

You can also convert your duotones to RGB format if you want to composite them with other images for multimedia use or output to a film recorder or some other RGB device. To do the conversion to RGB, just select Mode/RGB.

When working on a duotone or tritone, the Channels palette just displays a single channel, which is your original black-and-white image. When you print the tritone, this same black-and-white channel is printed 3 times, and each time the separate curve for

The final BurnleyGraveyard image created in Duotone mode as a tritone with black for the shadows, PANTONE 10 C for the midtones and PANTONE 422 CV for the highlights. It was later converted to CMYK for this final output.

IMPROVING COLOR AND MOOD WITH SELECTIONS AND MASKS

SELECTIONS, MASKS AND CHANNELS

Terms and Concepts for Working with Selections, Masks and Channels

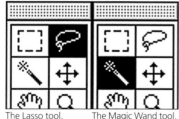

The Rectangular and Elliptical Marquees are the simplest selection tools. Double-click on the Rectangular Marquee, or type M, to change its option to Elliptical.

The Lasso tool.   The Magic Wand tool.

To understand all the possibilities, we need to first explain several important concepts. You need to understand the concept of a selection and how to make a selection using the Photoshop tools. You need to understand what a mask channel is, how to turn a selection into a mask channel and how to edit a mask channel using different tools to allow you to isolate the necessary parts of an image for a particular effect. This includes understanding what a selection feather or a mask blur is and how these affect the edges of blended selections. We will discuss the concept of opacity, which also affects image blending. We also show you how to effectively use the Channels palette.

MAKING SELECTIONS

Let's start out talking about the concept of a *selection*—an isolated part of an image that needs special attention. You may want to make this part of the image lighter or darker, or you may want to change its color altogether. You might also select something in an image that you wanted to copy and paste into a different image.

THE BASIC TOOLS

There are various tools for making selections. The simplest ones are the Rectangular and Elliptical Marquees, which allow you to draw a box or circle around something by clicking at one side of the area you want to isolate and then dragging to the other side. This will create a box or oval

shaped selection that is denoted by dotted lines around the edge. The next level of selection complexity is the Lasso tool that allows you to draw a freehand shape around the selected objects. With the Lasso in Photoshop, you can draw either freehand or straight line segments or combinations of both. Another selection tool is the Magic Wand, which allows you to click on a certain color within an image and automatically select adjoining areas based on that color. There are ways to increase the size of this selection and also to select all the objects of similar color within the image.

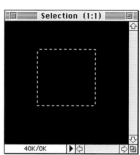

A selection made with the Rectangular Marquee.

WORKING WITH AND INVERSING SELECTIONS

Making a selection is like painting a wall when you want a straight line with blue on one side of the line and red on the other side. You put masking tape on the wall where you want the line to be, then you paint blue where the masking tape is not covering the wall. The area within a selection is the only area of the image that doesn't have masking tape on it. It is

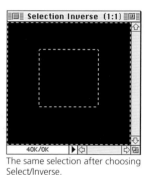

The same selection after choosing Select/Inverse.

the only area of the image you can paint or change with any of Photoshop's tools. Once you have painted the line or changed the image, then you can use Select/Inverse to inverse the selection. This is like taking the masking tape off the line on the wall then retaping over the area you just painted so you can now paint the other side of the line with red. When you inverse the selection, the masking tape then covers the previously selected area and everything that wasn't selected before is now selected.

CHANGING A SELECTION

Changing a selection is a lot easier than moving masking tape. You can add to a selection made with any of the Marquees, Lasso or Magic Wand selection tools by using any of these tools and having the Shift key down when you create the new selection. You can subtract from a selection by having the Command key down when you define the area to be subtracted using these same tools.

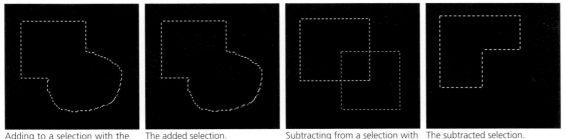

Adding to a selection with the Shift key down.　The added selection.　Subtracting from a selection with the Command key down.　The subtracted selection.

SETTING THE FEATHER VALUE

Using most of the selection tools in their default mode is similar to placing masking tape along the edge of the selection in that there is a defined sharp edge to the selection. It is like a line on a wall where on one side things are selected and on the other side they are not. This type of a selection is said to have a feather value of zero. The selection feather is something that determines how quickly the transition is made from being in the selection to not being in the selection. With zero feather, the transition is made instantly. You can change the feather of a selection using various commands in Photoshop. If you changed the feather of the selection to 10, that would mean that the transition from being fully selected to being fully uns-elected would happen over the distance of 20 pixels (actually, at least 10 pixels on either side of the zero feather selection line). If you used this type of feathered masking tape to paint the two colors on your wall, the feather would cause the two colors to fade together slowly over the distance of 20 pixels. Now, I wonder how one would measure 20 pixels on a wall?

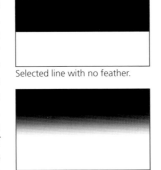

Selected line with no feather.

Selected line with 10 pixel feather.

PIXELS AND CHANNELS

A pixel is the basic unit of information within a digital image. Continuous tone digital images (scanned photographs of real objects) are a two dimensional array of pixels. If the image was 2000 pixels wide by

Blue fading to red over 20 pixel feather.

1600 pixels high and we were printing it at 200 pixels per inch, then the image would print at 10 inches wide by 8 inches high (2000/200 = 10, 1600/200 = 8).

If we are working with a black-and-white image, each one of these pixels contains one byte of information, which allows it to have 256 possible gray values. A black-and-white image has one channel where each pixel is one byte in size. A channel is just a term referring to a two dimensional array of bytes. If we are working with a RGB color image, it has three channels (one for each of red, green and blue). A CMYK image has four channels. You can see these channels by choosing Window/Palettes/Show Channels. In an RGB file, Channel #1 is red, Channel #2 is green and Channel #3 is blue. There is also an imaginary Channel #0 which allows you to see the red, green and blue channels at the same time. This is how you see color. The RGB channel, Channel #0, is an imaginary channel because it doesn't take up any additional space beyond that taken up by the red, green and blue channels.

CREATING MASK CHANNELS

When you make a selection, you are making what is called a mask. This is because the selection masks out the part of the image that is not selected. You can save a selection to a mask channel, which allows you to use it again later. To do this, choose Select/Save Selection or just click on the Selection icon at the bottom left of the Channels palette. The new mask channel would be named #2 if you were working in a grayscale image and #4 if you were working in an RGB image. Photoshop assumes Channel #1 is the image and Channels #2 and higher are masks when you are working with a grayscale image. In RGB, Photoshop assumes Channels #1, #2 and #3 are red, green and blue and that Channels #4 and higher are masks. You can rename a mask channel by double-clicking on the channel, entering the name you want and then clicking on OK.

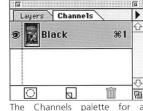

The Channels palette for a grayscale image with the single black channel, Channel #1, which is the image.

The Channels palette for an RGB image. Each of the red, green and blue channels is a grayscale image. You only see color when you view Channel #0, the RGB channel.

97

Image with dog selected.

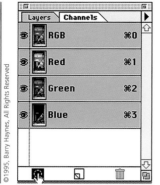

Saving this selection using the Selection icon.

The mask that gets saved for this selection.

The Channels palette after doing the Save selection and renaming Channel #4 DogMask.

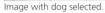

Load Selection the quick way; dragging the mask channel to the Selection icon at the bottom of the Channels palette. You can also hold the Option key down and click on the Mask channel you want to load.

Load Selection from the menu bar.

HOW MASKS WORK

A mask channel is just another channel like the others we've described. When you save a selection to a mask channel, the parts of the image that were selected show up as white in the mask channel and the non-selected parts (the masked parts) show up as black in the channel. When there is a blend between two things that are each partially selected, then this shows up as a gray in the mask channel. Selection areas that are feathered show up as gray. A mask channel has 256 possible gray values just like any other grayscale image.

EDITING MASK CHANNELS

You can actually edit a mask channel just like you would edit any grayscale image. Sometimes you may want to make a selection using one of the selection tools, save it to a mask channel, and then edit the selection within the mask channel using the pixel editing tools, like the Pencil or Paintbrush or Gradient tool, from the Tool palette. White in a mask means totally selected, and black means totally unselected. If you edit a white area to be gray, that makes it less selected or partially selected. You can edit a black area and make part of it white; this white part would be added to the selected area. You may be saving a selection in a mask channel so you can edit it there or you may just be saving it so you can use it again later.

We will do many things with mask channels in this book. Sometimes we use the terms *selection*, *mask* and *mask channel* interchangeably since they all refer to an isolated part of the image. When you want to turn your mask back into a selection again, you choose Select/Load Selection from the menu bar or you click on the mask channel you want to load and drag it to the Selection icon at the bottom left of the Channels palette. You can also load a selection by Option-clicking on the channel you want to load.

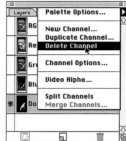

Deleting a mask channel from an RGB image using the Channels palette's pop-up window.

Deleting a channel from a grayscale image the quick way by using the Trash icon at the bottom right of the Channels palette.

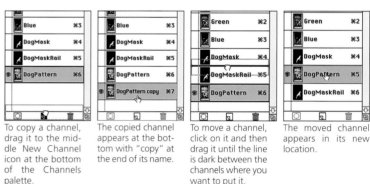

To copy a channel, drag it to the middle New Channel icon at the bottom of the Channels palette.

The copied channel appears at the bottom with "copy" at the end of its name.

To move a channel, click on it and then drag it until the line is dark between the channels where you want to put it.

The moved channel appears in its new location.

DELETING, MOVING AND COPYING CHANNELS

You can remove a mask channel by clicking on that channel and then choosing Delete Channel from the Channels palette's pop-up menu or by clicking on the channel and dragging it to the Trash icon at the bottom right of the Channels palette. You cannot delete the Red, Green or Blue channels this way.

You can make a copy of any channel, including the Red, Green and Blue channels by clicking on the channel and dragging it to the New Channel icon in the bottom middle of the Channels palette. You can also make a copy of a channel by choosing Duplicate Channel from the Channel palette's pop-up menu.

You can move a channel from one location to another by clicking on the channel you want to move and then dragging it until the line becomes dark between the two channels where you want to put this channel. Let go of the mouse at that point and the channel is moved.

98

USING THE CHANNELS PALETTE EYE ICONS

When you have saved a selection in a mask channel you can then work with it in a different way than by just seeing the marching ants lines around the edge of the selection. Notice that the Channels palette has two columns. The first column is the thin one that has the Eye icons in it. This column signifies the channels that you are currently seeing—the ones who's Eye icons are on. The second column is the one that has the name of the channel. When you click within the second column for a particular channel, that channel is grayed, which signifies that you are working on that channel. It is the active channel. Clicking in the second column for Channel 0, grays the Red, Green and Blue channels because Channel 0 represents all three of them. If you also have a mask channel defined, like the picture here with the dog mask, then there are different things you can do to work with that mask channel in relation to the other channels.

The Eye icons for the Red, Green and Blue channels are normally turned on, and those channels are grayed when you are working with an RGB image. The normal state is displayed here within this first picture.

If you click on the right of the second column of the DogMask channel, that channel becomes the active one. It shows up in black-and-white and if you do any editing with the painting tools, you will be editing in black-and-white within the DogMask channel. The Eye icons for the RGB channels turn off now. This state is displayed here in the second picture.

If you want to edit the mask while also seeing the RGB image, do the following. After making the mask the active channel by clicking in its rightmost column, you can then click on the Eye icon column of Channel 0. This will turn on the Eye icons for RGB. You will see RGB but these channels will not be active. Notice that they are not grayed. This means that you are seeing them but are still working on the grayed DogMask channel. The parts of the mask that are black will show up with a red overlay color. If you paint in black with the

Normal state for working in RGB, Channel 0, with Red, Green and Blue Eye icons on and the DogMask off.

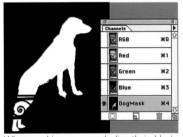

When working on a mask directly in black-and-white, you normally have its Eye icon on with its channel grayed. All the other channels have their Eye icons off and they are not grayed.

Paintbrush tool, you will be adding to this black part of the mask. The paint will show up in the red overlay color. If you paint with white, you will be adding to the selection, and this will subtract from the red overlay color. If you want to change the overlay color, double-click on the mask channel to bring up its channel options, click on the color swatch, and change its color in the color picker. You want to leave its opacity at lower than 100% so you can see the picture through the overlay.

If you want to, you can also see the DogMask while working on the RGB image. To get into this state, click on the rightmost column of Channel 0. This will activate the RGB channels, so when you paint with the Paintbrush, you will be modifying the RGB image. Now if you click on the Eye icon column of the DogMask channel, you will see this channel as an overlay while working in RGB.

FLOATING SELECTIONS AND FLOAT CONTROLS

When you have made any type of selection and it is highlighted on the screen with the dotted lines moving around it (marching ants), you can now choose Select/Float to float that selection. A floating selection is another copy of that selected area floating on top of the original image below. You also end up with a floating selection when you first paste one image, or a piece of an image, on top of another image using Edit/Paste. To learn more about floating selections and how you can move them around the image, see the Victorians and Clouds chapter. A floating selection is like a temporary layer and it actually shows up in the Layers palette. You will learn more about layers in the Layers for Compositing and Prototyping part of this book. Before Photoshop had layers, it always had floating selections. In older versions of Photoshop, all the things we do with layers today had to be done one at a time using a floating selection. You can only have one floating selection at a time and when you deselect it, by clicking outside it or choosing Select/None, it becomes embedded in the image. Then you can no longer move it. A layer, on the other hand, is like a permanent floating selection and you can have many layers. Layers don't go away like floating selections do when you save the file. Once you have created a floating selection, you can access the same controls that you have available with Layer Options by using Select/Float Controls. Float Controls is a new command available in Photoshop 3.0.4 that allows you to blend a partial range of the floating selection's pixels with those below it in the image. Float Controls does the same thing that Composite Controls used to do in the older versions of Photoshop. To learn more about what Float Controls can do, see the discussion about Layer Options in the Posterize, Bitmaps and Patterns chapter. You can always turn a floating selection into a full fledged layer by double-clicking on it in the Layers palette.

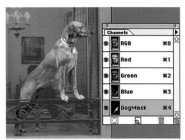

You can also work on a mask while looking at the RGB image too. To get into this state, first click in the second column of the Dog-Mask channel to activate the mask and then click in the first column of Channel 0 to turn on the RGB Eye icons without activating the RGB channels. Here you will be editing the DogMask channel.

If you want to work on the RGB channels while seeing the mask, first click on the right column of Channel 0 to activate RGB, then click in the Eye icon column of the DogMask channel. Here you will be editing the RGB channels.

You can use Float Controls to change the Opacity and Blend Mode of your floating selection. Using the two sets of sliders, you can also control which range of the 0..255 composited digital values appear from the floating selection or from the underlying image. See the Posterize, Bitmaps and Patterns chapter and its discussions about Layer Options to learn how to use these very powerful Floating and underlying sliders.

HANDS-ON SESSION: The Car

*Use the Magic Wand, the Lasso Tool
and Quick Mask Mode to
Select the Red Car and Change Its Color*

STEP 1: The original perspective Acura ad with the red Acura.

Let's say that the image for an ad has been created and the clients love it. They are ready to run the add and then the art director comes in with the boss and they both insist on having a purple car. You try to explain to them that red will really look better since the background is mostly purple but they insist on having a purple car. We don't want to have to go out and reshoot the car, that never happens in the digital world, so we will just select the car and change its color.

SELECTING THE CAR

STEP 1: The Magic Wand tool with its tolerance set to 75 and Anti-aliased on.

STEP 1: Open the RedAcura file from The Car folder. Double-click on the Magic Wand tool, set its tolerance to 75 and make sure Anti-aliased is on. The larger the tolerance, the more color the Magic Wand will select. Having the Anti-aliased feather on makes edges of the selection blend easier with their surroundings. Click down on the bright red color just to the right of the Acura emblem above the bumper. This will cause a selection of most of the bumper area to be made. Change the tolerance to about 45 and then Shift-click on the reddest part of the hood in the middle. Holding the Shift key down while making a selection adds that selection to what has already been selected. Continue to Shift-click on new areas with the tolerance set to 45. If adding any new area makes the selection lines go

STEP 1: This is about all the selection you should try to get with the Magic Wand. Now use the Lasso.

outside the area of the car, choose Edit/Undo (Command-Z) to undo that last part of the selection. Your previous selections should still be there. Once you have most of the red car selected without going beyond its boundaries, your selection should look like the one pictured here.

STEP 2: Double-click on the Lasso tool, make sure its feather is set to zero and that Anti-aliased is also on here. Again, hold down the Shift key first and then circle areas that were not selected by the Wand. You should zoom in closely to the area you are working on while adding to the selection with the Lasso tool. Make sure the Shift key is down or you might accidentally move the selection instead of adding to it. When the Shift key is down, the cursor will be either a cross-hair or the Lasso depending on how your preferences are set up. When the Shift key is not down, the cursor will be a right pointing arrow. Clicking and dragging at

STEP 2: The Lasso tool with its options.

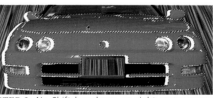

STEP 2: No Shift key down, so right arrow cursor moved selection. Choose Edit/Undo (Command-Z) immediately if this happens.

this point will move the selection. If you do this by accident, immediately choose Edit/Undo (Command-Z). Use Shift with the Lasso tool to circle all the areas that were not selected. When adding to the selection, first put the cursor on top of an area that is already selected, hold the Shift key down, and then press and hold down the mouse button while circling the areas you want to add. If you accidentally select something along a border that you don't want to select, move the cursor into an area nearby that isn't selected, hold the Command key down, press the mouse button down and use the Lasso to circle the part of that border area you want to deselect. When doing selections along a border with the Lasso tool, you have to trace the edge pixel by pixel. The Lasso tool has no intelligence to detect where color or brightness changes. This is a hand-eye coordination exercise. Make sure everything that is part of the red car is selected, even the reds that have a purple tone or are almost black. If they are part of the painted car, they should be selected. Just like an auto body shop that is putting masking tape on the chrome and other areas for a paint job, we need to make sure that all areas to be painted are selected and all areas that are not to be painted are not selected. Pretend that the unselected areas have masking tape on them.

SAVING AND LOADING YOUR SELECTIONS

STEP 3: After you have worked on this for a while, you may get nervous that all your hard work could be lost by a random mouse click. Remember, if you click without the Shift key down, this will make a new selection and the selection you have worked so hard for will be lost. If this happens by accident, choose Command-Z to Undo. Another protection against this happening is to save your selection into a mask channel. To do this, bring up the Channels palette, Window/Palettes/Channels (or F10 with ArtistKeys) and click on the Selection icon in the bottom left corner of the palette. A new channel will be added that is white where your selection is and black, or masked, everywhere else. If you want to save your selection a second time after progressing on it further, click on the Selection icon again and drag it and release on top of the mask channel, Channel #5, which you created the first time. This will overwrite the old saved selection with the

STEP 3: Click on the Selection icon to save your selection.

STEP 3: To load your selection again, click on the channel and drag it to the Selection icon at the bottom left or just Option-click on the channel.

new one. To retrieve your selection from the mask channel, Choose Select/Load Selection of a New Selection and set the Channel pop-up to #5. A shortcut for doing Load Selection is to hold the Option key down and click on Channel #5 in the Channels palette. The white parts in the channel will become selected. The mask channel called CarColor is a completed selection for you to check the accuracy of your selection. Leave this on the palette until the end, and then compare your finished selection to this for an idea of what you need to improve, if anything.

CHOOSING A NEW COLOR

STEP 4: When you think you have finished the selection process, with your selection loaded and active, choose Command-H to hide the selection edges. This will remove the marching ants and allow you to see the edges of your selection while you are changing the color of the car. If your selection is not correct, problems will usually show up along the selection edges. Now choose Image/Adjust/Hue/Saturation to bring up the Hue/Saturation dialog box. While you are in a color correction tool, the Eyedropper is automatically selected from the Tool palette. Click down with the Eyedropper on the red area of the car just above the Acura emblem. The Sample color swatch in the Hue/Saturation dialog will show this red. To use the swatch as a preview, you need to first set it to your starting color as we just did. Move the Hue slider, the top one, to the left until the number reads -70. Notice that the swatch changes from red to a purple color indicating that this change will make your reds purple. If the Preview button is selected, the car will also change to purple after a brief delay. When you are working on a large file, this delay can be long, so you might want to move the Hue slider back and forth with the Preview button off and use your swatch to get the new color within the ball park. The swatch will change instantly. When the swatch seems correct, click on the Preview button to see your selection change color. Turn the preview button on now if it wasn't before.

WORKING WITH QUICK MASK SELECTION MODE

STEP 5: While in the Hue/Saturation dialog with the Preview button on, use the Spacebar to scroll around the edge of your selection to make sure all of the red areas of the car changed to purple. You

STEP 4: The sample swatch changes to purple when you move the Hue to -70. With the Preview button on, the selected area will change also.

STEP 5: Unless your selection was perfect, you may have a red border around the edge and you may notice other areas that are still red after you turn the car to purple. Zoom in with Command-Spacebar-click to see selection edges closely.

Quick Mask mode selector

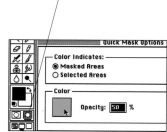

STEP 5: The Quick Mask mode selector is at the bottom right of the Tool palette. Here we see the color swatch in the Quick Mask Options dialog.

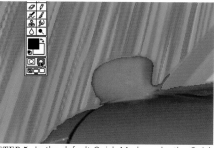

STEP 5: In the default Quick Mask mode, the Quick Mask icon has gray on the outside, a white circle on the inside, and a semi-transparent green mask that overlays the non-selected, areas. Painting here subtracts from the selection.

STEP 5: In the Selected Areas Quick Mask mode, the circle in the Quick Mask icon has gray on the inside and the green mask area overlays the selected areas. Painting here adds to the selection.

may notice a red edge around the car and in other areas, which indicates your selection is not perfect. If this is the case, hit the Cancel button in the Hue/Saturation dialog to return the car to red. We are going to use Quick Mask mode along with the Paintbrush tool to clean up your selection. Type a D to set the default black and white colors. In the Tool palette, double-click on the Quick Mask mode icon at the bottom right. This will bring up your Quick Mask options. Click on the color swatch and set it to a bright green. The default color for this swatch is red, which won't work here since we have a red car. The default for Quick Mask mode is that the masked area, the non-selected area, is covered by a colored semi-transparent layer. This is like seeing a rubylith in traditional masking. The selected area is not covered. When in Quick Mask mode you use the painting tools to add or subtract from your selection by painting with a brush. This gives you a finer pixel for pixel control than you can get with the selection tools.

When the masked areas are overlayed, the default, painting will subtract from the selection and add to the masked area. The default Quick Mask icon is gray on the outside. If you Option-click on the Quick Mask icon, it changes so the gray is on the inside and the selected areas are overlayed with green. When you paint in this mode, painting adds to the selection. Put yourself into this mode by Option-clicking on the Quick Mask icon until the circle in the middle of it is gray and the outside is white. Now the green overlay will be wherever your selection was.

STEP 6: Choose a 5 pixel brush, 3rd from top left in the Brushes palette (F12 with ArtistKeys), with the Paintbrush tool using Normal mode and 100% opacity in the Paintbrush options. If you see a red border around the edge of your selection, paint this border area with the brush. You may need to pick a larger or smaller brush. You can use the left and right bracket keys to change your brush size while painting. You can also double-click on any brush to change its size and attributes. See the earlier chapter entitled: The Tool Palette if you are not sure how to pick brush sizes and options.

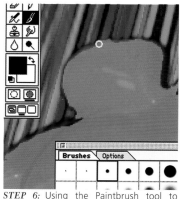

STEP 6: Using the Paintbrush tool to remove the red border from around the edge of the red car selection by adding to the selection.

Paint any red areas that still show up so they are overlayed in green. If you accidentally paint beyond the edge of the red area, you can Option-click on the Quick Mask icon and invert the overlay so you are subtracting from the selection instead of adding to it. A faster way to erase mistakes is to type an X, which exchanges the foreground and background colors. While in Quick Mask mode with selected areas overlayed, painting with black will add to the selection and painting with white will subtract from the selection.

When you have perfected your selection, the selection overlay should look like the diagram here. There should be no red border protruding around the overlay edge.

STEP 6: What the edge should look like with a perfected selection before switching back to Normal Selection mode.

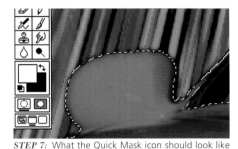

STEP 7: What the Quick Mask icon should look like (gray on the outside with a white circle inside) after switching back to Normal Selection mode.

RETURN TO NORMAL SELECTION

STEP 7: At this point, Option-click on the Quick Mask icon so the masked areas are overlayed and the icon is gray on the outside and white on the inside. When the Quick Mask icon looks like that, click on the Regular Selection icon to get the marching ants back around your selection. Save this selection by clicking on the Selection icon in the Channels palette.

FEATHERING THE SELECTION

STEP 8: Choose Select/Feather and put a 1 pixel feather on the selection border before going into Hue/Saturation. This may blend away very fine reddish hues along some edges of the car.

MAKING THE CAR PURPLE

STEP 9: Now choose Command-H to hide the edges of your selection, go back to Image/Adjust/Hue/Saturation (Command-U) and move the Hue slider back to -70. Your purple car should now look great and there should be no red edges. If this is so, choose OK from the Hue/Saturation tool. If it is still not perfect, Cancel Hue/Saturation (Edit/Undo if you already said OK), and go back to Quick Mask mode for more fine tuning with the Paintbrush. When you are done, choose File/Save As to save your final purple car under a different name.

STEP 9: The final purple Acura.

Removing Spots and Scratches with the Rubber Stamp Tool, Using Selections and Curves to Lighten Shadow Areas

The GrandCanyon image after the changes made in the Grand Canyon chapter.

In this example, we are making further improvements to the Grand-Canyon image using selections to dodge and burn. We will also remove the scratch, and spot the image.

SPOTTING THE IMAGE

STEP 1: Open the final color corrected version of the GrandCanyon image you created in the previous Grand Canyon chapter. After having done overall color correction on an image, you need to spot it and do any color fine tuning that might be needed using selections on specific items and color areas. Make sure your general preferences for tools are set up as recom-

mended in the Setting System and Photoshop Preferences chapter. Specifically, be sure that Painting Tools is set to Brush Size and Other Tools is set to Precise.

STEP 2: Put the image into Full Screen mode by clicking on the middle icon at the bottom of the Tool palette. Move the cursor to the sky in the upper right corner of the image, do a Command-Spacebar-click to zoom into that area and you will notice many dust spots. You should be zoomed in to 2:1 or 4:1. When you are in Full Screen mode, you can see the zoom ratio for your window in the Window menu.

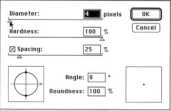

STEP 3: The Rubber Stamp tool.

STEP 3: Double-click on the Rubber Stamp tool and set the options as shown here. Make sure you are in Clone (aligned), Opacity is set to 100% and the Paint mode to Normal.

STEP 3: Rubber Stamp options

STEP 4: Now choose Window/Palettes/Show Brushes (F12 in ArtistKeys) and double-click on the third brush from the top left. Set a 4 pixel brush with the Brush Options that you see here. Refer to The Tool Palette chapter if you need help understanding the Brush Options.

STEP 4: The Brushes palette and your brush.

STEP 5: We're going to use the Rubber Stamp tool to remove the spots in the sky and also the scratch in the canyon. Move the cursor near a spot to be covered. You should be about 1/4 inch from the spot and over a color and texture that you want to fill that spot with. Hold down the Option key and click on the mouse. This tells the Rubber Stamp tool where to pick up image detail to use

STEP 4: The Brush options you want.

in removing the spot. When the Option key is down, the cursor turns into a cross-hair with a circle in the middle. Now move the cursor to the spot to

STEP 5: A spot to the left with the Option key down and cursor on the right. Option-click next to the spot to show Photoshop where to pick up color and detail.

STEP 5: Click on the spot without the Option key down, the cursor should look like this before you click and the spot should be removed when you click using the pixels from where you Option-clicked before.

be retouched and click on the spot without holding down the Option key. Without the Option key down, the cursor should be a clear white circle the size of the brush you are using. Image detail should now be copied over the spot from where you Option-clicked. If it is a big spot, you may have to move the cursor a little with the mouse button down to completely erase the spot. When you hold the mouse button down, you will notice a circle where the cursor is and an x where the Rubber Stamp tool is picking up the pixels to copy. As you move the cursor with the mouse button down, the x and the cursor move together showing you where the tool is copying from and to. This is why this mode of the Rubber Stamp tool is called Clone (aligned).

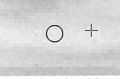

STEP 5: *The* circle and the cross-hair which you see while cloning with the mouse button down. Photoshop picks up detail from the cross-hair and places it down at the cursor circle.

STEP 6: Use the above technique to remove all the other spots in the sky on this image. Don't forget that you can scroll by pressing down the Spacebar, and then clicking and dragging with the Hand tool.

> *Another technique for removing dust is the Dust and Scratches filter. Select part of the sky and feather by about 4 first then do Filter/Noise/Dust and Scratches. It seems to do a good job on clouds and soft areas but it will blur areas that are sharp, so you don't want to run it on the entire image. You should test this on a particular selection by comparing the image with and without the Preview button on in the filter to make sure it doesn't blur the image too much. You can also try different radius and threshold values in the filter.*

REMOVING SCRATCHES

STEP 7: If you look in the rocky area to the right just below the horizon, there is a long white scratch. This is a one pixel wide scratch that we created to simulate the types of scratches you get when the film processor has dirt on it and puts a streak right across your favorite picture. We are going to remove that scratch, and you can use the same technique to easily remove film processor scratches. Before you remove this scratch, use Option-Spacebar-click to zoom out until the image is at 1:4 zoom ratio. In Full Screen mode, you can see the zoom ratio by clicking on the Window menu and looking at the name of this window; it will have a check mark next to it. Notice that at 1:4 ratio, only every fourth pixel in the image is displayed and the scratch is not visible. This is why when you are spotting or removing blemishes you should always be zoomed in to at least 1:1. Use Command-Spacebar-click to zoom back into 2:1 ratio.

STEP 7: You can see the zoom ratio, 1:2, in the Window menu.

STEP 8: Move the cursor to about 1/8 inch below the left end of the scratch line. Hold down the Option key and click on the mouse to tell Photoshop to pick up image detail here. Now move the cursor directly upwards and click on the left end of the scratch (no option key this time) with the cursor centered vertically on the scratch. A piece of the image is cloned here from below the scratch where you Option-clicked. Let go of the mouse button, move the mouse to the right end of the scratch, and then hold down the Shift key while clicking on the right end of the scratch. The scratch should be filled in with image data from right below the scratch as though you had cloned from below by holding down the mouse and drawing on top of the

STEP 8: First, Option-click below left end of scratch.

STEP 8: Second, click on left end of scratch, centered on scratch, directly above where you Option-clicked before.

STEP 8: Third, Shift-click on the right end of the scratch, centered on the scratch.

105

scratch from left to right. You may have to practice this several times to get it correct. Choose File/Save As and save this as GrandCanyonSpotted. You can now use File/Revert to return to this version if you make any mistakes during the rest of the exercise.

BURNING AND DODGING USING SELECTIONS

STEP 9: If the tree trunk, the big rock on the lower right side, the bushes on the lower left or some other parts of the image are too dark, you may want to lighten these like you would in a darkroom by holding something over the enlarger light source in that area while making the print. This is called dodging in traditional darkroom terms. I often burn and dodge using selections instead of the dodge and burn tools because this allows me greater flexibility with different types of effects that are always undoable. Double-click on the Magic Wand tool and set its tolerance to about 8. Lowering the tolerance to 8 will make this tool select a smaller range of colors. Make sure the Anti-aliased option is turned on. When Anti-aliased is on, the edge of the selection is given something like a very slight feather to blend changes you might make to that selected area with the background. Making a selection with Anti-aliased on produces a result that is different than a feather. Usually, when you are going to change something that needs to blend with the areas around it, you want Anti-aliased to be on. When it is not on, the edge of the selection is very abrupt; there is no blend between the edge and the background. Now click down in the dark part of the tree trunk with the Magic Wand. It will select the tree trunk and it may select more than that. If you don't like what it selected, type Command-Z for Undo and try again. You may want to select other dark parts of the tree trunk by holding down the Shift key while clicking on those parts. Remember, Command-Z will just go back to the last selection, so if you try to add a part and it messes up all of your selection, Command-Z is your friend. You

STEP 9: Tree shadow selection with anti-aliased on.

STEP 9: Tree shadow selection with anti-aliased off.

can also choose Select/None to remove this selection, change the tolerance on the magic wand and try again.

STEP 10: When you are happy with your selection, choose Select/Hide Edges (Command-H) so you can see how the selected part blends when as you work within Curves. Choose Image/Adjust/Curves (Command-M) and load the LockDownCurve. Use the Eyedropper to measure values in the tree trunk. Remember to click and drag on the trunk for the circle to show up in the Curve diagram. The values will be in the shadow parts of the curve, so click there and drag up and to the left to make the tree trunk lighter. Notice how the edges of the selection blend with other parts of the trunk and also the background. The preview button needs to be on for you to see this. If you do too much lightening, the edges start to distort. When you are

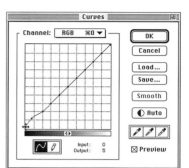

STEP 10: Curve adjustments we made to lighten the tree trunk.

STEP 10: The Channels palette at the end of step 10.

happy with the changes, click on the Save button to save this curve. Name it MagicWandCurve. Now choose OK to leave the Curves tool and accept your changes. Now you can toggle back and forth with Command-Z for Undo and Redo. This allows you to quickly see this change before and then after. We are going to show you another way to do this in Step 11, so undo your lightening effect for now. Click on the Selection icon at the bottom left of the Channels palette. This will save a mask of this selection in Channel #4. Double-click on Channel #4 and name it MagicWandMask. Choose Select/None (Command-D) to deselect this area in preparation for Step 11. Click in the rightmost column of Channel 0 to choose RGB for the next step.

STEP 11: Another method for dodging an image is to use the Elliptical Marquee tool to select a large area of the image around the entire tree with the center of this oval over the dark part of the tree bark. This dark part is the area that you really want to lighten. To do this, type an M, which gets you to the Rectangular Marquee, and then type another M, which will toggle to the Elliptical Marquee. If you continue to type M, you will toggle

STEP 11: *An oval selection of the darker parts of the tree.*

An oval selection with no feather saved as a mask channel.

The same selection with a 25 pixel feather.

A Curve to lighten causes spotlight effect with no feather.

The same Curve causes blended effect with the feather.

between the two Marquees. This is a good thing to remember since it is good to stay in one of these two tools whenever you are not using another tool in the Tool palette. It is difficult to accidentally damage your image with them and they are useful for other reasons. While in the Elliptical Marquee and holding the Option key down, click and drag an ellipse from the center of the dark tree trunk area. The Option key centers the selection where you first click down. After you have made this selection, or any selection for that matter, you can move the selection, without moving the contents of the selection, by holding the Command and Option keys down, and then clicking and dragging the selection marquee where you want it. If you click and drag without these keys down, the contents of the selected area will move and the background color will fill the vacated area. You usually don't want that to happen, but if you do it by accident, remember good old Command-Z.

STEP 12: Now choose Select/Feather and set the feather to about 25 pixels. This will smoothly blend the changes you are about to make in Curves over a large area. This technique is very similar to moving the dodging object up and down in the darkroom to make a soft edge when printing with an enlarger. Click on the Selection icon at the bottom left of the Channels palette. This will save a mask of this feathered selection in Channel #5. Double-click on Channel #5 and name it OvalMask. Choose Command-H so you can see how the selected part blends when you are working within Curves. Click on the rightmost column of Channel 0, the RGB channel.

When you put the large feather on the Elliptical selection, this causes the Curve effect to blend with the background. Here are two masks, the one on the right has a 25 pixel feather, the one on the left has no feather. We ran the same curve on the same image using each of these masks. You can see that the effect on the image to the left without the feather is a spotlight effect. The change on the right is more subtle and blended although more weighted towards the center.

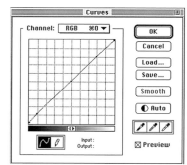

STEP 13: Curve adjustments to lighten oval selection of tree area.

STEP 13: Now go into Curves (Command-M) and use the Eyedropper to measure values in the tree trunk; remember to click and drag on the trunk for the measurement circle to show up in the Curve diagram. The values will be in the shadow parts of the curve, so click there and drag up and to the left to make the tree trunk lighter. Since we didn't load the LockDownCurve this time, a movement in the shadow part of the curve will also affect the rest of the image that is not a shadow. Although this selection is weighted by the feather towards the center where the dark trunk is, the area surrounding the trunk will also become lighter. The Preview button needs to be on for you to see the effect of this feather. If you click on a point in the middle of the curve and drag it back towards its original location, the lightening effect in the lighter parts of the image around the trunk will be lessened. I used a curve called OvalCurve, which is pictured here. You can load this area from the GrandCanyonTweaks Extra Info Files folder. This curve has two points on the bottom left that lighten the dark tree shadows, but it also has points in the middle of the curve that lighten the area surrounding the tree a bit. The effect should be similar to what you would get if you dodged this entire area in the darkroom. When you arrive at your final curve, click on the Save button in the Curves dialog and save this curve as OvalCurve. Now press the OK button to leave Curves with your changes

installed. You may want to try Command-Z several times to toggle between undoing and redoing this curve effect and comparing it to the Magic Wand technique to achieve a similar result.

DECIDING ON THE FINAL VERSION

STEP 14: We have now shown you several techniques with the Elliptical Marquee and Magic Wand for modifying selected areas of an image. Since you saved the selection masks MagicWandMask and OvalMask and you also saved the curves MagicWandCurve and OvalCurve, you can toggle between these two versions and decide which you like best. For instance, to go back to the Magic Wand version, first chose Edit/Undo (Command-Z) to undo what you just did with the Elliptical selection. Option-click on MagicWandMask in the Channels palette to load it. You have now reloaded your Magic Wand selection. Now choose Command-H to hide the selection lines followed by Command-M for curves. Use the Load button and

STEP 14: The Channels palette at the end of Step 13.

choose MagicWandCurve to reload the adjustments you made in step 10. At this point, you could go back to the Elliptical version in the same way.

STEP 15: You can now decide which technique to use as you lighten or darken various parts of this image to make your final version. I lightened the tree trunk using the Magic Wand and Curves. I also lightened the dark rock on the front to the right side. Save your final version of the Grand Canyon as GrandCanyonFinal.

STEP 15: The Grand Canyon after lightening specific areas and color adjustments. We sharpened this image with Unsharp Mask using settings of 150 Amount, 1.5 Radius and 8 Threshold. We also took a little of the Cyan cast out of the sky using the Selective Color tool with the technique described at the end of the Yellow Flowers chapter.

HANDS-ON SESSION: KANSAS—FINAL TWEAKS

*Use Selections with Curves, Hue/Saturation
and Unsharp Mask to Finish Color Correcting
a Problem Scan, Learn about CMYK Preview
Using Gamut Warning and Color Range to Deal
with Out-of-Gamut Colors*

STEP 1: Create the selection of the grass and trees with the Magic Wand.

In this chapter, we take the overall color correct image of Kansas and add color adjustments to specific areas using Curves and Hue/Saturation. This chapter also teaches you how to use the very important Unsharp Mask filter, the Gamut Warning and the CMYK Preview.

IMPROVING SELECTED COLOR AREAS

STEP 1: Open your corrected file from the Kansas chapter or use our version called KansasLev&HueSat. Double-click on the Magic Wand tool and make sure the Tolerance is set to 32 and that Anti-aliased is on, these are the defaults. We are going to select parts of this image and improve their color balance and/or density. We will start out with the green strip of grass that separates the field from the sky and also the two big trees next to the house. This whole area seems a bit magenta to me and the trees seem to be too dark. Click on the grass and then reclick with the Shift key down to add to the selection until all the grass and the two big trees are selected. Make sure you click only in the green areas and stay away from the parts of

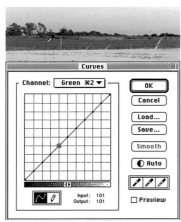

STEP 2: Measuring where the greens occur in the green grass.

the trees that are almost black. You can also use Select/Grow to increase the selection adjacent to areas already selected. If you accidentally select something that you shouldn't, choose Edit/Undo (Command-Z) then try again. You can also use the Lasso tool with the Shift key to add to the selection or with the Command key to subtract from the selection. Once you have this entire area selected, choose Select/Feather and enter 1 for a one pixel feather. This will blend the color changes you are making along the edge of the selection.

STEP 2: Choose Select/Hide Edges(Command-H) to hide the edges of the selection. This allows you to see whether the changes you will make to this area will blend properly with the surroundings. Choose Curves (Command-M) and load LockDownCurve from the Kansas Final Tweaks folder. Select the Green channel, and then click down on the Eyedropper in the area where the green grass seems magenta. Look at the circle on the curve and remember which point in the curve to change and then click on that point and move it up and to the left to add green to that part of the curve. Now measure the magenta in the darker parts of the big trees next to the house. Add green to that part of the curve too. Switch to the RGB curve (Command-0) and measure the brightness of the dark trees. Don't measure the totally black places since these are too dark to have any detail worth saving. Measure the medium to darker parts of the trees and see how the circle moves around on the curve as you move the cursor around over these parts of the trees. Move the points in these areas up and to the left to make the trees lighter. Notice that this also makes the darker bushes within the selection lighter. Turn on the Preview button so you can see the changes you have made within the selection and how they blend with the unselected, unchanged areas. If the borders are not seamless, you either made a poor selection or your changes are too radical. If you have problems with the way the border looks, first back off on the amount of change you made, and if this doesn't work, cancel the Curves command and go back to edit your selection.

STEP 3: Use the Magic Wand again to select the red parts of the red barn; this is most of it except for the roof. For this job, you may get better results if you set the Tolerance to about 8, and then use the Shift key with the Magic Wand to keep adding to the selection. Again choose Select/Feather of one pixel to soften the edge of the selection. Use Command-H to hide selection edges then choose Image/Adjust/Hue/Saturation and click on the

Red radio button. You will only be changing things that are red within this selection. Move the Hue towards Magenta by ten points (-10) and increase the saturation by 10 points. These changes will make the red more vivid. Make sure the preview button is on so you can see your changes. Click on the OK button and choose Select/None.

STEP 4: The gray roof on the barn has too much of a magenta tinge and also would look better if it was darkened a bit. Since this color is not like any of the solid colors in Hue/Saturation, we will use the Curves tool on the roof. Select the roof with the Magic Wand like you did the red parts of the building. Command-M will get you to Curves where you should load Lock-DownCurve again. Now click on the roof and measure around to see the roof's range of values on the RGB curve. Darken these parts of the curve by moving their lockdown points down and to the right. Now move to the Green curve and measure the parts of the roof that seem too magenta. Move them up and to the left to add green. If there are other parts of the roof that seem too green, move them down and to the right to add magenta. The two color areas should be in different parts of the curve. If you find it hard to get uniform color on the roof, you can also use Clone (aligned) in the Rubber Stamp tool at 50% opacity with the mode set to Color to add a color tint from one area to another.

STEP 5: The white buildings in this image are also not very clean. The building closest to the red barn is too dark and has a bluish cast. The other white buildings have various degrees of yellow tinge to them. Using similar

STEP 5: The Kansas image after specific color corrections using Selections.

techniques to what we have done with the grass and barn, first select the dark building and brighten it up using Curves. Then select all the yellow buildings and clean them up using either Curves or Hue/Saturation. Save this image as KansasRGBBeforeGamut.

OUT-OF-GAMUT COLORS

STEP 6: There are many vivid colors that you can see on the computer screen in RGB that can't be printed in CMYK on a press. If you are working in RGB to send your final output to a film recorder and color transparency film, you can get more colors on film than you can on a press. If your final output is some multimedia presentation, then you will also be able to get the colors there. You need to realize that each different type of computer monitor or digital color printer, or even press and paper combination, may have a different gamut. The color gamut of your output device is the range of colors it can actually print. For more information about these issues, see the Input, Calibration, Correction and Output chapter. If you are going to print this file on a press in CMYK though, you may want to check your out-of-gamut colors and see if you need to correct them. Refer to the Setting System and Photoshop Preferences chapter and make sure your CMYK preferences are set up correctly before using any of the CMYK Preview or Gamut Warning commands. Choose Select/Color Range, and then choose Out-of-Gamut from the pop-up mode selector within the dialog box. Click on OK and this will make a selection of all the colors that you can see in RGB but won't print exactly the same in CMYK. Choose Select/Hide Edges (Command-H) to hide the edges of this selection.

STEP 7: Some out-of-gamut colors, like red, often look quite different and usually muted when printed in CMYK. In many other colors, you may not notice the difference. Choose Mode/CMYK Preview and Photoshop will give you an estimate of what this image will look like when printed in CMYK. If you made the red barn really bright, you will notice it fades a bit. How many other changes did you see within the image? The sky may look a bit duller. Now choose Mode/Gamut Warning and all these out-of-gamut colors will change to gray or whatever gamut warning color you have set in Preferences. Remember that you have a selection that you made with Color Range of all the colors that are actually out-of-gamut. With Gamut Warning on, you can use this selection in conjunction with the Hue/Saturation command to fix a lot of this gamut problem. Colors are often out-of-gamut because they are too saturated. Choose Command-U for Hue/Saturation

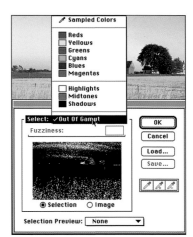

STEP 6: In Color Range, selecting out-of-gamut colors.

111

STEP 7: The CMYK Preview as well as the Gamut Warning in the Mode menu can help compensate for differences between RGB and CMYK color gamuts.

and move the Saturation slider to the left. Notice that the Gamut Warning areas get smaller the more you desaturate this selected out-of-gamut area. You may want to desaturate your out-of-gamut colors in several stages, or using the Sponge tool from the Tool palette, so you don't further desaturate colors that have already come back into gamut. To do this in stages, move the Saturation slider to the left, to, say, -10. Say OK followed by Select/None. Now go back to Color Range, Step 6, and choose the new smaller set of out-of-gamut colors. Reduce the saturation on these also by -10 and continue this iterative process until there are no more out-of-gamut colors or the out-of-gamut areas are so small they won't show.

STEP 8: I want to mention that Gamut Warning is a very useful tool for seeing colors that are going to be difficult to reproduce in CMYK. On the other hand, if you always desaturate all your colors so that no Gamut Warning areas show up, you may end up with duller colors on press than you would have gotten if you were a little less strict about dulling out all your RGB colors. I compared two conversions to CMYK of this image. The first had been pre-adjusted, via steps 6 and 7, to remove out-of-gamut colors. The second CMYK conversion was of the same image without the out-of-gamut adjustments. The pre-adjusted image didn't change much at all when it was converted to CMYK and this is good. The image that I hadn't pre-adjusted for out-of-gamut colors did change and got a little duller, like in the red barn, but overall it was a bit brighter and more vivid in CMYK than the pre-adjusted image. So if you work in RGB and use bright colors, even out-of-gamut ones, you may get brighter color results by going ahead and converting these to CMYK. You know that some bright colors may get a bit duller, but you can deal with those dull or changed colors once you are in CMYK mode—instead of dulling them ahead of time, by desaturating based on Gamut Warning, and possibly desaturating them too much. Do some tests to see what works best for you!

THE UNSHARP MASK FILTER

STEP 9: Here you will use Filter/Sharpen/Unsharp Mask to sharpen your image, either with or without the Gamut Warning adjustments, for final output. As a final step, you will often want to use the Unsharp Mask filter. The Unsharp Mask filter has three different settings (Amount, Radius and

Threshold) that affect different parts of the sharpening process. You will have to run some tests to determine what value to use in each of these settings. Since sharpening can take a lot of time, it is often useful to run tests on a small section of the image. Photoshop 3.0 does have a Preview button in the Unsharp Mask filter that allows you to see the filter happen in a selected area of the image, but this still doesn't allow you to compare one group of settings to another. The following method will allow this comparison.

Select a section of the image that can represent the entire image, and whose sharpness is most important, and make a copy of it using Edit/Copy. Now choose File/New (Command-N) to create a new file. Since you just made a copy, the new file will be the size of the copied section. Say OK to the new dialog and then do an Edit/Paste (Command-V) followed by Select/None (Command-D). Repeat this several times until you have 5 or 6 small files that can be placed next to each other on the screen for comparison. Now run different tests on each file so you can see what the three parameters of Unsharp Mask do.

AMOUNT: This setting controls the overall amount of sharpening. When you are comparing sharpening effects, you want to zoom into the image to at least 1:1 to be able to see all the detail. Compare different copies of the same image area using different settings for Amount. Sharpening an image is done by looking for edges within the photograph and enhancing those edges by making one side of them darker and the other side of them lighter. Edges are sharp color or contrast changes within an image.

RADIUS: This setting in the Unsharp Mask filter controls the width of pixels along an edge that are modified when the image is sharpened. Again, try running the filter with different settings and comparing two copies of the same image side by side.

THRESHOLD: When this setting is set to 0, then everything in the image is a candidate for being an edge and getting sharpened. If you set the Threshold to, say 10, then an edge will only be found and sharpened if there is a difference of at least 10 points (in the range from 0 to 255) in the pixel values along that edge. The larger value you give to the Threshold setting, the more contrasty an edge needs to be before it is sharpened and the more you are doing just Sharpen Edges.

When you find the correct Unsharp Mask values, use those to sharpen the entire file. The settings I use most often for 18 meg Photo CD files are 150, 1.5 and 8. If the original image is very grainy, I might increase Threshold, which will lessen the sharpening of the grain. If the file is very fine grain, I might decrease Threshold, which will allow me to sharpen the file a bit more without getting more than the normal grain appearance in the final image. Occasionally I will sharpen by 200% if I am trying to increase the size of an image and make it look sharp. You have to be careful not to over sharpen. If your final output is a halftone, you can get away with more

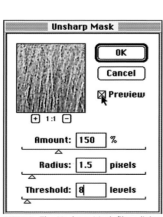

STEP 9: The Unsharp Mask filter dialog with its three settings.

sharpening than for a transparency film recorder or even digital print output. The screen angles and dots in a halftone tend to lessen some sharpening artifacts. All artifacts will show up if you output to a transparency film recorder. We usually use the Unsharp Mask filter instead of the other Photoshop sharpening filters because Unsharp Mask gives you much finer control over the many different types of images.

Another technique you can use for sharpening very saturated files is to use Mode/Lab Color to convert the file to Lab Color mode then sharpen the L channel. This will prevent your saturated colors from popping as much during the sharpening. You can then convert back to RGB.

| Image with no sharpening. | Unsharp Mask 150, 1.0, 8. | Unsharp Mask 150, 1.5, 8. |

| Unsharp Mask 450, 1.5, 8. | Unsharp Mask 150, 4.5, 8. | Unsharp Mask 150, 1.5, 0. |

SPOTTING WITH THE RUBBER STAMP

STEP 10: After you sharpen any file, you should zoom in to at least 1:1 and then step through each section of the file spotting it with the Rubber Stamp tool. Sharpening tends to enhance spots that may not have been obvious before. That is why you should leave spotting until after sharpening has been done. The procedure is the same as the spotting work done in the Grand Canyon—Final Tweaks chapter. Save your final spotted file as KansasFinalRGB, and then read the following step to convert to CMYK.

CONVERTING TO CMYK

STEP 11: Now you have your final color corrected version of the RGB image. If your final output device is an RGB device, like a film recorder or a video screen, you are finished. If you use a color management system, like the EFI system, which automatically converts your file from RGB to CMYK as you output it, then you are also done. If your final output device is CMYK and you are going to do the conversion from RGB to CMYK in Photoshop, then you need to make sure all the preferences are set up correctly for CMYK conversion (review the Input, Calibration, Correction and Output and the Setting System and Photoshop Preferences chapters). Choose Mode/CMYK to convert the image to CMYK. Once in CMYK, Photoshop will automatically adjust the image display on the monitor to try to simulate your actual CMYK printed output. Because of this, some of the brighter colors may get duller or change slightly. You may want to do additional small color tweaks now that you are in CMYK using the same tools you used in RGB. You can also use the Selective Color tool to tweak CMYK colors as explained at the end of the Yellow Flowers and Color Matching Cars chapters. For this particular image, we were happy with the CMYK version when it was converted from RGB. That is what is printed in this book. When you are happy with your CMYK image, save this as KansasFinalCMYK. See the Input, Calibration, Correction and Output chapter for further discussion on these final CMYK color tweaks.

STEP 11: The final RGB version of Kansas after all color corrections and using the Unsharp Mask filter.

HANDS-ON SESSION: YELLOW FLOWERS

*Using Color Range and Replace Color
to Change the Colors of Flowers and to
Enhance those Colors; Using Selective Color
to Improve the CMYK Version*

In this chapter we will be using the Color Range tool to select the flowers so we can change their color from yellow to orange. We will then enhance the color of the orange flowers using the Selective Color command.

ABOUT COLOR RANGE AND REPLACE COLOR

The first thing you need to do in this example is select all the flowers. There are two similar tools for making selections based on color in Photoshop 3.0. Select/Color Range allows you to specify a color using the Eyedropper tool, then shows you a mask of all the areas containing that color within the current selection. You can add to or subtract from that mask using + or – Eyedroppers, and when you leave Color Range, you end up with a selection containing the final colors you specified. Another new command that is similar to Color Range is Image/Adjust/Replace Color. This command allows you to make selections in a similar way and also change the colors of the selections at the same time using controls that are like those in the Hue/Saturation command but not quite as powerful. You can load and save color sets between these two tools, so it is important to understand the subtle but important differences between them.

The Color Range tool always returns a selection. You can then use this selection like you would any other to modify the selected areas using other Photoshop tools. Since Color Range is for making selections, it has some very useful

The Color Range tool is for making selections based on these different color choices. With the Sampled Colors choice, you click on the colors you want to select within the image.

Preview set to Quick Mask   Preview set to None

At the top of this image, the Selection Preview is None and you see the image. At the bottom of the image you see the purple Quick Mask preview, which is very useful.

Original version of the flowers picture.

features to help you see exactly what is selected. When you choose the Sampled Colors options from the Select pop-up menu in Color Range you select colors by clicking on them with the Eyedropper (you do the same in Replace Color). You can add to the colors that are selected with the regular Eyedropper by Shift-clicking and you can subtract from the selected colors by Command-clicking. There are also plus and minus Eyedroppers that always add to or always subtract from the selected areas. You see what colors are selected by looking at a black-and-white mask window within the dialog box. Here, white shows you the selected areas. To see the selected items in the most detail, choose the Quick Mask option in the Selection Preview pop-up and you will get a Quick Mask overlay on top of the areas that are not selected within the actual image window. If you choose the correct color for your Quick Mask (notice the purple in the diagram here), it is very easy to see when your

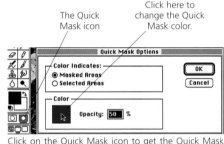

The Quick Mask icon

Click here to change the Quick Mask color.

Click on the Quick Mask icon to get the Quick Mask Options dialog and then click on the color square and select a new color with the Color Picker.

selection is complete. You choose the color for your Quick Mask by double-clicking on the Quick Mask icon at the bottom of the Tool palette. You need to do this before entering Color Range. See The Car chapter for a discussion of Quick Mask mode. By the way, the other options in the Select pop-up allow you to select all the reds, yellows, greens, cyans, blues, magentas, highlights, midtones, shadows or out-of-gamut colors within the part of the image that was selected before you entered Color Range. The out-of-gamut colors option is very useful (see the Kansas—Final Tweaks chapter for a discussion of this). Although Replace Color doesn't have these other Select options, you can get them by using the Save button in Color Range to save selections made with these options and use the Load button in Replace Color to load these selections.

The Replace Color tool also allows you to select colors with the Eyedropper in the same way as Color Range but there is no Quick Mask Preview mode and there are no Select options.

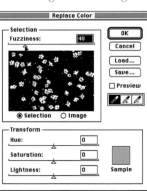

The Replace Color dialog with a mask showing the flowers selected.

Replace Color doesn't have as many options for selecting the colors or for seeing the selection. Once you make a selection in Replace Color or Color Range, you can click on the Save button to save the description of the selected colors. This allows you to select similar colors in other images or make the same color selection in this image from Color Range or from Replace Color by going into either tool and loading that color selection description using the Load button. When you have the selection you want, the Replace Color tool allows you to change the color of the selected items by using the Hue, Saturation and Lightness sliders at the bottom of the tool. The Preview box here shows you the color changes happening within the image on the screen. For changing color, this is even better than a selection preview because you see if the selection is correct as you actually change the colors you want. So, with Color Range you are selecting a range of colors in the image and you end up with a selection. With Replace Color, you select a range of colors and those colors are replaced at the same time. Now, let's try this out!

USING COLOR RANGE TO SELECT THE FLOWERS

STEP 1: Open the Flowers image in the YellowFlowers Example folder. Put Photoshop into Full Screen mode by clicking on the middle icon at the bottom of the Tools palette. Double-click on the Quick Mask icon, click on the colored square, and then set the color to medium blue or purple. Find a color that has no yellow in it so any flower parts that are not selected will show up easily. Make sure the Opacity is set to 50%. Say OK to these dialogs and click back on the regular Selection icon to the left of the Quick Mask icon. Now press the Tab key to remove all the tool windows from the screen. Choose Select/Color Range. Set the Fuzziness to 40. The Fuzziness, which works the same in Replace Color and Color Range, is like the Tolerance on the Magic Wand; the higher the Fuzziness, the more similar colors are selected. Unlike the Magic Wand, you can move the Fuzziness after making a selection, and the range of selected colors will change. Set Select to Sampled Colors and set Selection Preview to None for now. Use the Eyedropper to click on the yellow flowers and you will notice that wherever there is a flower, you should get some white showing up in the mask window. Hold the Shift key down and click on different areas of the flowers, adding more to the mask. If white areas or spots show up in

STEP 2: Part of the flower on the right is covered by purple. Shift-click on it to add it to the selection.

the mask window where there are not any flowers, hit Command-Z to undo that last Eyedropper click. When you think you have all the flowers selected without any areas that are not flowers selected, set the Selection Preview to Quick Mask.

STEP 2: In Quick Mask you will notice a see-through purple layer covering everything that is not selected by the mask. This is the Quick Mask preview. If you notice parts of the flowers that are covered by purple, Shift-click on them to add them to the selected areas. If you select a really bright part of the flower or a really dark part, you may also notice the purple overlay coming off other areas of the image that are not flowers. This means that you have selected too much, so type Command-Z.

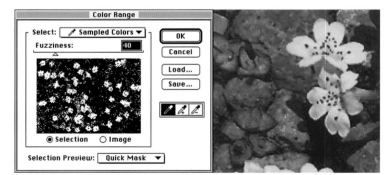

STEP 2: Here we have selected too much. You can see the mask coming off things that are not flowers, like the green leaves to the left of the flowers.

STEP 3: When almost all of the flowers are not covered by the purple mask and also when the purple mask is still over everything that is not a flower, this is the best you can do with Color Range to select the flowers. Click on the Save button and save this as ColorRangeToRC. Click on OK and you will end up with a selection of the flowers. If you wanted to work on these

selected items with one of the other color correction tools, like Hue/Saturation, this would have been a path you could have taken to get a selection of the flowers. We did the first step of this exercise in Color Range so you could see the differences between it and Replace Color. We could have done this whole exercise in Replace Color.

USING REPLACE COLOR TO SELECT AND CHANGE THE COLOR

STEP 4: We are now going to use Replace Color for the rest of this exercise. Choose Select/None since we are actually going to improve on this selection with Replace Color. Choose Image/Adjust/Replace Color and click on the Load button. Select the Color-RangeToRC file you just saved from Color Range. This will give you the same selection you just had, but this time you only see the black-and-white mask in the dialog. Hold down on the Shift key and click on a yellow flower at a place that is a middle yellow color. If you were going to have to pick one shade of yellow that best represented these flowers, Shift-click down at that point. Notice that the sample box at the bottom right of the dialog now has this yellow color in it. Getting this color into the sample box is why you Shift-clicked here. Shift-click adds a color to the color selection range instead of starting a new selection range. It does the same thing as the +Eyedropper. Now go down to the Hue slider and move it to the left to -20. The yellow sample is now orange. When you click on the Preview button, all the yellow flowers that are selected will turn orange. This is the one type of Selection Preview that you can't do in Color Range and it is very useful. If most of the flowers look orange but there is a little bright

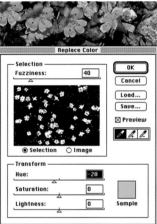

STEP 4: The Replace Color dialog with yellow to orange previewed.

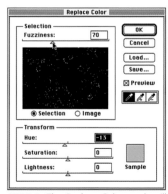

STEP 5: The Replace Color mask will have little dots all over it, like stars in the sky, when selecting just the yellow tips of the flowers. This time, you should not see whole flowers in the mask, otherwise you have reselected some of the parts of the flowers that are already orange.

The flowers after changing them to orange.

yellow around the tips of the flowers, you are about where you want to be. If all of the flowers are orange with no trace of yellow left in them, you should look around the rest of the image and make sure you didn't change the color of anything else that had some yellow in it but wasn't totally yellow, like the green leaves on the ground.

STEP 5: Click on the OK button to end this session of Replace Color. Now you need to change the yellow in the tips of the flowers to orange. Bring back the Tool palette by hitting the Tab key and double-click on the Eyedropper tool to set the Sample Size to Point Sample. This will allow you to select minute color differences that are only one pixel in size while in Replace Color. Hit Tab again to hide your palettes. Now go back to Replace Color and zoom in (Command-Spacebar-click) on any flowers that have too much yellow around the tips of their petals. Without the Shift key down, click on a yellow tip that was not changed to orange to begin your new color set. Hold the Shift key down as you carefully click on those yellow tip colors and add them to a new color set. The Preview button should be off to start with since this stops Photoshop from taking time to change the screen display. Once you have Shift-clicked on a lot of different shades of yellow in the tips, Shift-click again on that one that seems to represent an average of all of them. Its color will show up in the sample window. You Shift-click so you add this color to your set instead of starting a new set. Now click on the Preview button again and move the Hue slider to the left until the color sample looks like the orange flowers. Let up on the mouse

button and wait for the flowers to update. You can adjust the hue so the yellow tips match the orange that is in the rest of the flowers. You can also increase the Fuzziness and you will notice that more little dots show up as selected in the mask. This may also improve the blending of any remaining yellow in the flower tips. You may have to say OK to Replace Color several times, and then return to get the few last remaining yellow flower tips. Some of the brighter tips may actually just be highlights, so you don't need to change every last one. They just need to look natural as orange flowers. After you use Replace Color several times, there may still be flower tips that are just different from the rest of the flowers. It may be faster to change those using the Rubber Stamp tool, cloning color from another flower or another part of the same flower. You still will want to do this in the Clone (aligned) setting using either Normal or Color blend mode.

STEP 6: Use File/Save As to save this as Flowers-Orange, and then open the original Flowers file and compare the two. The flower colors and tones should look as natural in orange as they did in yellow. Bring back the Tool palette by hitting Tab and double-click on the Eyedropper tool to set the Sample Size back to 3x3 average.

USING SELECTIVE COLOR

STEP 7: When you are happy with the RGB version of this image and you have saved this version in Step 6, then you should convert it to CMYK using Mode/CMYK. You may notice a slight dulling of the flowers when converted to CMYK, although this orange color converts to CMYK quite well. Once in CMYK, you can use the Selective Color command to make further subtle tweaks on colors. This command will change a particular color based on the amount of each cyan, magenta, yellow and black that makes up the color. Bring up the Picker

STEP 7: After measuring the orange flowers, we notice in the Picker palette that this orange color is made up of 97% yellow and 52% magenta. We then choose yellow as the color to change with the Colors pop-up.

117

component of this orange color, it is 97% yellow, you should now choose yellow from the Colors pop-up. You will now be changing the percentages of other colors that make up your yellows.

STEP 8: Notice that this orange color is already very close to completely saturated in yellow but the magenta component is only 52% saturated. On the righthand side of the Picker palette, you see a swatch of the color where you last clicked. The Magenta bar in the Picker palette shows us that if we add magenta to this color the flowers will look a deeper orange and eventually reddish in color. If we take away magenta, the flowers will become more yellowish. Move the Magenta slider in Selective Color to the right to +20%. In our example, the Method radio button at the bottom of the dialog box is set to Absolute so this should mean that we are adding 20% magenta ink to the 52% magenta already in the yellows. We should get 72%. If Method were set to Relative, we would add 20% of the 52% percentage of magenta already there. This should bring us up to about 62%. Absolute mode actually brings the 52% magenta up to 61% and Relative mode brings it up to 57%. If you are trying to add a specific percentage, you should measure the results you actually get using the Picker palette instead of assuming the percentages in the Selective Color dialog box will be exact. Now subtract 25% magenta from these orange flowers and you will get the lighter, more yellowish orange you see in our third Selective Color illustration. This is how you use the Selective Color tool to make subtle tweaks in specific color ranges. When you set Colors to Neutral, Selective Color is also very good at removing color casts within the neutral areas. Photoshop is good at identifying which colors should be composed of equal quantities of cyan, magenta and yellow.

palette using the Window/Palettes menu or using Shift-F9 with ArtistKeys. Use its Options menu to change it to CMYK Display mode. Now choose Image/Adjust/Selective Color to bring up the Selective Color tool. With this tool, you have to select the main color that you would like to change using the Colors pop-up menu at the top. The choices are Red, Yellow, Green, Cyan, Blue, Magenta, White, Neutral and Black. If we want to change the orange flowers, orange is not one of these colors. Use the Eyedropper and click on an orange flower in a color area that is typical for the orange color of all the flowers. When you do this, you will notice in the Picker palette that this bright orange is made up of mostly yellow and magenta. Since yellow is the main

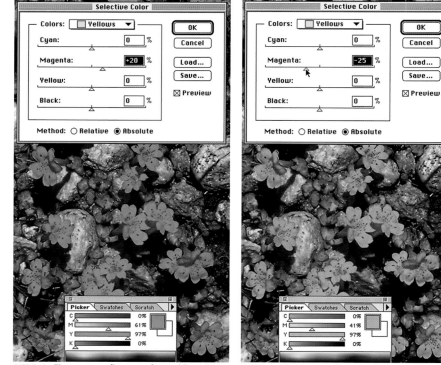

STEP 8: The orange flowers after adding 20% magenta. Notice that the Magenta value actually changed from 52% to 61%.

STEP 8: The orange flowers after removing 25% magenta. If you clicked on a sample color after entering Selective Color, the Picker palette will show you the actual new CMYK percentages as you make adjustments in Selective Color.

The orange flowers after final color correction choices have been made with Selective Color.

HANDS-ON SESSION: BUCKMINSTER FULLER

We start with a scan of an original black-and-white negative of Buckminster Fuller, and in order to make a fine print, we need to darken it and increase its contrast. We also want to brighten the white shirt and the candles a bit, and finally, add a little twinkle to Fuller's eyes, sharpen the center and burn in the edges of the print.

BRIGHTENING THE IMAGE

STEP 1: Open the Fuller file from the Buckminster Fuller folder on the Photoshop Artistry CD and use File/Save As to save it as FullerFixed.

STEP 2: Bring up the Info palette with Window/Palettes/Show Info, or F9 if you have ArtistKeys installed.

STEP 3: Choose Image/Adjust/Levels (Command-L).

STEP 4: Click down in the bright area of Mr. Fuller's collar and note the values that show up in the Info palette. They are not a very bright white. If we move the Input Highlight slider to the left, this would brighten the collar, but it would also blow out any remaining detail in the wall by the bright lamp. Instead, we are going to make a bright version of this image and then

Make a Fine Black-and-White Print the Digital Way: Increase Contrast, Brighten the White Areas Using Electronic Fericyanide and Burn in the Edges to Emphasize the Middle

(Original Concept by Bruce Ashley)

The original Fuller scan.

use that to selectively lighten (Electronic Ferricyanide) the shirt, candles and eyes. Adjust the Input Brightness/Contrast slider in Levels to the left to brighten the collar until the values in the collar that were 215 read about 235. The left set of Info palette values are the original values and the right set of values show the adjustments you made with this invocation of Levels. Exit Levels by clicking on the OK button to make the change.

STEP 5: Choose Edit/Take Snapshot to make a Snapshot version of the file. Then choose Edit/Undo Levels to undo the Levels change that you just made. You can use the Take Snapshot command without changing the state of what will happen when you choose Undo. The Snapshot is a special copy buffer that now remembers the lighter version of the file.

STEP 6: Go back into Levels (Command-L) and move the Brightness/Contrast slider of Levels to the right to adjust this image for greater contrast. Make sure large sections of the blackest blacks don't go below 2 or 3 in the Info palette. It is OK to have a few small sections that go to 0, but these should not be very large as they will show up as pure black in the printout. Exit

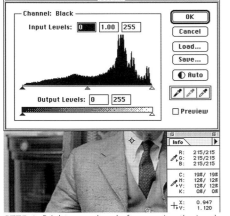

STEP 4: Brightness values before moving the Levels slider.

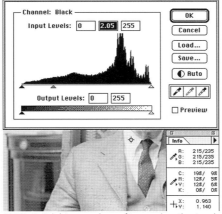

STEP 4: Brightness values after moving the Levels slider.

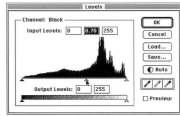

STEP 4: Levels slider adjusted for greater contrast.

119

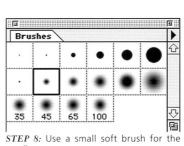

STEP 8: Use a small soft brush for the candles.

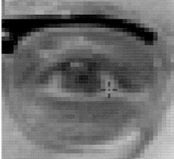

STEP 9: Zoom in to make the eyes brighter.

120

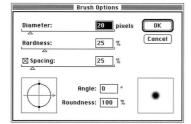

STEP 7: Choose From Snapshot as your Rubber Stamp option.

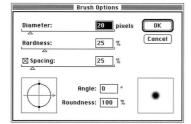

STEP 6: Start cloning with a large soft brush.

STEP 8: Set the Opacity to 30%.

Levels using OK. The overall effect of giving the picture more contrast is pleasing, but the whites of Fuller's shirt are now muddy. We will adjust the whites using the following "Electronic Fericyanide" technique.

STEP 7: Double-click on the Rubber Stamp tool to get the Tool Options palette and pull down the Option menu to From Snapshot. This will cause the Rubber Stamp tool to paint from the lighter Snapshot version of the image.

STEP 8: Choose Window/Palette/Show Brushes (F12 with ArtistKeys) and select a large brush with a soft edge. To fine tune the brush, double-click on it to bring up the Brush Options window. Start with a Diameter of about 20, a Hardness of about 25% and a Spacing of 25%. Click on OK in the Brush Options dialog box. In Rubber Stamp Options, set the opacity to 30%.

STEP 9: Lighten the collar and sleeve by painting on it with the Rubber Stamp. Each time you paint over a section it lightens it by using 30% of the light version in the Snapshot. If you want to remove the shadows on the white shirt next to his tie, several strokes there will turn them white. Now choose a two pixel brush and click on the

twinkles in Fuller's eyes to lighten them. Experiment with different size brushes and zoom in and out as you work. Command-Spacebar-click on the candles to zoom into the candles and continue to use the Rubber Stamp to clone from the Snapshot to lighten them. Pick a brush that is the width of a candle. Click on one end of a candle, and then Shift-click on the other end to draw a straight line the length of the candle. You may need to lower the opacity as you work to get more subtle shades of white. You may want to save your file now using File/Save (Command S). When you do a Save, this will flush the Snapshot buffer, so don't do it until you are finished lightening things.

BURNING IN THE IMAGE

STEP 10: Option-click on the Marquee tool in the Tool palette or type the letter M until the oval shaped icon is selected. Select from the center by positioning the cursor on the tip of Fuller's nose, holding down the Option key before you click, and then clicking and dragging to isolate the area you will want to sharpen and inversely burn in. If you've made the size and shape oval that you like, but it's not in exactly the position you want, use Command-Option along with a click and drag to move the selection. Don't forget that you need to click and drag inside the selection border

STEP 10: Make the Oval selection on Fuller look something like this.

to move it. Choose Select/Feather to set the feather to about 35 pixels. This will make a soft slow transition between the sharpened and non-sharpened areas and also the burned and non-burned areas.

STEP 11: Go to Filter/Sharpen/Sharpen to emphasize the center of the portrait by making it a little sharper. Then use Select/Inverse to invert the selection and select the outside of the image for burning. Choose Hide Edges (Command-H) from the Select menu to make your upcoming Curves changes easier to see.

STEP 12: Go to Image/Adjust/Curves (Command-M) and click the Preview checkbox to see how the changed area on the outside will blend with the unchanged area in the middle. Now adjust the Brightness/Contrast (move the center of the curve down) to make the outside of the image darker. Move the curve up and down until you like the amount of darkness. Click OK when you are happy.

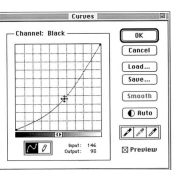

STEP 13: If you are not happy with the results, Undo (Command-Z) the curves, remake and refeather your selection and change your parameters in the Curves dialog.

STEP 12: Move the curve downwards to darken the edges. Make sure the Curves dialog box is out of the way so you can see most of Fuller.

STEP 14: Choose None (Command-D) from the Select menu to make your changes final.

REMOVING THE BANDAGE

STEP 15: If you have extra time, double-click on the Rubber Stamp tool and set it back to Clone (aligned). Now use this, with different size brushes and the Opacity set to 100%, to remove the bandage on Fuller's glasses. Copy skin at 100% opacity from different areas next to the bandage on top of the bandage. Don't copy the same piece of skin over and over again. To adjust skin shading, you can now change the Opacity to 50% and clone

lighter or darker skin areas over what you have already done, so the subtle shading on the head looks right. After cloning out the bandage, you may need to use the Blur tool at a low opacity to blend your changes together. As a final step, I selected the area that was changed, feathered the selection by 3, then I added about 5 of Gaussian Noise on top of the area that was cloned to make the noise there match the rest of the image.

Like all the exercises in this book, there are several ways that you could achieve the same result shown here. When you learn about layers later in the book, you might want to try this exercise using several layers and a layer mask.

STEP 15: Final adjustments were made to burn in edges. We also used the Rubber Stamp tool to remove the bandage.

HANDS-ON SESSION: COLOR MATCHING CARS

Measure and Adjust the Color of Objects so Different Colored Items Can Be Changed to Match, Do Subtle Color Tweaks After CMYK Conversion to Deal with Faded CMYK Hues

The long shot is a red car and we need to end up with two matching red CMYK images.

The closeup shot of a green car. You need to change its color to match the red car to the left.

STEP 1: Here is the color match spot in the red car.

STEP 1: Here is the color match spot in the green car.

Imagine that you want to create an advertisement using two photos of the Acura Integra. One of the photos was taken of a red Integra and the other was taken of a green one. You need to convert the green car photo so the color matches the red one. You will also convert both cars to CMYK and do some final color matching there.

CHOOSING A MATCHING COLOR SPOT

STEP 1: Open the RedAcuraCM and GreenDetail files from the Color Matching Cars folder. Find a spot on the red car where the color appears to be an average intermediate color that could represent the color you want for the whole car. Both of these photos have highlight and shadow areas and you are going to want them to match also. I've found that if you can locate a good midtone area in both images and get those midtone areas to match, the rest of the image will match pretty well also. I used the area on the front of the car to the right of the chrome Acura emblem just below where the word Acura is embossed in the red bumper. Since this spot exists in both photos and the lighting on it is similar, we can use this location on both cars to get the colors to match. We will call this location the color match spot. Bring up the Picker palette and set it to HSB mode. Put the Eyedropper over the color match spot and click to take a measurement. Hold the mouse button down and measure around a bit to make sure the spot you are using as this first measurement is an average measurement for this

STEP 1: The Picker palette in HSB mode. Write down the values you get.

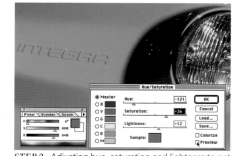

STEP 2: Adjusting hue, saturation and lightness to get the Hue/Saturation green swatch to match the red in the red car.

area. Double-click on the Eyedropper to be sure it is set to measure a 3x3 average of pixels. When you click and measure, that measurement is remembered in the Picker palette, even after you move the mouse. Write down the HSB values for that location.

STEP 2: Switch to the green car and find the same location right below the embossed Acura letters. Choose Adjust/Hue/Saturation (Command-U) then use the Eyedropper to click and take an average measurement in this area. Taking this measurement after bringing up the Hue/Saturation tool will fill the swatch color at the bottom of the dialog with green from this color match spot. Turn off the Preview button for a moment and move the Hue slider so the green swatch at the bottom middle of the dialog matches, as closely as possible, that same area on the red car. You will need to have the windows open on the screen so you can see both cars at the same time, and you might want to be zoomed in for now so you are looking at this part of both cars at the same time. Once the Hue/Saturation swatch matches fairly well, turn on the Preview button again and the green car will change to red. Now move the Saturation and Lightness sliders back and forth until you get Saturation and Lightness values in the Picker palette to match the numbers you wrote down for the color match spot on the red car. The Picker palette will continue to show you how the spot where you clicked in the green car has changed based on the Hue/Saturation slider movements. Don't worry about getting the hue numbers to match, they won't since they are degree rotation values based on changes in the original hue. Getting the saturation and lightness values to match is the key. You will notice that as you change one, the other will also change, so you will have to tweak both of them for a while until you get similar numbers to what you had in the red car. When you are happy with these adjustments, click on the OK button in Hue/Saturation.

STEP 3: Now convert the Picker palette to RGB mode. Measure the color match spot again in the original red car and write down the red, green and blue values. They should be around 213 for red, 23 for green and 31 for

blue. Switch to the green car, now converted to red, then go into Levels. Once you are in Levels, measure the color match spot within this image and make sure you can see the values in the Picker palette. Go into the Red channel and move the Input Brightness/Contrast slider, the middle slider,

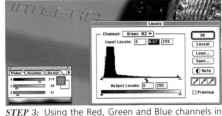

STEP 3: Using the Red, Green and Blue channels in Levels to match the green car's RGB values to the red car's values.

until the red value in the Picker palette matches the red value you wrote down for the original red car. Switch to the Green channel and do the same thing until the green values match. Finally do the same thing for the Blue channel. Now the two cars should match fairly well.

CONVERTING TO CMYK MODE

STEP 4: Convert the Picker palette to CMYK mode. Use Mode/CMYK to convert both cars to CMYK mode. The colors on the screen will now be as close as possible to your printed colors. You may notice the intense red of these cars fade somewhat. You will use the Selective Color tool to do final subtle tweaks of your red color in CMYK mode. Selective Color is a great tool for doing subtle adjustments to particular color areas within CMYK. Switch to the original red car, the long shot, then go into Image/Adjust/Selective Color. Make sure Colors is set to Red since we are going to

be adjusting the red colors within the car. Set the Method to Absolute. This will allow us to make the color adjustments more quickly. Take another measurement at the color match spot on this car and notice in the Picker palette that the color is made up mostly of magenta and yellow. The colors of the sliders on the Picker palette will show you how the color at the color match spot will change if you add or subtract more cyan, magenta, yellow or black ink. If the cyan value is greater than 0, subtract cyan using the Selective Color slider until the cyan value reads 0 in the Picker palette. This is adding red to the car color. Add magenta until the magenta value in the Picker palette is about 99. This will make the car a deeper richer color. Adjust the yellow until the yellow value in the Picker palette reads about 94. To get a slightly darker richer color, add some black until the black value in the Picker palette reads about 9. You don't have to use the exact same numbers that we have, just adjust the cyan, magenta, yellow and black percentages on the color match spot until you like this as the final redness of the car. Write down these final adjusted CMYK values from the Picker palette.

STEP 5: Switch to the close up shot and then again enter the Selective Color tool. Press down on the mouse button while taking a measurement of the color match spot within this image. Now adjust the cyan, magenta, yellow and black inks using the sliders in Selective Color until the percentages match the final adjusted percentages you just wrote down from the other image. We used Cyan = 0, Magenta = 99, Yellow = 94 and Black = 9, but your values can be different. You just want the two red colors to match and both look the way you like them. This is a good way to match the colors of objects that start out differently but have to end up the same.

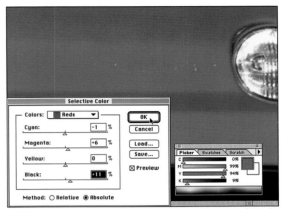

STEP 4: Using Selective Color and the Picker palette to adjust the CMYK version of the red color at the color match spot. This will change the makeup of all the reds.

The final green car after its conversion to red and CMYK adjustments.

The final longshot of the original red car after conversion and adjustment in CMYK.

HANDS-ON SESSION: COLOR CORRECTING AL

*Color Correcting this Difficult Exposure
and Scan and Using Threshold Masks
to Produce a Print with Natural, Consistent
and Pleasing Tones Overall*

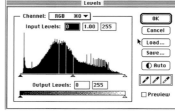

STEP 1: The initial RGB histogram.

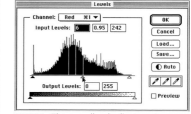

STEP 1: The overall red adjustments.

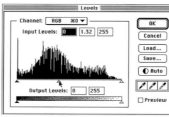

STEP 1: The overall green adjustments.

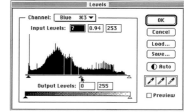

STEP 1: The overall blue adjustments.

One of my favorite pictures has always been this photo of my best buddy Al taken on a desert trip we made together back around 1980. I always wanted to make a print of it, so when I got my ProofPositive printer, I had it and a lot of other favorite pictures put onto Photo CD. When I brought in the photo, it was obviously oversaturated in the shadow area of the face. Since this is not a major area of the image, the first step to correct this is to do overall color correction to get the rest of the image to look correct.

OVERALL COLOR CORRECTION

STEP 1: Crop any areas from around the edge of the image that are not going to be in the print. In this case, my copyright notice is the only thing you need to crop. Use F9 to bring up the Info palette and Shift-F9 to bring up the Picker palette. Now go into Levels and use the steps outlined in the Grand Canyon and Kansas chapters to set the Highlight, Shadow, overall Brightness/Contrast, and finally the color cast. Here are the Levels settings I ended up with for Al. To set the highlight I used the Highlight Eyedropper in Levels and set it to the white

STEP 1: The original Photo CD scan of Al, during a desert camping trip back in the early days of Apple, has colors that are too saturated in the shadow areas on the face.

STEP 1: The overall RGB histogram. Notice how the values spread out just a little bit. We moved the large amount of data to the left of center a little more towards the center by this initial adjustment.

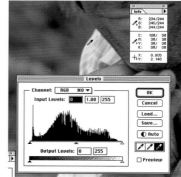

STEP 1: Setting the highlight by clicking with the Highlight Eyedropper on the whitest area of Al's shirt.

area on the tip of Al's right shoulder. For the shadow I used the Shadow Eyedropper and set it to the shadow on the black tuft of hair below Al's ear behind his neck. You may want to use the Save button in the Levels dialog to save your Levels changes so you can try them again later, starting with the same values, and then maybe adjusting a little differently the 2nd time. Click on OK in Levels to make your changes. Use File/Save As to save this as AlLevels.

MAKING A MASK OF THE OVERSATURATED AREAS

STEP 2: Look at the Red then Green then Blue channels of the image and see if one of them has a noticeable pattern in the area that is oversaturated.

STEP 2: The Red channel looks fine.

STEP 2: The Blue channel is dark in some areas.

STEP 2: The Green channel is dark in all the saturated areas. This is the best candidate to make the mask.

STEP 2: The mask made from a copy of the Green channel with the suggested Threshold setting.

You can see that the Green channel is very dark, magenta, in all the saturated areas. This will be a good channel to make a mask of the saturated areas, so drag this channel to the New Channel icon at the bottom of the Channels palette to make a copy of it. Double-click on it to name it Threshold Mask. Now choose Image/Map/Threshold and adjust the slider with the Preview button off until the saturated areas are black and the rest of the image is white. Click on the title bar to see a before/after of the image and compare your mask with the channel's details. If your computer doesn't support Video LUT animation, you will need to do all of your work in Threshold with the Preview button on. I used a setting of 47 to create my mask. Drag this channel to the New Channel icon to make a copy of the Threshold Mask so we can try different amounts of blur without damaging the initial mask. Now choose Filter/Blur/Gaussian Blur and blur the mask to a value of about 1.5. This will soften the transition between the masked and unmasked areas the same way Feather does with a selection.

STEP 3: Use Image/Map/Invert to invert the mask so the black areas are now white or selected. Type a D to get the default, white and black, colors. Use the Lasso tool with a zero pixel feather to select the parts of the white area you don't want to desaturate. Now Option-Delete to fill these with black. That is analogous to removing them from the selection. Name this channel Desat Mask.

STEP 4: Option-click on your Desat Mask to Load it as a selection. Type Command 0 to return to RGB. Now Image/Adjust/Hue/Saturation to desaturate the oversaturated areas of the face. With the Master button on, desaturate everything by -10%. Now click on the Red radio button and move the Red Hue slider towards yellow by 10% and desaturate the reds by -10% more and increase the Lightness on reds by +15%. The adjustments you

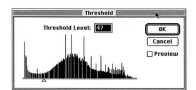

STEP 2: Adjust Threshold until the saturated areas and maybe a little beyond them are black, I used 47.

STEP 3: Use the Lasso to select the unrequired mask areas, and then Option-Delete to fill them with black.

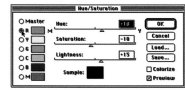

STEP 4: The adjustments made to the selected reds in the face.

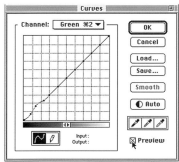

STEP 5: This part of the Green curve was moved away from magenta.

STEP 5: Al after the initial Levels, Hue/Saturation and Curves adjustments within the masked areas.

make may be a little different depending on the mask you create and the initial Levels adjustments you made.

ADJUSTING WITH CURVES

STEP 5: There were still parts of the face in the shadow areas that seemed too magenta. To fix this, go into Curves (Command-M) and load the LockdownCurve from the Al folder. Type Command-2, for the Green channel, click down with the Eyedropper in those areas and see where the circle shows up on the Green curve. Move this part of the curve up or down to add green or magenta. Adding some green here improved the areas that were still too magenta.

THE WHITES OF HIS EYES

STEP 6: Now use the Lasso tool to select the white part of Al's left eye. Use Select/Feather to put a 1 pixel feather on this selection. Go back into Hue/Saturation (Command-U) and try to brighten the white of Al's eye and make it more white. I added +15 to the lightness in Master mode, and then in Red mode I moved the red hues towards yellow by +10. This made the eye stand out a little better and removed some of the red tint it had.

CLEANING UP SOME BLEMISHES

STEP 7: Now use the Rubber Stamp tool with different size brushes and opacities to remove any blemishes and to also tone out areas that are too magenta. If you set the opacity to 30-50% then clone from an area next to the one you want to fix, it is easy to even out color areas that are not quite right without loosing the original detail in that area. You can also clone with the Blend mode set to Color to change the color of something without loosing its original detail. Remember that you can change the opacity by typing a number on the numeric keypad between 0 and 9. Zero is for 100%, 9 for

STEP 9: The final version of Al after cloning to even colors and blend out unwanted areas, then Sharpening and finally converting to CMYK.

90%, 8 for 80%, ...1 for 10%. You can also use the Bracket keys [and] to move to the next smaller or next larger brush. Make sure you have the preferences for Painting tools set to Brush Size. This way, if the cursor is over your image, you can see the brush size relative to your image and zoom factor as you change the brush size with the Bracket keys.

STEP 8: Go into Filter/Sharpen/Unsharp Mask and use the techniques learned in the Kansas—Final Tweaks chapter to find the right sharpening settings for Al. I used 150%, 1.5 and 8.

STEP 9: Save this as your final RGB version of Al, call it AlFinalRGB or something like that. Now use Mode/CMYK to convert Al to CMYK mode.

COMPOSITING IMAGES WITH
MASKS AND CHANNELS

HANDS-ON SESSION: VICTORIANS AND CLOUDS

*Using the Lasso Tool with
the Correct Feather to Combine Images
Along a Straight Sharp Edge with Basic Selection
and Compositing Techniques*

STEP 1: Victorians with original clouds.

STEP 1: We will use these clouds to replace those above the Victorians.

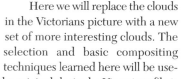

STEP 3: Use the Lasso tool with Anti-aliased and zero Feather.

Here we will replace the clouds in the Victorians picture with a new set of more interesting clouds. The selection and basic compositing techniques learned here will be useful in many places. Since the original sky in the Victorians file is not a solid color and the rooftops are very straight, we will get a better sky selection using either the Lasso or the Pen tool versus the Magic Wand. In this exercise, you are going to use the Lasso tool to make a selection along the edge of the building rooftops and then the entire sky. This selection will be used to replace the original clouds with those in the Clouds file.

SETTING THINGS UP

STEP 1: Open the Clouds file and then Victorians in the Victorians & Clouds folder. Victorians should be the active window, the window on top.

STEP 2: Click on the middle icon at the bottom of the Tool palette to put yourself into Full Screen mode and use Command-Spacebar-click to zoom into Victorians so it is at 1:1 or 2:1. Scroll using the Spacebar so the left edge of the picture is at the left of the monitor with the rooftops in the middle of the monitor.

STEP 3: Double-click on the Lasso tool from the Tool palette and check its options to make sure the Feather is set to zero pixels and that Anti-aliased is on. With this type of selection, it is best to make the selection using a zero pixel feather. You can adjust the feather later so the edges of the two composite images match the best.

SELECTING THE SKY

STEP 4: Push the Caps Lock key down to give you a cross-hair cursor instead of the lasso cursor. This is much more accurate. You can always have the cursor be a cross-hair by setting your Other Tools selection in General Preferences to Precise. If you have your preferences set that way, you don't need the Caps Lock key down. When using the Lasso tool, if you hold the Option key down, a straight line is drawn between each place you click with the mouse. If you hold the mouse button down and drag with the Option key still down, you can draw freehand. To make a selection with some straight line segments and some freehand segments,

STEP 4: Selecting the first section of the roof.

hold the Option key down while clicking and letting up on the mouse button between line endpoints, and then click and drag when you want to draw in freehand. When using the Lasso tool this way, you always want to draw a complete loop before letting go of the Option key. When you let up on the Option key as well as the mouse, the selection will be closed by a straight line between the end points.

STEP 5: Select the first section, and then bring up the Channels palette from the Windows Palette menu (F10 with ArtistKeys). In this image there are three channels for each of Red, Green and Blue. Choose Select/Save Selection or just click on the Selection icon in the bottom left corner of the Channels palette to add a Channel #4. Click on the rightmost column of Channel #4 in the Channels palette and you will notice that everywhere you selected is now white. This channel has remembered everything you

128

selected so you can return to it later should you accidentally loose it in the next step. Now click on the rightmost column of Channel #0 to return to your RGB image.

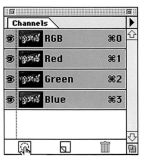

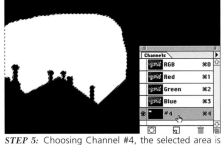

STEP 5: Just before saving your selection to Channel #4.

STEP 5: Choosing Channel #4, the selected area is white, and what is not selected is black. When choosing a channel, like Channel #4 here, click in the rightmost column of that channel in the Channels palette.

STEP 6: Scroll the image using the spacebar and continue to select the next section of the roofline. Do this using the Shift key with the Lasso tool. The Shift key adds to the selection. Without the Shift key down, go inside the existing selection and you will notice a right facing black arrow. If you press the mouse button now and move the mouse, the selected area will move. You don't want to do this!!! First press down on the Shift key and the cursor will change back to the lasso or cross-hair, now you can click and move the mouse to add to the selection. When the cursor gets to the edge

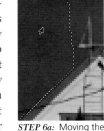

STEP 6a: Moving the right facing black arrow cursor moves the selection. Don't do this!

of the roofline and you want to again go into Option key mode, for straight line segments, hold the Option key down while keeping the mouse button down. After the Option key is down, you can let go of the Shift key and continue to add to the selection as you did the first segment. Just don't let go of the Option key until you have looped around the next segment. This is a tricky procedure if you haven't done it before. It is easy to make

STEP 6b: Press the Shift key to get the cross-hair cursor, then click and drag to add to the selection.

STEP 6c: Switch to the Option key here, before letting go of the Shift key!

a mistake and either lose the existing selection or move the selection. Adding to or deleting from a selection is a basic skill you need to know so hang in there and keep trying.

STEP 7: If you lose your selection, hold the Option key down and click on the right column of Channel #4 in the Channels palette. This will reload the selection you last saved. You can also choose Select/Load Selection from the menu bar to reload a saved selection. You can do another Save Selection each time you add to the selection. To save a new, improved selection over the existing one in Channel #4, just click on the Selection icon in the Channels palette, and then drag and drop this on top of Channel #4.

STEP 8: If you make a mistake in the middle of a section, like selecting too much or too little along the roof line, finish selecting that section without trying to fix the mistake. Just complete the rest of the area you were going to select, then go back and either add to the selection or subtract from the selection by using either the Shift key (add) or the Command key (subtract) along with the Lasso. When you add to the selection, the cursor should be inside the existing selection before you Shift-click. When you subtract, the cursor should be outside the selection before you Command-click. In either case you circle the amount you want to add or subtract.

STEP 9: When you get the roofline selected all the way across, zoom out (Option-Spacebar-click) so you can see the entire sky. Use Shift and the Lasso again to add any border areas around the edges of the sky. If you move the cursor out beyond the edge of the window, you are sure to get a straight line along the edge. Do this with the mouse button pressed down. (Don't try to draw the edge exactly, but drag out beyond the edge and it will be selected automatically.)

STEP 6d: Just don't let go of the Option key until you have looped around the next section.

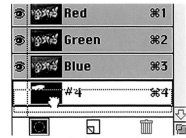

STEP 7: To load Channel #4 as the selection, click on #4 and drag to the Selection icon then release or just Option-click on Channel #4.

STEP 7: To make the current selection, overwrite the old Channel #4, click on the Selection icon and then drag this and drop (release the mouse button) on top of Channel #4.

STEP 9: The black line in the gray area shows the path of the Lasso tool to add the rest of the sky. Be sure you get all the edge pixels.

MASK INVERT VERSUS SELECTION INVERSE

STEP 10: Once the entire sky is selected, save this selection again on top of Channel #4. Double-click on Channel #4, name it FeatherZero, and then click OK in the Channel Options dialog. FeatherZero is called a mask since the areas where the selection was are white and the non-selected areas are black. The black area is "masked out" so you can't change it when the selection this mask represents is loaded. Choose Select/None to remove the marching ants from around the selection. Since the Channels palette has the FeatherZero channel selected, anything you do will only affect this channel. Choose Image/Map/Invert to turn everything in this mask channel into its opposite. What was white, the selection, is now black, no longer the selection. The old black area is now white. Option-click on the FeatherZero channel to load the selection. Notice that the selection loaded is the new white area, the buildings, the opposite of the sky. Now click on the right column of Channel 0, RGB, to see the colored Victorians image again. This now means that changes you make will affect all the Red, Green and Blue channels. Choose Select/Inverse and notice that the selection goes back to the sky again. Doing Select/Inverse on a selection (marching ants) is the same thing as doing Image/Map/Invert to a mask channel. We will be switching back and forth between selections and masks and using their terms interchangeably. A selection is a mask that hasn't been saved in a mask channel. A mask channel becomes a selection when you choose Load/Selection. Choose Edit/Undo (Command-Z) to put the selection back to the buildings.

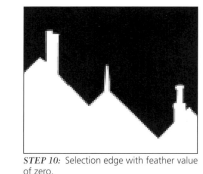

STEP 10: Selection edge with feather value of zero.

PICKING AN INITIAL FEATHER VALUE

STEP 11: Choose Select/Feather and set the feather of this selection to 2. Picking the right feather value is the most important thing, besides making an accurate selection, when compositing two images together. This is what makes the images seamlessly blend. Just click on the Selection icon, don't drag the icon on top of FeatherZero, to make Channel #5. Double-click on this channel and name it FeatherTwo. Choose Select/None (Command-D) to get the marching ants out of your way and zoom into the edge of the

rooftops to compare FeatherTwo with FeatherZero. Click back and forth between the two channels to see the difference. Blended areas are gray instead of pure white or black. When you make a selection and even add a feather to it, you don't need to save that selection to a channel to use it. If you want to see that selection, though, and see how the edges blend, it is easier look at a selection saved in a channel.

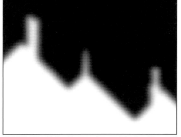

STEP 11: Selection edge with feather of two. Blended areas are gray, not black or white.

COMBINING THE IMAGES

STEP 12: Do a load selection of FeatherTwo, Option-click on the FeatherTwo channel, then click on Channel 0 to see RGB. Choose Edit/Copy and then switch to the Clouds image using the Window menu. Shrink this image with Option-Spacebar-click so it is all showing on the screen. Now do Edit/Paste to paste the Victorian buildings on top of the Clouds. The Victorians are now a floating selection. If you put the cursor on top of the floating selection and click and drag, you can change the location of the buildings. Let up on the mouse button when you like their new location.

Be careful with floating selections! If you click outside the floating selection, this does a deselect and makes that location of the buildings permanent. You can also do this by choosing Select/None or even by a quick click and release of the mouse on top of the selection without moving it. If you do one of these things by accident, choose Edit/Undo (Command-Z) to make the buildings float again. If this doesn't work and you are stuck with buildings where you don't want them, choose File/Revert to reload the Clouds from the disk. Then you can choose Edit/Paste again to get your floating selection back.

A safer way to move floating selections is to use the Move tool. Type a V to switch to the Move tool. It will move floating selections in the same way but won't deselect them. You can use Select/None (Command-D) to do the deselect.

STEP 13: Now move the Victorians around to the location you like best by clicking and quickly dragging. Photoshop shows you the outline of the floating selection as you drag it and then does a screen update when you release the mouse button. If you click and hold down the mouse button without moving it until the Clock icon stops, you can then move the entire selection in realtime on the screen. Try these two methods of moving a floating selection.

MAKING THE EDGE BLEND LOOK NATURAL

STEP 14: Zoom in on the edge between the rooftops and the new clouds and then choose Select/Hide Edges (Command-H) to conceal the marching ants. This allows you to see how the two images are blending together. With the two pixel feather you used along the edge, the blend is pretty soft—too soft to look real.

STEP 14: The two pixel feather is too soft!

STEP 15: Press on the Delete key to remove this floating selection with the two pixel feather. Use the Window menu to switch back to the Victorians image and do a Load Selection by Option-clicking on the FeatherZero channel. You will want less of a feather than two pixels but not as little a feather as zero. Since the two pixel feather is more blurry than what you want, you need to reload FeatherZero and then refeather with a softer edge. You usually want to make your initial selection with a feather value of 0 since this is the most accurate trace of the selection boundary. You can always take an accurate boundary, feather 0, and blur it to blend with a greater feather. Choose Select/Feather, enter .5 and choose OK. Photoshop will complain that you can only choose integer feather values between 1 and 250. Choose Cancel from the Feather dialog. It seems that a feather of 1 would still be too much, so let's use the Gaussian Blur filter to make a smaller feather using a mask channel.

GAUSSIAN BLUR FOR MORE FEATHER CONTROL

STEP 16: Choose Select/None (Command-D) to remove the selection. Click on FeatherZero in the Channels palette and drag it to the middle icon at the bottom of the window to make a copy of this channel. Choose Filter/Blur/Gaussian Blur, enter a value of .5 and choose OK. We are blurring this

mask channel since it is now the active (gray highlighted) channel. A Gaussian Blur of a certain value is the same as a feather of that same value. You do a Gaussian Blur on a mask channel, however, and then a load selection of that channel to turn it back into the feathered selection you need. You will later see that Gaussian Blur on a channel gives you much more control than Feather on a selection. Double-click on this channel and name it FeatherOneHalf. Drag it to the Selection icon or Option-click on it to do a Load Selection.

STEP 17: Click on the rightmost column of Channel 0 for RGB to make the RGB channels active. The copy function we are about to do will then copy the RGB color channels. Edit/Copy this selection then return to the Clouds image and do another Paste. Zoom into the rooftop boundary again and you will see that this feather should look more natural than the others. Use the Move tool to move the buildings to a place where you like the composition between their rooftops and the new sky. If you click and quickly drag the buildings to the bottom of the screen, and then let go of the mouse, the screen will refresh and you'll see most of the clouds. Now click and hold the mouse button down while keeping the mouse still until the Clock icon stops spinning. With the mouse button still down you can now move the buildings upwards while compositing with all the clouds in realtime. When you are happy with the position, release the mouse and choose Select/None.

STEP 18: Use the Rectangular Marquee tool to create a final frame for this image. Click in the bottom left corner, drag to the top right corner to define the frame, and then choose Edit/Crop to crop to this image. You can now use File/Save As to save your image with the new clouds under a different name.

STEP 17: Drag buildings to bottom and let go to see all the clouds for final composite.

STEP 17: Now click and hold until the Clock icon stops, then you can drag buildings in realtime.

STEP 18: The final cropped Victorians image with its bright new clouds.

HANDS-ON SESSION: BOB AND THE KESTREL

Using Threshold with
Hard- and Soft-Edged Masks
to Combine Images.

(Original Concept by Bruce Ashley)

The original Bob.

The original Kestrel.

This is a technique that would be difficult and tedious to do in the darkroom. Here, using digital imaging, it is easy. In this example we will create a complicated mask of the bicycle using Threshold and editing within a mask channel. We will then add a gradient to this mask and use it to seamlessly place Bob behind the bicycle.

PREPARING THE KESTREL IMAGE

STEP 1: Open the OrigKestrel file in the Bob & Kestrel folder. Choose File/Save As and save in Photoshop 3.0 format to your hard drive with the name Bob&Kestrel.

STEP 2: Crop the white and black borders from the file. Zoom in to 1:1 using Command-Spacebar-click. Use Filter/Sharpen/Sharpen Edges followed by Filter/Sharpen/Sharpen to sharpen this image. Whenever you sharpen something, you should be zoomed to at least 1:1 so you can see all the details. We normally use Unsharp Mask for sharpening, as in the

Kansas—Final Tweaks chapter, but this is simple and works well with these small images.

STEP 3: Type the letter D for the default colors. Use Image/Canvas Size to make the image window the same width but 750 pixels high. Put the image in the lower center of the canvas by clicking on the middle square at the bottom. It will turn gray to indicate where the original image will be in the new canvas.

STEP 3: Set up the canvas size to make room at the top of the file.

MASKING OUT THE BIKE

STEP 4: Go to Window/Palettes/Show Channels and drag Channel #1, the black channel, to the Channel Copy icon. You will use this new channel to create a mask to separate the bicycle from Bob. Double-click on this new channel and name it Bike Mask.

STEP 4: Make a copy of the Black channel to create a mask.

STEP 5: Using Image/Map/Threshold, adjust the slider until a good dropout of the bike frame is created. You don't want to etch too much from the edges around the bike frame and the seat. If gaps start to show on the edge, you have taken too much away. Don't worry about getting the tires completely; you can fix them later. Click OK to finish your Threshold selection. Now click in the Black/White box in the Tool palette, or type D, to make sure the foreground is black and the background is white.

STEP 6: Using the Lasso tool, draw freehand around the areas of black

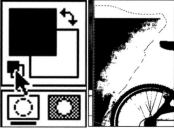

STEP 5: Move the Threshold slider until the best mask of the bike is created. About 127 worked for us.

STEP 5: Black/White box.   *STEP 6:* Selection to be deleted.

remaining in the background on the mask to select them, then use the Delete key to set them to white (only above the center of the wheels).

STEP 7: Go to Window/Palettes/Show Brushes and double-click on a brush to create a brush with a diameter of 5, 100% Hardness and 25% Spacing. Double-click on the Pencil tool and make sure the Auto Erase option is off. With the Pencil tool, add black to areas of the bike that are not filled in. The entire interior of the bike frame needs to be black so when the bike and Bob are combined, Bob will not show through those areas. This only needs to be done to areas above the height of the center of the wheel. Don't paint out beyond the edge of the original bicycle boundary. Without leaving the Pencil tool, you can switch between black, to fill in the bicycle, and white, to erase around the tires by Option-clicking on the color you want within the image. Option-clicking on a color while in a painting tool, brings up the Eye-dropper tool and selects that color as the foreground color. You can also toggle between the foreground and background colors by typing an X. Since you have done a lot of work editing this mask, do a Save to update your file on the disk in case you make a mistake in the following steps.

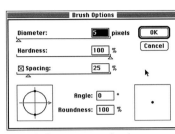

STEP 7: Create a custom brush.

STEP 7: The mask with the bicycle filled in.

CREATING A GRADIENT MASK

STEP 8: Make a copy of the Bike Mask by dragging the mask to the Copy icon at the bottom of the Channels palette. This will be Channel 3. Double-click on it and name it Gradient Mask.

STEP 9: Double-click on the Gradient tool and make sure its options are set as shown here. Notice that the Blend mode is set to Darken. You are going to use the Gradient tool to add a gradual blend from Bob at the top of the

STEP 9: Use these Gradient tool options.

image to the bicycle at the bottom of the image. We are doing this in a copy of the Bike Mask so if we make a mistake, we still have the original Bike Mask to try again. You use the Gradient tool by clicking in the place where you want 100% of the foreground color and dragging to where you want 100% of the background color. Everything between these two points will be a blend of the two colors. Everything outside these two points will be either 100% foreground or 100% background. The Darken option will make the gradient change the Bike Mask only when the gradient makes the image darker than what it was before.

STEP 10: Click on the Black/White icon at the bottom of the Tool palette or type D to set the foreground color to black and the background color to white. With the Shift key down, drag the Gradient tool from ¼ down from the top of the back wheel upwards to just above the seat. Release the mouse button before the Shift key to be sure the Shift key is applied. The Shift key forces the gradient line to be vertical. You should now have the final mask shown here. When you do a Load Selection on this mask, the white area at the top will be fully selected with the black areas fully not selected. The gray blend becomes less and less selected the darker it gets.

STEP 11: Click on Channel #1, the Black channel, within the Channels palette. Apply the Gradient Mask with Select/Load Selection or by Option-clicking on the Gradient Mask. Make sure you choose the Gradient Mask. The bottom of the gradient selection (the marching ants line) shows up at the 50% gray point. All of the gradient is actually selected, although it is only selected to a very small amount as it turns to almost all black.

STEP 10: To create the gradient, Shift-drag the gradient tool from ¼ down the wheel to just above the seat.

STEP 10: Your final gradient mask should look like this.

STEP 11: The appearance of the selection after doing a Load Selection.

133

The completed Bob&Kestrel image after it is cropped.

PUTTING BOB IN THE PICTURE

STEP 12: Open the OrigBob file from the Bob & Kestrel folder, and do a Save As naming it Bob PS in Photoshop 3.0 format. Crop the file to remove any white or black borders and the copyright notice. Zoom in to 1:1 using Command-Spacebar-click. Use the Sharpen Edges filter followed by the Sharpen filter to sharpen Bob.

STEP 13: Choose Select/Select All (Command-A), followed by Edit/Copy to place Bob on the clipboard.

STEP 14: Return to the Bob&Kestrel window and do Edit/Paste Into, not just Paste, to paste Bob into the selection loaded from the Gradient Mask. Bob is now a floating selection.

STEP 15: Choose the Move tool from the Tool palette (type the letter V). Click down on this floating selection and drag to adjust the position of Bob. Make sure there is no gray transition line visible at the bottom of Bob as he blends into the bicycle. It is easier to see this if you do Select/Hide Edges (Command-H) first to hide the edges of the selection. You need to drag him down until the bottom of his image reaches the place where the Gradient Mask turns completely to black. You can check that location in the mask channel by switching back there using Command-3 or by clicking on the channel you want within the Channels palette. You can see the selection while looking at the Gradient Mask by again doing Command-H to bring back the selection lines. Don't move the floating selection while viewing the mask channel. Do Command-1 to go back to the Black channel before moving Bob.

STEP 16: When Bob is in the correct location so the transition between him and the Kestrel is completely transparent, then make Bob permanent by choosing Select/None (Command-D). Crop and save this as Bob&Kestrel in Photoshop 3.0 format.

LAYERS FOR COMPOSITING
AND PROTOTYPING

INTRODUCTION TO LAYERS

Understanding the Terms and Concepts for
Working with Layers and Using
Layers for Prototyping and Effects Variations

When you are not using layers and you want to add a picture element, you have to paste a selection, add or delete from it, change its opacity, size it and move it around while it is still floating, and then finally drop it, which makes it permanent. If you want to change any of these things later, like when the art director looks at it, you have to start over or at least work with multiple versions. If you make the same image using Layers, all the above mentioned changes, and more, can be easily modified on the fly while the art director is watching. Layers is the most powerful new feature in Photoshop 3.0.

LAYERS AND CHANNELS

Layers are similar to channels in the ways you move them around, copy them and delete them. To work with layers, you use the Layers palette, which you can bring up from Window/Palettes/Show Layers or use Shift-F10 with Artist-Keys. If you are using layers and channels at the same time, which you usually do, you may want to separate the palettes so you can see

"Night Cab Ride in Manhattan" an image with many layers. Here we see all the layers. This image, called LayersIntro, is included in the Introduction to Layers folder on the CD. You may want to open it and play while reading this section.

them in different places on the screen. Just click on the Layers or Channels name tab at the top of that palette and drag it to a new place on the screen. You can then hide or bring up the Channels palette with Window/Palettes/Show Channels or F10 with ArtistKeys.

Each layer is like a separate Photoshop file that can be superimposed on top of other Photoshop layers within the same document. Take a look at the NightCabRide image at the beginning of this chapter; it was created using many layers. In an RGB file, for example, each layer has its own set of Red, Green and Blue channels. When working with layers, you can view one layer at a time, several layers at a time or all the layers at once.

HOW LAYERS WORK

Lets take a look at NightCabRide with several different layers and see how this works. Open the LayersIntro file in the Introduction to Layers folder, and try out the different options that we discuss here using that file. Make sure your Channels and Layers palettes are visible using F10 and Shift F10 if you have ArtistKeys loaded, or by going to Window/Palettes/Show Channels and Show Layers. In the Layers palette for NightCabRide, you see that this image has 6 layers. Currently we are looking at all of them since the Eye icons, in the left column of the Layers palette, are all on.

Imagine that all the layers are in a pile with the bottom layer, called All Black here, being at the bottom of the pile. As you add layers on top of this, like Canon, Building and Cab in this example, they are blended with the layers below. The active layer, the one that is highlighted, HeadlightsPizza, is the layer that is modified by changing the settings for Opacity and Composite Mode at the top of the Layers palette. You click in the right column of the Layers palette to make a layer active. The active layer will also be changed by anything you do with any other Photoshop tools, like Levels or Curves. If you do something

The Layers palette with the HeadLightsPizza layer active and all the Eye icons on.

Since all the Eye icons are on, the Channels palette shows you a view of the Red, Green and Blue channels as a composite image.

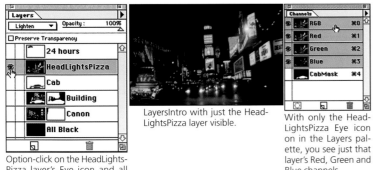

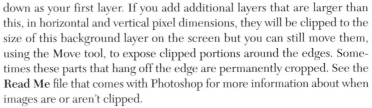

LayersIntro with just the Head-LightsPizza layer visible.

With only the Head-LightsPizza Eye icon on in the Layers palette, you see just that layer's Red, Green and Blue channels.

Option-click on the HeadLights-Pizza layer's Eye icon and all the other layers are no longer visible.

to the active layer while all the others layers' Eye icons are on, then you see the changes as they are combined with the other layers. The other layers themselves are not changed, only the active layer.

The Channels palette shows you the channels and Eye icon state for the layer you are working on. What you see in the Channels palette depends on the layer you have activated and which Eye icons are on in that layer and other layers. If you just want to work on that one layer and only see that layer, you can click on the Eye icons of the other layers to turn them off. You can also Option-click on the Eye icon of the layer you want to work on and all the other layers will be turned off. When you do this, the RGB display in the Channels palette also changes to show you just the Red, Green and Blue channels of this one layer. To turn all the other layers back on again, just Option-click again on the same layer's Eye icon. Then, the RGB display in the Channels palette will show a composite of all the visible layers.

Establishing a Background Layer

The Background layer, the one at the bottom, determines the physical dimensions of the entire document. Any image can be a background layer, it is just the first layer you start out with. If you open any single layer image into Photoshop and look at the Layers palette, you will notice that the image's layer is called Background. That is just the default name; you can double-click on this layer and give it a new name. When you are creating a composite image, it is important that you pick the right image for the

Background layer and that you size it correctly since this layer determines the canvas size for the rest of the layers. You want to make sure the canvas is large enough to encompass all of your picture elements. Because of this, you may want to put your largest picture element, which is often your main background, down as your first layer. If you add additional layers that are larger than this, in horizontal and vertical pixel dimensions, they will be clipped to the size of this background layer on the screen but you can still move them, using the Move tool, to expose clipped portions around the edges. Sometimes these parts that hang off the edge are permanently cropped. See the **Read Me** file that comes with Photoshop for more information about when images are or aren't clipped.

The Move tool.

When you turn off the other eyes and look at the Cab layer alone, you see the transparent area as a checkerboard.

Working with Additional Layers

When you add additional layers that are smaller than the background layer, or if you copy a small item and do an Edit/Paste Layer with it, the extra area around these smaller items shows up as transparent; this is a checkerboard pattern. When we look at just the Cab layer in this image, we see that all of it is transparent except for the cab itself. Through those transparent parts, when all the Eye icons are on, we will see the lights and buildings from the other three layers below the cab.

When you Command-click on an object with the Move tool selected, the current active layer will change to the one that contains that object. Command-Option-T will load a selection of everything but the transparent area in the active layer.

Additional layers are created in Photoshop by copying something from another image and then choosing Edit/Paste Layer. These layers can be named by double-clicking on them in the Layers palette. You can also click on a layer in the main document window, or the Layers palette in image "A", then drag and drop it on top of image "B's" main document window to create a new layer in image "B."

Layers can be moved from side to side or up and down using the Move tool. To do this, click to activate the layer you want to move within the Layers palette; it is highlighted when activated. Now select the Move

Moving the cab with the Move tool.

The moved cab.

The Layers palette setup for moving the cab. Notice that the cab opacity is set to 85%.

Lighten mode causes the headlights, and not their black background to show through the cab. Try Lighten mode instead of Normal mode here.

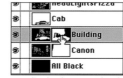

To edit the layer mask while still looking at the layer, just click on the layer mask's icon.

tool from the Tool palette, click and drag on the layer within the main document window, and then drag it to its new location. With all the Eye icons on, you will see its relationship to the other layers change.

Layers can be influenced by the Opacity and Blend modes. The Cab layer is partially transparent because its opacity is set to 85%. The reason that it looks like you are seeing headlights through the cab, however, is that the Blend mode on the HeadLightsPizza layer is set to Lighten.

CREATING AND EDITING LAYER MASKS

If you want part of a layer to be temporarily removed, or made invisible, you can add a layer mask to any layer. This allows you to instantly prototype a layer and its composite with the other layers, without seeing the masked-out part. If you later decide you want that part of the image back, just remove the layer mask. You can permanently remove that part of the image by integrating the layer mask into that layer. As you can see, a layer mask is a special mask that is attached to the layer it is associated with. When you activate a layer that has a layer mask, that mask is also added to the channels in the Channels palette. It only appears

in the Channels palette while you have that layer activated. If you want to edit the layer mask while still looking at the layer, just click on the layer mask's icon within the Layers palette. When you paint with black in the main document window, the black is added to the layer mask and those areas are removed from view in the layer associated with the layer mask.

If you want to edit the layer mask while looking at the mask itself, Option-click on the layer mask's icon within the Layers palette. The main document window will now just display the black-and-white mask and your Layers palette will have all the Eye icons dimmed out. The Channels palette will now have this channel selected with the Eye icon on. When you want to go back to editing the layer itself, Option-click on the layer's icon within the Layers palette. Don't worry, we will be using layer masks a lot in the exercises that follow and you will come to understand them completely.

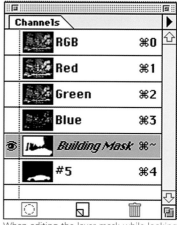

When editing the layer mask while still looking at the layer, the Channels palette will display the mask as above. The Eye icons are on for RGB, so you see those channels, yet you edit the mask since it is selected.

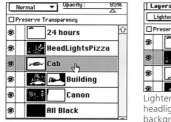

Adding a layer mask from the Layer menu.

The Building layer and its layer mask on the right.

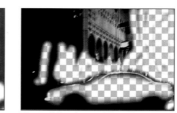

To edit the layer mask and see just the mask in the Document window, Option-click on the layer mask's icon. The layer Eye icon is now highlighted.

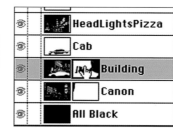

When editing the layer mask while looking at the mask, the Channels palette will display the mask highlighted with the Eye icon on as above. The Eye icons are off for the RGB channels since you don't want to see them.

138

The Building layer without its layer mask. Only the hole where the car will sit is transparent.

The Building layer mask.

The Building layer with its layer mask removing the newly transparent areas from the final composite.

THE LAYER OPTIONS DIALOG

If you double-click on a layer, you bring up the Layer Options dialog. This allows you to name a layer, group it with other layers or composite it using only a partial range of its 0..255 pixel values. The Posterize, Bitmaps & Patterns chapter explains Layer Options. All the layers features as well as the creation of a more complex

The Layer Options dialog.

version of the NightCabRide image are explained in the following chapters. Now let's talk about moving, removing and copying layers.

MOVING, REMOVING AND COPYING

You can remove a layer by clicking on it, choosing Delete Layer from the Layer palette's pop-up menu, or by clicking on the layer and dragging it to the Trash icon at the bottom right of the Layers palette.

You can make a copy of any layer by clicking on the layer and dragging it to the New Layer icon at the bottom left of the Layers palette. You can also make a copy of the active layer by choosing Duplicate Layer from the Layers palette's pop-up menu. The copied layer will have the same name with "copy" added to the end.

You can move a layer from one location to another within the Layers palette by clicking on the layer you want to move and then dragging it until the line becomes dark between the two layers where you want to put this layer. Let go of the mouse at that point, and the layer is moved. When you move a layer, it will change the composite relationship of that layer with the layers around it. Notice how the headlights no longer show through the cab since we moved them from above the cab to below the cab.

Deleting a layer the quick way by using the Trash icon at the bottom of the Layers palette.

To copy a layer, drag it to the New Layer icon at the bottom of the Layers palette.

To move a layer, click on it then drag it until the line is dark between the layers where you want to put it.

The moved layer appears in its new location now below the cab.

With the Cab layer below the HeadlightsPizza layer, the lights show through the cab.

After moving the HeadlightsPizza layer below the Cab layer, you can no longer see the headlights through the cab.

Using Threshold and Calculations to Create a Knock-Out of Bob, Introduction to Paths, Refining Selections with Paths, Clipping Paths to Quark and Illustrator and Using a Two Layered Document to Send Bob to Vegas!

Here we will explore various techniques to create a knock-out of Bob. We will show you how to use a Pen tool path as a clipping path to crop out a background in Quark or Illustrator. We will create a two layered document with Bob in one layer and Las Vegas in the other. A layer mask will then be used to send Bob to Las Vegas.

SETTING UP THE FILES AND CHANNELS

STEP 1: Open the file OrigBob and crop the image so there are no white or black edges around it. Run Filter/Sharpen/Sharpen Edges followed by Filter/Sharpen/Sharpen. It is easier to create a knock-out when you have a sharp image. Use File/Save As to Save this file as BobSharp.

STEP 1: Bob after cropping and sharpening.

STEP 2: Use Mode/RGB to convert Bob from Grayscale to RGB. Choose Show Channels from the Window menu to bring up the Channels palette.

STEP 3: Click on Bob's Red channel in the Channels Palette and drag it to the New Channel icon at the bottom middle of the palette. Double-click on this channel and name it LeftSide. Create another new channel in the same way and name this one RightSide.

USING THRESHOLD TWICE

STEP 4: Click on LeftSide and then choose Image/Map/Threshold. Make sure the Preview button is off and move the slider to the left until you have

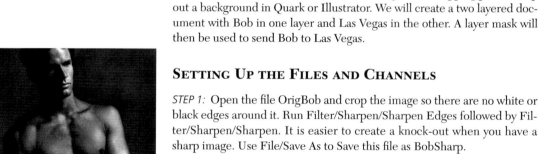

STEP 4: Using Threshold at 55 to create the mask for the left side of Bob.

a nice border between Bob and the background. Zoom in on Bob's neck and hair area. Click on the title bar to see before the mask, and release the mouse button to see after the mask. If you don't have Video LUT Animation, work initially with the Preview button on then use the Preview button here to see before and after. You can make sure the edge of the mask lines up with Bob this way. Click OK when the mask seems correct, around 55.

STEP 5: Use the Magic Wand to select the left edge then drag and drop the Selection icon onto LeftSide to save this selection.

STEP 6: Threshold at 100 for the right side of Bob.

STEP 7: Magic Wand for the right side.

STEP 5: Double-click on the Magic Wand and make sure its tolerance is set to 32. Click on the black area that defines the left side of Bob to select it only. Click on the Selection icon at the bottom left of the Channels palette and drag it over the LeftSide channel to redefine this as the selected area. Choose Select/None (Command-D).

STEP 6: Click on the channel named RightSide and use Threshold (Command-T) again to make a distinct edge on the right side of Bob. The value should be about 100.

STEP 7: Use the Magic Wand to select the white area that defines the right edge of Bob. Click on the Selection icon at the bottom of the Channels palette and drag to the RightSide channel. Now do Select/None (Command-D).

STEP 8: Now you want to combine the white areas of LeftSide and RightSide to get a complete knock-out of Bob. Use Image/Calculations with LeftSide and RightSide as the channels for Source1 and Source2. Set the Blending to Lighter and the Result to a new channel within the

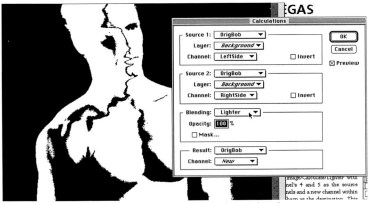

STEP 8: The Calculations command with its correct settings and result.

BobSharp file. You should be able to see the result if you have the Preview box checked. Double-click on the new channel and name it Both-Sides. The Channels palette should now look like the one to the right.

CLOSING UP THE BOTHSIDES CHANNEL

STEP 9: Now use the Lasso tool with a zero pixel feather to select the black areas in the middle of Bob in the BothSides channel. Type a D to set the colors to black-and-white. Hit the Delete key to turn this selected area to white also. Now you have the basic outline of Bob.

STEP 10: Click on the channel named LeftSide and drag it to the Trash icon at the bottom right of the Channels palette. Do the same thing to the RightSide channel. You no longer need these since you have BothSides.

STEP 8: BothSides after calculations.

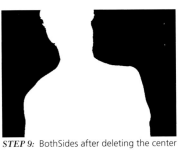

STEP 9: BothSides after deleting the center portion.

STEP 11: Choose Command-0 to switch to the RGB composite channel. Option-click on the BothSides channel. This will load the selection you just created. Use the Lasso tool with the Shift key down to add to the selection on the right shoulder and the right piece of hair. Threshold usually misses these since they blend into the background. Use the Lasso with the Command key down to subtract any required areas by the bottom of Bob's left arm. Resave your selection by clicking on the Selection icon in the Channels palette and dragging up to the BothSides channel again. This overwrites that channel with this new selection.

GETTING RID OF THE JAGGIES

STEP 12: Choose Select/None (Command-D), click on the BothSides channel and zoom in on Bob's right shoulder and neck area. Notice that the edge is sort of jagged. This is the kind of selection you get with Threshold. There is no anti-aliasing—no blending along the edge. Click on BothSides and drag it to the New Channel icon in the middle at the bottom of the Channels palette. Double-click on the copy and name it GausBlurMask. Choose Filter/Blur/Gaussian Blur and blur the copy by about 1.25 pixels. This makes a softer edge and gets rid of some of the jaggies. Let's try one more thing to get the absolute best edge on this selection.

IMPROVING SELECTIONS WITH PATHS

STEP 13: Option-click on BothSides to do a Load Selection. Enter Command-0 to return to RGB viewing. Choose Window/Palette/Show Paths (F11 with ArtistKeys) to bring up the Paths palette. Choose Make Path from its pop-up menu and set the tolerance to 2.0 pixels. The Path will be called WorkPath; double-click on it and rename it Bob Outline. We will edit this path to clean up the edges of Bob. First though, steps 14 and 15 will talk about creating a path from scratch. If you already know how to use paths, you can skip steps 14 and 15.

CREATING A PATH FROM SCRATCH

STEP 14: Click in the white space below Bob Outline to temporarily de-select Bob Outline as the path we are working on. We can now use the Pen

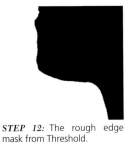

STEP 12: The rough edge mask from Threshold.

STEP 13: Make path from the Paths palette.

141

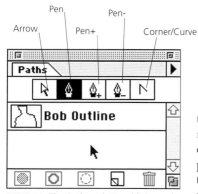

Arrow   Pen+   Pen-   Corner/Curve   Pen   Pen-

STEP 14: The Paths palette with its tools. Clicking in the white space below Bob Outline to deselect this path. NOTE: Adobe calls the Corner/Curve tool the Convert Direction Point tool.

142

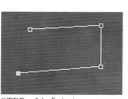

STEP 14: Entering corner points on a path.

STEP 14: Entering curve points on a path. The handlebars should be tangent to the curve shape you are trying to draw.

STEP 14: To close the curve, click on the first point a second time when you see the small circle next to the Pen icon.

tool to learn how to create a new path. Double-click on the Pen tool and make sure the Rubber Band option, in the Options palette, is on. This will cause the Pen to show you how a line or curve will draw between two points. The Pen tool allows you to make selections, called *paths*, by clicking to create points between either straight or curved lines. If you click on a point and immediately release the mouse, this is a corner point. If you click on a point and drag before releasing the mouse, that point becomes a curve point. When creating or moving a curve point, you will get two lines coming out of the curve point; I call these *handlebars*. The handlebars control the shape of the curve. Let's try this out! Its sort of like tracing but more fun!

Use the gray area above and to the right of Bob. Click with the Pen tool and immediately release to create a corner point. Click four or five corner points to create a box. When you put the last corner point on top of the first, a little circle appears next to the arrow indicating that you are closing the path. If you are going to turn your path into a selection, which we are going to do here, you usually want the path to be closed. After closing the first box path, move the cursor down below that box, and in a new area, click and drag to create a curve point. Where you click is the location of the point, and you affect the shape of the line segment between that point and the previous point as you drag out the handlebar beyond the point. Draw an oval shape by clicking and dragging four curve points. Close this path by clicking again on the original point. You now have a box path made up of corner points, and an oval path, made up of curve points. If you look at the Paths window, these are both there within a new path

called Work Path. Work Path is a temporary place where you can create a path without giving it a name. Actually, each of these two disjointed paths is a subpath of Work Path. Double-click on Work Path and rename it Play Path. Once you name a path, any changes to that path will be automatically saved as part of that path.

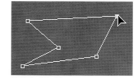

STEP 15: To move a corner point or a curve point, click on it and drag.

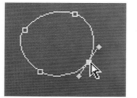

STEP 15: To adjust the shape of the curve, first click on the point whose handlebars affect the part of the curve you want to change. Second, below, click on the end of the handlebar and make it longer or shorter or change its angle. This will change the shape of the curve.

STEP 15: Moving a curve point to make the oval longer.

STEP 15: Now select the Arrow tool within the Paths palette and use it to edit the path. First click on the box shape you made with the corner points. When you click on this, its points will become highlighted. To move one of these points, just click on it, drag and then let go in the new location. This change will have already been saved in your Play Path. Click on the oval subpath now and its points will become highlighted. If you want to move one of these curve points to elongate the oval, just click and drag it like you would a corner point. To adjust the shape of the curve, first click on the point that is on one end of the curve segment you want to change. This will bring up the handlebars for that point. Then click on the end of the handlebar next to the segment you want to change and make it longer or shorter or change its angle to change the shape of the curve. Using the Pen tool in Photoshop is a lot like using the Pen tool in Illustrator but there are some differences. If you are not familiar with the Pen tool or if you want to know all the little details, read the chapter in the Photoshop manual about using paths.

EDITING THE BOB OUTLINE PATH

STEP 16: Click on Bob Outline in the Paths palette to make it the active path. Choose the Arrow tool from the paths palette and click on the Bob Outline path itself to activate the points along the path. Zoom in close on different areas of Bob to make sure the path lines up properly along the edge of Bob and that the curves of its line segments match his shape. You can click on a point to move it or to activate its handlebars. You can move the handlebars to change the shape of the curve.

You can also add points with the Pen+ tool and delete points with the Pen– tool. To add a point, just click along the line segment were there currently isn't a point using the Pen+ tool. You can access the Pen+ tool from the Arrow tool by holding the Command and Option keys down while over a location that doesn't already have a point. When the point is added, it will be a curve point. You can then change the shape of the curve by adjusting that point's handlebars. Command-Option with the Arrow over a location that already is a point will give you the Pen- tool and a click will remove that point. If you are removing a lot of points, you can just switch to the Pen– tool in the Paths palette. If you want a curve point to be changed to a corner point, or vice-versa, click on it with the

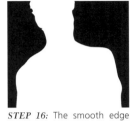

STEP 16: The smooth edge mask from the Pen tool.

Corner/Curve tool (Adobe calls this tool the Convert Direction Point tool). When changing a corner to a curve, you click and drag to define the length and angle of your handlebars. You can also access the Corner/Curve tool from the Arrow tool by holding down the Control key and putting the cursor over a point.

TURNING PATHS BACK TO SELECTIONS AND MASKS

STEP 17: Once you are happy with the shape of your Bob Outline path, choose Make Selection from the Paths palette's pop-up menu. Make it a New Selection with the feather set to 0 and Anti-aliased on. Once you have the selection, click in the Selection icon at the bottom of the Channels palette to save this as a new channel. Name this channel Path Selection. Now you can click in the white area at the bottom of the Paths palette to remove the path and its points from the screen. Click on the different mask channels to compare the Path Selection mask with the one made by Threshold and also the blurred Threshold version.

Paths make very smooth, elegant curves. We could have actually drawn the entire outline of Bob with the Pen tool instead of using Threshold. Very often though, it can take a long time to accurately draw a Pen tool path by hand when you can instantly create a mask using Threshold. Sometimes it makes sense to use the hybrid approach like we did here. It is very hard to select jagged edged things, like hair, using a path. Threshold can do a better job on these types of surfaces especially if you have a high resolution image that is very sharp. When

you use Threshold, there is usually a bit of editing required to perfect the selection. When you know a knock-out will have to be done, photographing objects with an entirely different color and brightness background can help make it easier to automatically do the knock-out using Threshold.

PUTTING LAS VEGAS IN THE BACKGROUND

STEP 18: Use Command-0 to return to the RGB view. Open the file called LasVegasNight and use the Shift key with the Move tool to click on it then drag and drop it on top of the BobSharp window. This creates a new layer with Las Vegas centered in the BobSharp document. Double-click on this new layer in the Layers palette to name it LasVegas. You really want this layer to be underneath Bob, the current background layer, but if you click and drag it down there, Photoshop won't let you move LasVegas to below the background layer. The name "Background" has a special meaning and Photoshop assumes you want it to be the bottom layer. Double-click on the background layer and rename it Bob. Now click and drag the LasVegas layer and place it below the Bob layer. Now it works! Click on the Bob layer to make it the active layer. Now choose Add Layer Mask from the Layer palette's menu. The layer mask should now be selected (its icon will have a dark border). Choose Image/Apply Image to copy the PathSelection channel to the layer mask. Use the settings shown here and you will see this PathSelection mask if you have the Preview button on. Click on the OK button and the layer mask will allow Las Vegas to show through as the background for Bob.

STEP 19: You may notice that there are some whitish halos around Bob's hair on the left side and there may also be some along his neck on that same side. You can clean these up by editing Bob's layer mask. Remember, wherever Bob's layer mask is black, you are going to see the Las Vegas scene and wherever it is white, you are going to see Bob. The white halos you see along the edge of Bob's hair are actually Bob's original gray background or they

STEP 18: These are the correct settings for Apply Image.

STEP 19: Your Layers and Channels palettes should look like this as you edit Bob's layer mask.

might be a highlight on Bob's hair that doesn't blend too well with the new black background of Las Vegas. Double-click on the Paintbrush tool and set the mode to Normal and the opacity to 50%. Double-click on the left-most brush in the second row of brushes and set it to 3 pixels wide and then select this brush. Type a D to get the default black-and-white colors. Click on Bob's layer mask so you are editing it but viewing the composite

of Bob and Vegas. Use Command-Spacebar-click to zoom in close. Painting on the halo areas with black as the foreground color will add black to the layer mask and will start to remove the light halo. The more you paint, the more the halo will be removed. If you remove too much, type X to exchange the foreground and background colors, and paint with white in the mask to bring back some of Bob. You may need to change the brush size and/or opacity to deal with the type of halo problem you have. I ended up using a big brush and painting with white to bring back the entire hairline and the edge of Bob's original background. Then I switched to smaller and smaller brushes with black as I slowly stripped the background and halo away. Use the bracket keys to change brush size and numbers to change opacity. If you are having problems getting this to work, look at Bob's layer mask in the BobVegas example file on the CD in the Extra Info folder.

Final version of Bob in Las Vegas.

STEP 20: Click on the Bob layer to select the layer, not the layer mask, and then use the Move tool to move Bob around in front of his Las Vegas background until you get him in the location you like best. Save this file as BobVegas in Photoshop 3.0 format. We will use it in a later chapter about Filters and Effects.

SAVING CLIPPING PATHS FOR QUARK OR ILLUSTRATOR

When you were finished editing the Bob Outline path at the end of step 16, it could have easily been used to knock out Bob as a clipping path within Quark or Illustrator. Importing with a clipping path into Quark or Illustrator would allow Bob to be placed as an object with a transparent background. This way text could be wrapped around him or he could be placed on top of a background created within Quark or Illustrator.

To save a path in this way, choose Clipping Path from the Paths palette Options menu. Choose the path you want for your clipping path from the Path pop-up. In this case, we would choose Bob Outline. We recommend leaving the flatness value blank to use the printer's default setting. For more info on flatness see the Photoshop manual. Save this file in EPS format and when you open it into Quark, Illustrator or other layout packages that support clipping paths, the background will be transparent.

144

HANDS-ON SESSION: VERSAILLES

This technique shows you how you can get more detail in a contrasty image by doing two scans, one for the highlights and another for the shadows, then combining the two images using Layers. Multiple layers of the same image will be exactly lined up with each other. We use this fact to our advantage in a lot of the techniques in this book and especially to get better effects with filters in this chapter.

SCANNING THE IMAGE IN LAYERS

STEP 1: Open the Sky file in the Versailles folder. This file was originally opened using the Kodak Photo CD Acquire module using a gamma of 1.4 and color temperature 5000, which gave the most detail in the sky but made the foreground look too dark. We will call this version of the image Sky.

STEP 1: The original Photo CD Acquire using gamma 1.4 to get the most detail in the sky.

STEP 2: Open the Buildings file. This file was originally opened using the Kodak Photo CD Acquire module using gamma 2.2 and color temperature 5000, which gave the most detail in the buildings and foreground but made the sky too light. We will call this image Buildings. If you were going to use this technique with two different scans of the same image, you would need to make sure both scans were pixel for pixel aligned. To do this, scan them at the same time and size without moving the original inside the scanner.

STEP 2: The original Photo CD Acquire using gamma 2.2 to get the most detail in buildings and foreground.

STEP 3: Make the Buildings image active and choose Select/Select All followed by Edit/Copy. Switch to the Sky image and choose Edit/Paste Layer.

Using Two Scans or Bringing the Image Up Twice from Photo CD to Get the Full Range of Detail from Brightest Highlights to Darkest Shadows in a High Contrast Image; Use Layers to Color Correct an Image by Combining Two Different Versions of the Image, and How to Apply Filters Selectively or Partially with Layers

Name this layer Buildings and double-click on the sky layer, currently called Background and rename it Sky. We now have a two layered document with the Sky layer as our background layer and the Buildings image as layer one. You could have also used the Move tool to drag the Buildings and then drop that image on the Sky file as a new layer. This is actually faster because it doesn't use the copy buffer. You can now close the original Buildings image since it is now a layer within Sky. Do File/Save As and save the two layered file in Photoshop 3.0 format calling it VersaiLayers. Use the Cropping tool to crop the black borders from around the image. Since you first made the Buildings image a layer on top of Sky, both images will be properly aligned and cropped exactly the same.

OVERALL COLOR CORRECTION

STEP 4: Do the overall color correction steps on each of the layers separately by first clicking on the layer you want to work on. With Levels: set highlight, set shadow, then set overall brightness and correct color cast; with Hue/Saturation: set overall saturation and adjust specific colors. See the Grand Canyon chapter if you need a review of

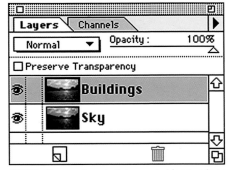

STEP 3: You now have both images inside a two layer document with the Sky image as the background image.

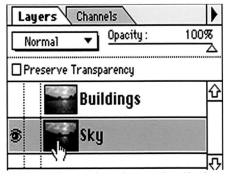

STEP 4: Make sure when color correcting either layer that only the Eye icon for that layer is on.

overall color correction. After I did my basic Levels adjustments, I then used Hue/Saturation on the buildings: I increased overall saturation by 20%, increased yellow saturation to 20% and moved yellows towards red by -10. I also moved reds towards yellow by +10. In the sky image I increased overall saturation by 20% and decreased overall lightness by -3. When you do this, you will focus on getting the part of each image you will use in the final composite to look color correct.

MASKING THE SKY FROM THE BUILDINGS

STEP 5: You now need to make a mask that separates the sky from the rest of the image. Look at the different color channels and find the one that has the most contrast between the tops of the buildings and the sky. In this case it is

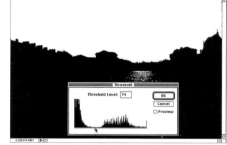

STEP 5: Use Threshold 74 to make a mask of the building/sky at the edges of the image.

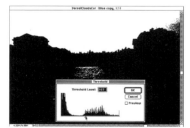

STEP 5: Use Threshold 107 to make a mask of the building/sky at the middle of the image.

the Blue channel from the Sky layer. The channels that show up in the Channels palette change depending on which layer is selected. Make sure the Sky layer is selected as shown here in Step 4 and then find the Blue channel in the Channels palette. Make two copies of this Blue channel using Duplicate Channel from the pop-up menu in the Channels palette or by dragging the Blue channel to the New Channel icon at the bottom center of the palette. Now use Threshold to make two masks using these copies of the Blue channel. You want these masks to separate the sky and the buildings. Zoom into different areas along the edge of this boundary and notice how different values of Threshold do a better or worse job of accurately defining this boundary. You can click on the title bar of Threshold (make sure the Preview button is off) to toggle between the mask you are making and the original Blue channel. This makes it easier to accurately see the boundary. If your computer doesn't have Video LUT Animation, work with the Preview button on and turn it off to see the original version.

Use a Threshold value of 74 in one copy of the Blue channel to get the most detail between the buildings and the sky at the edges of the image. In the other copy, use the value of 107 to get the best detail between the buildings and the sky in the lighter middle portion. If you need more

information on creating Threshold masks, see the Bob and the Kestrel or Bob Goes to Vegas chapters.

STEP 6: Type a D for the default colors. You will now combine these two masks to make your final Threshold mask. Choose Select all from the Select

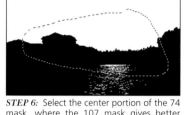

STEP 6: Select the center portion of the 74 mask, where the 107 mask gives better detail, using the Lasso tool with a feather value of 5.

Menu and then copy the mask where you used the 107 value. Select the center portion of the 74 mask, where the 107 mask gives better detail, using the Lasso tool with a feather value of 5. Do an Edit/Paste Into to replace this portion with that from the 107 mask. Name this combined mask HardEdge and use the Lasso with Option-Delete to fill any of the white reflections in the brick area in with black. The only thing you want selected here is the sky area. You can throw out the 107 Threshold mask by dragging it to the Trash icon in the Channels palette.

TWEAKING THE MASK WITH LASSO AND BLUR

STEP 7: Go back to the RGB channel (Command 0) and load the selection from your new HardEdge mask. Make sure the feather on the Lasso tool is set back to zero and then use the Lasso tool with the Shift key to add or with the Command key to subtract from the selection. Clean up any errors Threshold made in automatically making a mask to separate the sky from the clouds. You will probably have to spend some time on the scaffolding on the building to the right. Now save your edited selection to the HardEdge channel. After saving the selection, choose Select/None (Command-D) to deselect.

STEP 8: Make a copy of the HardEdge mask using the New Channel icon and Gaussian blur the copy with a value of about .5 to blend the edges. We do this blur on a copy of the original HardEdge mask in case we later decide to change the amount of the blur. Since we made the copy we can always go back to the sharp original and try a different blur on it. Double-click on this blurred mask and name it SoftEdge. We

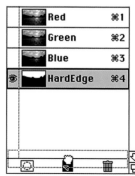

STEP 8: Drag HardEdge to the New Channel icon to make a copy of this channel.

will be able to use this mask to select either the sky or the buildings within a layer by inverting the mask to make the part we want to select white.

MAKING A LAYER MASK

STEP 9: Move to the Layers palette and click on the Buildings layer. Use the Layer Options pop-up menu to add a layer mask to this layer. Switch back to the Channels palette and you will notice that the layer mask is now the selected channel. Choose Image/Apply Image with the options shown here to copy the SoftEdge mask into the Buildings layer mask. Click on the Invert check box so the buildings will be chosen and not the sky. You can now view both layers at the same time with the Buildings layer mask showing you the details in the buildings from the Buildings layer and the details in the sky from the Sky layer. Try turning the different layers off and on using the Eye icons so you understand the control you have over viewing the different parts of the image.

TWEAKING THE LAYER MASK

STEP 10: You may notice some jagginess or tell-tale brightness variation along the edge between the original sky and the new foreground. Wherever the layer mask is black, you are seeing the sky from the underlying layer. Where the layer mask is white, you are viewing the Building layer. Type a D to set the default colors, and then you can use the Paintbrush to paint with black in the layer mask to see more from the darker sky image.You can also type X to exchange the colors then paint with white to see more from the lighter building image. Use a small brush and fine tune the mask along the edge to get even better blending between the two images. Remember that you can change the opacity of the Paintbrush by typing a number like 5 for 50%. Sometimes a partial opacity mask adjustment is just what you'll need.

MERGING THE LAYERS

STEP 11: Open the Channels palette and make a copy of the Buildings layer mask by clicking on it and dragging it to the New Channel icon in the middle at the bottom of the Channels palette. Name this SoftEdge Edited. We will now be merging the layers we have created so far, so you should do Command-S to save this version of the image with the different layers in case you want to go back to it later.

You can use the Gaussian Blur filter to reduce the edge jagginess further. When you do this, you will want to be blending the two layers along that edge. For this to happen correctly, we must first merge the

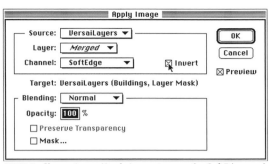
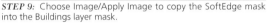

STEP 9: Choose Image/Apply Image to copy the SoftEdge mask into the Buildings layer mask.

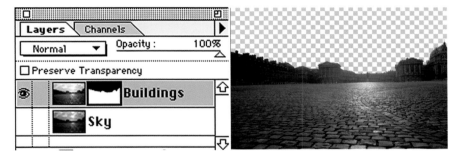

STEP 9: This is the Buildings layer with its layer mask selecting only the buildings. We can't see any sky since the Eye icon for the Sky layer is turned off.

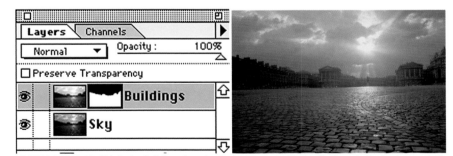

ZSTEPS 9 AND 10: This is the Buildings layer in the foreground with the Sky layer in the background. To see them together, make your Layers palette have both Eye icons turned on like the one here. With Layers set as in this image, you are seeing both layers and yet editing the Buildings layer mask. Use this setup to edit the layer mask as described in Step 10.

layers into a single new layer. Type Command-0 to return to RGB, and do a Merge Layers from the pop-up Options menu in the Layers palette. Save this under a different name (VersaiMerged) in case you need to return to the previous version that still has the separate layers.

STEP 12: Use this mask to blur the edges of the border you have merged together.

SMOOTHING THE BORDER

STEP 12: Now do a Load Selection from SoftEdge Edited to get a selection of the edge between the old layers. Choose Select/Modify/Border and set the border value to 3. This will select three pixels along either side of the border between the sky and the buildings. Use the Lasso tool with the Command key to remove the areas around the edge of the picture from the selection. Now do a Select/Feather of 1 to blend this border selection.

STEP 13: Now do a Gaussian blur of .25 along this border of the selection. This should reduce any jagginess that you see. Save this selection in a new mask channel and name it Border by double-clicking on the mask in the Channels palette and then entering its name.

IMPROVING THE FOREGROUND

STEP 14: We have now merged the two versions of this image together to get the best detail in the clouds and also in the foreground. Now we will use masks again to improve certain areas within the foreground image. Option-click to do a Load Selection from the old layer mask channel called Soft-Edge Edited. You may notice that the buildings and the brick courtyard on the left side and the right side of the image have a green tinge to them and they are also a little dark.

STEP 15: Use the Lasso tool with the Command key to delete the center area from the selection that you have loaded. You should now have a mask that selects these areas that are too dark and too green. You will want the edge of this selection that is along the roof tops to have the same feather as the mask you used to previously combine the two versions of this image. You will want the edge of this selection that is in the courtyard and on the buildings to have a much larger feather so the color and darkness changes will blend over a larger area. Do Selection/Save Selection on this new selection and name it GreenChange. Use the Channels palette to see this new selection channel by clicking on it. Circle the area where you want a

STEP 15: This is the mask to remove green and lighten the buildings and courtyard as selected using the Lasso tool. Below is the same mask after applying a Gaussian blur of 25 to the center portion. This acts like a feather to blend the changes.

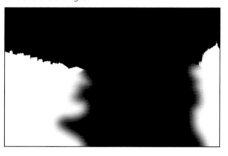

larger feather using the Lasso tool again with its feather set to about 4. You need a feather on the Lasso tool so there is a smooth transition between the sharp edge of the building tops and the soon to be heavily blurred area in the middle. Use the Gaussian Blur filter to experiment with the blur (which will become a feather after the selection is loaded) until it looks like it will give you a seamless change. Using Gaussian blur to create a feather within a mask channel has the advantage that you can see the feather while it is happening. You can compare your masks with the authors' by opening the file called 4.VersaiMerged in the Extra Info Folder.

STEP 16: Now Option-click on it to do a Load Selection on this Green-Change channel then move back to channel 0 (RGB) in the Channels palette (Command-0). With Levels you can now lighten this area by moving the middle slider to the left to about 1.13, while in RGB, and you can remove the green tinge by moving the Input Shadow slider to the right to about 3 while in the Green channel. This will subtract green and thus add magenta to the shadow parts of the GreenChange selection. I also found that things were improved if I moved the Output Shadow slider to 3 in the Red channel and the Output Shadow slider to 4 in the Blue channel. This will add red and blue to the shadow areas of this selection. This is a difficult area to correct so it is useful to zoom into the lower lefthand corner of the image while you are working on this. The numbers I have given you here will get you close, but the numbers you use will depend on how you color corrected your images and also upon your opinion about what looks better to you. When you think you have it right, hit the save button in Levels to save your settings and then click on OK.

Now you should zoom out so you can see the entire image and then toggle between Undo and Redo of this change by using Command-Z. If you made a good correction, you should see a significant improvement in the selected area of the image. If you are not happy, undo the change and try again by reloading your previous change with the Load button in Levels, and then modifying it.

STEP 17: The improvement in Step 16 fixed most of the green tinge but there was still some green in the deepest shadows. To fix this, I used the curve at the left and only changed the Green channel. This curve just adds some magenta to the darkest shadow areas. To create this curve, first load the Lock-DownCurve from the Curves tool. As explained in the color correction chapters, this curve allows you to easily isolate specific parts of the color and brightness range. While

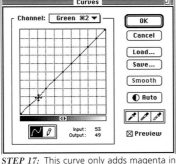

STEP 17: This curve only adds magenta in the very dark shadows.

in Curves, you now use the Eyedropper to measure the green shadow area area by holding down the mouse over that area. A small circle will show on the curve at the location that will affect that area of the curve. You can then create a curve, like the one here, that will only do a color change within the small range that you need.

SHARPENING AND SPOTTING

STEP 18: Do a Load Selection of the channel you called Border. Choose Inverse from the Selection menu to select everything except for the border. Now do Filter/Sharpen/Unsharp Mask of 150, 1.5, 8 to finalize this image. We didn't sharpen the edge along the border since we don't want

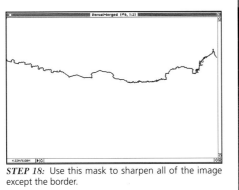

STEP 18: Use this mask to sharpen all of the image except the border.

to emphasize any imperfections that might be there from previously merging the two images. The Gaussian blur and Unsharp Mask have to be done after the Merge Layers for their effects to be properly seen along the edge of the selection.

STEP 19: Zoom into the image until it's 1 to 1 or closer. Double-clicking on the Zoom tool will automatically zoom the image to 1 to 1. Use the Rubber Stamp tool with a small brush to clone out any dust spots. It is best to do this after sharpening since sharpening can enhance dust spots that were previously not visible. Save this image in Photoshop 3.0 format along with its mask channels since we will use it in the next steps to create different looking versions of Versailles.

USING LAYERS TO APPLY FILTERS

By scanning, combining, color correcting and sharpening, we've created a great straight photograph that we could use as our final image. To

STEP 19: The Versailles image after removing the green tinge and lightening the edges and using the Rubber Stamp tool to remove any spots or blemishes. This version of the image was also sharpened using the Unsharp Mask filter with the 150, 1.5, 8 settings for basic sharpening.

149

STEP 25: Double-click on your new layer and rename it UM500,10,0. We are going to apply the Unsharp Mask filter to this layer and use it as a special effect. Click on this new layer so only it is active.

STEP 26: Choose Unsharp Mask from the Filters/Sharpen menu and set the parameters to 500 for the Amount, 10 for the Radius and 0 for the Threshold. Click on OK to run the filter on this layer. This gives the photo a dramatic effect, but we may not want this effect to be completely applied.

STEP 27: Now you have two copies of the final image with filters applied to them. The background final image and these new mask/filter layers can now be combined to produce a variety of effects.

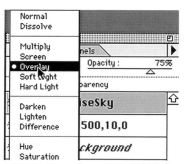

STEP 28: What we want to do now is apply the mask/filter layers at different opacities and using different composite modes until we get the effect we want. The noise filter was a little bit too grainy so I changed the composite mode to Overlay and changed the opacity to 75%. Since I had applied this layer using a mask of only the sky area, these changes only affect the sky.

STEP 28: Change the mode on the NoiseSky layer to Overlay and set the opacity to 75%.

STEP 29: The Unsharp Mask filter of 500,10,0 produced a dramatic effect but what I wanted to do was use this effect to slightly dramatize the image still leaving it in a more natural state. To do this, I selected the UM500,10,0 layer and set its opacity to 25%.

STEP 29: Change the opacity on the UM500,10,0 layer to 25%.

STEP 30: You can also turn on or off a particular layer completely by turning on or off the Eye icon for that layer. This allows you to see what the image looks like with or without a particular layer applied. It also allows you to look at just one layer. Try turning off or on particular layers and see how this affects your final image. Try changing the opacity of different layers and also changing the composite modes.

create a photo with a more surrealistic look, see the following steps which give you some ideas of how to use layers to enhance an image by applying filters with different opacities and blend modes.

STEP 20: Start with the final Versailles image from Step 19 of this chapter.

STEP 21: Do a Load Selection of the SoftEdgeEdited mask that separated the sky from the buildings. You can do this most quickly by Option-clicking on the the SoftEdgeEdited channel in the Channels palette.

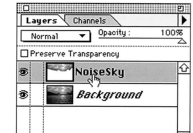

STEP 22: Choose Select/Inverse to invert the selection to the sky. Now copy the sky of the background layer. Follow this by a Paste Layer from the Edit menu. Name this layer NoiseSky by typing in the new name as part of the Paste Layer process. You will notice that since you did a Load Selection before the copy that only the sky was copied, and when you operate on this layer, only the sky area will be changed. Choose Select None from the Select menu and then click on the Eye icon of the background layer to turn off viewing of that layer. Make sure the NoiseSky layer is activated; it will be grayed in the Layers palette when it is active.

STEP 22: Make sure only NoiseSky is active. It will be highlighted in Layers when it is activated.

STEP 23: Choose the Add Noise filter from the Filter/Noise menu and choose Gaussian noise with an amount of 25. This will add a grainy appearance to the sky since the NoiseSky layer is active.

STEP 24: Activate the background layer again by clicking on it. Drag this background layer to the New Layer icon at the bottom of the Layers palette. This will make a copy of this layer called Background Copy.

STEP 24: To copy the background layer, drag it to the New Layer icon at the bottom of the Layers palette.

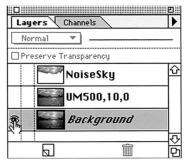

STEP 30: To just look at the background layer, Option-click on the Eye icon for that layer.

STEP 30: To look at the background layer with the Unsharp Mask layer applied at 25% on top, turn on the Eye icons of both layers.

STEP 32: The order of these layers that produced the final image here.

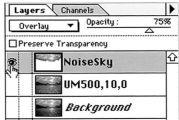

STEP 30: To look at the NoiseSky layer only, option-click on its Eye icon.

STEP 30: The NoiseSky layer by itself only shows you the sky since the foreground was not copied when this layer was originally created.

STEP 31: Besides changing the opacity and composite mode of your layers, you can also change the order of the layers. By applying the filters in different orders, the appearance of the final effect can be changed. To change the order of a layer, just click on the layer that you want to move and move it to its new location. When the line between the two layers you are moving it to becomes black, then you can drop your layer between the other two.

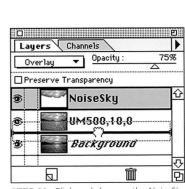

STEP 31: Click and drag on the NoiseSky layer to move it to the middle. When you see the line between layers turn black, that is when you let go.

STEP 32: I tried both orders for the NoiseSky and UM500,10,0 layers. This is the order for these layers that produced the final composite image.

The final version of this image along with the filter effects was produced by using three layers. The original background layer was the image from the first part of this example after we removed the green tinge and ran Unsharp Mask for basic sharpening. We then made a layer to add 75% of the noise filter to the sky using the Overlay Composite mode. The third and final layer adds 25% of the Unsharp Mask 500, 10, 0 to the entire image area. This makes the image more dramatic without taking away all the image detail that 100% of Unsharp Mask would have removed.

HANDS-ON SESSION: BRYCE STONE WOMAN

Advanced Color Correction Using
Threshold and Layers to Combine
Two Different Versions of a Nature Scene
to Get the Best Color.

The original Bryce Stone Woman scan is very dull, we will use some interesting techniques to greatly improve it.

This is one of my favorite photos. Color correcting with Layers, like I did here, is a technique that you may not have thought of for using Layers. Try it!

152

OVERALL COLOR CORRECTION WITH LEVELS

STEP 1: Open the BryceOriginal image from the BryceStoneWoman folder and crop out any black or white borders. Use Command-L for Levels and take a look at the histograms. All of them are short for this image, i.e. there is not a wide range of values from the brightest white to the darkest black. Looking at the Red, Green and Blue histograms separately, each one is a little different. In this image I tried to find a good white and black point for the Highlight and Shadow eyedroppers, but was not very happy with the results. Instead, I went into each of the color channels and brought the end points in so they would cause a full spread of detail without losing any important information. After this, the highlights seemed a little too bright

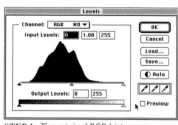

STEP 1: The original RGB histogram.

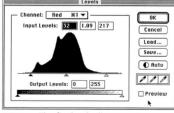

STEP 1: The final red adjustments.

STEP 1: The final green adjustments.

STEP 1: The final blue adjustments.

in the clouds in the top right corner so I backed each highlight value off by 10 points. It is still important to make sure that your blacks are black and your whites are white, so I used the Option-drag technique, described in the Grand Canyon chapter, to find a highlight and shadow and then checked the color balance of these using the Picker palette. Actually they were pretty good based on just initially moving the end points in. I then went back to the RGB channel and adjusted the overall brightness and contrast to bring out more detail in the green trees at top on the left side. Go into each of the Red, Green and Blue channels to adjust the color balance. The most important area to adjust for here is the red rocks since this is the largest area. Here are my final Levels settings for this initial adjustment. If you need more help with overall color correction, review the Grand Canyon and Kansas chapters as well as their Final Tweaks versions.

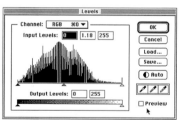

STEP 1: The final RGB histogram. Notice how the values are much more spread out. There is a small spike at the highlight end that indicates that we lost some highlight values to pure white. These are small areas in the clouds to the upper left and the bright white rock at the bottom right, and we decided that looked fine in this image. You can use the Load button to load this from Extra Info files, called InitialLevelsAdj.

STEP 2: The Bryce Stone Woman after Levels, Hue and Saturation then the 2nd incantation of Levels, called LevAdj2 in Extra Info.

STEP 2: After clicking on the OK button in Levels, use File/Save As to save this version as BryceAfterLevels. We may want to use it again later. Now go to Image/Adjust/Hue/Saturation (Command-U) and increase overall saturation of your colors by about 25%. Now click on the Red radio button and move the reds toward magenta by about 10%. Finally, click on the Yellow radio button and move the yellows towards red by 5%. Now the image looks very saturated but the highlights have become a little dull. Go back into Levels a second time and move the RGB Input Highlight slider to the left to about 231. This will brighten up the highlight areas and emphasize the places where the sun is shining on the rocks. I also moved the Input Brightness/Contrast slider to the right to .93 to darken the midtones a bit. I know this breaks the rule of only using Levels once and getting it right the first time, but occasionally, rules are made to be broken. The main thing we need to watch out for is that the final quality is excellent. Do another File/Saves As and save this as BryceAfterL,HS&Lev2.

LAYERS TO BRING OUT DETAILS

STEP 3: Leave this file open, reopen BryceAfterLevels and arrange both windows so you can see them. Switch to BryceAfterL,HS&Lev2 to make it the active window. Using the Move tool, click on BryceAfterL,HS&Lev2, then drag and drop it as a new layer on top of BryceAfterLevels. Save this as BryceLayers and close the other file. You now have the two versions of this image in registration on top of each other. The bottom layer is the less

bright version after just the first incantation of Levels. The top layer is the version you just finished in Step 2. This version has some very bright areas in the clouds at the top left corner and also in the greenish rock to the right of the stone woman.

You may want to tone down these areas somewhat. Add a layer mask to this layer using the Layers palette pop-up. The layer mask should now show the black outline around it indicating you are painting in the layer mask but seeing the layer. Use the Paintbrush with a fairly large brush, about 30-40 pixels, and paint with black at 50% opacity into the layer mask over the bright areas in the clouds . This will allow some of the detail from the underlying layer to show through. Also paint with 50% black into the layer mask to bring a little detail back from the underlying layer in the area of the white rock to the right of the stone woman. Now do a Flatten Image from the Layers palette pop-up to integrate these changes into one layer. If you didn't get enough detail from the underlying layer in the bright clouds area, you might want to now use the Rubber Stamp tool to clone some more detail from other parts of the clouds, at a lower opacity, into the brightest areas of these clouds. I found that parts of the rock to the right of the stone woman, and also the bright clouds in the upper lefthand corner also had a green tinge to them. You can select these areas then use the Curves tool with the LockDownCurve to remove this green tinge. For a review of using the LockDownCurve, see the Grand Canyon—Final Tweaks and Kansas—Final Tweaks chapters.

LAYERS AND MASKS TO TWEAK GREENS

STEP 4: Click on the background layer in the Layers palette and make a copy of it by dragging it to the Copy icon at the bottom left of the palette. Double-click on the background layer and name it Green. Double-click on the top layer and name it Red. Since we originally color corrected this image so the red rocks would look the best, we are now going to adjust the Green layer so the green colors in the trees and bushes look the best. Then we will make a mask to bring these two colored layers together and get the best of both in the final print. Turn the Eye icon off on the top Red layer. Click on the Green layer to make it the active layer; it should be highlighted in the Layers palette. Go back into Levels and adjust this layer so the green trees at the top left look really natural. I adjusted

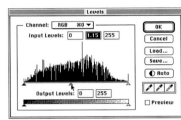

STEP 4: The RGB adjustments for green.

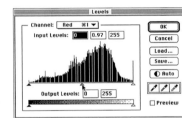

STEP 4: The Red channel adjustments.

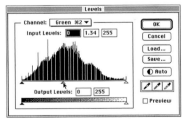

STEP 4: The Green channel adjustments.

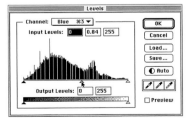

STEP 4: The Blue channel adjustments.

STEP 5: The Bryce Stone Woman after using the Paintbrush and the Red layer mask to bring out the green values from the Green layer underneath.

154

MASKING BY HAND

STEP 5: Turn the Eye icon back on for the Red layer and click on the Red layer to make it active. Use the Layers pop-up menu to add a layer mask to the Red layer. The layer mask will have a dark outline around it but the Eye icons in the Channels palette will be on for the RGB channels. You are now in the mode where you are seeing the Red layer but editing the layer mask. Type a D to get the default colors. Now use the Paintbrush to paint with black in the mask over the green trees and you will see the colors from the Green layer appear where you paint. Wherever the mask is black, you are seeing the Green layer below. Where the mask is white you are seeing the Red layer on

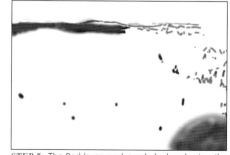

STEP 5: The Red layer mask made by hand using the Paintbrush tool.

top. While painting, you can switch between painting in white or black by typing an X. You can change the opacity of the brush by typing a number (0 is 100% opacity, 2 is 20%, 5 is 50%, etc.). If you paint black at 50% opacity, you are seeing exactly 50% of each layer, so you are blending them together. If that is not quite green enough, type a 2 for 20%, paint over that area again, and you will get 20% more of the Green layer. If that is too much green, type a 1 for 10%, type X to exchange the color to white, and then add 10% of the red back in.

only the Brightness/Contrast slider in each channel. In the RGB channel, I moved it to the left to bring out more detail in the trees. In the Red channel, I added a little cyan. In the Green channel, I added a lot of green, and finally, I added some yellow in the Blue channel. Here are the Levels changes I made to enhance the greens. They are in the Extra Info folder called Green-LayerLevels. Notice now that all the green plant areas of this layer look more natural. We will now combine them with the other parts of the Red layer.

Layer masks are very powerful tools for combining two layers. Also, while you are painting, you can change the size of the brush by typing with the right and left bracket symbols, [and]. The right bracket will move you to the next bigger brush and the left bracket to the next smaller brush. If your General Preference Painting Tools is set to Brush Size, then you can change the brush size as the brush is sitting over the area you want to paint. You'll see when you've reached the right size. If you are not clear how this two-layer thing works, click on the Eye icon for the Green layer to turn off that layer. Now you should see that the areas where the Red layer mask is black cause the Red layer to be transparent. That is why you see the green version in those areas when the Green layer's Eye icon is on.

When you are happy with your mask and image, bring up the Channels palette and make a copy of the Red layer mask by clicking and dragging it to the New Channel icon in the center at the bottom of the Channels palette. We are going to replace this mask in the next step, so we saved this one now in case we like it better. Do a File/Save on this version of the Bryce Layers document. We will now show you how to automatically create a mask for the green areas using threshold.

MASKING WITH THRESHOLD

STEP 6: Click on the Green layer and make sure the Eye icon is off for the Red layer. In the Channels palette, click on and compare the Red, Green and Blue channels of the Green layer and look for the channel that has the most contrast between the green parts of the image, where the trees are, and the rest of the image. The Red channel should be the obvious choice. Make a copy of the Red channel by clicking and dragging it to the New

STEPS 5 AND 6: The Layers and Channels setups you need for painting in the Red layer mask while seeing the composite of the Red and Green layers.

Channel icon at the bottom of the Channels palette. Double-click on this copy and rename it Threshold Mask.

Choose Image/Map/Threshold and adjust the Threshold slider until the areas of the trees and bushes are black and the rest of the mask is white. You want the Preview button off so you can click on the title bar of Threshold to see the Red channel before and after your slider adjustment. This will help you to see exactly where the trees and bushes are and more accurately gauge the border between them and the rest of the image. I ended up setting my Threshold slider to about 81. Now use Filter/Blur/Gaussian Blur to put about a 1.5 pixel Gaussian blur on this mask. That will soften the transitions between the areas of color. Option-click on the Red Layer Mask icon in the Layers palette to select that as the active channel. Now choose Image/Apply Image and this layer mask should be the Target. Set the Source channel to the Threshold Mask, set the blending

STEP 6: The original Threshold mask after the Gaussian blur of 1.5.

STEP 6: The final Red layer mask after Paintbrush edits are added to the above Threshold mask.

mode to Normal and the opacity to 100%. This will replace the layer mask you created by hand with this new Threshold version. After choosing OK from Apply Image, Option-click on the Red layer, not the layer mask, and you will see the composite with this new Threshold mask in place. It will probably do a better job than the hand painted mask in bringing the green up in all the small bushes, but you will have to modify it a bit in the big bush at the lower right and also remove some green in the background mountains that should be more bluish. Go back to the Paintbrush tool, click on the Layer Mask icon and use the same techniques you learned in step 5 to add black to the mask, to add more green, and white, which takes green away. I often use a final mask that is a combination of a Threshold mask and hand editing. Do another Save on your BryceLayers document.

FLATTENING THE IMAGE INTO A SINGLE LAYER

STEP 7: Now you need to Flatten your image into a single layer to do the final sharpening and conversion to CMYK. Choose Flatten Image from the Layer palette pop-up. Use File/Save As to save this under a different name like BryceFinalRGB. This way you won't accidentally overwrite your layered version in case you want to go back to it later. Choose Filter/Sharpen/Unsharp Mask to sharpen this image. Use the techniques described in the Kansas—Final Tweaks chapter to decide what settings are best for Unsharp Mask. I used 150, 1.0 and 8. Choose Command-S to save this final RGB version and do a Mode/CMYK to convert the image to CMYK. I found that this image did not change color much when converting to CMYK, so I did not tweak the CMYK version of the colors using Selective Color. If you do get a color shift after converting to CMYK, use Selective Color to adjust certain colors using the techniques explained in the Yellow Flowers and Color Matching Cars chapters.

The final CMYK, sharpened Bryce Stone Woman. The greens were a bit too intense so I went into Levels on the Red Layer Mask and moved the Output Shadow slider to 40. This lightened the blacks in the mask causing less than 100% of the green Layer to be used.

HANDS-ON SESSION: The Band

Create a Composite of the Band, Only Human,

from Non-Matching Original Files

Using Channels, Layers and Graduated Masks;

Color Correct and Adjust these Images

to Match as Closely as Possible

When you are compositing photographs together, you need to either color correct each of them separately before you composite them, or, if they are similar in color, you can combine them first and then color correct the final image as one. The Layers feature in Photoshop 3.0 will allow us to combine the images first and still color correct each of them separately after they are composited. This will allow us to do the color corrections while we are looking at how the images are combining. To do this example, you will be using the Photoshop 3.0 Tool palette, the Channels and Layers palettes, the Info palette and sometimes the Color Picker. Refer to the Navigating chapter to learn the most efficient ways to use these windows and the Setting System and Photoshop Preferences chapter to see how to set up Command keys to open and close them. You will also be using the Levels and Curves tools and should have already gone through the Grand Canyon chapter, which explains their basic functionality.

SETTING THINGS UP

STEP 1: Open the files Johnny, Chris and Beth from the folder The Band. Place them in order with Johnny on the left, Chris in the middle and Beth on the right. This is the order we will composite the photos together.

STEP 2: Click on Chris to make him the active window, and then go to Image/Canvas Size in the Image menu to change the

STEP 2: Chris will be in the center.

width of Chris to be 3 times the original width. We will be placing Johnny at Chris' left and Beth at Chris' right, so keep the gray area in the middle of the grid, which will add the extra white space evenly to either side of Chris. Just triple the value in the width field and click on OK. Now save this version of Chris in Photoshop 3.0 format and call it TheBand.

BLENDING JOHNNY INTO CHRIS

STEP 3: Use the Rectangular Marquee tool to select the right ⅓ or so of Johnny. We are using the selections here as a template for the area of Johnny that we are going to blend out. It is easier to make selections that go up to the edge of the image if you either put the image in Full Screen mode, by clicking on the middle icon at the bottom of the Tool palette or by making the window bigger than the image using the grow box. Both of these things will add gray space around the edge of the image area allowing you to start or end selections outside the image without the cursor getting confused about being in a scroll bar, the title bar or even another application. After selecting the right ⅓ of Johnny, click on the Selection icon at the bottom left of the Channels palette to save this selection as Channel #4. Choose Select/None from the Select menu and then click on Channel #4 in the Channels palette.

STEP 3: Select the right ⅓ of Johnny.

STEP 4: Click on the Black/White Default Colors icon or type D to force the foreground color to black and the background color to white.

STEP 5: Double-click on the Gradient Blend tool and make sure that it is set to a Linear blend with a midpoint at 50%. Use the tool while

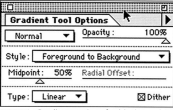

STEP 5: Gradient settings for black to white blend.

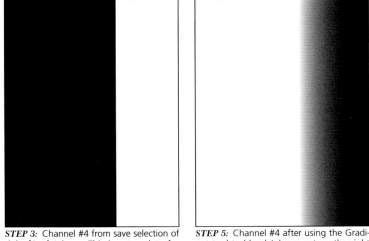

STEP 3: Channel #4 from save selection of right ⅓ of Johnny. This is a template for where the gradient blend will be.

STEP 5: Channel #4 after using the Gradient tool to blend Johnny out on the right side.

holding down the Shift key to create a blend from black to white starting on the right edge of the image area and moving left towards the inside. The shift key will constrain the blend to horizontal. You should let go of the tool when you reach the edge of the white space that was left by the selection. Most of the channel will now be white with a small area blended from white to black on the right hand side. This is the area where Johnny and Chris will blend together.

STEP 6: Do a load selection of Channel #4 by Option-clicking on it. Click on Channel #0 in the Channels palette to return to RGB viewing. Choose Edit/Copy to copy Johnny to the copy buffer.

STEP 7: Switch to the image of Chris, in TheBand, and do an Edit/Paste Layer, and name the new layer Johnny. You have now created a layer of Johnny on top of the layer of Chris. Use the Move tool and drag Johnny to the left until you notice a white halo area between Johnny and Chris. This is where Johnny has started to blend away and Chris is not below him. Move Johnny back to the right until the halo is completely gone and the two images have blended together smoothly. If you find that you are having trouble making subtle movements with the mouse, you can use the Arrow keys to move your selection one pixel at a time. We'll color correct Johnny after we add Beth to the image.

BLENDING BETH INTO CHRIS

STEP 8: Switch to the image of Beth and use the Rectangular Marquee tool to select the left ⅓ or so of the file. Again, you want to select the part of Beth that you are willing to blend out. Now click on the Selection icon at the bottom left of the Channels palette to save this selection as Channel #4 of Beth. Choose Select/None from the Select menu and click on Channel #4 in the Channels palette.

STEP 9: Click on the Black/White Default Colors icon or type D to force the foreground color to black and the background color to white. Use the Gradient tool again while holding down the Shift key to create a blend from black to white starting on the left edge of the image and moving right towards the inside. You should let go of the tool when you reach the edge of the white space. Most of the channel will now be white with a small area blended from white to black. This is the area where Beth and Chris will blend together.

STEP 10: Do a Load Selection of Channel #4 by Option-clicking on it. Click on Channel #0 in the Channels palette to return to RGB viewing. Choose Edit/Copy to copy Beth to the copy buffer.

STEP 11: Switch to the image of Chris and Johnny in TheBand. Click on the Background layer, to make it active, then do Edit/Paste Layer, naming this layer Beth. You have now created a layer of Beth between the Layers of Johnny and Chris. Use the Move tool and drag Beth to the right until you notice a white halo area to the left of Beth. Move Beth back to the left until the halo is completely gone and the two images have blended together smoothly.

There are several ways to create gradient mask channels and layers in Photoshop. A gradient mask can be created while viewing the image by adjusting the Eye icons in the Channels palette. Layers can be dragged and dropped instead of copied and pasted. These techniques were chosen here because they have proven to be less error prone in a classroom situation.

STEP 8: Beth with the area to be blended selected.

STEP 9: Final version of Beth's mask selecting the area to the right.

STEP 13: Adding a layer mask to Beth's layer.

STEP 14: With Beth's layer mask activated, edits will change only the mask, which will add or subtract things to the appearance of Beth's layer without actually changing her layer. Since the Eye icons are selected on all the layers and all the channels, you will see everything while this is happening. Only the activated (grayed) channel is actually changed.

REMOVING PICTURE ELEMENTS

STEP 12: Click on the Rectangular Marquee tool and frame the three images without any of the white borders. Choose Edit/Crop to crop the image so you just see the band. Double-click on the Background layer in the Layers palette and rename it Chris. You now have the three images blended together and cropped in their final size. Do a File/Save As at this point and name this TheBand.1. Now you can revert to this version of the image if you are not happy with the following changes.

STEP 13: At this point we have a problem with Beth's image since the amplifier covers up Chris' arm and cymbal. Click on the righthand column of Beth's layer in the Layers palette. This allows you to work on Beth's layer without changing Johnny or Chris. If you click on the Eye icon of Beth's layer it will turn off and you will see that Chris' layer is black below where the amplifier is added by Beth. If we could just remove the area of Beth's image where the amplifier is and see Chris' image in its place, that would solve our problem. To do this, we will use a layer mask. Click on the Eye icon of Beth again to make her layer visible. Her layer should also be the active layer, the one that is grayed. Choose Add Layer Mask from the Layer Options menu. The layer mask will appear to the right of Beth's layer icon. Arrange things on your monitor so you can see all of the Layers palette and the Channels palette at the same time. Depending on the selection in the Layers palette, it is important that you understand which channel(s) are actually being edited versus the channels that are being viewed. Only the edited channels can be changed.

STEP 14: Anything that is black in the layer mask will make the corresponding part of Beth's layer not show. Click on Beth's layer mask and this will allow us to edit only that mask even though we are still viewing all the layers together. Use the Paintbrush tool with 100% opacity and a large brush to paint over the amplifier with black as the foreground color. As you paint, the painted

STEP 14: Option-click on the layer mask to see it by itself.

STEP 14: The amplifier before it is removed by the layer mask or with the layer mask not applied.

STEP 14: The amplifier after it has been removed by the layer mask.

parts of Beth's layer will disappear and Chris' layer will show through from below. Paint over the amplifier and also over Chris' shirt and arm in the area where Beth's black background overlapped Chris. Now type a 5 to set the brush to 50% opacity and use this to blend in the two backgrounds above where the amplifier used to be. As you move farther away from the amplifier you may want to use only 30% opacity, type a 3. Blend the two images around the edges of the area you removed. Now Option-click on the layer mask and you can view the mask alone without the layers. Notice how the black and gray areas in the mask are causing the two layers to blend.

STEP 15: Option-click back on Beth's layer icon and this will allow you to edit the layer with the mask applied. Notice that all three RGB channels are now highlighted (active, grayed) in the Channels palette. This shows you that if you edit anything, these channels, within Beth's layer, are the things that will be changed by the editing. You will still see all the channels and layers that have their Eye icons turned on.

STEP 16: If you Command-click on the layer mask, a red X is drawn through it and it is no longer applied to Beth's layer. This would allow you to show a client or art director the image with

STEP 15: With Beth's layer activated, edits will change the actual contents of Beth's layer; only the highlighted (grayed) channels. Since the Eye icons are selected on all the layers and all the channels, you will see everything while this is happening.

or without the amplifier and decide which version they like better. If you are not sure if you want to remove an element, just use a layer mask to remove it, then you can decide later whether to make the removal permanent. Now you should Command-click on this layer mask again to reapply it.

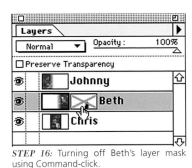

STEP 16: Turning off Beth's layer mask using Command-click.

COLOR CORRECTING THE IMAGE

STEP 17: Notice that the coloration on Johnny is much redder than that of Chris or Beth. He was standing under a red light when photographed. Since he is so different, we should color correct him to make him look closer to the others before proceeding with overall color correction. All these photos were taken without flash using ASA 1600 film. Click on the right column of Johnny's layer making it active (gray) and allowing us to edit this layer while still seeing the others. Click in the righthand column in the Channels palette of each of the channels: Red (Command-1), Green (Command-2), and Blue (Command-3). You will notice that the Red channel of Johnny has lots of detail but the Green and Blue channels have very little detail especially when compared with those channels of Beth and Chris. This is why Johnny looks so red and so flat. Since Johnny doesn't have detail in the Green and Blue channels, we will first have to add some detail there to be able to color correct him in the normal way using Levels or Curves.

STEP 18: We are going to modify the channels of Johnny to make them look more like the channels of Chris and Beth. Click on the Johnny layer to make sure it is the active layer. Choose Red (Command-1) from the Channels palette. Use the Image/Adjust/Brightness/Contrast slider and move the contrast to the left to about -7 and the brightness to the right to about +12 to make the Red channel of Johnny have similar brightness and contrast to the Red channels of Chris and Beth. You want the Preview button on so you can see the changes made to Johnny without any screen changes happening to Chris and Beth. Click on OK in the Brightness/Contrast tool. Type a D to get the default colors. Choose RGB, Command-0, from the Channels palette to select the Red, Green and Blue channels of Johnny. Choose Select/All, Command-A, from the Select menu, followed by Edit/Stroke and stroke the border with a 100% opacity, normal stroke of 2 pixels on the inside of the selection. This will draw a black two pixel border around the

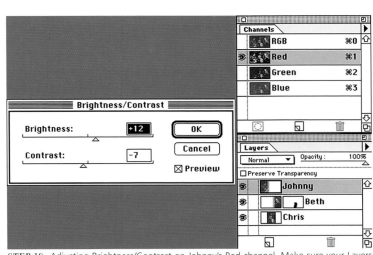

STEP 18: Adjusting Brightness/Contrast on Johnny's Red channel. Make sure your Layers and Channels palettes look like this.

entire image. Now choose the Red channel of Johnny again (Command-1) and do a Select/All followed by Edit/Copy to make a copy of the Red channel of Johnny. The black border needed to be drawn to remove transparency from the outside of the channel, so when we paste this channel on top of the Green channel, it goes down in exactly the same place.

STEP 19: Switch the Channels palette to the Green channel (Command-2). Paste Johnny's Red channel on top of Johnny's Green channel. In the Layers palette, change the opacity of the floating selection (Johnny's old Red channel) to somewhere around 52 percent. Change the opacity until Johnny's Green channel looks like and blends well with Chris and Beth's. Look at the tone and brightness of Johnny's face and also make sure the backgrounds look similar as they blend together.

STEP 20: Switch to the Blue channel (Command-3) and notice that the

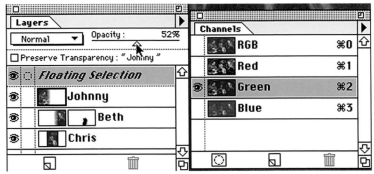

STEP 19: Change the opacity of the floating selection to about 52 percent.

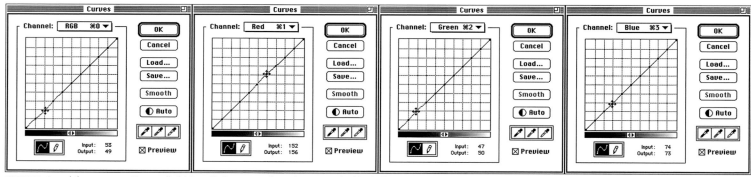

STEP 21: I used these curve settings, called JohnnyFixCurve, to adjust Johnny to make him look more like Beth and Chris. These settings are in the Extra Info Files folder for this chapter on the CD. Your changes may be different if you used different Brightness/Contrast and opacities on Johnny.

selection got dropped and made permanent. Now paste the Red channel on top of the Blue channel and adjust the opacity to make Johnny's blue look like the Blue channel of Chris and Beth. Set it to somewhere around 18.

STEP 21: Using the Channels palette again, switch back to the RGB channel (Command-0). Now Johnny should look much closer to Chris and Beth than when we started. Johnny is never going to look as good colorwise as Chris and Beth since we are making most of his color from the Red channel. Don't try to be a perfectionist here, just get them close and understand the process for future corrections of your own. Now use the Rectangular Marquee tool to crop the 2 pixel black border from around the image. Make a selection just inside this border and choose Edit/Crop. Now that there is color information in each of Johnny's channels, you can use the other color correction tools to make him seem even closer in color to Chris and Beth.

At this point, I used the Curves settings here, which improved Johnny considerably.

I started the Curve adjustments by entering Curves, Command-M, then using the Load button to load the LockDownCurve. This curve allows you to measure specific areas in the image using the Eyedropper, then make a subtle adjustment to just that area. For more information on using Curves and the LockDownCurve, refer to the Grand Canyon—Final Tweaks and Kansas—Final Tweaks

chapters. The change made in the RGB curve was to darken the background of Johnny (measure the top left corner area) to make it match the other images better. The adjustment to the Red channel was to make Johnny's face (measure his face) a little redder. The adjustments to the Green and Blue channels were to remove a purple tone from the background behind Johnny (measure the top left corner area). The adjustments that you make may be different depending on exactly what you did to Johnny when working with the channels.

STEP 22: Once Johnny looks as close as possible to Beth and Chris, you now want to do overall color correction for the entire image. You have the choice here of merging the channels first so there is just one layer and then correcting the image as one unit, or you can correct each image layer separately while looking at the merged image to make sure the corrections match. This second approach gives you more control and demonstrates an advantage of leaving the image in Layers until the last possible minute. Do a File/Save As to save this version as TheBand.2.

TRANSPARENCY AND BACKGROUND

STEP 23: Now you will adjust the overall contrast and color balance of each of the layers using Levels, with the techniques discussed in the Grand Canyon chapter. Click on the Chris layer to make it the active layer. Choose Command-L for Levels and look at the histogram of Chris. Notice the large white spike at 255 on the right. Cancel from Levels and Option-click on the Eye icon for Chris' layer. This will show you his layer without the other layers. Notice that he is surrounded by two large white areas that end up below Beth and Johnny. Option-click on Beth and Johnny's Eye icons and you'll notice that they have a checkerboard pattern in their

TheBand after step 21 and before final overall color correction.

unused areas. The checkerboard pattern means that those areas have no value, they are transparent. If the checkerboard is placed on top of another layer, you can see through it. When you look at a histogram, the checkerboard does not affect that histogram. Let's turn Chris' white area into a checkerboard to get a more accurate histogram of Chris.

STEP 24: Option-click on the Chris layer Eye icon again so you see Chris. Use the Rectangular Marquee tool to exactly select the image area of Chris in the middle. Be careful to include all of Chris' image area and none of the white space. Choose Select/Inverse to invert that selection to all the white space. Hit the Delete key to turn the white space into checkerboard. When you have a layer named "Background", the default name, the Delete key will fill a selected area with the background color. When you rename that layer to another name, you are turning it into a normal layer. From this point on, the Delete key will fill that new area with transparency instead of the background color. Had we renamed Chris' one layer to Chris, instead of Background, in Step 2 before adding the canvas, then the new canvas area would have come in as transparent.

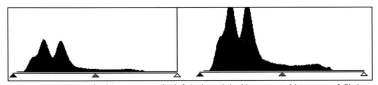

STEPS 24 AND 25: The histogram to the left is the original inaccurate histogram of Chris. To the right we see the improvements after filling the unused areas with checkerboard.

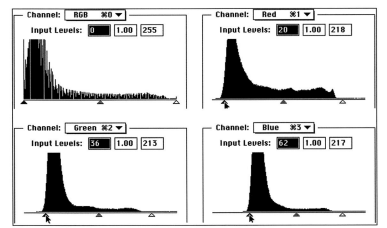

STEP 25: My final Levels color correction settings for Chris. Yours may be different.

STEP 25: Option-click on the Chris layer Eye icon again to see all the layers and choose Command-L. Notice the Levels diagram no longer shows the white area, which really wasn't part of the image we were trying to color correct.

OVERALL COLOR CORRECTION

Now we will do the standard overall color corrections to each of the three layers matching them as we go. Since Chris is in the middle, lets first set the white and black points. Use the Option key, as described in the Grand Canyon chapter to decide where to set the white and black points. I set the white to the brightest place on his shirt using the Highlight Eyedropper and the black by moving the Input Shadow slider on each of the Red, Green and Blue channels to the right until it reached the histogram data for each color. I decided not to use the Shadow Eyedropper to set the black since the blacks in this image are not very consistent. By moving the Shadow Eyedroppers over to where the data starts in each color, you get a definite dark value. You then need to look at and measure the black values on the screen and adjust them so each of Chris, Beth and Johnny have a visually matching black. I actually moved each of Chris' black values over 5 more points to the right. Once the overall white and black are set, adjust the Input Brightness/Contrast slider in RGB mode then go back to the individual channels to correct for color casts. Review the Grand Canyon chapter if you have any questions on overall color correction.

STEP 26: Say OK to the Levels tool for Chris and then click on Beth's layer to color correct it next. Go back into Levels and use the Preview button when you want to see the changes to Beth relative to the rest of the image that will not be changed by this invocation of Levels. I set the white point with the Highlight Eyedropper in RGB on Beth's forehead but not at the absolute brightest spot there. You don't want her whole forehead washed out, but a little bright spot there looks good. Remember, where you set the

STEP 27: Now we need to adjust Johnny to make him look like Chris and Beth. As usual, Johnny will be the hardest image to adjust. Again, you want to switch the layer you are working on to Johnny. Now go into Levels and look for a white and black point. The only white point on Johnny is the reflection in his guitar, and this is pretty much a specular highlight. It is most important to make sure that the lighting on Johnny's face matches Chris and Beth as much as possible. To set the highlight, I moved the Input Highlight sliders for each of the Red, Green and Blue channels over to the left until they were at about 225. This made Johnny's face look the best. I set the shadows on Johnny again by moving the Input Shadow sliders over to the right until the data started and then a little bit more, moving each slider by the same increments. Then it's back to RGB to adjust the Brightness/Contrast slider in the middle and at the same time moving the Input Shadow slider (RGB) to the right to darken the shadows a bit more in all colors. Go back and forth between these two sliders so the shadows and the brightness/contrast looks like the best match with Chris and Beth. Remember to leave the Preview button on. Now go back into the individual color channels and make any color cast adjustments. After saying OK to Levels on Johnny, I made a selection using a 4 pixel feather with the Lasso tool around Johnny's face and then used Curves to make a small contrast and color adjustment just to the face area. Again, this was to better match Johnny to Chris and Beth.

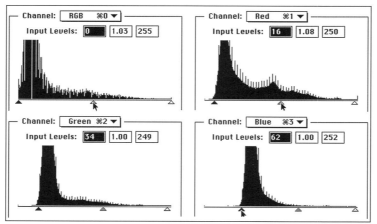

STEP 26: My final Levels color correction settings for Beth. Yours may be different.

white point is the last place where you see detail, and everything brighter than that will be pure white with no dots. If you set it on the absolute brightest spot, there will be no specular highlight and that is not really what you want here. I set the black on Beth in the same way I did on Chris by moving the Input Shadow sliders for each color channel to the right until the data starts. I then adjusted the color balance on Beth to match Chris—his face, lighting and background. After saying OK to Levels, Beth may be improved by using Hue/Saturation to clean up the yellows in her hair. Some of the yellow hair looked green to me, but adding magenta in Levels messed up the rest of the image. Here are the Levels and Hue/Saturation adjustments I did for Beth.

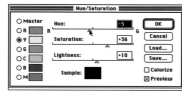

STEP 26: Final Hue/Saturation/Lightness changes for the yellows in Beth.

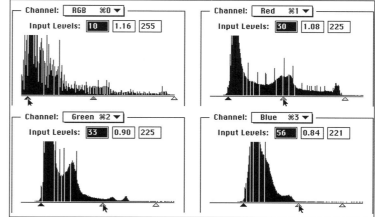

STEP 27: My final Levels color correction settings for Johnny called, JohnnyFinalLevels in the Extra Info Files for this chapter on the CD. Notice how little data there is in the Blue channel here. Your settings for Johnny will probably be different because each of us have already adjusted Johnny in a slightly different way.

MAKING FINAL ADJUSTMENTS

STEP 28: Now you have completed the compositing and color correction steps. Use File/Save As to save a version of this image and call it The-Band.FinalLayers. You can use this version to show your clients the image with or without the amplifier, and you can also use the Move tool to move Johnny and Beth up and down and in closer to Chris. If you want to move Beth and Johnny out farther away from Chris, drag Chris' layer to the New Layer icon at the bottom of the Layers palette. This will make a copy of Chris' layer right above the current one. Select the bottom version of Chris and fill it with Chris' background color. Now, if you move Johnny or Beth outward, instead of the white halo you got before, you just get more of Chris' background and it looks pretty natural.

STEP 29: Before spotting this image, you need to choose Flatten Image from the Layers palette pop-up menu. This will merge everything back into a single document that you can save as a TIFF, EPS or in some other format. Save it under a different name if you want to still be able to play with your layers version. Now that you have just one layer, use the Rubber Stamp tool to remove any scratches or spots or imperfections in the image. There is a hairline scratch from the top to the bottom of the image just to the right of Johnny's face. Beth has a black hole in the corner of her lip and there are various dust spots and lines. These all need to be removed.

STEP 30: Save the final version of the file. You can compare your different versions of this image to the ones of the same name that I created. They are in the Extra Info Files folder.

STEP 30: The final completed version of TheBand.

163

HANDS-ON SESSION: NIGHT CAB RIDE IN MANHATTAN

Learn Most of the Features of Layers as We Show You the Creation of the Image Night Cab Ride in Manhattan

In this example, we will create this final version of Night Cab Ride in Manhattan with its many layers.

In this example we are going to be compositing a lot of different images using the Layers features of Photoshop 3.0. All the images used in this example were taken by Barry during one cab ride from uptown Manhattan down Broadway to the Lower East Side. The film was Kodak Lumiere X and the scans are all Photo CD scans done at Palmer Photographic in Sacramento California. The image of the cab and the New York Convention Center started as a 1024x1536 pixel, Photo CD scan and all the other images started as 512x768 pixel, Photo CD scans. Some of these were resized up to 1024x1536. pixels, which is the final canvas size for this image. Barry wanted most of the neon signs to have sort of a soft effect, so resizing the smaller files up achieved this.

Since this is a long chapter and not really about color correcting, many of the files have been color corrected ahead of time. If you are not sure how to do some of the steps mentioned here, you should refer back to the Introduction to Layers chapter that shows you the basic concepts and functions for working with layers. This chapter is complicated and written more for advanced and/or patient users.

CREATING YOUR BASE IMAGE

STEP 1: Open the Canon file in the Night Cab Ride folder, which is a picture of Times Square where the Canon sign is the most prevalent. This file is already 1536x1024 pixels, which is the final canvas size. Choose Shift-F10, assuming you have ArtistKeys keys installed, to bring up the Layers palette. Double-click on the Background layer and rename it Canon. Now choose New Layer from the Layers palette menu and name the new layer All Black. Click on this new layer and move it to the bottom

of the Layer palette below the Canon layer. Click on the White/Black icon in the tool palette, (or type D) to force the foreground color to black and background color to white. Choose Select/All, (Command-A), to select all of the All Black layer and then Option-Delete to fill this with black. In this example we will be adding various layers of neon using the Lighter and Screen Layer modes and we'll remove parts of some layers, so if we have pure black as the bottom layer, we can be sure to create a pitch black night effect. Choose File/Save As and save this as NightCabRide.

ADDING THE CAB

STEP 2: Open the Cab&Building file and bring up the Channels palette, (F10 with Artist-Keys). You are going to copy just the cab from this file and make it a separate layer. Option-click on the CabMask channel in the Channels palette. This loads the selection that was previously made of just the cab. If you are using the JPEG compressed versions of the images, you

STEP 2: Make sure the Canon layer is activated by clicking on the rightmost column in the Layers palette.

The final Layers window for this image with the Eye icons for the accepted layers on.

will need to open the CabMask file, then switch back to the Cab&Building window and choose Select/Load Selection to get the selection from the separate mask file. Now choose Edit/Copy and then switch windows back to NightCabRide. Make sure the Canon layer is the active one (the gray one) by clicking on the rightmost column in the Layers palette. Choose Edit/Paste Layer and name the new layer Cab. Type V to select the Move tool and move the cab down to the bottom of the screen.

TIMESSQUARE IN SCREEN MODE

STEP 3: Open the TimesSquare file and position it so you can see its window and the window for NightCabRide at the same time. Click with the Move tool on the Background layer of TimesSquare, its only layer, and drag it until you can drop it on top of the document window for NightCabRide. Let go of the mouse button and you will copy TimesSquare as a new layer in NightCabRide. Double-click on this new layer, which was called Layer 1, and rename it TimesSquare. Now change its mode to Screen. The

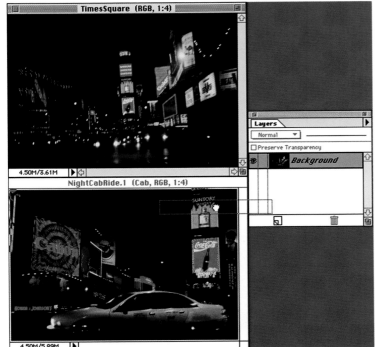

STEP 3: Dragging the TimesSquare layer from its window to a new layer within Night-CabRide. You can drop it when you see the Fist icon.

Screen mode is like projecting this new layer up on a screen using one slide projector with the composite of the previous layers also projected using another projector. This allows the bright parts of Times-Square to show through the previous layers, but the dark parts don't really affect the previous layers. Notice that the headlights in the TimesSquare layer now show through the cab in the Cab layer. To get a better understanding of the composite modes, read the chapter entitled: Blend Modes, Calculations and Apply Image.

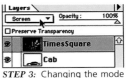

STEP 3: Changing the mode of the TimesSquare layer to Screen.

While TimesSquare is still the selected layer, use the Move tool to move it a little to the left so the headlights shine through the cab in a pleasing location and so the signs from the two Times Square shots line up nicely. Click on the Cab layer to activate it and then set its opacity to about 85%. This will allow more of the TimesSquare layer and also a little of the Canon layer to show through the cab. Use the Move tool to reposition the cab if necessary. Save this on top of the previous NightCabRide using File/Save (Command-S).

STEP 3: Setting the Opacity of the Cab layer to 85%.

WORKING WITH THE BUILDING LAYER

STEP 4: At this point you can close the TimesSquare file, but you are going to use the Cab&Building file again to create another layer. Go back to the Cab&Building file, choose Select/None (Command-D), click on its Background layer and drag it on top of the NightCabRide window to create yet another layer. Double-click on the new layer and name it Building. We are going to scale this layer and use only the New York Convention Center building from it. Notice that

This is how NightCabRide should look after step 3.

the Building layer is now on top and since its mode is Normal and opacity is 100%, we can't see the other layers below it. If you click on its Eye icon, you will turn off viewing of this layer and you will again see the other layers below it. Notice that there is a lot of black sky in the lower layers above the neon signs. We are going to use this building to fill some of that black sky. Leave the Eye icon for the building layer on for now so we can just work on that layer.

STEP 5: Use the Rectangular Marquee to select the part of the Building layer that you want to use as a backdrop in the black sky. Select from just below the cab and just behind the cab up to the top of the image. See the

STEP 4: Leave the Eye icon on for now so we can just work on the Building layer.

STEP 5: Select this part of the Building layer to move and stretch.

STEP 5: The Floating Selection of the stretched building before choosing Command-D.

STEPS 5 & 6: Building layer after first part of stretch, Step 5, with second part of stretch, Step 6, selected.

STEP 6: Here is the stretched image after dropping the floating selection.

suggested selection here. Set the mode for this Layer to Screen and then turn off the Eye icons on all the other layers except for the Cab layer. This will allow you to see the Building layer at the same time as the Cab layer. We are going to use the cab within this selected part to make a ghost image behind the Cab layer.

With the Building layer selected in the Layer palette, click on and move the selected part so the cab in the building Layer is just above and slightly behind the cab in the cab layer. Choose Image/Effects/Scale and you will get the four little handles, small white squares, in the corners of your selected area. Click and drag on the bottom right of these, drag directly right to the edge of the image area and then release. This stretches out the ghost cab and building to make it a little longer. Now click and drag upwards on the top right handle, to make the ghost cab a little bit taller, and then release. Click in the center of the selection when you see the Gavel icon to make this part of the scale permanent. Notice at the end of the Scale command that this selected area now shows up as a floating selection within the Layers window. It is a floating selection on top of the Building layer. Choose Select/None (Command-D) to permanently integrate this floating selection into the Building layer. Now the Building layer will be the selected, grayed, layer.

STEP 6: Turn off the Eye icon on the Cab layer. Make a selection over the entire width of this image starting from just above the top of the cab and ending at the top of the building. We are going to stretch this building until it reaches the top of the image window. Choose Image/Effects/Scale, click on the top right handle and drag it to the top right of the image area and let go. Move the cursor to the middle of the selected area and click when you see the Gavel icon. Now your Building layer should fill most of the screen with the cab towards the bottom. Choose Command-D to drop the floating selection.

STEP 6: The image after Step 6 with all the Eye icons now on.

FIXING THE GHOST CAB

STEP 7: Option-click on the Building layer's Eye icon to turn on the Eye icons for all the lower layers, and you should now see an image that looks like the one above. The building looks good rising up in the sky in the middle although it is a bit too bright. Use the Opacity slider to change the Building layer's opacity to 70%. The ghost image of the cab within this layer is a bit too much. It might look better if we only see the outer part of it. Option-click on the Building layer's Eye icon again so you are just looking at this layer. Double-click on the Lasso tool and make sure it is set to zero pixel feather with Anti-aliased on. Make a selection around the inside of the car within this layer and then click on the Selection icon at the bottom left of the Channels palette to save this selection. When you save the selection to a channel, you can try different feathers on it without loosing your original selection. Click on this new mask channel and copy it by dragging it to the New Channel icon at the bottom middle of the Channels palette.

Choose Command-D (Select/None) and then choose Filter/Blur/Gaussian Blur and blur this by 20. In this type of situation, I like to look at a blurred black-and-white mask channel better than guessing at a selection feather or using Quick Mask mode. You really see the area that the blur is affecting and can better estimate how it will cause your blend to fade. Option-click on the blurred channel to load selection. Now click on the RGB channel, Channel #0, and then press the Delete key, which will remove the center part of the ghost cab causing

STEP 7: While working on Step 7, the Layers palette should look like this with the Building layer active. Here we have set this layer to Screen mode with opacity at 70%. The Eye icons for the other layers may be on or off depending on what you are trying to see.

STEP 7: The transparent part of the ghost cab created by deleting your blurred selection. Once you delete this, you can't put it back.

166

it to be transparent. Now Option-click on the Building layer's Eye icon again and you will see the effect of making the center of the ghost cab transparent. All you see now is the faint edge of the ghost cab. Removing the cab in this way does not allow you to put it back later. Type Command-D to Select None.

LAYER MASKS FOR CLEANUP

STEP 8: The building this layer adds in the middle of the night sky is an interesting addition to this image but some of the layer's other effects tend to confuse the neon signs that are already in the composite. Using a layer mask, we can selectively remove parts of this layer and then put them back again if we don't like their removal. From the Layer palette's menu, with the Building layer active, choose Add Layer Mask. The layer mask comes up to the right of the Building Layer icon in the mode where you are editing the mask. Double click on the Paintbrush tool and make sure the mode is Normal and the opacity set to 100%.

Pick a large 100 pixel brush or make a 200 pixel brush with the hardness set to 0 and the spacing set to 25%. This will paint a large area but with a soft edge. Type D to set the foreground and background colors to black-and-white. Paint on the composite image with black and this will add black to the mask. Wherever the mask is black, those parts of the image will be temporarily removed. Paint with the brush to remove the bright windows on the right side of this layer and also the bright arches on the left side. With

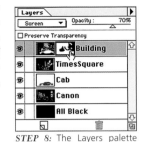

STEP 8: The Layers palette after adding the Building layer mask. The layer mask comes up in the mode where you are editing the mask but seeing the composite image.

STEP 8: Just the Building layer with its layer mask applied.

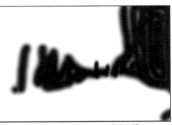

STEP 8: This is the layer mask itself.

STEP 8: Here is the composite image with the Building layer mask applied.

these removed, you will see the neon signs from the other layers better. Be careful not to remove the outline of the cab or the main convention building in the middle of the sky. If you remove something by accident, just type X to switch the foreground and background colors, and you will be painting in the mask with white. Paint with white wherever you want to bring something back. Remember that you can change the size of the brush while painting by using the left and right bracket keys.

To see just this layer while painting the layer mask, Option-click on its Eye icon. To see the layer mask itself while painting, Option-click on the Layer Mask icon to the right of the Layer icon. When you click back on the Layer icon, you will be able to see the layer again and Option-clicking on the Layer icon will actually have you painting in the layer and not in the layer mask. You can temporarily turn off a layer mask by Command-clicking on its icon. This will put a red X through the layer mask and you will again see all of this layer. Command-click again and the layer mask is reapplied. When you want to make a change to a layer and you are not sure you want to keep the change, always use a layer mask. If we would have done step 7 with a layer mask, we could have returned the center of the cab to this layer again. It is usually better to use a layer mask and keep your options open.

STEP 9: Activate the Canon layer and choose Add Layer Mask. Use the Paintbrush again to remove the bright yellow piece of building in the upper left corner of the image. Since we are sure we want this building to be removed, we can now integrate the layer mask back into this layer. Click on the rightmost icon for the layer mask, not the layer, and drag it to the trash. When you do this, you will be asked the question "Apply mask to layer before removing?" If you click on the Apply button, the area that is black in the mask will be turned transparent in that layer. If you click the Discard button, the layer mask is thrown away without affecting your image. In this case we want to choose the Apply button to permanently remove the yellow building from the corner of this layer. It will be replaced by the checkerboard transparent area.

STEP 9: Remove the Yellow building in the Canon Layer.

ADDING SOME NEON

STEP 10: Now that we have completed the major background parts of this image, we will be adding small sections of neon to certain areas. These additions will be done so they can be easily removed and put back to show variations of this image to an art director, boss or whoever you need to please. Open the file called 24 Hours. Use the Lasso tool to select just the Open 24

STEP 10: Use the Lasso to select Open 24 Hours only.

STEP 10: The final modification and location of this Open 24 Hours addition.

White Lights

STEP 11: Lower left corner before Leon's Pizza is added.

STEP 11: Lower left corner after Leon's Pizza is added and the white lights are removed.

Hours sign from this file. The closer you make the selection, the better. Copy this, switch back to NightCabRide and do Edit/Paste Layer. Name the new layer 24 Hours and set its composite mode to Lighten. This will make the neon part of the sign show up without the black area around the sign changing the rest of your composite, since your composite is already black or a value lighter than black. You want the 24 Hours layer to be on top of the Building layer. If the Building Layer was active before you did the Paste Layer, then 24 Hours is in the right place since new layers are created on top of the current active layer. Otherwise, click on the new layer in the Layers palette and drag it to place it on top of the Building Layer.

Use the Move tool to move this new sign to the top left black sky area. Make sure 24 Hours is the active layer in the Layers palette. Use Image/Effects/Scale to stretch the sign horizontally and vertically; you have to make it quite a bit bigger. Go into Levels and move the Input Shadow slider to the right to darken the background of the sign until it is totally black (0, 0, 0 for RGB values). Use the Rubber Stamp tool in Clone Aligned mode to remove any non-black areas around the neon text or to clean up any of the letters that are damaged. I wanted the sign to be more blurry, so I did Filter/Blur/Gaussian Blur of 2 on the entire sign area. I also did a Filter/Blur/Motion Blur of about 14 pixels with the angle set to 8 degrees. This made the text softer still. When you are happy with the size, blur and location of the text, do another save on your NightCabRide file.

STEP 11: Now we will add Leon's Pizza to the lower left corner of this image. Open the Topless/Pizza file and select Leon's Pizza shop with the Lasso tool. Choose Select/Feather to feather your selection by about 5 pixels. Copy this area, switch to Night-CabRide and do another paste layer on top of the 24 Hours layer. Name this layer Pizza and set its mode to Lighten so only its bright neon will show on top of darker places on the previous layer. Use the Move tool to move this into place in the lower left corner of the image.

You may notice the Howard Johnson's sign that blends in from the Canon layer. I think this looks pretty good here but there are also some white lights that blend in from the Times Square layer that I'd like to get rid of. To remove the white lights, select the Times Square layer and add a layer mask to this layer. Now use the Paintbrush and paint with black over the white lights while the layer mask is selected as the paint target. You should be able to paint while looking at the composite until the white lights are gone. Let's say that having these white lights gone or not gone is not an option you want to give to the art director. In this case, drag the Times Square layer mask to the Trash icon at the bottom of the Layers palette and choose the Apply button when the dialog gives you the choice of applying or discarding. If you now look at the Times Square layer by itself, you will see that the area where the white lights were is now transparent.

STEP 12: Before the Topless sign is added.   STEP 12: After the Topless sign is added, rotated and blurred.

STEP 12: Use the same sequence of steps to select the Exotic Show Girls Topless sign from the same Topless/Pizza file and to add that as the Topless layer on top of the Pizza layer. There is no layer mask needed for this step. When you get this sign in place, you can use the Image/Rotate/Free Rotation tool to rotate the sign so it is tilting down slightly. Then you should also do a Gaussian blur of one pixel on this layer to make this sign stand out a little less. Do all of these steps with the Topless Layer selected.

STEP 12: Do all of this with the Topless layer selected.

STEP 13: Open the file XXX and select the neon sign and theater front as shown here. Feather the selection by 8 pixels and then copy it. Do another paste layer on top of the Topless layer, name this one XXX and set the

STEP 13: The selection, feathered by 8 pixels, for the XXX image.

mode to Lighten. Move this sign over to the lower right of the image as shown here. This sign blends in better if you set the opacity to 80% and do a Gaussian blur on this layer of .5 pixels. Remember, you can turn each one of these pieces on and off for the art director, or yourself, by just using the Eye icon

STEP 13: The final Location for XXX.

for its layer. As an artist creating this image, I did this so I wouldn't have to decide until the end which parts I wanted in the final image.

STEP 14: Open the file CoffeeCup and do the same basic process here to select around the cup, feather of 5, copy it, paste layer on top of the XXX layer and name this layer Coffee Cup with the mode set to Lighten. To make the cup look better, you need to go into Levels and darken the shadows considerably. Just move the Input Shadow slider to the right in RGB until the shadows around the cup look close to black. You also need to use the Rubber Stamp tool to replace the part of the cup's neon that is missing in the upper left corner and to do some other cleanup on the cup. It is easier to do all of these things working on the cup with the other layers turned off. To do this, just Option-click on the Coffee Cup layer's Eye icon. When the cup has been cleaned up and darkened, Option-click on its layer's Eye icon again and then move it

STEP 14: The cup before, left, and after the cleanup.

STEP 14: Working with just the Cup layer visible.

into place above the cab's front window. I found that the cup looked best with its opacity set to 90%.

STEP 15: The process for the Late Show image is again the standard select, feather of 5, copy, paste layer, name it Late Show, use Lighten mode, and then move the sign into place within the bigger Cannon sign. The only thing I did to this Late Show layer was a Gaussian blur of 1 pixel to make its sharpness match the surrounding signs. Do a save at this point since this may be your final version of NightCabRide.

STEP 15: Placement of the Late Show in the Canon sign.

PLAYING WITH THE CAB LAYER

Let's say right now you are happy with this image but you know that your boss, art director or whoever passes judgement on your artistic taste is (as always) going to want to modify your image in some way. Once they do this, they are happy. You have learned by now if you put something in the image that is a little bit tacky, something glaring you really want this person to remove, 80% of the time this item can get removed and your art critic's ego issues about having some influence on the project will be satisfied. Do people really do things like this? Anyhow, this process will show you some neat possibilities for using the Clipping Group features of Layers.

STEP 16: Select the Cab layer, then click on the New Layer icon at the bottom left of the Layers palette. The New Layer dialog will come up, and within this dialog you need to name this layer RedCab, set the mode to Color and click on the Group with Previous Layer check box. The new layer should come in right above the Cab layer. You will notice that the line between the two layers is dotted instead of solid and Cab is underlined. This means that the RedCab layer will have the same transparent areas, the same clipping mask, as the Cab layer. Leave this Red-Cab layer as the active layer. Click on the foreground color to bring up the Color Picker and pick a deep bright red as the new foreground color. Choose Select/All (Command-A) and then Edit/Fill. Fill this layer with 100% of this red color with the fill mode set to Normal. After waiting a minute for the screen to

STEP 16: The New Layer setup for the RedCab layer.

STEP 16: The Cab and Red-Cab layers are a clipping group. Notice how the line between them is dotted and the bottom Cab layer is under-lined since it defines the clipping mask for the group.

STEP 16: With the RedCab layer's Eye icon on, the cab looks red.

STEP 18: Details of the striped pattern added to the cab.

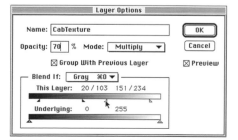

STEP 17: These are the options you want for the Gradient tool.

STEP 17: The RainbowCab layer when viewed by itself.

170

STEP 17: With the RainbowCab layer's Eye icon on, the cab is a rainbow color.

Layer Options

Name: CabTexture

Opacity: 70 % Mode: Multiply

☒ Group With Previous Layer   ☒ Preview

Blend If: Gray ⌘0 ▼

This Layer: 20 / 103 151 / 234

Underlying: 0   255

STEP 18: Final Layer Options for the CabTexture layer.

refresh, you will notice that the car is now painted with a red tint. Since the layer mode was set to Color, only the hue and saturation was changed and the details of the car remain the same. If you turn off the Eye icon for the Red-Cab layer, the cab will return to yellow. Let's play with the cab color some more!

STEP 17: With the RedCab layer still selected, choose New Layer again and call this layer RainbowCab with the mode set to Color. Also check Group with Previous Layer. Turn off the Eye icon for RedCab and make RainbowCab the active layer. Set both the foreground and background colors to the brightest red you can find in the Color Picker. They both need to be set to exactly the same bright red, the exact same numerical values. Double-click on the Gradient tool and set the options to Linear, CounterClock-Wise-Spectrum, Midpoint at 50%. Now create a gradient by clicking on the front of the cab and dragging to the back of the cab. Wait for the screen to refresh and your cab will now be a rainbow color. Since the RainbowCab layer is above, the cab will still be this color even if the Eye icon for the RedCab layer is also on. When you turn the RedCab layer's Eye icon off, it just makes it faster for Photoshop to redraw because it doesn't have to do the calculations for the RedCab Layer.

STEP 18: With the RainbowCab layer selected, again choose New Layer but this time set the mode to Multiply and choose Group with Previous Layer. Name this layer CabTexture and type a D to set the foreground color to black and the background to white. Option-click on the Eye icon for this new layer so you are just viewing it for now. Choose Select/All (Command-A) followed by Edit/Fill. Fill this with 100% of the background color in Normal mode. Now choose Filter/Noise/Add Noise and add Gaussian noise of about 100. This will fill this layer with colored dots. Choose Command-D (Select/None) and then use the Rectangular Marquee to select a thin

STEP 18: Turn on these layers to see the above image.

rectangle from the top to the bottom of the layer on the left side. Make sure the screen is zoomed so you can see the whole layer. It makes it easier to make this type of selection if the window is bigger than the layer size (or in Full Screen mode), so there is some gray to select in around the edge of the layer.

After making this selection, choose Image/Ef-fects/Scale and grab the top right handle and stretch it directly to the right all the way to the other side of the layer. We are taking a thin rectangle of colored spots along the left edge of the layer and stretching it out to make a pattern of colored stripes. Click in the middle of the screen on the Gavel icon to finish the Scale command and then choose Image/Rotate/Free to rotate the striped lines. The cab in this image is rotated so the front of it is pointing slightly down. Click on the top right handle and move it upwards to rotate the stripes so they are parallel with the angle of the cab. Click again on the Gavel and wait for the Rotate to finish.

Now you can see the effects of this added texture by Option-clicking back on this layer's Eye icon, which will turn the Eye icons for all the other layers back on. Zoom in to 1:1 so you can see the details of the stripes on the cab as you change the options. You can turn the Eye icons off for the RainbowCab layer and the RedCab layer one at a time to see this striped effect added to each color of cab. To get the most from the striped effect, double-click on the CabTexture layer to bring up the Layer Options dialog. Use the This Layer sliders to remove parts of the 0..255 range of pixel values from the compositing of the current layer. I moved the left (Shadow) slider to the right to 20. This removed all the deep shadow values from 0..20 from the stripes. I then moved the right (Highlight) slider to the left to 234, which removes values from 234..255.

To smooth out these transitions, hold down the Option key while clicking and dragging on the right side of the left slider again. This will cause the slider to split. Drag the rightmost section of it to 103. This

STEP 19: Layer Eye icons and image with the Topless and XXX layers removed.

means that the values from 0..20 are still completely removed and the values from 20..103 are slowly blended out. If you Option-click and drag on the Highlight slider, (the rightmost one), and drag the left half of it to 151, you are slowly blending out the values from 234 down to 151. For a final tweak on this effect, I then set the opacity to 70% with the mode still being set to Multiply. The mode and opacity within this Layer Options dialog are the same controls that are at the top of the normal Layers palette. Now you have completed all the layers within this example. Choose File/Save (Command-S) to save this final layered version.

DECIDING ON THE FINAL VERSION

Now it is time to play with your creation. You may have an art director or some clients you want to show several variations of the project. This example represents that situation. Let's go through some of these variations, how to show them and what they look like. With the Car layer and the other layers in its clipping group, you have a lot of options.

STEP 19: To show the client the basic final image, turn on all the Eye icons except for RedCar, RainbowCar and CarTexture. Now click on the Eye icon for CarTexture to add the striped texture to the yellow car. Click on the RedCar layer to show the client a red version. Click on the Rainbow-Car Eye icon to show them that version. Any car color can be shown without the stripes by just clicking on the Eye icon for the CarTexture layer. If the client likes the striped look, you can Option-click on the line separating the CarTexture layer from the RainbowCar layer and this will remove CarTexture from the clipping group. The effect here will be to add the stripes to the entire image. If you want to explore this effect, double-click

on CarTexture and modify the Layer Options blending numbers to better suit the entire image. If you want to put the CarTexture layer back into the car's clipping group, just Option-click again on the line between it and the RainbowCar layer. If your client is concerned about some of the more risqué aspects of New York nightlife, you can click on the Eye icons for the Topless and XXX layers to remove these from the image. Have Fun!

STEP 20: Once you, or you and your client, decide that certain layers are going to be used in the final image, those layers can be merged together into one. Turn the Eye icons on for the layers that you want to merge. Make sure one of the layers whose Eye icon is on is the active layer by clicking on it. The other layers will be merged into the bottom layer whose Eye icon is on. Now choose Merge Layers from the Layers palette menu. Here we are merging the top six layers that were just adding particular items to the image. If all those items are accepted as part of the final image, and you won't want to change this later, there is no need to keep them as separate layers. When you merge layers together, remember that the final merged layer will only be allowed one opacity, mode and set of layer options. The layer options, mode and opacity of each layer that was set when you merged will be applied at the time of the merge to the set of layers that were merged. The mode of the merged layer is then reset to Normal and its opacity to 100% and all its layer options are set to the

STEP 20: Merging the six item Layers into the one 24 hours Layer.

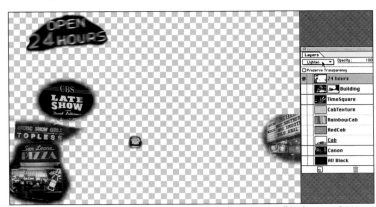

STEP 20: After you merge the 6 item layers together, they are now all in the same 24 Hours layer. Make sure you make the mode for this new combined layer Lighten.

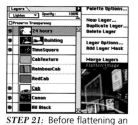

STEP 21: Before flattening an image, turn on the Eye icons for the layers you want in the final image.

STEP 21: File/Save a Copy is a way to quickly get a flattened copy of your image and still keep your multi-layered version.

default. This can cause a different effect when the Eye icons for the other layers are turned back on. Be careful when you do this. Here, we need to make sure the mode for the new layer is set back to Lighten.

STEP 21: When you are done with the project and you are sure you will never need the layers again, you can select, by turning the Eye icons on, the layers you want in the final image. Choose Flatten Image from the Layers palette menu. If you did not select all the layers, you will be asked "Discard Hidden Layers?" and if you choose OK, those layers will be thrown out. After flattening the image, it looks like a single layer image with just a background layer. Sometimes you want to keep your multi-layered version, but you need to print a version with some of the layers on and some of them off. To do this, just turn the Eye icons on for the layers you want in this version and then choose File/Save a Copy. This command allows you to save a flattened copy of the image under a different name without removing the layers from your original image.

172

STEP 21: The final flattened image with all the layers merged into one Background layer. The effects will have been thrown out for any layer whose Eye icon was not on before the flatten.

BLEND MODES, CALCULATIONS AND APPLY IMAGE

How Each of the Blend Modes Work;
the Subtleties of Using Modes in Calculations,
Apply Image, Layers, Fill and the Painting Tools;
When and How to Use Calculations vs
Apply Image vs Layers

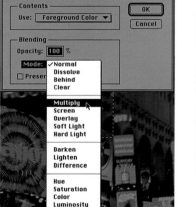

The Blend modes for the Fill command.

The Blend modes for the painting tools.

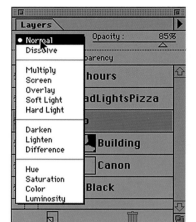

The Blend modes for the Apply Image command.

The Blend modes for Layers.

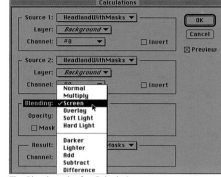

The Blend modes for Calculations.

Image and the Calculations command. Not all of the blend mode options are offered in each of these areas. As we explain each blend mode, it will be easier to see why some of them make more sense in one or another area. All of these options also offer you a way to use a mask while you are combining the two groups of image information. The mask will affect the parts of the two groups that are combined.

THE TOOLS FOR BLENDING

First we will discuss the different tools and methods for blending and when it makes the most sense to use each of them. Later we will discuss each of the blend modes and its unique applications within each of the different blending tools. In the Calculations folder on the CD are many of the images we use in this chapter. Although this is not a step by step hands-on, we encourage you to play and explore these techniques with the images. By playing on your own, you learn new things, and it can be a lot of fun.

THE FILL COMMAND

The Edit/Fill command is used to fill a selection, or the entire image if there is no selection, with something like the foreground or background color or from the pattern, snapshot or last saved file. The mode and opacity within Fill just determines how this filling image will combine with what was there before. Normal, at 100% opacity, completely covers what was there before with the new color or image. An opacity of 50% will give half what was there before and half the new filled image or color. We usually use Fill to completely cover a selection or the entire image with a solid

The blend modes are used to determine how two groups of image information combine. The two groups of image information could be of various types within Photoshop. The first type could be a photographic image with the second being a solid color that is painted or filled on top of that image. This could be done using one of the painting tools or the Fill command. If you created a layer that was a solid color, then you could also combine this layer with a photographic image on a second layer using a mode in the Layers palette. In the Layers palette you can determine which mode will be used to combine two photographic images within the same layered Photoshop 3.0 document. You can use the Apply Image command with different modes to combine two color photographic images that are in separate documents that have the exact same pixel dimensions. Finally, you can use the Calculations command with modes to combine two images of the same size when you want a black-and-white mask channel as a result. The blend modes appear in the painting tools, the Fill tool, the Layers palette, Apply

174

Here's how we created the highlighted pop-ups on the previous page with Fill.

The Las Vegas Night image.

The Century Plant image.

The Vegas Lights mask.

color or a tint. We also use Fill a lot to revert to the previously saved version of a file within a selected area. When you use Fill, you need to pick an opacity and Fill mode before you do the operation, and then you have to undo it if you want to change it. Only use Fill when you are sure of the look that you want. We used Fill to get the highlight effects in the pop-up dialog on the previous page. Since we wanted them all to look the same, we just used the Rectangular Marquee to select the Blend Mode pop-up menu, used Select/Inverse to invert that selection, and then used Fill with 40% black in Normal mode to get the effect. If you need to prototype the opacity or mode of your Fill, use the layer techniques we'll show you later.

THE PAINTING TOOLS

You use a painting tool when you want to apply an effect by hand and softly blend it in and out, like you would do with an airbrush or paintbrush. These tools in Photoshop have a lot more power, however, due to the magic of digital imaging and the blending modes. Go through The Tool Palette chapter to learn about the subtleties of each tool. With the Blend Mode options with the tools, you don't just lay down paint, or even a previous version of the image. Instead, you can control how this paint or image combines with what is already there.

COMBINING IMAGES USING LAYERS

Layers is the most powerful way to combine two or more images while keeping the most options open for further variations and many versions of your composite. Sometimes we use Layers even when we are dealing with a pattern or solid color. The reason is that with Layers you can always go back and change something, move something, change the opacity or blend mode without having to totally redo your image. You can try an effect and be able to turn it on and off at will. Layers gives you the most sophisticated control of the blending modes as well as many other capabilities at the same time. If you don't understand Layers, and if you haven't read the Introduction to Layers chapter, you should read that chapter now before

The Night Cab Ride image produced with many layers.

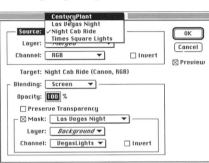

Here we see most of the possible options of Apply Image. Before we entered Image/Apply Image we made Night Cab Ride the active document in Photoshop. Canon was the active layer within that document. This active item is always selected as the Target of Apply Image so you will be changing that document, channel or layer. The Source pop-up window shows you only documents that are the same pixel size and dimensions as the target document. Here we chose the Century Plant as the Source. The Blending pop-up is where you choose the Blend mode. There is an optional mask, selected here, which causes the blending to only happen within the areas of the mask that are white. If the Preview button is on, you see the results of the Apply Image within the Target window. This way you can try different options and see what they do.

The results of the Apply Image settings shown in the previous illustration. The Century Plant image is brought into the Night Cab Ride composite where the Las Vegas Night mask was white. In that area, it is blended with the Canon layer using the Screen Blending mode.

you continue. When you use Layers, your files will get much bigger since every layer adds at least the original size of the file in that layer to your document size. Layered documents have to be saved in Photoshop 3.0 format to maintain the flexible layer information. Still, layers are WAY COOL!

COMBINING IMAGES, LAYERS AND CHANNELS USING APPLY IMAGE

The basic function of Apply Image is to copy one image, layer or channel, called the Source image, and use it to replace another image, layer or channel, the Target image, of exactly the same pixel resolution. To combine two items with Apply Image they have to be exactly the same width and height in pixels. The two images are combined using a blending mode and opacity that are chosen from the Apply Image dialog. You can optionally

175

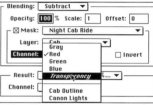

Here we see a more simple application of Apply Image. The source, target and resulting images are shown here. The Screen Blending mode is analogous to taking transparencies of the two images and projecting them onto the same screen from two different slide projectors. The light areas of the images are emphasized. Setting the opacity to 85 percent made the Las Vegas Lights a little less bright within the composite image below.

The Times Square Canon image.

The Las Vegas Night image.

choose a mask, which will combine the images only where the mask is white. Apply Image is useful when copying a channel or layer from one place to another especially when you want to put it on top of an existing channel or layer and combine the two with a blend mode.

Before you enter Apply Image, you should choose the Target image, layer or channel. This will be modified when you leave Apply Image with OK, so you may want to first make a copy of that Target item.

Actually, if you hold down the Option key while selecting Apply Image, you get an extra Result pop-up menu at the bottom of the dialog that allows you to direct the result of Apply Image to: the Current Target, a New Document, a New Layer, a New Channel or a Selection. If you choose either New Layer, Channel or Selection, these end up within the Target image.

If the Preview button is on, you can see the results of the operation within the Target window. In choosing the Source, you can pick any open document, layer or channel so long as it is the same exact pixel dimensions as the Target. Like the Source, the mask can be any open document, layer or

Using the Layer pop-up you can select the Merged layer or any individual layer within a layered document.

channel that is the same pixel dimensions as the Target. The Preserve Transparency options will stop the Apply Image command from changing any transparent areas within a layer. Both the Source and the mask have an Invert check box which will turn that selection to its negative if checked.

In this chapter, we will be using three images that we have cropped to be exactly the same pixel size. They are the Las Vegas Night, the Century Plant and a modified Night Cab Ride image from the Introduction to Layers chapter. As mentioned before, read the Introduction to Layers chapter now if you haven't already. The Las Vegas Night Image has a mask, called VegasLights, that is white where the neon lights are. There are no particular masks in the Century Plant image. Here are some other examples of using Apply Image, using the same three images, so you can get an idea what the command does. If you want to get a result that is more than one channel deep, you need to use Apply Image instead of Calculations. The effects you can create with Apply Image can also be achieved with Layers by first copying the different components into a layer document. Layers has more flexibility since the different layers don't have to start out being the exact same size and they can be moved around side-to-side as well as above-and-below with relationship to each other. Effects within layers can also be done and undone in multiple combinations using the Eye icons.

Apply Image should be used mostly in cases where you already know the spatial relationship between the objects being combined, and the operation has to be quickly done for some production purpose. Motion picture and multimedia work (where you are compositing many frames of two sequences together that have been pre-shot in registration, to be lined up exactly), is a good example of how you

With a Channel pop-up you can select any channel including Transparency and layer masks.

Here are the Calculations settings to produce the mask of the glow on the next page. When doing a Subtract, the item that you want to subtract from should be in Source 1. The item you are subtracting from should be in Source 2. In this case the result was a New channel. Depending on the choice we make for the Result file and Channel, the result could have replaced any existing channel within any file of the same pixel dimensions, or, by choosing Selection, it could have been loaded as a selection.

176

The Headland sign, we want to make a mask of just the glow without the sign.

We have a soft-edge mask of the glow including part of the sign. We put this into Source 2.

We have a hard-edge mask of just the sign. We put this into Source 1.

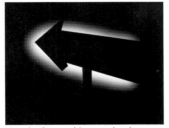

Here is the resulting mask where we subtracted the hard-edge mask from the soft-edge mask.

channel, which is a mask of any transparent areas within the chosen layer. This interface allows you to blend any two documents, layers or channels that are open using the blending modes and put the result into any channel that is open. These open items must have the same pixel dimensions as the active window. The blending interface also allows an optional mask, which will force the blending to only happen in the areas that are white in the mask. Both source items and the mask have an Invert checkbox to optionally invert any of them before doing the composite. We will learn more about Apply Image and Calculations as we go through each of the blend modes next. If you hold down the Option key when selecting Calculations, a smaller version of the dialog will come up.

UNDERSTANDING EACH BLEND MODE

Let's start out with the blend modes listed in the Edit/Fill command, which would have the same effect as the blend modes used by the painting tools if you were painting with the same color, pattern or image that you were filling with. When using the Fill command you are filling a selected area. You can fill with the foreground or background colors as well as from the Snapshot, from the last saved file and from a pattern. All these options are available to paint from by using different flavors of the painting tools. The Rubber Stamp tool gives you the most options. When painting you are selecting your "fill area" as you paint instead of from a selection. In either case, the modes will work in the same way. Some of these modes also apply to Layers and the Calculations and Apply Image commands. Their differences will be explained for these situations also.

NORMAL

When painting or filling in Normal mode, you are filling the selected or painted area with the foreground or background color or from the snapshot, pattern or saved file. Normal mode for a top layer in the Layers palette means that the top layer at 100% opacity will be opaque. You will not see any of the layers below through this layer. You use Normal mode in Calculations or Apply Image to copy the Source layer or channel to the Target or destination layer or channel without any blending. This totally replaces the the Target or destination with the Source.

would use Apply Image. This process could be automated over hundreds of frames using QuickKeys, Photomatic or some other application automation software.

COMBINING CHANNELS USING CALCULATIONS

The main purpose of the Calculations command is to use the blend modes to combine images, layers or channels and end up with a single black-and-white channel as the result. When you need a color result, use Apply Image, when you need a channel result, use Calculations. Calculations provides for two source files, Source 1 and Source 2, and a Result file. When you enter Calculations, all three of these will be set to the active window within Photoshop. You can use the pop-up menus to change any of these to any other open file that has the same pixel dimensions. The source files are the two that will be combined using the blending mode that you choose. The Layer pop-up on each of these is available for layered documents and allows you to choose the merged layer, which is the composite of all layers that currently have their Eye icons on or any other layer within the document.

The Channel pop-up allows you to choose any channel within the chosen file or layer. To access a layer mask channel, you need to first choose the layer that owns that layer mask. You can also choose the Transparency

✓ Normal
Dissolve
Behind
Clear

Multiply
Screen
Overlay
Soft Light
Hard Light

Darken
Lighten
Difference

Hue
Saturation
Color
Luminosity

The green circle is in the top layer with red in the bottom layer. Now both layer's Eye icons are on.

Here is just the circle with the Red layer turned off. The transparent area shows up as a checkered pattern.

We have painted black into this transparent area using Behind mode with a large soft brush.

Here we see the shadow without the background color. When painting in Behind mode, we didn't have to worry about painting on top of the green. It is automatically masked out since it is not transparent.

DISSOLVE

Depending on the opacity of dissolve, this mode appears to take the opacity as a percentage of the pixels from the blend color and place them on top of the base color. The base color is the color or image that was there before the dissolve. The blend color is the color or image that is being dissolved on top of the base color or image. Try this with two layers setting the mode between them to Dissolve. If you set the opacity to 100%, you get all of the top layer and don't see the bottom layer. The same thing happens with a fill of 100% or painting at 100% in Dissolve mode. When you set the opacity to 50% and look at the pixels up close, you will see that there are about 50% pixels from the top layer and 50% from the bottom. Set the opacity to 10% and only 10% of the pixels are from the top layer or color.

With Dissolve the pixels seem to be entirely from one image or the other; there don't seem to be any blended pixels. On first impression, the dissolve appears to be random. If you do a 50% dissolve between two layers and then zoom out to 1:2 or 1:4, you will notice a pattern in the dissolve. It looks like Photoshop creates or uses some fixed dissolve pattern over and over again across the screen. You probably wouldn't see it if you were painting with a soft brush over not too large an area. Still, this pattern doesn't look good over the entire screen between two layers. If you want this type of look between two images without an obvious repeating pattern, create a layer mask on the top layer filled with solid white.

Now go into the Add Noise filter and add Gaussian noise to the layer mask. Where the noise is black, the bottom layer will show through and you will get an effect similar to Dissolve but this time without the annoying pattern. The more noise you add, the more you will see the bottom layer. Also, in this case, some of the pixels are actually blends between the layers. Dissolve is not an option with Apply Image or Calculations but you can get a similar effect here by using a Gaussian noise mask as you combine images, layers and channels.

BEHIND

This blend mode is used to paint into the transparent part of a layer. It is only available from Fill and the painting tools and only if the layer has a transparent area. It is not available if the Preserve Transparency checkbox is checked for that layer. Behind allows you to paint a shadow or color behind an object, like a circle, in the layer using a painting tool or the Fill command. The actual image in the layer won't be affected because Behind only paints into the transparent area. Painting in Behind mode is like painting on the back of the acetate. Here we see a shadow that was added to a circle using Behind mode with a large soft brush and the Paintbrush tool.

CLEAR

The Clear mode is only available when in a layered document from the Fill command, the Paint Bucket and the Line tool. It will fill the selected area, the line in the case of the Line tool, with transparency. This is the little checkerboard pattern that means you can see the layers below through the transparent areas. Clear is also available as a menu item from the Edit menu although the Edit/Clear behaves a little differently depending on whether you are in a layered document or not. When in a layered document, Edit/Clear fills the selected area with transparency. When in a normal document, without layers, Edit/Clear fills the selected area with the background color.

This brings up an interesting thing about Photoshop and how it deals with layers and the special layer called the Background layer. When you open a TIFF file or some other file that doesn't contain layers into Photoshop then go into the Layers palette, you will notice that these files contain a single layer called *Back-ground*. This isn't really a layer in the true sense of the word because it can't have any transparent areas. If you make a selection in a Background layer of an image and then choose Edit/Clear, the selected area will be filled with the background color. You will notice that Clear does not show up as an available option for a Background layer within Fill or the Line and Paint Bucket tools. If you double-click on this special Background layer within the Layers palette and rename it something else, it will turn into a real

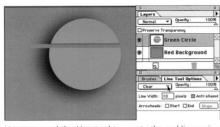

Here we used the Line tool to create the red line going across the circle by drawing the line in Clear mode.

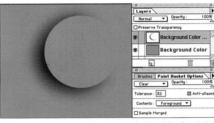

Here we clicked on the green circle with the Paint Bucket in Clear mode leaving only the shadow with this nice effect.

layer. Now, Edit/Clear will fill a selection with transparency and Clear is available in the Line and Paint Bucket tools. Until you rename the Background layer and make it a real layer, you can't interchange its order in the Layers palette with other layers.

MULTIPLY

Multiply is a blend mode that is very useful and is available within all the blend mode pop-ups. When you Multiply two images together, it is analogous to what you would see if both the images were transparencies and you sandwiched them together and placed them on a light table or projected them onto a screen. Anything that was black in either image would be black in the resulting composite image. Any-thing that was white or clear in either image would let you see what was in

A Multiply of the Century Plant and Las Vegas Night images, from the 2nd page of this chapter, emphasizes the darker areas of each image.

the other image in that area. When you multiply two images together, the 0..255 values of the corresponding pixels in each image are actually multi-plied together using the following formula:

(Source 1) x (Source 2) / 255 = destination

Just like doing a multiply in mathe-matics, the order of the Source 1 and Source 2 images doesn't mat-ter. Dividing by 255 at the end forces all the values to be in the 0..255 range. You can see that when either Source value is 0, black, you are going to get 0 as the result. When either Source value is 255, white, you are going to get the other Source value as the result, because 255/255 = 1, so you multi-ply the other Source value by 1.

SCREEN

Screen is sort of the opposite of Multiply in that when you do a Screen between two images, any-thing that is white in either of the images will be white in the result-ing image. Anything that is black in either image will show the other image in that black area. Screen, like Multiply, is also available in all the different blend mode pop-ups. When you Screen two images together it is analogous to what you would see if both the images were projected from two different slide projectors onto the same screen. The formula for Screen is:

255 - ((255-Source 1) x (255-Source 2) / 255) = destination

The original Glow mask we want to drop a gradient into.

Unwanted Halo Effect

Doing a Load Selection on the glow, left, and dropping the gradient into the selected area, produces the halo around the glow at the back of the arrow.

Create the gradient in a separate mask channel and use Calculations to Multiply for the effect at right.

A Calculations Multiply of the Gradient and Glow mask channels drops the gra-dient into the glow area without a halo.

A powerful use for Multiply is to seamlessly add a gradi-ent to an existing selection. Let's say we wanted to use the Glow mask to create a glow that was bright at the front of the arrow and fading towards the back. To do this, we would want to drop a gradient into this mask. If you do a Load Selection on the mask and then create the gradient within that selection, you will get a light halo around the edge of the gradient towards the back of the arrow. This is caused by the loaded selection. To avoid getting this halo, just create the gradient in a separate channel and then multiply the two channels together giving you a better fade.

A screen of the Century Plant and Las Vegas Night images emphasizes the lighter areas of each image.

You can simulate the Screen command using the Multiply command if you first invert both of the Source images then multiply them together and finally invert the result of that multiply. That is exactly what this formula for Screen does: (255 - Source1) does an Invert of Source 1. With the Screen formula then: the Invert of Source 1 is multiplied by the Invert of Source 2 and then is divided by 255. That part of the formula does the multiply of the two inverted images. Finally, subtracting that result from 255 at the end does the Invert of the result of that multiply giving you a Screen. The important thing to remember between Screen and Multiply is that a Screen of two images will emphasize the lighter areas and a Multiply will emphasize the darker areas.

SOFT LIGHT

In Soft Light mode, the original image is blended with the blend color, pattern or image by either making the original image lighter or darker depending on the blend image. If the blend image is lighter than 50% gray, then the original image is lightened in a subtle way. Even where the blend image is pure white, the resulting image will just be lighter than before, not pure white. If the blend image is darker than 50% gray, then the original image is darkened in a subtle way. Even where the blend image is pure black, the resulting image will just be darker than before, not pure black. The tonal values and details of the original are fairly preserved, just subtly modified by the blend image. If you add a 50% gray layer above an original image and set the blend mode to Soft Light, you can then use a soft brush and paint with white or black to dodge or burn the image by lightening or darkening this gray layer. Use less than 100% opacity on your brush to get more subtle effects. This is better than using the dodging or burning tool and infinitely adjustable because you are not actually changing the original image. When you get an effect you like, just merge the layers to get a new final image. You can easily get a 50% gray layer by using the New Layer option in the Layer palette's pop-up, choosing Edit/Fill and filling with Use: 50% Gray, Opacity: 100% and Mode: Normal.

HARD LIGHT

In Hard Light mode, the original image is blended with the blend color, pattern or image by either making the original image lighter or darker depending on the blend image. If the blend image is lighter than 50% gray, then the original image is lightened and this lightening is a contrast effect. If the blend image is pure white, the resulting image will be pure white. If the blend image is darker than 50% gray, then the original image is darkened and this darkening is a contrast effect. If the blend image is pure black, the resulting image will be pure black. In Hard Light mode, the resulting image seems to take its lightness value from the blend color, pattern or image. Since the tonal values of the original are not very preserved, this is a radical adjustment. If you add a 50% gray layer above an original image and set the blend mode to Hard Light, you can then use a soft brush and paint with white or black to dodge or burn the image by lightening or darkening this gray layer. This will be a radical, contrasty dodge and burn. Use less than 100% opacity on your brush or you will get pure white or black. Remember that this effect is infinitely adjustable because you are not actually changing the original image. When you get an effect you like, just merge the layers to get a new final image. See the Soft Light section for how to get a 50% gray layer above the image.

Apply Image was originally used to prototype the Paris Dog examples. The mask used to isolate the dog is seen here but we Invert it to actually get the effect in the background.

The Dog mask before inverting.

OVERLAY

Overlay does a combination of Multiply and Screen modes. The dark areas of an original image are multiplied and the light areas are screened. The highlights and shadows are somewhat preserved since dark areas of the image will not be as dark as if you were doing a Multiply and light areas will not be as bright as if you were doing a Screen. The tonal values and details of the original are preserved to some extent, but this is a more contrasty transition than Soft Light just not as radical as Hard Light.

The original ParisDog image.

The original Dog pattern.

The examples shown here use Apply Image and Layers to combine my ParisDog image with a pattern that I created in Photoshop and a mask that stops the dog itself from being affected by the pattern. I initially tried this out using Apply Image. The original ParisDog image, the grayscale DogPattern and the DogMask were all in the same file. Before entering Apply Image, I selected the RGB background of ParisDog, this made that the Target. For the Source, I selected the DogPattern, which applies the pattern on top of the ParisDog. I set the mode to Overlay and then decided that I didn't want the pattern on the dog. Choosing the Mask option allowed me to pick the Dog mask, and the Invert checkbox was turned on because the mask was actually white in the dog area. Turning on Invert made the mask white in the back- ground and the white area of the mask is where the

181

Overlay: this is contrasty but it still pre- serves some of the tone and detail from the original.

Multiply: notice how dark the shadows are compared to Overlay.

Screen: notice how bright the highlights are compared to Overlay.

Soft Light: this preserves the most tone and detail from the original.

Hard Light: the highlight and shadow val- ues and the lightness values come pretty much directly from the pattern.

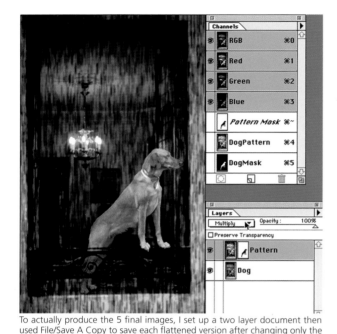

182

To actually produce the 5 final images, I set up a two layer document then used File/Save A Copy to save each flattened version after changing only the mode between each save. That was just a better production choice.

image is applied. With the Preview button on, I tried all the different blend modes and could see that I wanted to use this as an example. At this point I was going to have to produce 5 versions of this image, one for each blend mode. When you use Apply Image, it actually changes the Target image, so to do 5 versions with Apply Image I would have had to make 5 copies of the ParisDog, one for each blend mode.

A more efficient way to do this, after prototyping the effect with Apply Image, was then to create the 5 versions from a layered document. The bottom layer was the ParisDog image. I added a layer above this for the Dog-Pattern, and to this layer I added a layer mask for the inverted DogMask channel. For more information on using layer masks, see The APDA Magazine Cover or Night Cab Ride in Manhattan chapters. Now to produce the 5 different versions, all I had to do was change the blend mode in the Layers palette once for each version and choose File/Save A Copy for each version to make a flattened TIFF copy with all channels and layers removed.

Again, Photoshop Layers are a great prototyping and production tool! When I took this photo on a residential alley in Paris, the dog was in this pose as I walked by. I pointed and focused my camera and then the dog went back inside just as I was about to shoot. I stood there for a bit with the camera ready, and, sure enough, the dog returned and posed for me. It has always been one of my favorite shots.

DARKEN AND LIGHTEN

The Darken and Lighten blend modes are pretty easy to understand. In the Darken mode, each of the corresponding pixels from the original image and the blend color, pattern or image are compared, and the darker of the two is chosen for the result. In the case of Lighten, the lighter of the two pixels is chosen for the result. Within Apply Image and Calculations, these modes are called Lighter and Darker. These blend modes are most useful in combining masks to create new masks. An example of this, shown

The shoes and the glasses have each been pasted in here separately.

One mask was saved for the shoes.

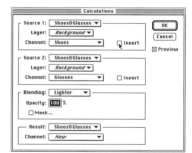

Another mask was saved for the glasses.

These Calculations settings using Lighter will create the new mask below to the left.

This mask of both shoes and glasses was created with Calculations using Lighter.

To create this background mask with a single calculation, invert both the source masks and use Darker instead of Lighter.

here, would be the situation where you have pasted two objects into a composite scene and for each object you did a Select/Save Selection to save the selection of that object. You have a mask of each separate object, and now you need one mask that contains both objects at the same time, because you want to drop in a new background behind the objects.

Using Calculations to do a Lighter between these two objects will create the mask of both the objects. You can then use the inverse of this mask to give you a mask of the background. If you select the Invert checkboxes on both the Source channels within Calculations, the inverse is done for you in the one calculations step. In this case, since both the Source masks have been pre-inverted, you would have to use Darker to combine the two masks and get the final mask with the white background.

DIFFERENCE

Difference is one of the most useful blending modes. Difference compares two images and gives you a mask that is black where each of the two images are exactly the same and is non-black and closer to white the more the images are different from each other. The formula for Difference is:

| Source 1 - Source 2 | = Destination

Difference is similar to Subtract but the results are never inverted; they are always positive because the two vertical bars stand for absolute value and make the result positive. With a little photographic planning, you can use Difference to automatically separate an image from its background. When you are shooting from a tripod, first shoot the background without the objects to be placed on that background. Pick a background that is quite different in color and brightness from the objects to be shot. Without moving the tripod or changing the lighting, place the objects and shoot them. If these two photographs are scanned in register, then doing a Difference between them can often automatically give you a mask of just the objects. The two objects in the example here were shot on a tripod using a Kodak DCS electronic camera. When using an electronic camera, scanning the images in register is no problem because they are sent directly from the camera to the computer. In this case, we had the computer in the studio so we could try Difference and then adjust the lighting and exposure to make sure we'd get an automatic knock-out. Actually, to create the final mask of the objects, we brought the Difference mask into Levels and increased its brightness slightly. Then we did some quick editing of the masks of the actual objects. Still, this process was faster using Difference than if we had done the knock-out by hand.

A digital camera hooked up to a computer will be a part of the standard photography studio of the future, and it is starting to become a reality for more and more photographers today, especially those that do a lot of repetitive catalog work. Also, consider the motion picture industry where artists or technicians might have to knock out hundreds or even thousands of frames to composite two sequences together. With Difference and a little computer controlled camera work, this situation could also be automated. Say you are shooting some guys on horses riding across a field that you will later want to superimpose on another scene. Have a computer remember all the frame by frame motion of the camera while shooting the scene. Now immediately, while the lighting hasn't changed, use the computer to move the camera back to the original position at the beginning of the scene. With computer control, reshoot all those frames without the horses to just get the backgrounds. Now using Difference, and maybe QuickKeys to automate over hundreds of frames, you can quickly create a knock-out of all those frames.

The objects as originally shot with the Kodak DCS system.

The background shot with the same lighting and camera position.

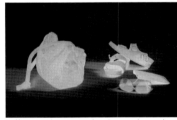

Difference between the Green channels of the background and the object shots.

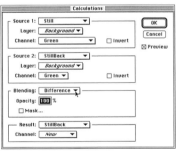

These Calculations settings using Difference will create the mask to the left.

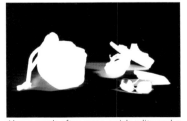

Above mask after some quick edits and a brightness adjustment with Levels.

New background placed behind the objects using an inverted version of the mask to the left.

The Las Vegas Night image.

The Century Plant image.

ADD AND SUBTRACT

Add and Subtract are only available within Apply Image and Calculations. Add takes the corresponding pixels of the original and blend image and adds them together using the following formula:

Add = (Source 2 + Source 1) / Scale) + Offset = Destination

Subtract takes the corresponding pixels of the original and blend image and subtracts them using this formula:

Subtract = (Source 2 - Source 1) / Scale) + Offset = Destination

Scale and Offset are additional parameters that you use with these blending modes within Apply Image or Calculations. The normal values for Scale and Offset for both Add and Subtract are 1 and 0. The order of the Source 1 and Source 2 parameters doesn't matter with Add but with Subtract it definitely does. The Source 1 parameter is always subtracted from the Source 2 parameter, and the result has to be in the 0..255 range. When Source 1 is white, 255, which represents a selection, the result of the Subtract will always be black. The effect of the Subtract is then to remove the selected areas of the Source 1 mask from the selected areas of the Source 2 mask. This is a very useful function. Of the two, Subtract is the blend mode I use more often, and I usually do Subtracts between masks. See the example of Subtract with Calculations on the Headland sign earlier in this chapter.

When doing either an Add or a Subtract, the Offset value will make the resulting mask lighter if the offset is positive, and darker if the offset is negative. The offset is a number, in the 0..255 range, that will be added to the result of each corresponding pixel's calculations. If we do an Add of two images and set the scale to 2, we are getting an average of the two. This would give us the same result as doing a Normal mode paste of one image on top of the other at 50% opacity. With the Add command, you have the additional control of using the Offset parameter to make this resulting image either lighter or darker.

HUE, SATURATION, COLOR AND LUMINOSITY

These blending modes will effect the original image by using either the hue, saturation, color or luminosity of the blend color, pattern or image as the hue, saturation, color or luminosity of the original image. In these examples, combining the two sides of the desert (the original desert Century

Plant and Las Vegas), you can see how the Century Plant scene is modified by the hue, saturation, color and luminosity of the Las Vegas Night scene. The Las Vegas scene has very intense hues that are also very saturated so it is easy to see what happens with these two images. We placed the Las Vegas scene as a layer on top of the Century Plant layer and just changed the layer blend mode of the Las Vegas layer to get the different effects. In Hue mode you see the hues from the Las Vegas scene but the saturation, the intensity, of those hues and all the details come from the Century Plant scene. In Saturation mode the highly saturated values from the bright neon lights intensify the more subtle hues and details from the Century Plant scene. Color mode combines the hue and saturation from Las Vegas with the details, or luminosity, of Century Plant. When you

The Las Vegas hue with the Century Plant saturation and luminosity.

The Las Vegas saturation with the Century Plant hue and luminosity.

The Las Vegas hue and saturation, Color, with the Century Plant luminosity.

The Las Vegas luminosity with the Century Plant hue and saturation.

put the Las Vegas scene in Luminosity mode, then you are seeing all the details from that Las Vegas scene but the more subtle hue and saturation values from the Century Plant. Within the Las Vegas scene there are large black areas. These have no hue or saturation values, which is why they show up as gray when in Hue, Saturation or Color modes.

A more interesting way to combine these two images is to double click-on the Las Vegas layer to bring up the Layer options. Moving the left, Shadow, slider to the right in the This Layer part of Layer Options, removes the black part of the Las Vegas scene from the composite. In the final example of this image we have used the Move tool to move the Las Vegas layer up a little bit. Now Las Vegas is at the end of the trail in the desert. We then double-clicked on the Las Vegas layer to bring up its Layer options. We are in Luminosity mode but the colors of the Century Plant image show through in the black areas of Las Vegas because we have moved the Shadow sliders of This Layer over to the right.

First we moved the Shadow slider to the right to 10. That removed all the digital values from 0 to 10 from the composite allowing the Century Plant to show through. This produces jaggy edges on the transition between Las Vegas and the Century Plant backgrounds. By holding down the Option key and sliding the rightmost part of the Shadow slider further to the right, the Shadow slider has now split. We moved the rightmost part of this slider to 25. The meaning of this is that the black values in Las Vegas from 0 to 10 are completely removed and the values from 11 to 25 are blended out making a softer edge

between these two images. The Luminosity values in Las Vegas from 26 to 255 are still retained within this composite. For more information on this very powerful Layer Options dialog, see the Introduction to Layers chapter and also the Posterize, Bitmaps and Patterns chapter.

Have fun with all the Photoshop blending modes!

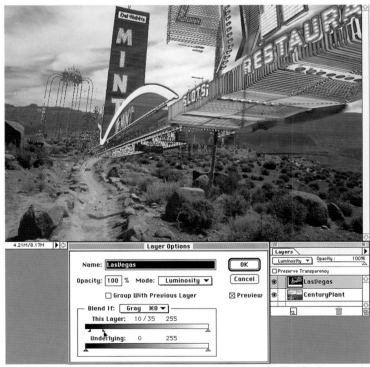

Here we see the results of using Layer Options in Luminosity mode to completely remove the black values in the 0-10 range and to blend out the black values in the 11-25 range from the composite of Las Vegas and the Century Plant. We double-clicked on the Las Vegas layer to get the Layer Options dialog.

HANDS-ON SESSION: BIKE RIDE IN THE SKY!

*Two Color Images Are Combined Using Two
Gradient Masks to Create a High-Flying Bicyclist,
Three Text Treatments Create Different Effects*

The original bicycle.

Yes, the same clouds!

I was playing in Photoshop one day, a long time ago, and created one of my favorite images using two gradients to blend a cyclist into the clouds. Multiplying this image with its negative made it even more interesting. Here we use this image to play with some text effects.

COMBINING THE IMAGES WITH GRADATIONS

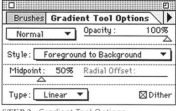
STEP 1: Create a new channel from the Channel Menu palette.

STEP 1: Open the Clouds and BikeRider files in the Bike Ride in the Sky folder. Click on the BikeRider file to make it active. Choose Window/Palettes/Show Channels if the Channels palette is not currently visible. In the Channels options choose New Channel and say OK to the default options or click on the New Channel icon in the middle of the bottom portion of the palette.

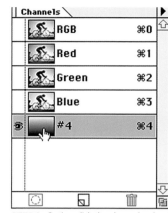
STEP 3: Option-click the channel to load the selection.

blend from black at the bottom edge of the channel to white at the top. Make sure you finish your blend exactly at the top edge of the file. If you increase the window size to slightly larger than the file itself, finding the edges will be easier.

STEP 3: Drag the channel to the Selection icon at the bottom left of the Channels palette, or just Option-click on Channel #4 to load this selection. Now click on the RGB channel (Command-0) and choose Edit/Copy to copy this file.

If you go to the Clouds file and Edit/Paste you will notice the bike rider fades out toward the bottom. Since we want a more dramatic fade-out with the wheels disappearing into the clouds, hit the Delete key to get rid of the bike rider for the moment.

STEP 4: In the Clouds file, make a new channel and do a Gradient Blend in this channel just as you did in Step 2 with the bike rider. Load this channel as a selection.

STEP 5: You still have the bike rider in the copy buffer but instead of just pasting the file, choose Edit/Paste Into. The already faded bike rider is being pasted into a graduated version of the Clouds file so fewer and fewer of the pixels in the lower portion of the Clouds file are affected by the Paste Into command. By doing the Load Selection on the bike rider before copying him, you are applying a mask. Doing the Paste Into applies a second mask to the image and fades it further at the bottom.

STEP 6: Move the bike rider and then crop the image and save.

STEP 2: Gradient Tool Options.

STEP 2: Double-click on the Gradient Blend tool and set the options to Linear, 50% midpoint skew, and Foreground to Background as shown. Type D to make sure the foreground color is black and the background color is white. Click at the bottom of the channel and hold down the Shift key as you drag to

STEP 2: Channel with gradient blend.

STEP 6: Use the Move tool to Move the bike rider into a position that you like and Select/None to paste him permanently. Use the Cropping tool to crop the composite to

186

your liking and save this file in Photoshop 3.0 format under a different name than the original clouds. We used NewBiker.

USING MULTIPLY FOR A MORE INTERESTING EFFECT

STEP 7: Click on the Layers tab in the Channels palette, or, if your palette does not show a tab for Layers, chose Window/ Palettes/Show Layers (Shift-F10 with ArtistKeys). You will have only one layer currently named Background. Click on this layer (click on the layer name) and drag the layer to the New Layer icon at the bottom left of the window to make a copy of this layer. Double-click on the layer name and rename this layer Inverse.

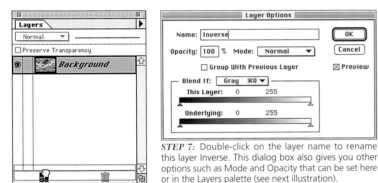

STEP 7: Make a copy of the Background layer.

STEP 7: Double-click on the layer name to rename this layer Inverse. This dialog box also gives you other options such as Mode and Opacity that can be set here or in the Layers palette (see next illustration).

STEP 8: The Inverse layer is now active (highlighted). Go to Image/Map/Inverse or type Command I to make a negative of the image. Change the mode of the layer from Normal to Multiply. This does a Multiply of the pixels in this layer with the corresponding ones in the underlying layers. We will be using Levels to make this picture more interesting, but first you must Merge Layers in the Layers options or you will only be running the Levels changes on the Inverse layer. To merge the layers, choose Merge Layers from the Layers Options triangle on the Layers palette.

STEP 8: Change the mode to Multiply.

STEP 9: Go to Image/Adjust/Levels in the RGB channel and move the sliders to create

more vivid color and contrast. Move the Input Highlight slider to the left until you reach the beginning of the histogram information, then adjust the Brightness/Contrast (middle) slider to the right until you have an effect that you like. You may want to move the Shadow slider a bit to the right also. Click on OK in Levels.

STEP 10: Double-click the Lasso tool in the Tool palette and set a feathered edge of about 5 pixels. Lasso a portion of the clouds, hold down the Option key and then click and drag a copy of the clouds over to cover what remains of the men holding up the bicycle. Use Command-H to hide the edges of your dragged patch; this makes it easier to see how it blends. You may have to take portions of several clouds to make the image look smooth. You can use the Rubber Stamp tool to clone/align portions of the clouds, the Smudge tool to soften the effect, or the Blur tool to smooth transitions at this point also. Choose File/Save As to save this file as New Biker.

TEXT EFFECT ONE

This first type of text technique was originally learned from Kai Krause's helpful tips on channel operations that have been posted on America Online for the last few years. Check out the keyword Photoshop on America Online for all of Kai's interesting techniques and lots of useful Photoshop info from all over. The steps we are using here are somewhat different from Kai's channel operations and they are made easier to understand by doing them using Layers.

STEP 1: Use File/New to make a new grayscale document 600 pixels wide by 150 pixels high with a resolution of 72 dpi. Make the background white. Click on the default colors box or type D to make sure the foreground color is black. Click

STEP 8: Choose Merge layers.

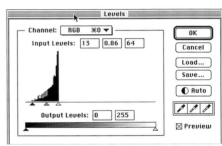

STEP 9: Adjusting levels makes this picture more interesting.

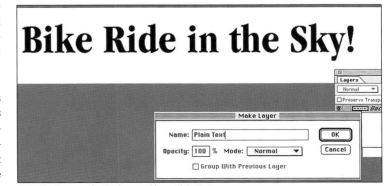

STEP 1: Rename the Background layer Plain Text.

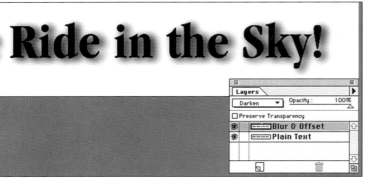

STEP 2: The Blur & Offset layer set to Darken mode.

STEP 3: Equalize the Multiply layer .

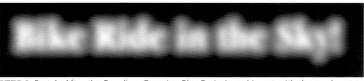

STEP 3: Part 1, After the Equalize, Gaussian Blur 5 pixels and Invert with the mode set to Normal.

STEP 3: Part 2, Finally, the above image after changing its mode to Multiply. That multiplies this layer with the step 2 results in the lower layers.

188

down with the Text tool to bring up the Text dialog box and type "Bike Ride in the Sky!" in Times Bold 60pt with Anti-aliased chosen. Position the type in the center of the background and deselect it. Double-click on the background layer and name it Plain Text. Make a copy of this layer by dragging it to the New Layer icon at the bottom of the palette and name it Blur & Offset.

STEP 2: Click on and activate the Blur & Offset layer, do a Filter/Blur/Gaussian Blur of 5 pixels and a Filter/Other/Offset of 6 pixels to the right and 4 pixels down. Make sure Repeat Edge Pixels is chosen in the Offset filter. Now make the mode for the Blur & Offset layer Darken. This chooses the darker parts of the two layers. If you wanted black text with a gray drop shadow, you could stop now. We'll go further.

STEP 3: Make a copy of the Blur & Offset layer and rename it Multiply. Set its blend mode to normal. Choose Image/Map/Equalize, to spread the blur even further, Gaussian blur this layer by 5 pixels to soften this spread, and finally choose Image/Map/Invert. We invert this blur at the end because we will eventually want to colorize it as a glow, and for that purpose we need a light gray text blur area. We also want the area surrounding the glow to be black so we can later remove it. Now, set the mode to Multiply. Remember that Multiply will emphasize the dark areas of either image.

STEP 4: Make a copy of this Multiply layer Using the New Layer icon. This actually copies Step 3: Part 1

(see illustration). Change the blend mode to Difference and name the layer Difference. File/Save this layered version and then use File/Save A Copy to save a flattened version of the image called SkyText.

STEP 4: The result of a difference between Step 3 Part 1 and Step 3 Part 2. When you do a Difference, areas that are the same become black and areas that are far apart become white to gray depending on how far apart their corresponding pixels are.

STEP 5: Final text after Hue/Saturation.

STEP 5: Open the flattened Sky Text file. Go to Mode in the main menu, change the mode to RGB and open the Hue/Saturation dialog box (Command U or Image/Adjust/Hue). Click on both the Colorize and the Preview boxes and drag the Hue slider to the left until you get a nice purple. You may also want to lower the saturation and the lightness values to get a deeper, darker purple. Say OK. Go back to the Layers palette and click on the Background layer and drag and drop a copy of this layer into your NewBiker image.

STEP 5: Move the Hue slider to colorize text.

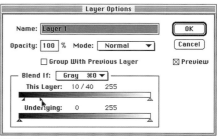

STEP 5: Blend out black on the text layer gradually with Layer Options.

Use the Move tool to move the text to a location you like. Double-click on this new layer and name it SkyText. You will now be in the Layer Options box. Drag the leftmost This Layer slider to the right slightly until most of the black background is removed. Hold down the Option key and drag just the right side of that slider triangle further to the right until you get a shadow effect that you like. Save this as NewBiker1.

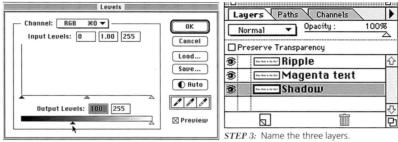

STEP 2: Move the Output Shadow slider to right.   STEP 3: Name the three layers.

The final Text One effect.

TEXT EFFECT TWO

STEP 1: Make a new RGB file 600 pixels by 150 pixels at 72 dpi with a transparent background. Click on the Black/White default colors icon or type the letter D to make the foreground color black. Choose the Type tool and click in the file to bring up the Type dialog box. Use Times Bold 60 pt. and type "Bike Ride in the Sky!" Type Command-D to Select/None.

STEP 2: Go to Image/Adjust/Levels (Command-L) and drag the Shadow Output slider (the bottom left slider) to the right to about 100 or 110 to make the text a middle gray. Say OK.

STEP 3: Drag this layer to the New Layer icon twice. Name the original layer Shadow. Name the first copy Magenta Text and the second copy Ripple.

STEP 4: Click on the Shadow layer, go to Filter/Other/Minimum and use 3 pixels to add bulk to the letters. Next, use Filter/Blur/Gaussian Blur by 5 pixels to soften the text. Finally, go to Image/Adjust/Hue/Saturation and click on the Colorize and Preview buttons. Move the Hue slider to the left to about -79 to colorize the text purple for the Shadow layer.

STEP 5: Turn off the Eye icon for the Ripple layer to see how the colors of the bottom two layers will work together. Click on the Magenta layer then go to Image/Adjust/Hue/Saturation (Command U) again and colorize this layer magenta by moving the Hue slider to about -50.

STEP 6: Turn on the Eye icon for the Ripple layer and click on that layer to make it active. Go to Filter/Distort/Ripple and use 80 Large to distort this type. Colorize to a light magenta using Hue/Saturation with the settings Hue -50, Saturation 100 and Lightness +35. Finally, change the opacity of this layer to about 65%.

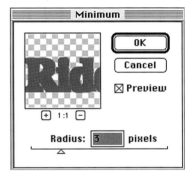

STEP 4: Use the Minimum filter to fatten the text.

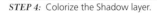

STEP 4: Colorize the Shadow layer.

189

STEP 1: Text with a transparent background.

STEP 5: The Shadow and Magenta text layers after colorizing Magenta text.

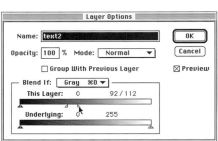

STEP 6: The Ripple layer after the Ripple filter.

STEP 7: Experiment with Layer Options to get effects like the cut-out text below.

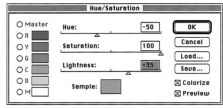

STEP 6: Colorize the Ripple layer.

STEP 7: You can now go back into any of the 3 layers and change colors, modes, or opacity. You might also use the Move tool in conjunction with the Arrow keys to move one or more layers 1 pixel at a time. Merge all 3 layers and drag this layer to your copy of New-Biker image. Double-click on your text layer to use Layer Options to experiment further. Save this as NewBiker2.

STEP 6: All three text layers active after steps 4, 5, and 6.

STEP 7: Result of the above Layer Options

STEP 6: Merged text layers on New Biker image.

TEXT EFFECT THREE: PHOTOSHOP AND ILLUSTRATOR

Now we will be switching between Photoshop and Illustrator. We will be using both programs for several reasons: first, we want to set our type on a path; second, we want our type to print at a very high resolution to avoid looking jagged; third, Illustrator will allow us to easily kern and resize our type; fourth, we'd like the ability to make further corrections to the underlying Photoshop file without disturbing the text. So fasten your seatbelts!

STEP 1: Reopen a third copy of your New Biker image. Open the paths palette by going to Window/Palettes/Show Paths (F11 with ArtistKeys). Click on the Pen tool. If you haven't used the Pen tool before, it might take several tries to get used to the feel of the tool but keep at it. If you need to, go back to the Bob Goes to Vegas chapter and reread the Creating a Path from Scratch section on using the Pen tool. This tool is a very powerful feature of Photoshop and once you get used to using it, you'll wonder how you ever worked without it.

STEP 1: The mighty Pen tool!

STEP 2: You are now going to build a path on which you will set type. You want the path to curve over the back of the bicyclist, so click the Pen tool underneath the bicycle seat to set the first point on the path and drag a handle from this point at about a 45° angle towards the upper left corner of the file. Then, let go of the mouse button and click and drag a point somewhere near the biker's shoulder. Drag this point almost directly horizontal and to the right. You'll see the actual path grow and curve as you manipulate this handle. Now, click on the selection arrow in the Paths palette to modify the curve until you get a curve that matches the biker's back and is offset from his shape several pixels. Save this path as Path 1. Click in the white space below Path 1 in the Paths palette to deselect that path.

STEP 3: Choose Select All to get the outline of your file and click the middle icon at the bottom of the Paths palette to make a new working path with this selection. Name the new path Path 2. An alternate method is to Select All

and then make a path using the Make Path option in the Paths palette menu with the tolerance set to 2.

STEP 4: Once you have named this second path you should save this Bicyclist image as NewBikerCurve in Photoshop 3.0 format. Go to File/Export/Paths to Illustrator, choose All Paths from the right pop-up item and click on Save to save a new file. This will give you the default name, which is the name of the current file with the extension .ai. If you have enough memory to run Illustrator at the same time you have Photoshop open, start Illustrator now. If not, you'll have to quit Photoshop to work in Illustrator and return to Photoshop to do your effects later. If you have no experience using Illustrator, try not to get frustrated with this part of the exercise. Illustrator, like Photoshop, is a large and wonderful program with lots of power and places to make mistakes.

STEP 5: From Illustrator, open the file you just exported, NewBikerCurve.ai. When the file opens you will probably only see four sets of cropmarks and the outline of the page size that you have set in your document layout option. Don't worry about how things look for now. Just go to View/Artwork and you should see a rectangle the size of your Photoshop file and the path that you drew for the type.

STEP 6: Use the Magnify tool, same as Photoshop's, to get close to the path for the type. Click on the Type tool and you will notice that the horizontal baseline under the tool becomes wavy as you put the Type tool on top of the path. This is the Path Type tool. Click down on the

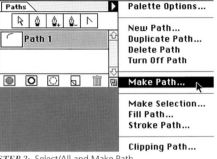

STEP 3: Select/All and Make Path.

191

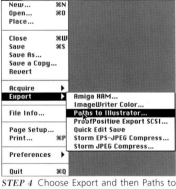

STEP 4 Choose Export and then Paths to Illustrator.

STEP 2: The first click and drag.

STEP 2: The second click and drag.

STEP 9: You may now use any technique to achieve a special shadow or glow effect. In this example, we made a copy of the text, ran a minimum filter of 3 pixels, Gaussian blurred 5 pixels, adjusted Levels to a middle gray, then used Hue/Saturation to colorize the shadow. The opacity of this layer was adjusted to 75%.

STEP 10: Once you have made your shadow layer or layers, resave the file. Your goal now is to create an image you can import into Illustrator with the shadow for the text created in Photoshop. The actual text will be created and output from Illustrator because it can then be output at Imagesetter resolution. Next, throw away any extra channels or unused layers, like the actual text but not the shadow, and then flatten the image. Save this file under a different name as an EPS with either a Mac 8-bit or Mac JPEG preview. Close Photoshop if necessary.

STEP 8: Make the floating text a new layer by dragging it to the New Layer icon.

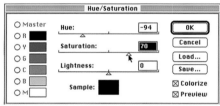

STEP 9: Colorize the shadow.

STEP 11: Go back to Illustrator and place this art. If you are still in Artwork mode you will see a bounding rectangle with an X

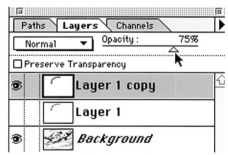

STEP 9: Opacity of shadow set to 75%.

across it. Use the Selection tool, the top left tool in Illustrator's tool palette, and the Arrow keys to position this rectangle exactly above the existing rectangle. For accuracy, you may want to zoom in considerably. When the file is in position, send it behind the type by using Arrange/Send to Back or by typing Command –. Then, use View/Preview to switch to Preview mode. You can use the Selection tool to click on the type baseline and change the color with the Paint Style dialog at this point. If you do further

---

STEP 6: Click on the path with the Text tool.

STEP 7: Command A to Select/All.

192

path near the bottom left point and you get a flashing insertion point. Type "Bike Ride in the Sky!".

STEP 7: The Type Specs dialog box in Illustrator.

STEP 7: Text kerned and resized.

STEP 7: Then, with the Text tool still selected, do Command-A (Select All) and Command-T to bring up your type specs dialog box. Change the type face to Times Bold at a point size where all the type fits and looks good (or go wild, choose Futura or some nice fat face). If you know how to use Illustrator, kern and resize the type to your heart's content, and then use Command-S to save the file with the same name.

STEP 8: Back in Photoshop, reopen NewBiker-Curve if needed, go to File/Place and choose the Illustrator file. You will get a bounding rectangle with an X over it to show the size of the EPS file. In this case, it is exactly the same size as the Photoshop file. Gavel this down and you will see a floating selection of the text that you just typed. In the Layers palette, make this a new layer.

revisions to the Photoshop file, or have other versions of the file that you would like to try, you can click on the Photoshop image, go to File/Place Art, and Illustrator will ask you if you want to replace the artwork that you have selected. If you say Replace to this prompt, your new artwork will pop into place automatically.

When you are done with your final Illustrator file, save this. It, along with the Photoshop EPS file, can now be printed to an imagesetter from Illustrator to get much finer edges on your text with PostScript text output.

STEP 11: Click on the baseline to change the color of the type.

STEP 10: EPS file with the image and shadow to be placed in Illustrator.

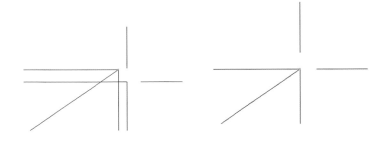

STEP 11: Your file may place like this.

STEP 11: Use the Selection tool and Arrow keys to line up the file.

STEP 11: Final Text Three effect.

HANDS-ON SESSION: POSTERIZE, BITMAPS AND PATTERNS

Create Interesting Images Using Posterize,
Bitmaps and Patterns Along with
the Layers and Calculations Features

STEP 1: The original photo of the Packard.

194

STEP 3: The Layers window should now look like this.

STEP 3: A section of the image with the 40% mezzotint pattern applied using Multiply mode.

There are many ways to create and integrate patterning into Photoshop images. Here we use Bitmaps, Filters and Layer Options to add texture effects to images.

STEP 1: Type the letter D to get the default colors. Open the Packard image within the Posterize Bitmaps & Patterns folder and bring up the Layers palette (Shift-F10 with ArtistKeys). Double-click on the background layer and rename it Packard. Choose File/Save As and save this as PackardLayers. Choose Image/Duplicate and name the duplicate copy PackardMezzo. Use Mode/Grayscale to change the mode on the duplicate copy to Grayscale and say OK to Discard Color Information. Choose Flatten if asked about flattening the image. Choose Select All (Command-A) then Edit/Copy and finally File/New (Command-N) to get a grayscale file the same size as the other Packard files. Before clicking on the OK button in the New dialog, name the file MezzoTint and make sure the White radio button is selected to fill this copy with white. Choose Filter/Noise/Add Noise and add 100 Gaussian noise. This is sort of a mezzotint pattern. Choose Command-A again to select all of the grayscale pattern. Now choose Edit/Define Pattern to make this the pattern Photoshop is now using. You should now have three windows on your screen. The original color Packard, now called PackardLayers, the grayscale PackardMezzo and the MezzoTint pattern.

DIFFUSION DITHER BITMAPS AND MEZZOTINT PATTERNS

STEP 2: Go back to the PackardMezzo window and choose Mode/Bitmap and you will get a dialog box with a lot of options. Choose Diffusion Dither and say OK; the image will be zoomed to 1:1 because diffusion dithers don't look right unless the image is seen at 1:1 or closer. A diffusion dither bitmap is an image made up of only black and white dots, there are no grays. The Bitmap mode contains one bit of information for each pixel; it is either on or off, black or white. These images are very compact. A regular grayscale image contains 8 bits per pixel, so each pixel can have 256 different gray values. You can display a diffusion dither on any computer monitor, so they are very useful. Now choose Command-Z to undo the diffusion dither, choose Mode/Bitmap again and this time pick the Custom Pattern option. This will make a bitmap that uses the MezzoTint pattern you created and saved as the default pattern. Choose Select All, go to Edit/Copy and then switch to your original color Packard image and do an Edit/Paste Layer. Name this layer MezzoPattern.

STEP 3: With the MezzoPattern layer active and both Eye icons on, change the opacity to 40%. Now you can see the original Packard layer with MezzoPattern on top of it. The colors on the Packard will be muted since you are in Normal mode. Change the mode to Multiply and this will make the black dots more black. It will also bring out better color saturation in the non-black areas, and you will see better colors from the original Packard. Choose File/Save to update your file.

A Subtle Posterize Effect

STEP 4: Click on the Packard layer to make it the active layer, and then drag it to the New Layer icon at the bottom left of the Layers palette. Double-click on this new layer and name it Posterize. Option-click on its Eye icon to turn off the other layers for now. Choose Image/Map/Posterize and set the Levels to 6. This reduces each color channel in the Posterize layer to only 6 levels of gray and will give this layer a posterized look. Now click on the Eye icon in the Packard layer to make that layer visible, but leave the Posterize layer active (highlighted in gray). Move the Opacity slider to 40%, which will show 60% of the original Packard layer from below. This will give you a subtle posterize effect while still maintaining most of the original image from below. Now turn the Eye icon of the MezzoPattern layer on and you will see all three layers together.

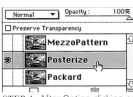

STEP 4: After Option-clicking on the Posterize Eye icon, the other layers are not visible.

STEP 4: Seeing Posterize and Packard at the same time with Posterize being active at 40%.

Streaked Patterns

STEP 5: Now we will create another pattern and add some more layers to give you other options with this image. When we add the next layer, we want it to be added above the MezzoPattern layer, so click on the Mezzo-Pattern layer to make it the active layer. Switch windows back to the MezzoTint file and zoom out so you can see the whole file on the screen. Use the Rectangular Marquee tool to make a long skinny selection on the left edge of the file the full height of the file. This rectangle should be about 1/4 inch wide. Now use Image/Effects/Scale and grab the top right handle and drag it across the screen to the right side of the window. This stretches out the dots within this 1/4 inch selection and gives you a streaking pattern. Click on the gavel to finish the scale process. Now choose Filter/Stylize/Emboss and Emboss this pattern by 4 pixels, 300% at 135 degrees. Your file should still be selected, so now choose Edit/Define Pattern to make this the current Photoshop pattern. Choose File/Save As and name this pattern MezzoStreaks. Use Command-O to reopen the original

Packard image. Use Mode/Grayscale to convert it to grayscale and then use Mode/Bitmap to convert that to another bitmap again using the Custom Pattern option. You will now get a streaked version of the Packard. Use File/Save As to save this as PackardStreaks.

STEP 6: Click on the MezzoPattern layer in PackardLayers to make it the active layer. Arrange the PackardStreaks document and the PackardLayers document so you can see both of them on the screen at the same time. You may need to re-size the windows to make them fit concurrently. Make PackardStreaks the active document, use the Move tool to click on the PackardStreaks Main Document window and then drag it and drop it on top of the PackardLayers Main Document window. The cursor will change from the Move tool double arrow to a white hand when you can release the mouse and drop the new layer. This will make a new layer in the PackardLayers document above the MezzoPatternlayer. Double-click on this new Layer and name it StreakPattern. When you double-click on a layer, this brings up the Layer Options dialog. After typing in the new name, move this dialog out of the way so you can see the PackardLayers document as well as this dialog. From the Layer Options dialog, we can change the Opacity and Composite modes. There are two sets of slider bars that are very cool—This Layer, which allows you to remove some of the pixels in the 0..255 range from the active layer, and Underlying, which allows you to specify the pixels from the underlying layers that will definitely be in the composite. Move the rightmost highlight slider on This Layer until it says 247. This means that all the pixels from 248 through 255, the white pixels, will be removed from this layer in the composite. Now you see black streaks added to the composite image as the colors and pattern from below show through the white areas. Now change the opacity to 50% and the black steaks turn to gray. Click on the OK button, and then do a Save (Command-S).

Blurring Bitmaps to Add Gray Values

STEP 7: Click on the StreakPattern layer and drag it to the New Layer icon at the bottom left of the Layers palette. Double-click on the new layer and use the Layer Options dialog to name this new layer, which should be above the StreakPattern layer, StreakPatBlur. Set its opacity back to 100% and move the rightmost This Layer slider back to 255. Say OK. Turn off the Eye icon on the StreakPattern layer and then click on the StreakPat-Blur layer to make it active. Use Filter/Blur/Gaussian Blur of 1 pixel to blur

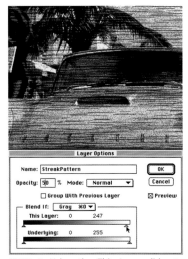

STEP 6: Using the This Layer slider to remove the whites from the pattern.

this new layer. Now double-click on it to bring up the Layer Options dialog again. The original StreakPattern layer was either black or white, there were no gray values. By blurring this layer, we have added some grays.

STEP 8: Now we can use the This Layer slider bar to do a lot of different types of effects. Move the left shadow slider on This Layer to the right until it reads about 39. This removes the dark shadow values from 0 to 38. Now move the rightmost highlight slider to the left until it reads about 226. This removes the bright highlight values from 227 to 255. Notice that this modified pattern contains jaggy edges where the whites and blacks have been removed. While holding down the Option key, click on the right side of the left shadow slider and slide it to the right, which will split the slider in two. Drag the right side of the left slider until it reaches 116. Option-click on the left half of the rightmost slider and drag it until it reads 162. The numbers on the This Layer slider should now read, from left to right: 39, 116, 162 and 226. The meaning of this is that the shadow values from 0 to 38 are completely removed. The values from 39 to 116 are blended out slowly, which removes the jaggy edges. The values from 117 to 161 are completely opaque. The values from 162 to 226 are blended out, and the values from 227 to 255 are completely removed. Try changing the mode between Normal, Multiply, Screen, Lighten, Darken and Difference until you get the one you like best. You can also re-adjust the Opacity for each different mode you try. Press on the OK button in the Layer Options dialog when you are happy with this layer's effect. Do Command-S to save this version of the document.

The Float Controls dialog in Photoshop 3.0.4 allows you

to have Layer Options type controls with a floating selection. You can convert a floating selection into a Layer by double-clicking on it or dragging it to the New Layer icon in the Layers palette.

TIME TO PLAY WITH LAYERS AND OPTIONS

STEP 9: Now you have several layers and effects that you can adjust until you get the final image you want. Remember that you can turn off any layer by clicking on its Eye icon. Play with Opacity, Mode, This Layer slider and Underlying slider in the Layer Options dialog for each layer until you get the final combined effect you like. Remember, the Underlying slider bar in the Layer Options dialog forces pixels of lower layers into the composite. In the StreakPatBlur layer, if you move the rightmost Underlying slider to the left until it gets to 128, then all the values in the final composite from 128 to 255 will come from the lower layers, they will not come from the StreakPatBlur layer. Play with this until you understand it. When you are happy with a particular effect, you can use File/Save A Copy to save a flattened version of the file using only the layers that are currently visible. This way, you can save many variations of this multi-layered document.

STEP 8: The StreakPatBlur layer with its Layer Options and the state of the Layers palette.

My favorite layer combination has the Posterize layer set to 50%, the MezzoPattern to 20%, and the StreakPattern and StreakPatBlur layers both to 40 %. I left the Layer Options and the modes for each layer as they were in the directions.

HANDS-ON SESSION: FILTERS AND EFFECTS

The best way to learn the simple filters is to just play with each of them. Try out each filter and the different features of each filter and compare them on the same image. This is something you can easily do yourself. In *Photoshop Artistry* we are going to concentrate on how to use layers and masks to combine filters in interesting ways. We are also going to talk about some of the more complicated filters and how to understand and make the best use of them.

A Tour of Some of the More Versatile 3.0 Filters (Wave, Displace, Lighting Effects, Others) as Well as Many Useful Layer and Blending Techniques for Getting the Most Out of All the Filters

GETTING BOB READY

STEP 1: Open the final file BobVegas from the Bob Goes to Vegas folder. Click on the Bob layer in the Layers palette to make it the active layer and Option-click on Bob's layer mask to work on it. Type D for the default colors. Use the Rectangular Marquee to select any sections of this mask that are white around the edge and Option-Delete them to turn them black.

STEP 1: Open BobVegas from the Bob Goes to Vegas chapter.

The white edges were added to Bob's layer mask when you moved Bob's layer around with the Move tool. Click on Bob's layer mask in the Channels palette and drag it to the Copy icon at the bottom of the Channels palette. Name this copy Bob/Vegas. We can use this Bob/Vegas mask in different ways to run different effects on either Bob, the background or some combination.

STEP 2: Option-click on the Vegas layer then use the Eyedropper to select a bright red, green or yellow from the Las Vegas background as the foreground color. Click on the Bob layer, not the layer mask, choose Edit/Fill (F3 with Artist-Keys) and fill Bob in Color mode with 20% to 30% of this color. This should give him an interesting glow.

STEP 2: Adding a red glow.

STEP 3: The Bob/Vegas/Blur mask channel.

STEP 3: Click on the Bob/Vegas mask and make another copy of it called Bob/Vegas Blur. Choose Filter/Blur/Gaussian Blur and put a 25 pixel blur on this mask channel.

STEP 4: Make a copy of Bob's layer by dragging it to the New Layer icon at the bottom of the Layers palette. Name the copy Bob/Edges. Command-click on the Bob/Edges layer mask to turn it off and Option-click on the Bob/Edges layer to make it active. Run Filter/Stylize/Find Edges on this layer followed by Command-I to invert it. Now go into Levels and notice how you can emphasize the main edges by moving the Input Highlight and Brightness/Contrast sliders to the left and the Input Shadow slider to the right. Choose OK when the edges look right to you. Now Command-click on the Bob/Edges layer mask again to turn it back on. Now turn off the Eye icon for the Bob layer and see the Bob/Edges version on top of Las Vegas.

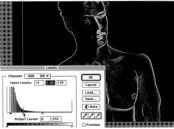

STEP 4: Using Levels to emphasize the main edges of the Find Edges filter.

STEP 5: To blend Bob/Edges and Vegas together a bit, Option-click on the Bob/Edges layer mask and choose Image/Apply Image. Set the Source to the Bob/Vegas/Blur channel, which will blend Bob/Edges with the Las Vegas scene and make the top layer slightly transparent.

STEP 5: Bob/Edges blended with Vegas.

STEP 6: Your layers and channels should look like this after Step 6.

STEP 6: Now change the mode on the Bob/Edges layer to Difference and see Las Vegas through the middle of Bob. Turn on the Eye icon for the Bob layer and at least Bob is no longer see-through. Now his skin looks sort of hard baked.

STEP 6: Bob/Edges In Difference mode with Bob partying in Las Vegas.

STEP 7: The new background with the motion blur effect.

MOTION BLUR

STEP 7: Turn off the Eye icons for all the layers except the Vegas layer. Drag that layer to the Copy icon at the bottom of the Layers palette. Name the copy Vegas Motion Blur. Use Filter/Noise/Add Noise to add 35 of Gaussian noise. Now use Filter/Blur/Motion Blur of 40 at 23° to blur the Las Vegas street in the direction of motion down the block. Change the blend mode to Luminosity and you will get an interesting effect between the blurred Las Vegas and the original Las Vegas.

STEP 8: 20% Radial Blur, Spin Draft mode on Bob's left eye then inverted.

STEP 8: With other layers on, set mode to Hard Light.

RADIAL BLUR

STEP 8: Make of copy of the Bob layer and call it Bob Radial Blur. Option-click on its Eye icon to turn off the other layers for now and Command-click on the layer mask to turn it off, too. Use Filter/Blur/Radial Blur and set the center of the blur to Bob's left eye. This may take you a couple of times to get

right. Use Spin of 20 in Draft mode. The other modes will take forever but don't forget that they are there when you need the absolute best quality radial blur. Use Command-I to invert this image to complete the first part of this step. Now Option-click on the Eye icon of this layer to turn the other layers back on. Set the mode of this layer to Hard Light, then set the opacity of the Bob layer to 50% and you get the second effect of this step.

STEP 9: What the Layers palette should look like after Step 8.

STEP 9: Choose File/Save to save your creation so far. Turn off the Eye icons of the top two layers and set the opacity of the Bob layer to 70%. Choose Image/Duplicate and select the Merged Layers Only checkbox to create a merged copy of the bottom three layers. Choose Flatten Image from the Layers palette of this copy. Choose Select/All and then Edit/Copy to copy this new composite image. Switch back to your layered document, make sure the top layer is active and do an Edit/Paste Layer. Name the new layer Comp layer and leave its mode and opacity at Normal and 100% for now. We just created a single new layer that is a composite of three previous layers.

THE WAVE FILTER

STEP 10: Now choose Filter/Distort/Wave and look at the many options within this dialog. The first step in understanding what the Wave filter can do for you is to simplify the options. Set the number of generators to 1, the type to Sine, both wavelengths to 30 and both amplitudes to 50. Just make waves

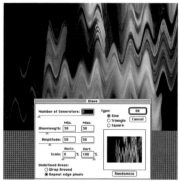

STEP 10: The Wave filter with the options simplified. The wavelength of a sine wave goes from one high point to the next. The amplitude is from the top to the bottom of a wave. It is a bit easier to see what the wave looks like because we are just doing it in the vertical direction.

for now 100% in the vertical dimension. Getting simple sine waves across the screen makes it easier to see what this filter actually does. Change the type to Triangle waves and you can see that they look like the stitch of a zig-zag sewing machine. Try the square shape, my favorite. It makes the image look like it went through a shredder and then was put back together again. Play around with these parameters but keep it simple until you understand what each one does. They can be combined in interesting ways to create all sorts of wave shapes.

Go back into the Wave filter and set the shape to Square. Set the number of generators to 1, all wavelength and amplitude values to 50, and then set 100% Vertical and 50% Horizontal. Repeat Edge Pixels should also be turned on. This is a cool effect just by itself, but now try the different blend modes and also different opacities to get lots of other neat effects. The one I liked best is shown here with blend mode set to Overlay and Opacity set to 100%.

LINE DRAWING

STEP 11: Now let's open a different image and try some other types of filters and effects. Open the file called ParisDog from the Filters and Effects folder. Notice that it already contains a mask of the dog and a pattern that we created in Photoshop. See the Posterize, Bitmaps and Patterns chapter for some ideas about how to create patterns like this in Photoshop. First we will show you how to turn this image into a line drawing. Double-click on the Background layer and rename it Orig Dog. Make a copy of this layer by dragging it to the Copy icon in the Layers palette. Name the copy Dog Edges. Use Filter/Stylize/Find Edges on the Dog Edges layer to find the edges of this image and use Image/Map/Invert (Command-I) to invert those edges. Use Command-L for Levels and move the

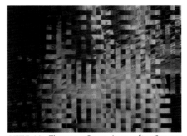
STEP 10: The new Comp layer after Square wave with the Blend mode set to Normal.

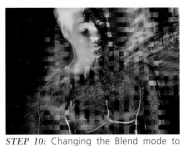
STEP 10: Changing the Blend mode to Overlay brings in the lower layers in an interesting way.

STEP 11: The original Paris Dog image.

Input Highlight and Brightness/Contrast sliders to the left and the Input Shadow slider to the right to emphasize the main edges. You can also use the Load button to load the LevelsIsolateEdges preset levels settings from the Extra Info folder. Click on OK in Levels.

STEP 12: Choose Duplicate Layer from the Layers palette pop-up with a new destination to make a copy of this layer in a separate file. Use Mode/Grayscale to turn the copy into black-and-white. You need to do this in a separate file or else all the layers will be turned into black-and-white. You will now have white lines against a black background. Use the Move tool to click on this grayscale file and then drag it and drop it back on the Paris Dog file. Now you should have a new black-and-white layer on the top so name it Dog Edges B&W. You should now have Orig Dog as the bottom layer, then Dog Edges and finally, Dog Edges B&W on top. Turn off the Eye icon for Dog Edges and set the mode for Dog Edges B&W to Darken. Darken mode will give you a black background with colored lines where the white edges were. To get a different effect, use Command-I to invert Dog Edges B&W

STEP 11: The Dog Edges layer after Find Edges, Invert and Levels.

STEP 12: The Dog Edges B&W layer by itself after being Inverted.

STEP 12: Dog Edges B&W combined using Lighter with the Orig Image channel.

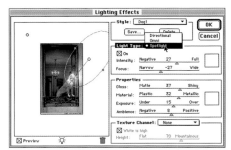

200

STEP 13: The Dog Edges B&W Fat layer combined using Lighter with the Orig Image channel.

STEP 14: The Lighting Effects filter with texture created by the Lines Thin pattern.

and change the mode to Lighten. This will give you a white background with colored lines. I like this effect a little better.

STEP 13: Now make another copy of the Dog Edges B&W layer, call it Dog Edges B&W Fat and make sure that is now the top layer. Turn the Eye icon off for Dog Edges B&W. You should now have the Eye icons on for Dog Edges B&W Fat (the active layer), and for Orig Dog. Run Filter/Other/Minimum of 1 on Dog Edges B&W Fat. This will make the edges here a minimum of 1 pixel wide and will give a chalk drawing type effect. The mode should still be set to Lighter, so you will see more color detail with these thicker lines.

LIGHTING EFFECTS

STEP 14: Click on the Dog Edges B&W layer, go into the Channels palette and make a copy of its Red channel using the New Channel icon at the bottom of the Channels palette. Name this copy Lines Thin. We are going to use this as a pattern in the Lighting Effects filter. In the Layers palette, make another copy of the Orig Dog layer right on top of that layer and call it Dog Pattern. Option-click on its Eye icon to turn off all the other layers for now.

Choose Filter/Render/Lighting Effects and notice the many options in this filter that allow you to add lighting with different types of lights to your image. The Photoshop 3.0 manual has a good description of this filter, which you should read if you want to understand all of its features. We are going to try some of them here. Set the light type to Default and click on the white circle over the dog preview in the dialog box. This is the original light. Drag it and place it on the dog's shoulder. Click on the other end of the line that is leading out of the white spot and move it around so it ends up above and to

the right of the dog's head. This is a spotlight pointing at the dog and coming from above and to the right of the dog. Set its intensity and width as shown here. You change the width by clicking on the sides of the oval then dragging to make the oval wider or thinner.

Now add a new light by clicking on the Light-bulb icon at the bottom of the dialog. Set its light type to Directional and place it at the top left of the image near where the chandelier meets the ceiling. Drag the line coming out of the spot far above and a little to the right. This creates a light coming from above at a subtle angle. Set its parameters as shown in the dialog. Click on OK to see the effects of these lights in more detail. Choose Command-Z to undo these effects. Type Command-Option-F to bring up the Lighting Effects filter again and change its options. Go down to the Texture Channel pop-up and select the Lines Thin channel you

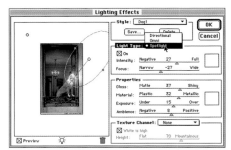

STEP 14: The different light types in the Lighting Effects filter.

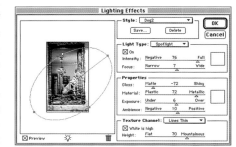

STEP 14: The Spotlight.

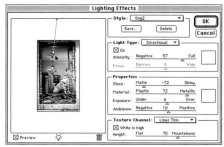

STEP 14: The Directional light and Texture Channel set to Lines Thin.

created at the beginning of this step. Set the parameters as in the illustration here. Now choose OK from the Lighting Effects filter and you will see a texture formed around the line edges.

STEP 15: Choose Command-Z to undo the previous incantation of Lighting Effects and Command-Option-F to go back into the filter. Change the Texture Channel to Dog Pattern and set the parameters as shown. Click on the OK button. Now turn on the Eye icon for the Orig Dog layer underneath.

STEP 15: The Lighting Effects filter with texture created by the Dog Pattern pattern.

STEP 15: The Dog Pattern Lighting Effects combined with Orig Dog using Soft Light mode at 70% Opacity.

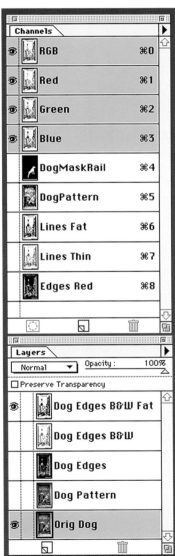

STEP 15: The final Paris Dog layers and channels.

STEP 15: The setup for the Texture Channel and Dog Pattern.

With Dog Pattern as the active layer, set the mode to Soft Light and the opacity to 70% to see the final effect pictured here. You should try some of the textures on the Photoshop 3.0 Deluxe CD-ROM with the Lighting Effects filter.

DISPLACEMENT MAPS

STEP 16: Now let's play with displacement maps. Go to the Channels palette and choose New Channel from the pop-up. Type D to get the default colors then use the Gradient tool to do a linear gradient with 50% midpoint skew from black at the bottom to white at the top. Use Command-M to enter Curves, click on the Load button and load the Displace Curve from the folder for this exercise. This will create a displacement map that is black in the center and white at the top and bottom. Using this as a displacement map will cause any value that is less than 128 to displace in a negative direction and any value that is greater than 128 to displace in a positive direction. Use the Duplicate Channel pop-up to copy this channel to a separate, new destination file and save it in Photoshop 3.0 format. Name this new file Left/Right Flop. Any Photoshop 3.0 file can be a displacement map. Make the Dog file active, choose Filter/Distort/Displace and set the

STEP 16: The Left/Right Flop displacement map.

STEP 16: The dog after being displaced by 20 horizontally.

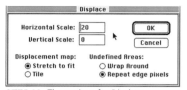

STEP 16: The settings for Displace.

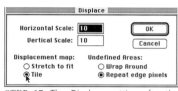

STEP 17: The Displace settings for the Chain Displacement map.

STEP 17: The dog after being displaced by the Chain Displacement map.

parameters to displace as shown here. Make sure Stretch to fit and Repeat Edge pixels are turned on. When asked for a displacement map, open the file you just saved, Left/Right Flop. Notice that the pixels in the image whose corresponding pixels were less than 128, in the displacement map, moved to the right, and those that were more than 128 moved to the left. Use Command-Z to undo this. Now, try Displace again, but this time use -20 as the horizontal value. That causes the image to flop in the opposite direction.

STEP 17: Again, use Command-Z to undo the last Displace. Now use the Rectangular Marquee to select the rightmost small chain hanging down to the bottom left of the window. Also select a little of the gray around the chain. Edit/Copy this, do Command-N and OK for a new file, and then paste this section of chain in the new file. Save this as ChainMap in Photoshop 3.0 format. Now choose Filter/Distort/Displace again but this time change the settings to 10 in each of the horizontal and vertical directions and turn on the Tile setting. This will cause the same displacement map to be repeated over and over again until the image is covered. Choose the ChainMap for your displacement map and you will get the image shown here. Try some other patterns for a displacement map. When there are two or more channels in the displacement map, the first channel is used to displace in the horizontal direction and the second channel is used to displace in the vertical direction. Displace is a very powerful and fun filter that can be used for a lot of great effects. You just need to create the displacement map that is appropriate for your needs!

STUDENT CREATIONS

While teaching Photoshop since 1990, I have saved various student creations. A few of these follow on the next three pages. Some of these were done using the files from my courses (the many variations of Bob), and some were done using files the students brought to class.

FACING PAGE

Effects done by students in Haynes' advanced courses where the students bring in their own projects and images. The image on the top left is by Susan Holland, the top right is by Will Croff, the bottom left and bottom middle are by Jeffrey Myers and the bottom right is by Marita Gootee.

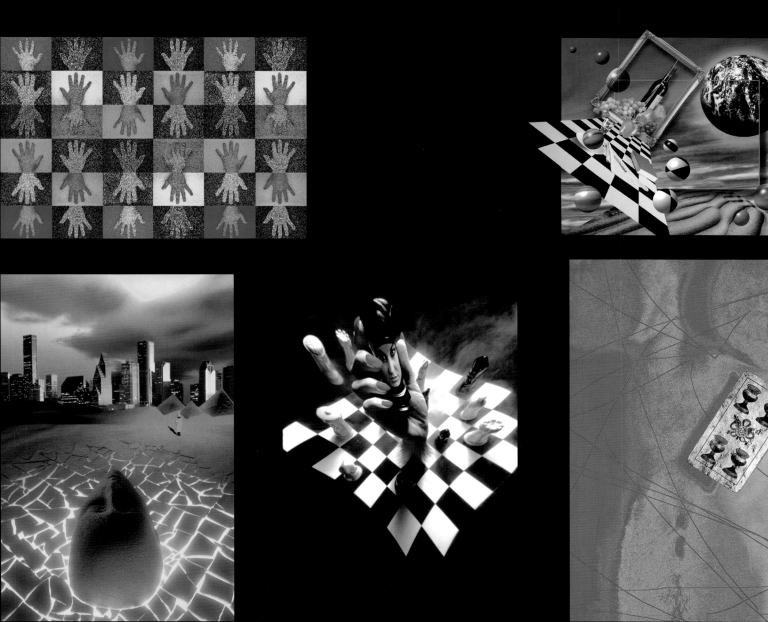

Radiation Bob by Robert Chaponot

Twistin Bob by Pat Kirk

By Jim Ferry

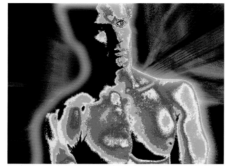

Ramblin Gamblin Bob by Ed Birmingham

Sharp Bob by Merin Mcdonell

WindBlownBob by Hillary Granfield

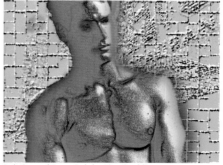

By Mariam Wiegel

By Mariam Wiegel

Bob Several From Bob by Lisa Conklin

Damage From Bob by Darren Bradley

Pasty Bob by Lisa Conklin

Hot Pink Bob by Carrie Bahnsen

Bob's Fantasy World by Linda Danialy

AlienBob by Becky Collins

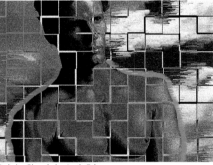

Bob in Clouds by Ipek Erk

By Mathew Foster

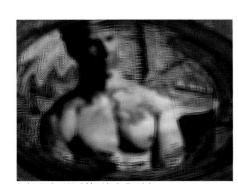

Bob's Noisy World by Linda Danialy

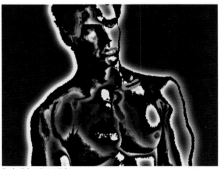

Bob E by Pat Kirk

HANDS-ON SESSION: THE APDA MAGAZINE COVER

*Create an Image from Components for a
Specified Canvas Size, a Magazine Cover;
Work with Drop Shadows, Knock-Outs, Motion Effects,
the Pen Tool and Layers for High Quality Output*

(This magazine cover was produced for the Apple Programmers and Developers Association)

The original photograph of the computers by Marc Simon Photography. We'll refer to this as Computers in the example.

This example describes the production of a published magazine cover for the February 1993 issue of the Apple magazine *APDA*, Apple Programmers and Developers Association. This magazine is a catalog of tools and information for Macintosh software developers. This cover was to introduce some new QuickTime multimedia tools for writing software for the Macintosh and Windows. Dan Auvil, from Crane Auvil & Associates in San Francisco, came up with the concept for the cover, which he sketched to scale on an 8.5x11 sheet of paper. Dan then hired Marc Simon, also in San Francisco, to shoot the original photographs—the two computers and the multimedia objects that would be flying into the computer screen. The objects were shot together like this so the lighting and shadows on each object would look correct in relationship to each other when they were composited in the computer.

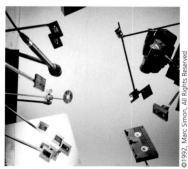

The original photograph of the multimedia objects by Marc Simon Photography. We'll refer to this as Objects in the example.

Marc had recently taken a Photoshop class from Barry, so he hired Barry to do the compositing on the Macintosh. Like many photographers today, Marc was considering purchasing a computer to add to his bag of darkroom tools. Since this project, Marc has purchased his own Macintosh and is now among those leading edge photographers who do great studio

The final February 1993 APDA magazine cover image as delivered to the advertising agency, Crane Auvil & Associates. They added text titles and logos using QuarkXPress to produce the final cover. This is the image you will produce in this example.

work and also digital imaging. While working on this project, Barry and Marc had to look at Dan's hand drawn sketch and produce the concept to scale with Marc's images on the computer screen. We will go through the steps to do this here.

PRODUCING THINGS TO SPEC

One of the things we want to learn in this example is how to produce things to scale to a spec. Since the final magazine cover has already been produced, we will use that as a target to emulate instead of working from the hand drawn sketch. The files in this example are in CMYK format because they were scanned from a high-end scanner where the operators guaranteed that the color of the scan would match the transparency. Because of the high-end CMYK scan, we just had to do the compositing and effects, we didn't have to worry about color correcting.

SETTING UP THE CANVAS

STEP 1: Open the files ComputersOrigScan, PartsOrigScan and FinalAPDA from the APDA Magazine Cover folder on the CD. What we want to do in this example is create the FinalADPA image from the other two files. For the original magazine cover all the files were 300 dpi, we have reduced them to 150 dpi and JPEG compressed them here so they are not quite so big to work with.

STEP 2: The final cut magazine cover is 10.8 inches by 8.4 inches. We want to produce something a little bigger than this since the cover is a full bleed and there needs to be some leeway around the edges. We will make the final canvas size 9 by 11 inches keeping in mind that it will be cropped to 8.4 x 10.8 when it is printed. Switch to the file ComputersOrigScan and choose Image/Canvas Size. Set the height to 11 inches and put the gray box in the bottom center so the new height will be added above. Leave the width as is and choose OK. Now double-click on the Rectangular Marquee and set its options to fixed size with the width being 1350 (9x150) and the height being 1650 (11x150) pixels. Zoom out so you can see the entire image on the screen. Click down in the top left hand corner of the screen to place the fixed size selection box and then drag with the mouse button still down to the location you want to crop. Now choose Edit/Crop (F4 with ArtistKeys) to crop the image to your 9 x 11 x 150 pixel size. Choose File /Save As and save this as WhiteCanvas. You will turn this into your final canvas for this project.

STEP 3: Arrange WhiteCanvas and FinalAPDA on the screen so you can look at all of both folders at once. Bring up the Info palette (F9 with ArtistKeys) and in Palette options, set its bottom measurement area to inches. Double-click on the Line tool and set the line width to zero with no arrowheads. We will use the Line tool as a ruler to measure the distance from the bottom of the keyboard to the bottom of the FinalAPDA image. To do this, just click at the bottom of the keyboard in the rightmost computer and drag to the bottom of the image area with the Shift key down to force a vertical line. It should be about 1.813 inches shown as delta Y in the Info palette. Now measure this distance on the WhiteCanvas image; it will be less. Figure out the difference between 1.813 and the distance on WhiteCanvas and write this down. Set the Rectangular Marquee tool back to Normal mode and use it to select the part of the WhiteCanvas image that was there originally before we increased the height in Canvas Size. Select the full width. Move the selection upwards then, after starting the move, put the Shift key down to force the movement to be only vertical. Move it upwards the calculated distance so the total distance from the bottom of the keyboard to the bottom of the image is 1.813 or very close to it. You can see the moved distance as delta Y in the Info palette. Delta X should stay zero; having the Shift key down after you start the move will force this. Do Command-S for Save.

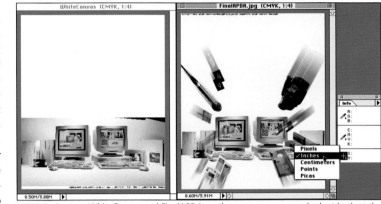

STEP 3: Arrange WhiteCanvas and FinalAPDA on the screen so you can look at both at the same time. Set the Info palette to measure in inches.

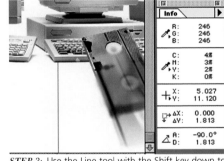

STEP 3: Use the Line tool with the Shift key down to measure the distance from the bottom of the keyboard to the bottom of the image.

KNOCKING OUT THE BACKGROUND

STEP 4: Now you will use the Pen tool to make a selection around all the computers and other objects in the image. We want to knock out the background, and unfortunately, we can't do it automatically, because it is not a different enough color from the computers and equipment. Put yourself in

Trace up the left side of the rightmost monitor, down its other side and over the tops of the books on the right side. Now come along the bottom of the mice and keyboards. When you are selecting shadow areas, include all the shadow in your selection. This is very important! Move to the left along the front of the keyboards and then finally up the left side of your original book until you complete the path by clicking again on the first path point. When you get to that point, a little white circle will appear to the right of the pen nib to tell you the path has been completed. Choose Save Path from the Path palette's menu and name it Computers Outline.

STEP 5: With this path still selected, use the Pen tool again to add the two hole areas below and to the left of the leftmost monitor and below and to the right of the rightmost monitor. These areas will be holes in your final selection. Now click on the Arrow tool and click on the first big path you made around all of the equipment. This will bring up the points again and you should scroll around the screen looking at each point and the adjoining lines carefully and moving any points that need to be moved. Remember that you can get the Pen+ tool while using the Arrow by holding Command-Option down when on a line. You get Pen- with Command-Option when on a point and the Convert Direction Point tool with Command-Control when on a point.

STEP 6: Since you named your path, it and all its changes have been saved under the name we gave it in the Paths palette. When your path is completed, click with the arrow tool on the background image outside the path to deselect any subpaths that could be selected. Now, click on the Selection icon in the middle at the bottom of the Paths palette to turn the entire path into a selection. Bring up the Channels palette (F10 with ArtistKeys) and click on the Selection icon at the bottom left of it to save this selection to a channel. Name this channel HardEdgeMask and then choose Select/None (Command-D) to remove the selection. Go to Image/Map/Invert to invert

STEP 4: Start and end your path here at the top left of the leftmost book.

STEP 4: Make sure you select the shadows below the keyboards, mice and other items.

Full Screen mode using the middle icon at the bottom of the Tool palette. Hit the Tab key to close all your palettes. Choose Window/Palettes/Show Paths to bring up the Paths palette. Select the Pen tool and use Command-Spacebar-click to zoom into the top of the leftmost book at the left of the White-Canvas image. Start tracing the image around the edge between the books, computers and other objects and the background. We want to make a path that selects all objects but no background. Use the Spacebar to scroll, Command-Spacebar to zoom in and Option-Spacebar to zoom out as you move around the edges of the objects making a path to eliminate the background. If you misplace a single point, you can Undo (Command-Z) to remove that one point and redo it. If you mess up several points, just continue and fix them later. Trace the path to the right across the books, up and around the leftmost monitor and down its right side getting the nook areas between the monitors. Don't forget to use click and drag around the corners and on curves to get an accurate path for each type of shape. Remember to use the Spacebar and mouse drags to scroll around the image as you work.

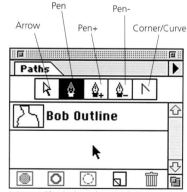

STEP 4: The Paths palette with its tools.

STEP 6: Here is the finished selection as saved in the Paths palette and converted to a selection then saved as a channel.

the mask so the selected area, the white area, is the background of the image instead of the computers. We are now going to blur the areas that were shadows in the original image so when we knock out the background with a solid color, the original shadows remain.

BLURRING TO KEEP THE SHADOWS

STEP 7: Make a copy of HardEdge-Mask by dragging it to the New Channel icon in the middle at the bottom of the Channels palette. Name the copy SoftEdgeMask. We will blur parts of the copy so we can start over with the HardEdgeMask if we make a blurring mistake. Hit the Tab key to bring back the Tool palette if it is still hidden. Double-click on the Lasso tool and set its feather to 2 and make sure Anti-aliased is on. Click on Channel #0, CMYK, and select the shadow under one of the mice. Select very wide around the shadow where it blends into the white background and then select more exactly the shadow edge where it meets the non-shadowed mouse. Look at the example selection here. Now click on Channel #6, SoftEdgeMask, and you will use this selection to blur the mask. Enter Command-H to hide the selection edges and then Choose Filter/Blur/Gaussian Blur and do a Gaussian blur of 3 pixels on this selected area. Notice in the diagrams shown here what this does to the mask.

STEP 7: Select the shadow below the mouse with a selection like this.

STEP 7: Switch to Channel #6 then Command-H to hide selection edges. Here is the mouse before the blur.

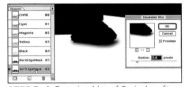

STEP 7: A Gaussian blur of 3 pixels softens the shadow area below the mouse in the mask channel.

STEP 7: When you are finished with the mask, it should look like this.

Now you need to repeat this process for all the shadows that occur at the bottom of the objects in the foreground. The shadows below the keyboards, the mice, the CD and any other objects need to be done. The steps are: select the shadow area while in Channel #0, Command-6 to switch to the mask, Command-H to hide the selection edge so you can see if the blur looks clean, Command-F to run the same Gaussian blur of 3 pixels, and then Command-0 to switch back to Channel #0 and select the next section. Don't forget about using the Option key with the Lasso tool to get straight sections. You can review this in the Victorians and Clouds chapter. If you are not sure how the mask should look, compare it to the sample version called WhiteCanvasBackgroundMask in the Extra Info Files folder for this chapter on the CD.

STEP 8: Once you have finished blurring the shadows in the mask, do a Load Selection on this SoftEdgeMask by Option-clicking on it in the Channels palette. Click on the background color at the bottom of the Tool palette and set its CMYK values to 5,3,3,0. Click OK in the color picker. Now all you have to do is hit the Delete key and the background of your image will be filled with its final background color of 5,3,3,0, which is the brightest neutral white that will still hold a dot on most sheet-fed presses. You don't want solid white in this area because it will stand out too much and the blurs that you are going to do later will look a lot better against a white that still has a dot in it.

SAVING YOUR BASE CANVAS

STEP 9: Save your completed WhiteCanvas file. Since you will be adding objects to this file from now on, it may be easier to recover from a mistake by reverting areas back to this original WhiteCanvas. To save space and time, you may want to save the SoftEdgeMask in a separate file in case you ever need it later. Saving it in a separate file stops Photoshop from taking

STEP 8: The WhiteCanvas with the selection loaded before the delete changes the background color.

STEP 8: The WhiteCanvas after the delete changes its background color.

the time and space to compress it and add it to the file every time you do a Save for the rest of this project. I often save my masks in separate files when I think I'm done with them just in case I need them for an effect later. Click on the HardEdgeMask in the Channels palette and drag it to the Trash icon at the bottom of the palette. Now click on the SoftEdge-Mask and choose Duplicate Channel from the Channels palette's menu. Set the destination to New and call it WhiteCanvasBackgroundMask. This will open up in a new window as a grayscale Photoshop file. Save it in Photoshop 3.0 format and it will be greatly compressed since it is a mask. Now go back to your WhiteCanvas and drag SoftEdgeMask to the trash. Save this without any mask channels attached. This will make subsequent saves of WhiteCanvas faster and make the file smaller. If you ever need to use that SoftEdgeMask background mask again, just open the file and either copy it as a new channel back to White-Canvas or do a load selection from one window to another. Just as long as neither the mask nor the WhiteCanvas file have been cropped since they were separated, the mask will still line up exactly.

STEP 9: The Duplicate Channel dialog box. Set Destination to New to move the channel to a new window.

ADDING THE MULTIMEDIA OBJECTS

STEP 10: Now that we have completed our final canvas, it is time to start adding the multimedia parts that are to be flying into the computer screens. Switch to the file PartsOrigScans and bring up the Paths palette (F10 with ArtistKeys). Since you have already had a goodly amount of exercise with the Pen tool, we won't make you outline all these parts. Notice that the path for each of the parts is already in this file. Just remember though, if you are trying to figure out how long it will actually take to do a job like this, each of these objects will have to be carefully outlined with the Pen tool. Click on the path called Video8 and you will notice it highlighted on the bottom right. You want to turn this into a selection so click on it and drag it to the Selection icon in the middle at the bottom of the Paths palette. Now choose Edit/Copy to copy this first object. Switch to the WhiteCanvas, do Edit/Paste Layer and name this layer Video8. We will make each of the objects a separate layer so we can move them around and change them for the art director and even his/her boss.

STEP 11: Look at the position of the Sony Video 8 cassette within the file FinalAPDA and then use the Move tool to move the Sony cassette in the Video8 layer to the same location in WhiteCanvas. Since we have made this object a layer, we can always move it again later for our client's final approval. Choose Edit/Paste Layer again and name this layer Video8Blur. Choose Image/Effects/Distort and distort the Video 8 cassette so it is massively stretched along its longest axis, but the shortest axis, the vertical, is not changed in size (see the diagram here). Click on the Gavel to finish the distort. If necessary, use the Move tool to first move the disk to the middle of the screen so there is enough room to distort it as much as needed. Now choose Filter/Noise/Add Noise and add Gaussian noise of about 50.

Now choose Filter/Blur/Motion Blur and do a motion blur of Distance 32 whose Angle is parallel with the direction of motion of the cassette. You change the angle by clicking on the line in the circle and rotating it so it is parallel with the direction of motion. The motion blur will cause the pieces of noise we just added to look like streaks. Now set the opacity of this layer to 50% and then use the Move tool to move the blur on top of the Video8 layer. With the opacity at 50%, you can see through the Video8 Blur layer to see if it is lined up and sized correctly with the Video8 layer. At this point you will probably need to do Image/Rotate/Free to get the angle of the blur to exactly match the Video8 layer below. First you grab the top left corner handle and drag it to rotate the blur the desired amount. If you wait a minute, Photoshop will give you a low-res prototype of the new rotated blur. If the angle doesn't seem correct, you can again grab the handle and adjust the rotation amount. When the low-res prototype seems correct, click on

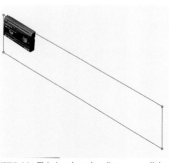

STEP 10: Turning the Video8 path into a Selection.

STEP 11: This is what the distort parallelogram of Video8 should look like.

the Gavel icon in the middle of the rotation area to complete the rotate and see it in hi-res. After the angle looks correct, you may need to use Image/Effects/Scale to scale the blur so it is exactly the same width as the Video8 cassette. When scaling this, use the handle on the lower left corner with the Shift key down to scale proportionately. You will probably need the scale because the Distort command usually changes the width somewhat. When the blur is lined up correctly, it should look like the diagram here.

STEP 11: This is what the blur will look like when it is rotated, scaled and lined up on top of the Video8 Layer.

STEP 12: The blur should be lined up on the Video8 layer so the white hub of the leftmost tape reel blurs off below and to the right. Set the feather on the Lasso tool to about 10 and use it to select the portion of the blur that is hanging off above and to the front of the Video8 layer. You want to select widely around this area so the 10 pixel feather doesn't affect the area you want to remove beyond the front edge of the Video8 cassette. The feather should cause the removal to slowly fade from a sharp front edge of the cassette on the Video8 layer into the blur caused by the Video8 Blur layer. Once you make the selection correctly, hit the Delete key to remove this part of the blur. Again, see the diagram here for details on how to make this selection. After deleting this area, choose Select/None (Command-D) so the blur you are about to do affects this entire layer. Now, for the final finishing touches, I set the opacity on the Video8 layer to 80% and that on the Video8Blur layer to 60%. I also did a Filter/Blur/Gaussian Blur of 1 on the Video8Blur layer to soften the streaking effect.

STEP 12: Here is the selection, with 10 pixel feather, of the area we are going to remove from the Video8 blur layer.

ADDING THE SLIDES

STEP 13: This is the basic process for the effect of objects flying into the computer screens. The Video8 cassette is about the simplest object to do since it has a very symmetrical shape and it was easy to get a blur effect

that looks good and also lines up with the original object. Many of the other objects presented specific problems due to their shape. The technique for the slides at the bottom left is about the same as Video8 but they need to be done in three different parts. First do the single slide, called Slide in the PartsOrigScan Paths palette, and paste two layers like you did for Video8. To avoid too much distortion when you stretch the slide to make the blur, you may want to first rotate it so its bottom side is horizontal and the left and right sides are vertical. You can then use Image/Effects/Scale to stretch it straight down instead of using the Distort command. When the Slide layer and its blur layer look correct together, go back and do Slides in a similar way. Copy all of the slides and paste them down as the Slides layer. Now edit that layer with the Rubber Stamp tool to remove the prop objects that are visible separating the front two slides from the back three. Now do one blur layer for the blur effect on the back three slides and then do a separate blur layer for the blur effect on the front two slides. Once you have these slide layers looking correct together, you can merge them into fewer layers to reduce the total number of layers. Try these slides next and then we will move on to some more complicated objects.

FADING THE BLUR

STEP 14: The Dat tape, diskettes, video tape and cassettes all use some variations of the technique we used for the Video8 and the Slides files. The Dat tape is the simplest, just do the same thing again. The cassettes are difficult because the two blurs melt together awkwardly; still, I think you can figure this out. The video tape has a weird shape with dark holes in its bottom that don't blur very nicely. You will have to change their shape and remove some dark parts before you can get a blur that looks good. With the diskettes the problem is getting the chrome sliding doors to look correct in the blur. One thing all these objects and the transparencies have in common (we didn't do this with the Video 8 cassette) is that their blurs fade away as they get further from the object. The following steps cover a general technique to fade the blur (using the Dat tape as an example) that works with all the objects we have mentioned so far.

STEP 15: As in Video8, we start by making one layer called Dat in which we place the Dat tape copied from PartsOrigScan. Then we create a second layer called Dat Blur where the blurred Dat effect was created. So far this

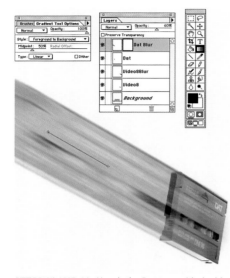

STEP 17: Double-click on the Layer Mask icon to get the Layer Mask Options. Set Position Relative To: to Image to move the layer mask separately from its layer.

STEPS 15 AND 16: Here is the Dat tape with the blur effect as we fade the blur. To set up for fading, we use the Gradient tool with the above options and a layer mask. We click down in Gradient where we want the blur to be 100% gone and drag to where we want it to be 100% there.

STEP 16: The layer mask that caused the blur to fade as pictured to the right. Wherever the mask is black, the blur is completely gone.

STEP 16: The blur after the Gradient tool fades it with a layer mask.

is exactly like Video8 and here is what it looks like. To fade the blur we need to add a layer mask to the Dat Blur layer from the Layers palette menu. The layer mask has been added to the right and it is highlighted, so we are editing the layer mask while watching the layer and all the layers below it.

STEP 16: We need to double-click on the Gradient tool and make sure we are doing a Linear gradient from Foreground to Background at 100% Normal. Our foreground and background colors have been set to black and white. We now click down on the far end of the blur where we want it to have faded completely away, and then drag parallel to the blur towards the Dat tape and let up where we want the blur to still be 100% there. Voila, instant fade! It will have faded along the length of the gradient line.

STEP 17: Remember, when you add a layer mask, the things that are black in the layer mask are removed from the layer. Pictured in Step 16 is the layer mask that removed the tail of this blur. If you are not happy with the length of the blur fade-out, you need to redo the gradient to make a longer or shorter distance in the transition from black to white. If you are not happy with the location of the blur fade-out, you can move the layer mask separately from the layer it is masking and change the location of where the fade starts and ends. To do this, double-click on the layer mask icon and then set the Position Relative To option to Image instead of the

default Layer. Now you can use the Move tool to move the layer mask. If you move the mask to the left, the tail on the Dat will get longer, and if you move it to the right, the tail will get shorter. Try it! When you are happy with how the blur fades, you can click on the layer mask and drag it to the trash at the bottom right of the Layers palette. If you choose Apply instead of Discard when you are given the choice, the areas that were removed from the blur by the layer mask will become permanently removed from that layer. They will become transparent so you can see the layers below through them. You may not want to remove and apply the layer mask until the art director or person who needs to approve the project has seen it. You can always make a layer mask temporarily disabled by Command-clicking on the Layer Mask icon. This would bring back the full length of the tail in this case.

When you have completed an object layer and its blur layer, you could use Merge Layers to combine them into one layer. This would make the file smaller but wouldn't give you the maximum flexibility if you later wanted to change the blur or the object by itself.

MORE DIFFICULT EFFECTS

STEP 18: The most difficult objects are the CD, the video camera and the microphone. Let's start out with the microphone. Go to the PartsOrigScan file and load a selection for the mike by clicking on it and dragging it to the Selection icon at the bottom of the Paths palette. Copy this as usual and do an Edit/Paste Layer on top of all the other layers you have done so far. Name this layer Mike and use the Move tool to position the mike in the correct location based on the FinalAPDA file. The first thing you need to do now is straighten out the cord that leads from the end of the mike off the screen to the left. Set the Lasso feather to 0, select the cord area and rotate it so it looks straight. I also had to copy a straighter part of it next to the mike and use that to lengthen the rest of the cord and also make it look straight. You will probably have to use the Rubber Stamp tool to do some cleanup when you are done creating the basic straight cord.

THE BLURRED MIKE

STEP 19: To create the blur effect on the mike, we tried all sorts variations and the thing that looked the best was actually stretching out part of the wire mesh that you speak into on the head of the mike. To do this, select the wire mesh with the Lasso tool as shown here. Copy this, choose File/New (Command-N) and create a new CMYK file that is about 1000x1000 pixels. Paste the wire mesh there, and then do the following contortions to it while it is a floating selection to create the blur effect. Use Image/Rotate/Free to rotate it so it is vertical. Use the Command key with the Rectangular Marquee to crop it further so the vertical sides are straight. Now do Image/Effects/ Perspective and click on the top

STEP 19: Here is the wire mesh selection we used to create the wire mesh blur.

right handle to stretch the right side up and down, so it is more symmetrical to the left side. Move this to the left side of the window and then use Image/Effects/Scale to stretch all the way to the right side of the window.

Now use Select/Feather to set the feather to 10 and run Filter/Stylize/ Wind Blast to the left on it. Use Filter/Noise/Add Noise with Gaussian noise of 20. Run Filter/Blur/Motion Blur of 30 at 0 degrees two times. Now copy this strange shape and do an Edit/Paste Layer on top of the Mike layer.

Call this new layer Mike Blur. Use Image/Rotate/Free to rotate this so it is parallel with the movement of the mike in the Mike layer. Use the Move tool to put it on top of the mike then set the opacity to about 17. Use the Lasso tool with a feather of 3 to select then delete the part of the blur that protrudes from the front of the mike. Add a layer mask to the Mike Blur layer and use this with the Gradient tool to fade the blur towards the back of the mike.

You might also use the Paintbrush with a soft brush and also some of the other editing tools to

STEP 19: The wire mesh selection and how it is distorted to make the blur effect. The rotate step has already been done here.

edit the layer mask to fade the blur in towards the back of the mike and the cord. Have fun, you can spend hours playing with the possibilities! Save the file in Photoshop format when you are done.

THE FLYING CD

STEP 20: To create the effect of the CD flying into the computer screen, first load the selection of the CD from the Paths window on the Parts-OrigScan file. Copy the CD and then switch to White-CanvasLayers and do an Edit/Paste Layer on top of your topmost layer so far. Use the Move tool to move the CD into position flying into the leftmost computer. Name this layer CD and then add a layer mask to it. While editing the layer mask, set the feather on the Lasso tool to 1 pixel and use it to make a selection of the right part of the CD that you want to remove. The edge of the selection on top of the CD should be straight. With black and white default colors, Option-Delete to turn that area black in the mask and thereby remove the right part of the CD. Imagine that the computer screen is water and the CD is flying into the water. The image you see on the screen is just a reflection in the water.

STEP 20: This is the selection that deletes the front part of the CD by turning its layer mask black when you Option-Delete.

Ponder what would happen to that reflection when the CD creates a wave while flying into the water. We will use the Zigzag filter to create that effect.

First use the Elliptical Marquee (type M until the top left tool icon is the Elliptical Marquee) to make a selection that would be the area of the screen wave. Use Select/Feather to set a feather on this of about 5 pixels. Make the base layer, where the computer screen is, the selected layer by clicking on it, and then type Command-H to hide the selection edges. Now choose Filter/Distort/Zigzag and go into this filter. Start by using Out From Center, Amount 30, Ridges 4 and then change the options until the wave looks correct to you. You may need to play with the options and/or your selection to get what you want.

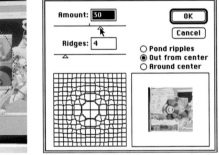

STEP 20: This is the selection that defines the area of the wave effect on the computer screen.

STEP 20: Here are the settings in the Zigzag filter to get the wave effect on the computer screen.

THE VIDEO CAMERA

STEP 22: Load the selection and copy the video camera from PartsOrigScan. Do an Edit/Paste Layer of it on top of your topmost layer and call it Camera. Use the Move tool to position it appropriately. Double-click on the Lasso tool and set the feather to 3 pixels. We want to remove the piece of the tripod that is still attached to the bottom of the video camera. Use the Lasso tool to select a dark area from the bottom of the camera—above and to the right of the tripod. Hold down the Option key while you click and drag that area and then move it to partially cover the tripod. Option-dragging a selection makes a copy of the selection while leaving the original selection there. If you Option-click and drag the copied area, it will make another copy of it, and you can use it over and over again to completely cover the tripod. You will also need to cover the white text that is partially obliterated by the tripod. Once all these areas are covered, use the Rubber Stamp tool to blend out any blemishes along the edges of the covering patches you put in. The feather of 3 should have done most of this for you if you selected the right dark area to use as a patch.

STEP 22: Underside of camera showing the tripod and the selection we used as a patch to cover the tripod.

STEP 22: The same area as above with the tripod now removed.

STEP 23: Make a copy of the Camera layer on top of the Camera layer by clicking on it and dragging it to the New Layer icon at the bottom left of the Layers palette. Name this copy CameraBlur. Option-click on the Eye icon of this layer so you just see it for a while. Use the Lasso tool with a 3 pixel feather to delete the top and bottom of the camera within the CameraBlur layer so it looks like the one pictured here. Since the camera has such a varied shape with varied light and dark portions, we get a better blur effect by just blurring this part of the camera. When we did this job, it took a lot of experimentation to discover this. Use Image/Rotate/Free to rotate this chopped camera so the left and right edges are vertical. Use the Move tool to move this to the top of the layer and then choose Image/Effects/Scale and click on the bottom right handle dragging it all the way to the bottom of the layer. Click on the Gavel icon in the middle of the scaled area to finish the scaling process.

STEP 21: With the CD still in the copy buffer, do another Edit/Paste Layer on top of the CD layer and call this layer CD Blur. Use Image/Effects/Distort to stretch the CD out to make a blur. Use Filter/Noise/Add Noise to add about 20 Gaussian noise then Filter/Blur/Motion Blur to blur about 30 in the direction of CD motion. I did motion blur of 30 twice because a bigger value started to cause distortions in the blur. Move the blur into place above the CD and set its opacity to 50% so you can see through to the CD. Use Image/Rotate/Free to rotate the blur and Image/Effects/Scale to scale the blur so it fits the CD well where they overlap. I also darkened the center portion of the CD blur by using Color mode to fill a selection of that area with some darker colors from the CD. I used Image/Adjust/Hue/Saturation to saturate the colors in the entire CD blur. Add a layer mask to the CD blur layer. Use the Lasso tool to edit the layer mask while viewing the CD layer and select the part of the blur you want to remove in front of the CD. A feather of about 3 seems to work well here. Option-Delete will make the layer mask black in this area and thus remove the front part of the blur in the layer.

Now use the technique described in steps 15 to 17 to have the tail of the blur slowly fade away. Since you have already used this layer mask to get rid of the front of the blur, you should apply it before using it again to get rid of the tail, or do the work on the tail within a selection that only includes the tail area. If you don't do this, the white part of the gradient may extend across the mask and wipe out the work you just did to remove the front part of the blur. Look at the layer mask in my example WhiteCanvasLayers file if you are not sure what the problem is here. The final opacity I used for the CD blur layer was 40%. It is easier to see exactly what you want for opacity and saturation once the front and tail of the CD are removed.

STEP 21: The CD blur layer before its layer mask is applied to remove the black mask areas.

STEP 21: The CD blur layer mask which removes both the front of the CD blur to the right and the tail to the left.

STEP 23: The cropped and rotated camera part before scaling it.

STEP 23: The final CameraBlur layer if viewed by itself without its layer mask.

STEP 23: The final layer mask for the CameraBlur layer.

We rotated the camera first so we could use Scale instead of Distort to stretch it. That way it doesn't get too distorted when stretched. Use Filter/Noise/Add Noise to add 50 Gaussian noise then use Filter/Blur/Motion Blur to blur it by 30 at an angle of 90%. Do the Gaussian noise and motion blur steps a second time. Set the opacity of the blur layer to 50% for now. Option-click on this layer's Eye icon to turn on viewing of all the other layers again. Now use the Move tool to move the blur back on top of the camera in the layer below. Use Image/Rotate/Free to rotate the blur back to the correct angle to match the camera and you may also need to use Image/Effects/Scale to scale the blur so it is the correct width to fit exactly on top of the camera. Move the blur back and forth until you find the location that best matches the lighting paths from the camera body.

Add a layer mask to this CameraBlur layer and you will be set up for editing the layer mask while viewing the rest of the composite image. Use the Lasso tool set to an 8 pixel feather to circle the front part of the blur that you want to delete. Choose Option-Delete to fill the layer mask with black and mask out this front part of the blur. Now make a rectangular selection of the tail of the blur to protect the rest of the layer mask from the Gradient tool. Now use the technique described in steps 15 to 17 to fade out the tail of the blur using the Gradient tool. I then set the opacity of the CameraBlur layer to 40%. Save this final WhiteCanvasLayers in Photoshop format so you can turn on and off individual layers, or layer masks, change opacities or move layers until you and your client are happy with a final image. For more information on how to do these things, see the Night Cab Ride in Manhattan chapter. Here is the final Layers palette showing the layers for the objects we added here with

STEP 23: The Layers palette for the layers we have added here in the directions.

detailed instructions. You can use the same techniques to add the rest of the objects to complete this magazine cover project.

LINKING LAYERS TO MOVE THEM TOGETHER

STEP 24: One advantage to having each of these objects and its blur in a separate layer is that each of these items can be changed and moved separately while showing them to your client or just trying different alternatives for the final effect. If you want to move an item and its blur together to a new place on the screen, there is a way to link the two layers together and move them at the same time. First click on one of the two layers (the item you want to move) to make it the active, grayed, layer. Click in the Link column, the middle column of the other layer (that item's blur), and you will notice that the Link icon turns on in both these layers. Now you can use the Move tool to move this item and its blur together to the left, right, or up and down within your image area. If one of these layers has a layer mask, like the CameraBlur does here, that will also move in unison with the linked layers. You can link more than two layers by just clicking in the Link column of additional Layers. To unlink a layer, just click in the Link column again and that layer will be unlinked.

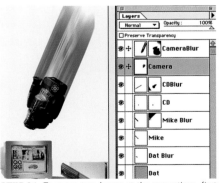

STEP 24: To move two layers at the same time, first click in one of the layers to make it active, gray. Then click in the Link column, the middle column, of the layer(s) that you want to move with this active layer. Now use the Move tool to relocate the position of these layers within your document window.

HANDS-ON SESSION: CREATING SHADOWS

Different Techniques to Create and
Refine Drop Shadows and Cast
Shadows, Including Objects That Cast
Shadows with Irregular Shapes

Here are a variety of techniques to add shadows to objects. This can be done in many different ways and people need to do it a lot. We believe one of these techniques will meet your needs. You should also check out the technique for preserving shadows that is used in The APDA Magazine Cover chapter and also the technique for doing automatic knock-outs using Difference in the Blend Modes, Calculations and Apply Image chapter.

DROP SHADOW ONE

This technique is fairly quick and simple but does not give as much flexibility or control as other techniques.

STEP 1: Click on the background color square and type in these values in the Color Picker dialog: C 5, M 3, Y 3, K 0. This gives you a background white that still has a halftone dot. Choose File/New to create a new CMYK document of 300 pixels by 300 pixels at a resolution of 150 dpi with this background and name the file Shadow2. Now use File/Open to open the PartsOrigScan file from the Creating Shadows folder. Go to Window/Palettes/Show Paths and click on the path named Slide. Drag it to the Selection icon in the middle at the bottom of Paths palette. This will turn this path into a selection. Edit/Copy the slide and paste it on the new document. While the slide is still a floating selection, go to the Channels palette and click on the Save Selection icon at the bottom of the palette to

STEP 1: Create a channel for the slide as well as a new layer called Slide.

make a channel named Slide. Next go to the Layers palette and click on the New Layer icon to make the floating selection a new layer called Slide. File/Save and name this file Slide 1.

STEP 2: Use the Paintbrush or the Airbrush tool. For either tool, choose a large soft brush about 25 to 30 pixels. The hardness should be set to 0 to give you the absolute softest edge. Now choose the color for your shadow, set the opacity of the Paintbrush to about 50-60%, or the pressure of the Airbrush at about 20%, and set the painting mode to Behind.

STEP 3: Make sure the Slide layer is active. Use either the Paintbrush or the Airbrush tool to paint your shadow. I prefer the Airbrush tool for its softer, more diffuse edge, but see what works best for your image. Begin inside the object that you want to shadow. Paint freehand or click with the Painting tool. Let go of the mouse button, move the cursor and Shift-click with the tool to create straight lines. If you can draw the shadow with one stroke, you can undo it if you don't like the effect. If not, Select/Load Selection, load an inverse selection of your object, delete the shadow and

STEP 3: If you use the Paintbrush, lower the opacity to about 50%. Behind mode only paints on the transparent part of the layer.

STEP 3: This brush works well right out of the palette.

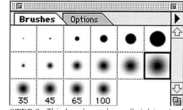

STEP 3: If you use the Airbrush make its pressure about 20%.

STEP 3: Paint in the shadow with the Airbrush or Paintbrush.

start again. With a little practice you can create quick, cheap drop shadows at will.

STEP 4: File/Save As to save this file as Slide1Shadow.

> *If you want your shadow to be only on the Black printing plate, force the color of the shadow to 0,0,0,100 by clicking on the foreground color square and entering those CMYK values. The default black is a mixture of the 4 process inks. When you have a black shadow, sometimes creating it only on the Black plate will avoid gradient color blending problems associated with using a combination of 4 inks.*

DROP SHADOW TWO

STEP 1: File/Open Slide1 that you created in the previous exercise, make a second copy of the Slide layer and name it Shadow.

STEP 2: Go to Edit/Fill (F3 with ArtistKeys) and make sure that you turn on the Preserve Transparency option in the Fill dialog box. Fill this layer with 100% black (the default foreground is CMYK black) or any other color that you wish to use as your shadow.

STEP 3: Offset this layer in the direction of the shadow using either the Move tool or the Offset filter. Now, click and drag the Shadow layer in the Layers palette to move your Shadow layer below the Slide layer.

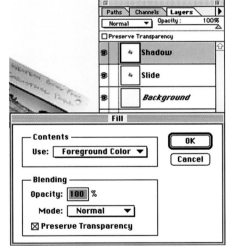

STEP 2: Fill the Shadow layer with 100% Black.

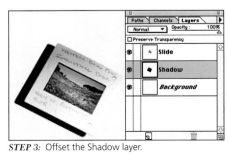

STEP 3: Offset the Shadow layer.

STEP 4: Make sure Preserve Transparency is off. When you have your shadow in position, use Filter/Blur/Gaussian Blur to soften the edges of the shadow. The amount of blur is dependent on how far from the original object you place your shadow—the further away, the softer the shadow. I used 4 pixels for this illustration. With the Preview button on, you see the shadow form and change with different amounts of blur.

STEP 5: Finally, change the opacity of the Shadow layer. Once again, this is dependent on how close the shadow is to the object. A short, sharp shadow will be darker than a shadow cast from a distant light source. I used 45% opacity here.

STEP 6: Save the file.

STEP 5: Final version of the file using an offset and blurred layer described in Drop Shadow Two.

DROP SHADOW THREE

STEP 1: Use the Slide 1 file that you just saved, but turn off the Shadow layer by clicking on its Eye icon in the Layers palette.

STEP 2: Go to Window/Palettes/Show Paths and make a path along the edge of the object where you want your shadow. Double-click on the name in the Paths palette and name this path Shadow path.

STEP 3: Make sure the Background layer is the target (active) layer.

STEP 4: Use the Airbrush tool with a large soft brush, about 25 pixels with a Hardness of 0. Set the pressure to about 20-25%.

STEP 5: Set the painting mode to Normal. Type D to make sure the foreground color is black, or set the foreground color if you want something other than a black shadow.

STEP 2: Name the path Shadow path.

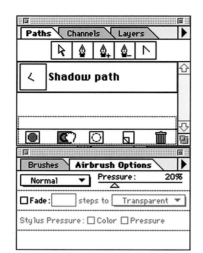

STEP 6: With the Airbrush as the active tool, drag your Shadow path to the Stroke Path icon at the bottom of the Paths palette.

STEP 6: Final version of the file using a stroked path.

STEP 6: Go back to the Paths palette and drag your path down to the Stroke Path icon at the bottom of the palette. If you are unhappy with the shadow, Edit/Undo the stroke (Command-Z) and change the shape of your path, the size of your brush, the pressure of the Airbrush, or the color of the foreground color.

DROP SHADOW FOUR

STEP 1: Click on the background color to bring up the Color Picker and create a color that has the values 5, 3, 3, 0 for cyan, magenta, yellow and black. Choose OK to make this your background color. Open the PartsOrigScan file from the Creating Shadows folder on the CD and bring up the Paths palette (F11 with ArtistKeys). Click on the path named Slide and drag it to the Selection icon in the middle at the bottom of the Paths palette. This will turn the path into a selection. Now do a copy of the slide and choose File/New. Create a new file that is 500 by 500 pixels in size and choose to fill it with the background color. Paste the slide into this new file and move it to the left ⅓ of the window. Bring up the Channels palette (F10 with ArtistKeys), and click on the Selection icon at the bottom left of this Palette to save a mask of the slide selection. Double-click on this mask channel and name it Slide & Tapes. Now use Command-D to Select/None. Use Command-S to save this file as DropShadows.

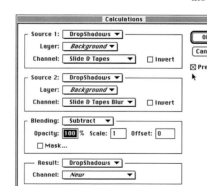

STEP 4: Here are the settings for the Calculations Subtract command.

STEP 2: Go back to PartsOrigScan and load a selection of the path called Tapes by clicking on it in the Paths palette and then dragging it to the Selection icon at the bottom middle of the palette. Copy this then switch back to your new file and do another paste. Again save your selection, but this time hold the Shift key down, click on the Channels palette Selection icon and then drag it and drop it on top of the Slide & Tapes channel. This will add the tapes to the mask of the slide. The Shift key adds the current selection to a mask and the Command key subtracts the current selection from a mask.

STEP 2: Here is the CMYK image after step 2.

STEP 3: Click on the Slide & Tapes channel and drag it to the New Channel icon at the bottom of the Channels palette. Double-click on this new channel and call it Slide & Tapes Blur. We are going to turn this channel into a shadow. Choose Filter/Other/Offset to offset this channel by -6 to the right and 5 down. Make sure Repeat Edge Pixels is chosen. This will make the shadow below and to the left of the objects. Use Filter/Blur/Gaussian Blur of 7 pixels to turn this into a shadow.

STEP 4: Now what you want to do is subtract (turn to black) the selection indicated by the Slide & Tapes channel from the Slide & Tapes Blur channel. This will just leave the shadow, the blur, around the edge of the objects. Choose Image/Calculations and set up your calculations dialog with the Slide & Tapes channel as your Source1 channel, the Slide & Tapes Blur as your Source2 channel, Blending set to Subtract with Scale set to 1 and Offset set to 0, and Result set to a New Channel. Double-click on this new channel and name it Shadow.

STEP 5: Set the feather on the Lasso tool to 5 pixels and type a D to get the default colors. Using the Lasso tool, select the parts of the Shadow channel that are above and to the right of the objects. To be realistic, you really don't want to add shadows in these areas. Option-Delete these areas to set them to black. The 5 pixel Lasso setting blends out the deleting of these areas along the edges like a soft shadow. Choose New Channel from the

Channels palette menu, and if this channel is not already black then choose Select/All followed by Option-Delete to turn it black. Now choose Copy to copy this black patch into the copy buffer.

STEP 5: These are the parts of the shadow that don't need to be there.

STEP 6: Now click back on Channel 0 and do a Load Selection on the Shadow channel by Option-clicking on it. Choose Edit/Paste Into to paste the patch of blackness into the shadow area. By doing the Paste Into, instead of a Fill, you can now change the opacity of your shadow using the Opacity slider for the floating selection at the top of the Layers palette.

STEP 7: You may notice a thin white line between the shadow and the tapes. Notice that there is no such line on the slide. Since the tapes are black and the shadow is black, the mask for the shadow needs to be perfect. Choose Command-Z to undo the Paste Into of the shadow, go back to the Shadow mask channel and use Filter/Other/Off-set of 1 to the right and -1 up. Now redo step 6 and you will notice that this problem has gone away in most areas. There are still several small areas where you can see a white line. Choose Command-Z again and then go back to the mask. Edit these small areas using the Rubber Stamp tool in Clone (aligned) mode with about a 4 pixel hard edge brush to copy white areas of the mask where you need to add more shadow in a white line area. Use the Paintbrush and paint black with a soft brush into the mask where you want to remove edges of the shadows. When you believe your mask is correct, repeat Step 6 until you end up with a mask that looks as good as the ShadowModified-Final mask in the sample DropShadows file on the CD.

STEP 7: Here is the final mask after using the Rubber Stamp and Paintbrush to make subtle corrections on the shadow areas.

STEP 7: Here are the final images with shadows after applying step 6 to the final mask.

CAST SHADOW ONE

If the object that you wish to shadow is on its own transparent layer, make a new layer of the object. If not, select the object, copy it and paste it as a new layer into a new file with the background you want to use.

Use Image/Effects/Distort or Image/Effects/Perspective to change the shape of this layer. How you change the shape will depend on the direction of the light source and its closeness to the object you wish to shadow. Here are some different possibilities.

STEP 1: Open the Ball file from the Creating Shadows folder. Select/Load Selection, which is an outline of the ball, and use Image/Rotate/Free to rotate the ball until the light source comes from above.

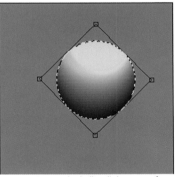

STEP 1: Rotate the ball so light comes from above.

STEP 2: Make a copy of the Ball layer by dragging this layer to the New Layer icon at the bottom of the Layers palette. Double-click on the new layer and name this layer Shadow.

STEP 3: Deselect and Edit/Fill (F3 with ArtistKeys) the Shadow layer with 100% Black (or other shadow color). Make sure you turn on the Preserve Transparency option in the Fill dialog. Use Image/Effects/Perspective to flatten and widen the shape of the ball. Begin changing the perspective by pulling one of the bottom handles out horizontally.

STEP 4: Use the Layers palette to move this layer between the ball and the background.

STEP 5: Filter/Blur/Gaussian Blur (F14 with ArtistKeys) the layer about 8 pixels.

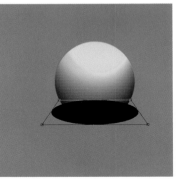

STEP 3: Use Image/Effects/Perspective to flatten the shape.

219

STEP 7: Experiment with the placement, opacity and softness of the shadow to achieve the effect of distance from the background and closeness of the light source.

STEP 6: Change the opacity of the layer to about 60%.

STEP 7: Use the Move tool to position the shadow. Remember, the further away from the shadow the object is positioned, the larger and softer the cast shadow. An item further away from its shadow is also further from the plane upon which the shadow is cast. Therefore, an item that casts a large soft shadow, which does not touch the shadow itself, indicates that the item "floats" away from the projection plane. Experiment with moving the shadow closer or further from the ball to see how this affects the depth perception of the object to its shadow.

STEP 8: Save the file as Shadow Above.

CAST SHADOW TWO

STEP 1: Reopen the Ball file. Here we have an object lit from the upper right. Therefore, we will have a cast shadow that goes down and to the left at an opposite angle.

STEP 2: Make a new layer of the ball by dragging this layer to the New Layer icon at the bottom of the Layers palette. Double-click on the layer and call it Shadow.

STEP 3: Edit/Fill (F3 with ArtistKeys) this layer with black. Make sure the Preserve Transparency option is on. Use Image/Effects/Distort to change the shape of the shadow. You may have to try the

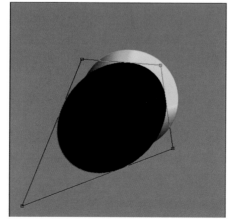

STEP 3: Use Image/Effects/Distort to change the shape of the shadow.

Distort several times. Photoshop only gives you a rectangular shape to use as the basis for your distort, and it's difficult to get an accurate read on what your distorted shape will actually look like. I brought the upper right point inside the shape of the ball, the upper left and lower right points in on a diagonal but still outside the shape of the ball, and the lower left point out and down in a diagonal the opposite direction of the light source.

STEP 4: When you get a shape that you're happy with, use the Layers palette to move the shadow shape below the ball.

STEP 5: Use the Transparency option in the Layers palette to change the opacity and the Move tool to position the shadow. Filter/Blur/Gaussian blur the shape. Remember that the distance from the object dictates how soft the shadow should be. The closer the shadow, the sharper the shadow. If the rotation of the shadow does not match the direction of the light, use Image/Rotate/Free to get the angle which matches.

STEP 6: Use File/Save As and name the file Ball Cast Shadow.

 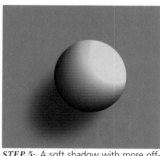

STEP 5: A hard, dark shadow seems to place the ball directly against the background.

STEP 5: A soft shadow with more offset gives the appearance of the ball floating above the background.

Cast Shadow Three

This technique is similar to Cast Shadow Two but incorporates a fade from the front of the shadow to the back.

STEP 1: Reopen the Ball file.

STEP 2: Make a new layer of the ball and call it Shadow. Edit/Fill, turn on Preserve transparency inside the Fill Command and fill the shape with 100% black.

STEP 3: Use Image/Effects/ Distort to change the shadow shape. It will be a similar distort to the previous technique but will probably be wider and longer than your last cast shadow.

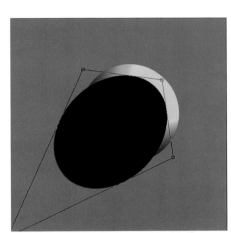

STEP 3: Distort the shadow considerably if you are going to have a fade out.

STEP 4: Make sure the Preserve Transparency option for the layer is off in the Layers palette and then Filter/Blur/Gaussian Blur this layer by a large number of pixels, say 15.

STEP 5: Make sure only the Shadow layer is active by Option-clicking on its Eye icon and go to the Channels palette. Make a copy of the Red channel by dragging it to the New Channel icon at the bottom of the palette. Double-click on this channel and call it Shadow Shape. Choose Image/Map/Invert to invert the channel so the shadow area is white (selected).

STEP 6: Go back to Layers and select the Shadow layer. Move this layer below the Ball layer. Edit/Fill (F3 with ArtistKeys) the Shadow layer with 100% of the Foreground but make the mode Clear.

STEP 7: Select/Load Selection to load the Shadow Shape channel. Type G to access the Gradient Blend tool and set the options to: Normal, 100%, Foreground to Transparent, Linear blend, 50% Midpoint. Now, do your blend from slightly inside the shape of the ball and outward in the direction

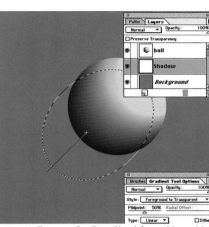

STEP 7: Try your Gradient Blend from this position and with these options.

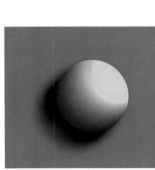

STEP 7: Change the opacity of the layer to get a softer fade.

of the distort. You should get a shadow that is soft on all sides but has a more pronounced fade at the tail. You may want to experiment with starting and ending your blend at different points as well as further distortion of the layer to soften or enlarge your shadow.

Cast Shadow Four

Occasionally you need a cast shadow that is an irregular shape where neither Distort or Perspective gives you a realistic shadow. Try this technique in those instances.

STEP 1: Open the Video Tape file from the Creating Shadows folder on the Photoshop Artistry CD.

STEP 2: Show Paths (F11 with ArtistKeys) and use the Pen tool to draw the basic shape of the object creating the shadow. In this example, it is the top of the tape cartridge that actually casts the shadow. Look at the light source. It is coming from the upper left edge of the object, therefore our cast shadow will be down and to the right. Also look at the bottom edge of the cartridge. Since it is totally in shadow, the cast shadow must start

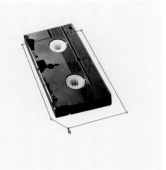

STEP 2: Modify the Tape Top path so the path is larger than the actual tape.

at the left edge of the cartridge to be believable. Save the path you create as Tape Top and then use the selection arrow of the Paths palette to modify the shape for the shadow. Make the shadow area for the tape wider than the tape itself. Click on the Selection icon at the bottom of the Paths palette to turn this path into a selection.

STEP 3: The Shadow Shape channel.

STEP 3: Go to Window/Palettes/Show Channels and click the Selection icon at the bottom of the palette to turn this selection into a channel. Name this channel Shadow Shape.

STEP 4: Go to the Layers palette and make a new transparent layer and make sure that this layer is active. Call this layer Shadow. Option-click on the Shadow Shape channel to load the selection to this layer.

STEP 5: Use Select/Feather to feather the selection by about 9 or 10 pixels.

STEP 6: The shadow overlaps the tape.

STEP 6: The Shadow layer before the layer mask.

STEP 6: Edit/Fill this selection with 100% black. Make sure the Preserve Transparency option is off. Change the opacity of the Shadow layer to 65%. You now have a basic shadow but there is shadow area on the left of the tape that needs to be deleted.

STEP 7: From the Layers palette, add a layer mask to this layer. Now use the Paintbrush with a large soft brush and 100% black to paint out areas of the shadow on the left edge. You may need to change brush sizes or switch to the Airbrush tool to get the desired softness or sharpness to your edge.

STEP 8: Finally, for this image, I noticed that there is a gray hairline at the bottom of the tape that interferes with the shadow, so I added a layer mask to the Tape layer and used a small brush to "erase" the edge so the shadow layer shows through.

STEP 7: The Shadow layer after painting the layer mask.

BIBLIOGRAPHY

Adams, Ansel with Mary Street Alinder. *Ansel Adams: An Autobiography*. Boston, MA: New York Graphic Society Books, 1985.

Adams, Ansel with Robert Baker. *Ansel Adams: The Camera*. Boston, MA: New York Graphic Society Books, 1980.

Adams, Ansel with Robert Baker. *Ansel Adams: The Negative*. Boston, MA: New York Graphic Society Books, 1981.

Adams, Ansel with Robert Baker. *Ansel Adams: The Print*. Boston, MA: New York Graphic Society Books, 1983.

Blatner, David, Phillip Gaskill, and Eric Taub. *QuarkXPress Tips & Tricks: Industrial-Strength Techniques, 2nd Edition*. Berkeley, CA: Peachpit Press, 1994.

Burns, Diane and Sharyn Venit. *The Official QuarkXPress Handbook, Macintosh 3.2 Edition*. New York, NY: Random House Electronic Publishing, 1994.

Cohen, Luanne Seymour, Russell Brown, Lisa Jeans, and Tanya Wendling. *Design Essentials*. Mountain View, CA: Adobe Press, 1992.

Cohen, Luanne Seymour, Russell Brown, and Tanya Wendling. *Imaging Essentials*. Mountain View, CA: Adobe Press, 1993.

Dayton, Linnea and Jack Davis. *The Photshop Wow! Book*. Berkeley, CA: Peachpit Press, 1993.

McClelland, Deke. *Macworld Photoshop 3 Bible, 2nd Edition*. San Mateo, CA: IDG Books Worldwide, 1994.

Rich, Jim and Sandy Bozek. *Photoshop in Black and White: An Illustrated Guide to Reproducing Black-and-White Images Using Adobe Photoshop*. Berkeley CA: Peachpit Press, 1994.

Tapscott, Diane, Lisa Jeans, Pat Soberanis, Rita Amladi, and Jim Ryan. *Production Essentials*. Mountain View, CA: Adobe Press, 1994.

White, Minor, Richard Zakia, and Peter Lorenz. *The New Zone System Manual*. Dobbs Ferry, NY: Morgan Press, Inc., 1976.

Wilhelm, Henry with Carol Brower. *The Permanence and Care of Color Photographs: Traditional and Digital Color Prints, Color Negatives, Slides, and Motion Pictures*. Grinnell, IA: Preservation Publishing Company, 1993.

INDEX

231

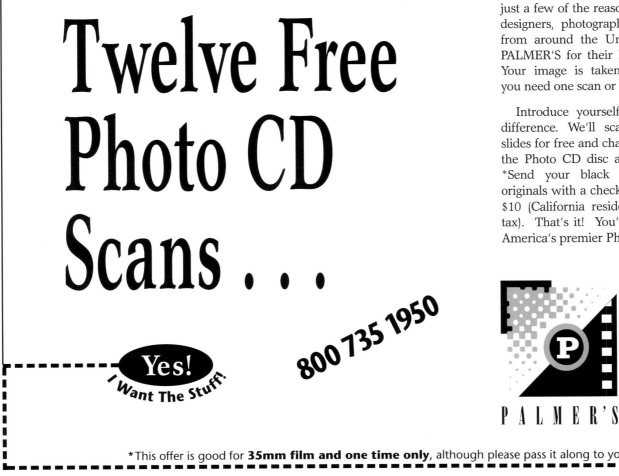

ABOUT THE AUTHORS

Barry Haynes uses digital technology to print, show and sell his photography. In addition to his love for creating photographs, Barry teaches digital photography, creates commercial special effects and does digital image consulting. He has been teaching Photoshop courses since 1990 to clients including Apple, Kodak, Nikon, Pacific Bell, Sony, Tandem, Super-Mac, The San Jose Mercury News and many others. He teaches regular digital photography workshops for the University of California Santa Cruz Extension, The Palm Beach Photographic Workshops and AD Vantage Computers in Des Moines, Iowa. He has given talks or workshops for the MacSummit conference, Seybold Seminars, the Center for Creative Imaging, the Digital Photography Conference, the American Society of Magazine Photographers, advertising agencies, design firms and other organizations.

He has written articles for desktop publishing magazines and his imaging effects have appeared in brochures and on magazine covers for companies including Apple and Tandem. Barry has a degree in computer science and spent 10 years, from 1980 to 1990, doing software development and research at Apple. There he did research involving desktop publishing, digital imaging and high speed networks and before that he worked on Pascal and Object Oriented software development environments for Apple including Macintosh Smalltalk, MacApp, the Lisa Workshop and Apple II Pascal.

Wendy Crumpler has been in advertising and design since 1980. She has worked in print, television, CD-Interactive, interactive television and computer-based training. Prior to her discovery of the computer in 1981 and the Macintosh in 1986, she was an actress and teacher. Since her involvement in digital imaging she has done production, illustration, design and training for a variety of clients using Quark, PageMaker, Illustrator, Freehand, Photoshop and other applications. Recent clients include: Angotti Thomas Hedge, Boardroom Reports, Deutsch Advertising, J. Walter Thompson, TBWA Advertising, Wechsler Design, AT&T, Manhattan Transfer, Wells Rich Greene, Canon, Parke Davis, Saab, Dow Jones, IBM, Shearson and AT&T.

Wendy Crumpler in Manhattan hired Barry Haynes from California to teach Photoshop workshops for her New York clients. During the three days he was in New York, and the many hours they spent on the phone they fell in love! Now they are married, living in the Santa Cruz mountains of California and expecting their first child. Who says long distance romances can't happen?

LET US KNOW WHAT YOU THINK

There's been a lot of student and reader involvement in the shaping of this book. Listening to people who use these techniques helps us to refine and dig deeper to find solutions to our clients' and students' problems. And, we get smarter in the process. We love what we do and invite you to become part of the digital revolution with us. Let us know what you think of the book, what was helpful, what confused you. We are committed to empowering people to use their computers and their software to advance their own artistic abilities and to make a difference on this planet.

SERVICES AVAILABLE FROM THE AUTHORS:

As imaging consultants, we have the know-how to create or help you create the effect you want. In producing photographic effects and also brochures and publications, we can do it all or just the parts where you need help.

Besides teaching at digital imaging centers around the country, we also teach more personal Photoshop, Quark and Illustrator courses in our own studios and courses tailored to your special needs at your business location.

WE LOOK FORWARD TO HEARING FROM YOU!

For further information, fax (408) 338-6571
America Online or Internet at
WECrumpler@aol.com, BarryHayne@aol.com
AppleLink at Barry.Haynes

Wendy Crumpler Enterprises
Barry Haynes Photography
820 Memory Lane
Boulder Creek, CA 95006
(408)-338-4569

COLOPHON

How and Where this Book Was Produced and a Special Word of Thanks to Our Publisher

This book was produced almost entirely on two machines: first, a Quadra 900 accelerated with a Daystar PowerPro 601 Power PC board, 112 Mb RAM, Radius/SuperMac Thunder/24 video board and 20" Trinitron Dual Mode monitor, Micronet Raven disk array, Bernoulli 230 Mb transportable drive and a Micronet CD drive; and second, a Mac IIci with 20 Mb RAM, 210 Mb hard drive, a 230 Mb Bernoulli transportable drive, a 44 Mb Syquest drive, and an E-Machines T-16 monitor. Tape backups were made to a Micronet DAT tape drive using Retrospect.

Each chapter of this book was set up as a separate document in QuarkXPress. The text was input directly into Quark using a template document with Master pages and style sheets. As design decisions changed, the template document was updated. When necessary, text and pictures were stripped out of old documents and reflowed into the new template. Style Sheets and H&J settings were appended to each document when changes occurred. Charts were done in Adobe Illustrator and color correction and separation was done, of course, from Photoshop using the methods and settings described in this book.

Screen captures were done with Screenshot™, Exposure Pro™, and occasionally with the Mac's Command-Shift-3 command. Low res RGB captures were placed in the original documents and sized in Quark. After design decisions were made as to size and position, the resolution was changed to 400 dpi and photos were sharpened, separated and saved as CMYK Tiffs in Photoshop. Photos were reimported into Quark at 100%. Two black-and-white 600 dpi versions of this book were printed at Kinkos on the Xerox Docutech before final design decisions were made. These were used for classes, pre-publicity and prototypes.

Most photographs in this book are from Photo CD or Pro Photo CD scans from 35mm slides done primarily by Palmer Photographic in Sacramento. Several, including the cover, were from scans done by Robyn Color on a Howtek D4000 drum scanner. Original color proofing for critical color pages and for the cover of the book were output to the Radius/SuperMac ProofPositive Two-Page dye sublimation printer and color corrected using the GTI Soft-View D5000 Transparency/Print Viewer.

Film output was done by Strine Printing on the Agfa SelectSet 7000. Most pages were output at 2400 dpi using a 200 line screen and Agfa Balanced Screens. Section opening pages and the cover were output at 3600 dpi with a 200 line screen. Proofing was done using both the Kodak Approval Proofing system and the Kodak Contract Proofing system. Once

again, color corrections were done by calibrating these proofs to our Radius/SuperMac monitor using the GTI Soft-View D5000 lightbox and the Gamma Control Panel with the techniques discribed in this book.

Transfer of files was done primarily using Bernoulli 230 disks which were sent FedEx between the printer and the authors. Files were sent as Quark documents with high-res photos in position. We sent a FileMaker Pro document which delineated the names of each chapter, and the page start and length of the document. Film was set in signatures of 16 pages starting with the most color critical signatures first. In some instances, images and Quark files were sent via America Online from the authors to the printer.

Printing was done by Strine Printing of York, PA on 3 Heidelberg Speed Master presses. The book is printed on 80lb Vintage Velvet and the cover is 12pt C1s with a gloss coating.

Typefaces are New Caledonia, New Caledonia SC&OSF, Frutiger, and, on the cover, Industria, all from Adobe.

A word about publishers. You can, these days, publish a book completely by yourself. Friends have done it, and we considered it ourselves. Over the years, we've been offered contracts for this or similar books by several different publishers. We turned them down, because we had a vision of what we wanted and could not get a publisher to agree to support that vision in their contract. SYBEX had the courage to back up their proposals with a clearly written and specific contract that gave us both the freedom and the support needed to produce this book. Their guidance was invaluable—their patience, outstanding. We hope they feel as happy with the final product as we are. We are grateful for this opportunity to work with them.

PHOTO CREDITS

Bruce Ashley
© 1995, Bruce Ashley, All Rights Reserved
Bob: ix, x, 132, 134, 140, 141, 143, 144, 197, 198, 199, 204, 205
Kestrel: ix, 132, 133, 134
Fuller: viii, 119, 120, 121
Gears: 67

Marc Simon
© 1992, Marc Simon, All Rights Reserved
Flying Books: 56, 58, 60
Headland: 177, 179
Computers: xii, 206, 207, 208, 209, 213
Multi Media Parts: xii, 206, 207, 210, 211, 212, 213, 214, 215, 216, 217, 218, 219, 221, 222

Wendy Crumpler
© 1995, Wendy Crumpler, All Rights Reserved
Men In Boat: 34, 35
Boats In Harbor: 173

Adobe Systems Incorporated
© 1989, Adobe Systems Incorporated, All Rights Reserved
Olé No Moiré: 56, 58, 60

Jeffrey Myers
© 1995, Jeffrey Myers, All Rights Reserved
ChessQueen: 203
Head and City: 203

Will Croff
© 1995, Will Croff, All Rights Reserved
Wine Grapes & Checkerboard: 203

Marita Gootee
© 1995, Marita Gootee, All Rights Reserved
Cardline: 203

Susan Holland
© 1995, Susan Holland, All Rights Reserved
Hands: 203

Barry Haynes
All other photographs in this book and on the cover:
© 1995, Barry Haynes, All Rights Reserved

WARRANTY

SYBEX warrants the enclosed disk to be free of physical defects for a period of ninety (90) days after purchase. If you discover a defect in the disk during this warranty period, you can obtain a replacement disk at no charge by sending the defective disk, postage prepaid, with proof of purchase to:

SYBEX Inc.
Customer Service Department
2021 Challenger Drive
Alameda, CA 94501
(800) 227-2346
Fax: (510) 523-2373

After the 90-day period, you can obtain a replacement disk by sending us the defective disk, proof of purchase, and a check or money order for $10, payable to SYBEX.